THE BROTHERS
POWYS

Author of

Lawrence of Arabia and his World
A. E. Housman: The Scholar-Poet

THE BROTHERS
POWYS

RICHARD PERCEVAL GRAVES

Charles Scribner's Sons
New York

For my own brothers and brothers-in-law
Simon William Graves
Charles Macartney Graves
Jan Lewis Fortescue
Thomas Richard Fortescue
and
Paul Howard Goodchild

Contents

Plates

Between pages 202 and 203

1 The Vicarage, Montacute [courtesy Kenneth Hopkins Esq.]
2 The Powys brothers at Montacute [courtesy Francis Powys Esq.]
3 Theodore and Violet Powys, with Dr O'Neill [courtesy Mrs Isobel Powys Marks]
4 Thomas Hardy [Dorset County Library]
5 Llewelyn Powys [courtesy E. E. Bissell Esq.]
6 Louis Wilkinson [courtesy Oliver Wilkinson Esq.]
7 The Sherborne 'Prep' [courtesy E. E. Bissell Esq.]
8 Group photograph at Montacute, *c.* 1911 [courtesy Mrs Isobel Powys Marks]
9 Frances Wilkinson [courtesy Oliver Wilkinson Esq.]
10 Isadora Duncan [BBC Hulton Picture Library]
11 John Cowper Powys with Louis and Frances Wilkinson [courtesy Oliver Wilkinson Esq.]
12 Edna St Vincent Millay [Library of Congress]
13 Sylvia Townsend Warner [National Portrait Gallery]
14 Phyllis Playter [courtesy Francis Powys Esq.]
15 Phyllis Playter in Breton costume [courtesy Francis Powys Esq.]
16 Llewelyn Powys in the Rockies [courtesy E. E. Bissell Esq.]
17 Alyse Gregory on her wedding-day [courtesy Miss Rosemary Manning]
18 Theodore Dreiser [University of Pennsylvania]
19 Gertrude Powys in 1926 [courtesy Francis Powys Esq.]
20 Gamel Woolsey [courtesy Kenneth Hopkins Esq.]
21 Llewelyn Powys with Gamel Woolsey [courtesy E. E. Bissell Esq.]
22 Phudd Bottom in winter [courtesy E. E. Bissell Esq.]
23 Theodore Powys with David Garnett and Richard Garnett [courtesy Richard Garnett Esq.]

It has not been possible to trace all the copyright owners of these photographs, but if further information becomes available they will be acknowledged in future editions.

Acknowledgments

The author and publishers would like to thank the following for permission to reproduce copyright material: The University of Texas [as owners only] for quotations from Powys manuscripts held in the Humanities Research Center; Laurence Pollinger Ltd for Kenneth Hopkins and the Estate of Gamel Woolsey for extracts from 'Gamel Woolsey to Alyse Gregory, Some letters 1930–1957', ed. Kenneth Hopkins, in *The Powys Review*, no. 8, ed. Belinda Humfrey, and from Gamel Woolsey's poems in the following Warren House Press publications: *Twenty-Eight Sonnets* (1977), *The Last Leaf Falls* (1928), and *Middle Earth* (1979); Laurence Pollinger Ltd and Oliver Marlow Wilkinson for extracts from 'A Rival to Jack' by Oliver Marlow Wilkinson in *Recollections of the Powys Brothers*, ed. Belinda Humfrey (Peter Owen, 1980) and from 'John Cowper Powys in Love' in *The Powys Review*, no. 2, ed. Belinda Humfrey; Laurence Pollinger Ltd and Mary Barham Johnson for extracts from Miss Johnson's 'The Powys Mother' in *The Powys Review*, no. 8, ed. Belinda Humfrey; Laurence Pollinger Ltd and Kenneth Hopkins for extracts from *The Powys Brothers* by Kenneth Hopkins (Warren House Press, 1972), from the Introduction to *Llewelyn Powys: A Selection of his Writings* by Kenneth Hopkins (Macdonald, 1952), and from *Advice to a Young Poet*, ed. R. L. Blackmore (Fairleigh Dickinson University Press, 1969); Laurence Pollinger Ltd and the Estate of Louis Wilkinson for extracts from the following works by Louis Wilkinson: *Swan's Milk* [under pen name Louis Marlow] (Faber & Faber, 1934), *Forth, Beast!* [under pen name Louis Marlow] (Faber & Faber, 1946), *The Buffoon* (Village Press, 1975), *Welsh Ambassadors* [under pen name Louis Marlow] (Village Press, 1975), and from A note in Mappowder church; Laurence Pollinger Ltd and the Estate of Malcolm Elwin for extracts from *The Life of Llewelyn Powys* (John Lane at The Bodley Head, 1949); Laurence Pollinger Ltd and the Estate of John Cowper Powys for extracts from the following works by John Cowper

Acknowledgments

Powys: *Autobiography* (Colgate University Press, 1968), *Odes and Other Poems* (Village Press, 1975), *Poems 1899* (Village Press, 1975), *Wolf Solent* (Penguin Books, 1964), *Lucifer* (Village Press, 1974), *Romer Mowl and Other Stories* (Toucan Press, 1974), *The War and Culture* (Village Press, 1975), *Visions and Revisions* (Village Press, 1974), *Wood and Stone* (Village Press, 1974), *Wolf's Bane* (Village Press, 1975), *One Hundred Best Books* (Village Press, 1975), *Rodmoor* (Macdonald, 1973), *Suspended Judgments* (Village Press, 1975), *Mandragora* (Village Press, 1975), *The Complex Vision* (Village Press, 1975), *After My Fashion* (Pan/Picador, 1980), *Samphire* (Village Press, 1975), *The Owl. The Duck. and-Miss Rowe! Miss Rowe!* (Village Press, 1975), *Psychoanalysis and Morality* (Village Press, 1975), *James Joyce's Ulysses: An Appreciation* (Village Press, 1975), *Ducdame* (Village Press, 1974), *The Meaning of Culture* (Village Press, 1974), *In Defence of Sensuality* (Village Press, 1974), *A Glastonbury Romance* (Pan/Picador, 1979), *Dorothy Richardson* (Village Press, 1974), *Weymouth Sands* (Pan/Picador, 1980), *An Englishman Upstate* (Village Press, 1974), *The Art of Happiness* (Village Press, 1975), *Maiden Castle* (Macdonald, 1966), *Morwyn* (Sphere Books, 1977), *Owen Glendower* (Pan/Picador, 1978), *Porius* (Village Press, 1974), *Obstinate Cymric* (Village Press, 1973), *The Brazen Head* (Pan/Picador, 1978), *Homer and the Aether* (Macdonald, 1959), *Letters to Louis Wilkinson* (Village Press, 1974), *Letters to his Brother Llewelyn*, volume I (Village Press, 1975), *Letters to Nicholas Ross* (Bertram Rota, 1971), *Letters to Clifford Tolchard* (Village Press, 1975), *Letters to C. Benson Roberts* (Village Press, 1975), *Confessions of Two Brothers* (The Manas Press, 1916), and from the words of John Cowper Powys as quoted in 'John Cowper Powys in America to T. F. Powys: letters 1923–1929' in *The Powys Review*, no. 2, ed. Belinda Humfrey, in 'Wolf Solent: a letter from John Cowper Powys to his brother Llewelyn' in *The Powys Review*, no. 7, ed. Belinda Humfrey, in *Essays on John Cowper Powys*, ed. Belinda Humfrey (University of Wales Press, 1972), and in *Recollections of the Powys Brothers*, ed. Belinda Humfrey (Peter Owen, 1980); Chatto & Windus Ltd on behalf of Miss Susanna Pinney and Mr William Maxwell, the executors of the Sylvia Townsend Warner Literary Estate, for extracts from the following works by Sylvia Townsend Warner: an unpublished letter to Alyse Gregory, 'Theodore Powys at East Chaldon' in *Recollections of the Powys Brothers*, ed. Belinda Humfrey (Peter Owen, 1980), and 'Theodore Powys and Some Friends at East Chaldon, 1922–1927', in *The Powys Review*, no. 5, ed. Belinda Humfrey; Dr and Mrs Clifford Musgrave and Peter Owen Ltd for an extract from Clifford and Margaret Musgrave: An Interview', in *Recol-*

lections of the Powys Brothers, ed. Belinda Humfrey (Peter Owen, 1980); Peter Owen Ltd for an extract from 'The Books in My Life' by Henry Miller, from *Recollections of the Powys Brothers*, ed. Belinda Humfrey (Peter Owen, 1980); Lloyds Bank Ltd and the Estate of A. B. Gourlay for an extract from *A History of Sherborne School* by A. B. Gourlay (Sawtells, 1971); A. P. Watt Ltd for lines from a poem by W. B. Yeats; Mr Albert S. Krick for extracts from a recorded talk; The George Arents Research Library, Syracuse University [as owners only] for a letter of Norman Denny; Mr Raymond Garlick for extracts from his essays 'Blaenau Remembered' in *Recollections of the Powys Brothers*, ed. Belinda Humfrey (Peter Owen, 1980) and 'Powys in Gwynedd: the last years' in *Essays on John Cowper Powys*, ed. Belinda Humfrey (University of Wales Press, 1972); The Society of Authors and Mrs Evelyn Elwin for extracts from unpublished letters of Llewelyn Powys, and from his published writings as follows: 'Conversations with Theodore Powys, Summer 1931' in *The Powys Review*, no. 4, ed. Belinda Humfrey, *A Baker's Dozen* (Village Press, 1974), *Damnable Opinions* (Watts, 1935), *Ebony and Ivory* (Richards Press, 1960), *Dorset Essays* (The Bodley Head, 1935), *A Pagan's Pilgrimage* (Longmans, Green, 1931), *Apples Be Ripe* (Longmans, Green, 1932), *The Cradle of God* (Jonathan Cape, 1929), *The Pathetic Fallacy* (Watts, 1931), *Impassioned Clay* (Longmans, 1931), *Now that the Gods are Dead* (The Bodley Head, 1949), *Glory of Life* (The Bodley Head, 1949), *Love and Death* (The Bodley Head, 1950), *The Letters of Llewelyn Powys*, ed. Louis Wilkinson (John Lane at The Bodley Head, 1943), *Confessions of Two Brothers* (Manas Press, 1916), *Skin for Skin* (Village Press, 1975), *Black Laughter* (Macdonald, 1953), *The Verdict of Bridlegoose* (Village Press, 1975), *So Wild A Thing*, letters to Gamel Woolsey, ed. Malcolm Elwin (The Ark Press, 1973), and a letter to *The Times*; Chatto & Windus Ltd and A. P. Watt Ltd for extracts from 'The Familiar Faces' by David Garnett which appeared in *Recollections of the Powys Brothers*, ed. Belinda Humfrey (Peter Owen, 1980); The Colgate University Library [as owners only] for unpublished material by Louis Wilkinson, Albert S. Krick, Alyse Gregory and Malcolm Elwin; Mr Gerard Casey for extracts from his letter to the editor in *The Powys Review*, no. 4, ed. Belinda Humfrey, and from his article 'A Double Initiation' in *Recollections of the Powys Brothers*, ed. Belinda Humfrey (Peter Owen, 1980); Faber & Faber for lines from 'Autumn Sequel' taken from *Collected Poems* by Louis Macneice; Mr Jeffrey Kwintner for an extract from *A Visit to John Cowper Powys* by Oloff de Wet (Village Press, 1974); Miss Catherine Morton for an extract from 'T. F. Powys: A

Few Recorded Memories' by Elizabeth Muntz which appears in *Recollections of the Powys Brothers*, ed. Belinda Humfrey (Peter Owen, 1980); Victor Gollancz Ltd for an extract from 'Too Late to Lament' by Maurice Browne, which appeared in *Recollections of the Powys Brothers*, ed. Belinda Humfrey (Peter Owen, 1980); Rosemary Manning for extracts from unpublished writings by Alyse Gregory, for extracts from her own: 'Alyse Gregory: A biographical Sketch' in *The Powys Review*, no. 3, and for extracts from the following published works by Alyse Gregory: *The Cry of a Gull*, ed. Michael Adam (The Ark Press, 1973), and 'The Character of Llewelyn Powys', 'A Famous Family', 'The Character of Theodore' and 'Recollections from Her Journals: 1940 and 1953', from *Recollections of the Powys Brothers*, ed. Belinda Humfrey (Peter Owen, 1980); Laurence Pollinger and Francis Powys for extracts from 'Mr Weston's Good World' in *Recollections of the Powys Brothers*, ed. Belinda Humfrey (Peter Owen, 1980), and from a sermon by Charles Francis Powys in *The Powys Newsletter*, no. 3, (Colgate University 1972–3); Laurence Pollinger and the Estate of Louis Wilkinson for an extract from an unpublished letter by Louis Wilkinson; Mrs Isobel Powys Marks for extracts from the following works by Littleton C. Powys: *The Joy Of It* (Chapman & Hall, London, 1937), *Still The Joy Of It* (Macdonald, London, 1956), and *The Powys Family* (Western Gazette, Yeovil, 1952); Francis Powys and Chatto & Windus for extracts from the following works by Theodore Francis Powys: *An Interpretation of Genesis* (Chatto & Windus, London, 1929), *The Two Thieves* (Chatto & Windus, 1932), *Soliloquies of a Hermit* (Village Press, 1975), *Mr Tasker's Gods* (Trigon Press, 1977), *The Left Leg* (Chatto & Windus, 1923), *Mockery Gap* (Chatto & Windus, 1925), *Mr Weston's Good Wine* (London, Heinemann Educational Books, 1974), *Fables* (New York, The Viking Press, 1929), *Kindness in a Corner* (Chatto & Windus, 1930), *Unclay* (Chatto & Windus, 1931), and 'The Child Queen' in *The Powys Newsletter*, no. 1, (Colgate University, 1970); Mark Holloway for an extract from his 'With T. F. Powys at Mappowder' in *Recollections of the Powys Brothers*, ed. Belinda Humfrey (Peter Owen, 1980); and Norma Millay Ellis for permission to reprint part of the poem 'The Ballad of Chaldon Down' by Edna St Vincent Millay in *Collected Poems*, Harper & Row, copyright 1939, 1967, by Edna St Vincent Millay and Norma Millay Ellis.

The author and publishers acknowledge the use of material from an extract from *Privileged Spectator* by Ethel Mannin (Hutchinsons) which appeared in *Recollections of the Powys Brothers*, ed. Belinda Humfrey

Acknowledgments

(Peter Owen, 1980); from 'T. F. Powys and the Theatre' by Michel Pouillard in *The Powys Review*, no. 5, ed. Belinda Humfrey; from 'John Cowper Powys and Theodore Dreiser: A friendship' by Marguerite Tjader in *The Powys Review*, no. 6, ed. Belinda Humfrey; from 'The Powys Family: Some Memories of the Mid-Forties' by Denys Val Baker in *The Powys Review*, no. 7, ed. Belinda Humfrey; and from Derek Langridge, *John Cowper Powys: A Record of Achievement* (The Library Association, 1966).

The author and publishers would like to acknowledge the use of material by the following authors, for whom, despite strenuous efforts, the copyright holders could not be traced: Norman Denny, and Gerald Brenan.

Introduction

*The great works of art are not motivated by the clairvoyance of malice;
they are motivated by the clairvoyance of love. It is only in the inferior
levels of art that malice is the dominant note.*

John Cowper Powys in The Complex Vision

Charles Powys's eleven children form one of the most remarkable
literary families of modern times. Seven of them wrote books, and of
their books more than a hundred appeared in print between 1896 and
1960. Three of the family have won an enduring reputation: John
Cowper Powys, author of *Wolf Solent*, *Weymouth Sands*, and *A Glastonbury Romance*; Theodore Francis Powys, author of *Unclay*, *Kindness in a
Corner*, and *Mr. Weston's Good Wine*; and Llewelyn Powys, author of
Dorset Essays, *Somerset Essays*, and *Skin for Skin*.

At first there appears to be a sharp contrast between the solidly
mid-Victorian vicarage childhood of the brothers Powys, and the
insecure, colourful, and sometimes strangely unreal world which they
inhabited in later life; but even in their childhood they were a little out
of step with the times in which they lived. With his inherited wealth
and aristocratic connections, their father was securely placed in the
upper echelons of a rural society that in most important respects was
unchanged since the agricultural revolution of the eighteenth century.
Their childhood was spent in villages and small market towns in the
heart of the Derbyshire, Dorset, and Somerset countryside; and the
increasing industrialisation which was the predominant feature of the
nineteenth century largely passed them by. In their home they lived
very much in their own world; and as they grew older they learned to
share their father's preference for much that was old-fashioned. Their
lives spanned a period of immense change: John Cowper Powys
(1872–1963), born while Livingstone was still alive in central Africa,
lived to see the first man in space; but although he himself was
intellectually adventurous throughout his adult life, he never used a

typewriter, never drove a car, never flew in an aeroplane, and wrote long letters rather than use a telephone.

John and his brothers were brought up as gentlemen: they began their adult lives with moderate private incomes, and even when those incomes failed their status was not severely affected, for during the first half of the twentieth century it was still possible in England to live in 'genteel poverty'. However, poised as they were between the old and the new, they were not unaffected by the modern world; and although they remained unmistakably gentlemen, they reacted strongly against the social conventions and religious beliefs of their childhood. Llewelyn (1884–1939) made frequent attacks upon the church and Christian morality; Theodore (1875–1953) castigated the rural clergy and squirearchy; and John was prepared to advocate full-scale revolution as the prelude to a more equitable society.

All three of them abandoned orthodox Christianity, but in their own fashion all three remained deeply religious; and the central quest of their lives was both religious and philosophical, as they attempted to find meaning and purpose in a post-Christian universe. As they elaborated their individual beliefs, all three of them became preachers or prophets; and as such they are set apart from most of their literary contemporaries.

Certainly, they came into contact with numerous writers, artists and philosophers of their day: between them, they met such diverse figures as Sigmund Freud, T. E. Lawrence, Charlie Chaplin, and Scott Fitzgerald, and they numbered among their friends and acquaintances Thomas Hardy, Bertrand Russell, Arnold Bennett, Isadora Duncan, Augustus John, Edna St Vincent Millay, David Garnett, Sylvia Townsend Warner, Theodore Dreiser and Dorothy Richardson. But none of the brothers produced work which fits clearly or easily into the body of twentieth-century literature. Theodore has sometimes been bracketed with Mary Webb as a 'rural novelist'; but that is hardly an adequate description in view of the highly original and unorthodox philosophy which fills his novels and short stories. Llewelyn, born only two years after James Joyce, made no similar innovations in his craft; he was inspired by the essayists of earlier centuries, and the best of his prose has a clarity and grace to which his contemporaries rarely aspired. John Cowper Powys owed much to his elders, in particular to Thomas Hardy, but his writing is very different from that of his own most famous contemporary, H. G. Wells, who was concerned primarily with sociological and scientific themes. John admired the work of many other living writers, but did not emulate them; he had his own ideas about the scope and function of the novel, but did not found a new school of writing though he was an important influence on the novelist Angus Wilson. John's endeavours to analyse human relation-ships might be compared with those of D. H. Lawrence, who was Llewelyn's contemporary; and his efforts to breathe new life into ancient mythologies with those of Robert Graves, a much younger man; but when his work is taken as a whole, it stands alone. Even John's *Autobiography* is most unusual: he was not unique in relating the difficulties for a sensitive child of being brought up in the upper-middle class of Victorian society – one thinks for example of the autobiography of Laurence Housman, some seven years his senior – but never since Rousseau's *Confessions* in the eighteenth century had a writer been prepared to acknowledge his manias and obsessions so frankly, and similar revelations are unlikely in the post-Freudian era.

Since the three brothers were usually concerned with the unchang-ing nature of the human condition rather than with passing social problems, they continue to speak directly to fresh generations of readers. Llewelyn's philosophy has now become the philosophy of many people who have abandoned formal religion, but believe that life is worthwhile, and must be enjoyed to the full in defiance of estab-lished conventions of all kinds. Theodore's philosophy, informed by his unpleasant awareness of the darker side of existence, is both more disturbing and more profound, a formidable intellectual and spiritual challenge to our comfortable pretensions and delusions. John's philo-sophy has an increasingly widespread appeal for those who believe that the universe is too complex to be explained by conventional science, and who discover in his novels a remarkable blend of insight into human nature, and apparent knowledge of the occult.

Many critical appreciations of the brothers' work have appeared; and in 1967 Kenneth Hopkins published 'a biographical introduction', which he 'modestly offered as a guide or introduction' not only to their work, but to their lives. That book, *The Powys Brothers*, has served a valuable purpose for fifteen years: but it does not attempt to be more than an introduction.

There are still no full-scale lives of either John or Theodore, and none seem likely to appear for many years. Malcolm Elwin's excellent *The Life of Llewelyn Powys*, published in 1946, is in need of revision because Mr Elwin very properly withheld information relating to people then living which might have caused them considerable embarrassment.

In these circumstances my aim has been to provide a joint survey of the lives of the brothers Powys which not only revises Mr Elwin's portrait of Llewelyn, but also provides what are likely to be the definitive portraits of John and Theodore for many years to come. It is important to state at once that this must be treated in some respects as a work in progress. I believe that I have discovered the most significant facts about the lives of all three brothers; but some documents have been withheld from me; and although he has been most helpful in every other respect, Mr Francis Powys, John and Theodore's literary executor, has not allowed me to make quotations from the vast mass of unpublished material which I have studied. I have not seen John's diaries, or many of his letters to Frances Wilkinson; and no doubt when these are in print it will be necessary to make some revisions to the text of the present work. However, John was so prolific a letter-writer, so many of his letters are either in print or available for inspection in university or private collections, and he was so devastatingly honest in, for example, his later correspondence with Louis Wilkinson, that it is unlikely that there is anything of great biographical significance still waiting to be discovered. As for Theodore: I have read a remarkably frank collection of his letters to John in the University of Texas, spanning the years from 1914 to 1952; and I have also had access, through the generosity of Count Potocki of Montalk, to a copy of the original typescript of a life of Theodore written by his adopted daughter. The version of this life which has recently been serialised in *The Powys Review* has been heavily rewritten, had many controversial details or opinions removed and is a far less valuable document.

So far as published material goes, I have read more than one hundred and twenty books from cover to cover. My main reading of unpublished material has been done in the three principal American collections at the Universities of Texas, Colgate and Syracuse; I have also had the benefit of conversations with Mr Oliver Wilkinson, son of the Powyses' great friend Louis Wilkinson; with their nephew, Mr Peter Powys Grey; and with their niece, Mrs Isobel Powys Marks. Mr Kenneth Hopkins has been an invaluable help, suggesting books for me to read, lending many of them to me if they were out of print, and commenting on those parts of my typescript which related to Llewelyn's mistress Gamel Woolsey; he has also gone to considerable trouble to introduce me to people whom he felt I should meet both in England and in America; and his *The Powys Brothers* has been constantly at my side.

I owe an equally great debt to Mrs Evelyn Elwin, Llewelyn's literary executor. She has allowed me to quote freely from his published and unpublished writings, and to read important correspondence in her possession. She also lent me a typescript copy of the then unpublished second volume of the letters from John Cowper Powys to Llewelyn Powys, covering the years from 1925 to Llewelyn's death in 1939. Without the knowledge which I have gleaned from those letters, it would have been impossible to give an accurate account of John's life between those years. Mrs Elwin has also been most hospitable, and given me a great deal of encouragement with what has proved to be an enormous undertaking.

Anyone writing about the Powys brothers owes a considerable debt to Mr Jeffrey Kwintner of the *Village Press* for bringing so many of their works back into print; to Miss Belinda Humfrey who, apart from reprinting published material, has discovered and published so much new biographical and critical material in *Essays on John Cowper Powys* (1972), in *Recollections of the Powys Brothers* (1980) and in the excellent *The Powys Review* (1977–) which she edits; and of course to John Cowper Powys himself for his remarkable *Autobiography*, which has been the single most important source for the early chapters of the present work. I owe an additional debt to Mr Kwintner for his close interest in the completed typescript.

Others whom I thank personally for providing me with information include Mr Charles Lock, Dr Susan Wharton, the Rev. Anthony Butler, Ms Penny Smith, Mr Donald Kerr, Mr Glen Cavaliero, Miss Mary Barham Johnson, Mr Richard Taylor, and Professor G. R. Wilson Knight. I also thank Mr Gerald Pollinger and Mr Victor Bonham-Carter for their helpful efficiency in dealing with copyright matters.

I thank most warmly all those who offered me their friendship and hospitality during my research trips in England and America; and I make particular mention of Dr Francis E. McIntyre, a most civilised gentleman, who welcomed me into his home in the autumn of 1980, and gave me a memorable introduction to the high society of Austin, Texas.

Finally I thank my wife Anne, who read the book in draft, made numerous valuable suggestions, and typed out the final version.

CHAPTER ONE

1797–1885

Aristocratic connections of the Powys family.
Charles Powys, born in Dorset, is ordained, and in 1871 marries Mary
Cowper Johnson.
They move to Derbyshire where John Cowper Powys is born in 1872,
and Theodore Francis Powys in 1875.
In 1879 Charles becomes heir to a fortune, and they return to Dorset.
In 1883 John is sent to boarding school • Llewelyn Powys is born in
1884 • and in 1885 they move to Somerset.

John, Theodore, and Llewelyn – polytheist, heretic, and atheist – were
the sons of a sturdily conventional Victorian parson, the Reverend
Charles Powys. The Powys ancestors had been prosperous country
gentlemen with estates on the Welsh Borders: Charles's great-uncle
Thomas had been created the first Lord Lilford in 1797, and Charles's
branch of the family remained highly proud of their aristocratic connections, and of a shared though probably fictitious descent from the
ancient Welsh princes of Powysdom.

Charles's family was both well-connected and rich. His father, on
giving up a fellowship at Corpus Christi College, Cambridge, and
becoming rector of the Dorsetshire village of Stalbridge, had married
an extremely wealthy widow. Mrs Knight brought with her not only
riches, but a daughter named Pippa, and a strain of masochism so
powerful that some of her descendants made puns about the deadly
nightshade in their blood.[1]

Charles, born in 1843, eventually went up to his father's college;
though he was intellectually a late developer, and his main pleasures at
Cambridge were boxing, walking and rowing. He expected that the
family fortune would go to his elder brother Littleton, whom he greatly
admired, and who had taken a commission in the army; while he

himself, declining a teaching post at Repton, was ordained and became curate-in-charge of Bradford Abbas, a very small Dorset village not far from Sherborne. In 1869, returning to Cambridge to take his Master's degree, he went on to spend a few days' holiday with the family of the Norfolk parson who had tutored him before he first went up to the university. On Whit Sunday Charles impressed them all by preaching 'a simple, earnest Gospel sermon'.[2] Now aged twenty-six, he was indeed:

> an impressive figure, well nigh six feet tall, with high, broad shoulders and a deep chest. . . . He had an arresting face, a broad, not very high, forehead with beetling brows that overhung his deep-set grey-blue eyes, wavy . . . hair and side whiskers, a good nose and a long upper lip which he had a way of pulling down and making still longer when stirred by any strong emotional feeling; he had a determined chin and jaw and no-one who saw him could fail to recognise his powerful personality.

During this visit, Charles was strongly attracted to one of the parson's daughters, Mary, a girl of twenty who:

> was of medium height and moved easily and unaffectedly. She was always simple, modest and neat in her dress. . . . But she could not fail to make an impression . . . with her striking face, with its good brow crowned with lovely rippling hair, parted madonna-like in the middle . . . the deep-set brown eyes were perhaps her chief feature, and a good nose, a mobile mouth, and a well-shaped chin completed her pleasing oval face.

Mary was not only attractive, but witty and accomplished. She drew and painted and loved music; and she had attended lectures at the Royal Institution in London, where she stayed with an uncle and was described as being: 'quite delightful. We all compare her to a mountain spring – it is so refreshing to fall in with her. Her conversation flows on so prettily with quaint little sparkles of fun every now and again.'[3] At home she was 'a most entertaining narrator of incidents in the village life', and she was devoted to literature.

This was not altogether surprising: Mary's family had long prided itself on taking an interest in literature. They knew that they were descended from a branch of the family which had produced the poet John Donne; and Mary's grandfather Dr John Johnson was so proud of being the second cousin of the poet William Cowper – who called him affectionately 'Johnny of Norfolk' – that he had named Mary's father William Cowper Johnson. William had carried on this tradition by giving Cowper as Mary's middle name.

Mary Cowper Johnson, as one of her sons later wrote, 'seemed made for an artistic life'. Unfortunately her family shared some of William Cowper's less desirable traits. Mary's father was liable to fits of nervous depression, and she herself had a morbidly self-doubting and fatalistic streak, not very obvious in those days – though an aunt found her 'inclined to rebel against the botheration of being made to think about *herself*, and take care of herself' – and deriving partly from the shock of an older sister's death from tuberculosis.[4] For the sake of the security and strength which Charles Powys offered her, Mary was prepared to sacrifice most of her artistic interests, 'divert[ing] her burning zeal for the arts into the channel of her devotion to him and the life that was his'.

In 1871, after a courtship of two years, Charles and Mary were married in her father's church at Yaxham. Although Charles was only six years older than his new wife, he had known her since the time when she was still a child, and he was already a young man. This made it easier for him to assume the same position of unquestioned authority, within his own sphere, that his father had exercised over his own very much younger wife. Mary, for her part, had grown up in a household where her father had set very high standards; and it was partly her fear that she would prove unable to live up to these standards[5] which had given her the tendency towards a somewhat masochistic resignation in the face of personal difficulties. Their children later applauded the dominating strength and the 'massive simplicity' of their father, while regretting the obvious self-sacrifice of their mother.

Charles, in his efforts to be a good Christian, had developed a saintly delight in depriving himself of things which a normal man might reasonably have enjoyed without guilt. He made 'bread and butter . . . his staple diet', tasted 'alcohol only as a priest at the altar', and conveyed to his children the impression that sexual pleasures were not in fact very agreeable. Mary encouraged him in all this, appearing to think more highly of renunciation and even of failure than of acceptance and success. In her own mind, as even her most orthodox son admitted, 'there may well have been questionings and [religious] doubts which she shared with no one'; but she rested securely upon

3

her husband's simple faith and unshakeable convictions. At the same time, Mary's love and interest was of the utmost importance to Charles: after her death, another of their sons was shocked to find him with tears pouring down his cheeks as he raked the drive. On being asked what the matter was, Charles lamented: 'There is nobody now to come and see what I do!'

Early in 1872, a few months after their wedding, the Rev. Charles Powys was appointed vicar of Shirley in Derbyshire, a living which was in the gift of his half-sister Pippa, now married to an Oxford don. It was at Shirley, in the large eighteenth-century vicarage, that Mary awaited the birth of their first child. It is recalled in the family that she was 'full of foreboding and did not expect to survive';[6] but on 8 October 1872, she gave birth quite safely to a healthy boy. Retaining the 'Cowper' conceit, Charles and Mary named him John Cowper Powys. There were few obvious pressures on the family: they had servants to help them look after the comfortable house and extensive gardens; they lived in peaceful seclusion, a quarter of a mile across the fields from the small village, and not far from some of the finest scenery in England: one of John's earliest memories was of the rocky valley of the Dove, and of the 'dim feeling of *immensity*' produced in his mind by the grassy hill in the neighbourhood of Dovedale which is known as Mount Cloud. Although Mary continued to fear childbirth,[7] John soon had some companions: in 1874 Littleton Charles was born; and on 20 December 1875, Theodore Francis. But despite being a member of a happy family, in a peaceful country setting, John later recalled that his early childhood was so unhappy that he would never wish to live it over again.

John was sensitive and imaginative, and there were several incidents which cast a gloom over his seven years at Shirley. The most memorable of these occurred when he and his family joined a larger party to enjoy a picnic on the banks of a private lake in nearby Osmaston Park. John, playing happily, threw a rotten stick into the water; and a foolish adult said that he 'had better look out. The police would have him for throwing things into the pretty lake!' For the remainder of his time at Shirley, John lived in fear of being taken away by the police. Night after night, from his cot opposite Littleton's cot, he lay awake suffering from a 'dark unrevealed, unspoken terror', which was only occasionally alleviated when a hymn calling on God to 'Keep me . . . beneath Thine own almighty wings' was recited over him as part of his bed-time prayers.

Perhaps to combat this fear, John played with the idea of having magical powers himself: his head may have been filled with odd ideas by his Nanny, Maria Brocklehurst, who was 'a most competent intellectual', but had 'a mania for . . . Phrenology . . . the pseudo-science of "feeling your bumps"';[8] and once, walking down the narrow lane which led to the church, a little ahead of the pram in which Littleton was being pushed, 'I turned to the nurse-maid who was pushing it and announced triumphantly that I was "the Lord of Hosts".' The idea that he might possess magical powers was a dream to which John clung for the rest of his life.

Another upsetting element in John's childhood was very closely associated with his awareness of his father. Although on the surface there was usually nothing but kindness from Charles Powys, there was a sense of some great force dammed up in him that was frightening for a child. Fifty years later, recalling his father 'as vividly from that early time as . . . from all the later periods of my life', John wrote that: 'Enormous emotional and magnetic explosiveness, held rigidly under an almost military control, was the most characteristic thing that emanated from Charles Francis Powys.'

But on one of the rare occasions when this explosiveness was not held under control, Charles displayed a violent temper. John had been indulging 'the most wicked pleasure then known to me, of transferring tadpoles from the pond in the field to the puddles left by the rain at the side of the drive', when Charles arrived and was shocked by his son's brutality. Dragging John away, he took him to where he himself had been chopping down some laurels, 'moved by a natural desire that his son should behold these deeds of devastation and glory in his begetter's skill and strength.' Then Charles gave John a present, which he had carved himself from the laurel wood: it was an axe. For a sensitive three year old, the incident as a whole was a thoroughly disturbing experience; and it was one which John never forgot. His father, angry with him for his cruelty to the tadpoles, had shown him a scene of devastation which was the result of his own violence, and had then given him a weapon for further destruction. The creation of the sweet-smelling laurel axe was the only positive part of the story; and in later years, recalling his loss of the axe, it came over John 'that I had lost – for ever and for ever lost – a mystery that would have guarded me all my days.' All else was violence, or suppressed violence; and John's mind became seriously thrown off balance.

Looking at one of his picture-books, and seeing an eagle seize upon a lamb, John became thrilled by a sadistic feeling; and for much of the remainder of his long life he was obsessed by sadistic images. Excited by these images, he developed 'the habit night by night of making my little cot shake with the feverish intensity of my infantile eroticism'; and this led to further trouble: for when this habit was reported to his father, John 'would be asked every morning if I had been "doing that"' and when he confessed, as he invariably did, ice-cold water would be poured over him.

This punishment did not deter John from the fantasies he enjoyed each night, in which he was in control of a world which normally frightened him; and sometimes such fantasies spilled over into his day-time games. On one occasion this almost had fatal results: playing the hangman, John very nearly killed his brother Littleton, who began to turn purple as he swung from the bellrope in the passage at the top of the stairs.

Although John was disturbed by the 'frightening' aspect of what might lie beneath his father's self-control, that self-control was so rigorous, and Charles Powys's simple convictions were so unshakeable, that less sensitive children, such as Littleton, were able to grow up relatively unaffected by any underlying tensions in his character. The strength of these convictions was remarkable. Many of them, including his 'fierce, inarticulate, irrational loyalty' to old things and old customs – 'old-fashioned' was his strongest word of praise – were associated with his family pride. On his shelves he kept a volume of Burke's Peerage; and John remembered how his father's eyes burned 'with a fire that was at once secretive and blazing, like the fire in the eyes of a long discrowned king, when he told us how we were descended from the ancient Welsh princes of Powysland.' With this enormous pride went a 'child-like sense of the incredible romance of his own existence upon earth'. Delighting in the mere fact of being alive, he had an intense interest in all natural things, and, though he despised science, he knew all the common names for rocks, flowers, birds or butterflies. He had a fine collection of birds' eggs, and would recount proudly the dangers which he had overcome to collect them; while he rarely came home 'without a small bunch of wild flowers in his hand'. But this sense of romance went further than an interest in natural history:

> Every person of his life, every place he had ever lived in, took on
> for him the importance of something tremendous and

mythological! His pride and his egoism in this ultimate matter were absolute. He had only to link up any human being, any place, with the experiences of his own life, and that person and that place assumed a curious fairy-like quality, *beyond normal reality*.

The children's Johnson grandparents were still living in Norfolk, and the Rev. Charles Powys occasionally took his wife and family by train to visit them in their Yaxham rectory. John later recalled wandering around the village with Littleton and Theodore, amusing them by pretending to be a steam-engine, and fishing for newts in the village pond; but the new landscape made the greatest impression on him, 'lying almost at sea-level, and where nothing but poplars and alders and willows obstruct the rising and sinking of the sun'.

There were other holidays: the children's Powys grandfather had died in the year before John was born, so none of them ever knew him; but their grandmother was now living in retirement at Weymouth on the south coast. Each year, the Powys family visited her house in Brunswick Terrace. Here, from a drawing-room where the fragrance of old wood mingled with the sharper scents of the sea, they could look out across the narrow esplanade to the sea shore. From shelving banks of pebbles the water grew deep so rapidly that the fishermen chose this place to draw in their nets; and beyond them the children could see the great chalky outcrops of Portland to the west, and the White Nose and St Alban's Head to the east. Sometimes they walked to the sandy beaches for which Weymouth is famous; and with their father they explored the harbour, travelled on ferries, went out rowing, examined sea-anemones, and collected shells: in particular, cowrie shells, which Charles would hold 'with exquisite care in one of his broad palms . . . saying with intense pride: "My brother tells me they use cowries as money in India."'

This brother was the children's uncle Littleton, now a captain in the 59th Regiment, and a man who had seen a good deal of active service in the East. He came to stay with them once at Shirley, where he impressed John as 'a dignified, bearded man, with a square forehead . . . I recollect well the vicious pleasure I got when seated on his knee in the evening, he permitted me to pound his bearded face with my fists to test the courage of this officer of the Queen.' When Littleton returned to his regiment he was stationed in Afghanistan at Kandahar, from where he kept up a regular correspondence with his brother.

Early in 1879 Littleton was pleased to hear that Charles intended to leave Shirley:[9] not only was he 'young and strong and felt a call to work in a larger sphere'; but he began to feel that it was time to keep a closer watch on their elderly mother, and so he had accepted a subordinate post as curate only eight miles away from Weymouth in the pleasant country town of Dorchester.

While Charles was still planning the move, he heard the news that his brother Littleton had died of cholera; and he himself was now sole heir to a fortune of some £40,000. Charles now decided to purchase the lease of a substantial house which was then being built in a good part of Dorchester: for with the birth of Gertrude in 1877, and of Eleanor, or 'Nelly' in 1879, he was already the father of five children. They had to leave Shirley before their new home was ready, and so were able to spend several enjoyable months at Weymouth before moving into Rothesay House.

It was here, at the age of seven and a half, rather late for a clever child, that John learned to read. At Shirley, perhaps not long before the move, he had listened while his father had read from Aytoun's *Scottish Cavaliers*: a warlike poem in which the Rhine was crossed by exiled Highlanders in the service of the King of France; and he later wrote that Aytoun's verses, and the illustrations in the book, had not only made him 'an obstinate, incurable romanticist', but had given him his 'first impression of the enchantment of literature'. Stimulated by this, he learned to read for himself: and his first choice was *Alice Through the Looking Glass* by Lewis Carroll. He read it from cover to cover, sitting in his father's study on a wet afternoon; and at once, together with its companion volume *Alice in Wonderland*, which had already been read out to them, it became a part of the children's private world.

For John, in particular, this was a happy world. He left behind some of his childhood fears at Shirley; and he was to remember the first two years at Rothesay House as 'the most important, most significant, and certainly most happy of my whole life'. He and Littleton had not yet gone away to boarding school, but attended a small private Dame's school in Dorchester. Sometimes, like any normal children, they behaved mischievously; but their parents gave them a great deal of freedom to roam the town and surrounding countryside. From Rothesay House in respectable South Walks Road they could walk northwards into the town centre to where their father's church, St Peter's, stood at a central crossroads dominating High West and High East Streets; and beyond the church they could find their way along a lane which led to the River Frome, and the watermeadows where they liked to catch minnows. Or they could walk south along the Weymouth Road: this rapidly brought them to Maumbury Rings, an old Roman amphitheatre dating back to the days of the walled town of Durnovaria; and two miles further on, they could turn aside to the vast prehistoric earthworks of Maiden Castle, an Iron Age hill-fort which had first been occupied around the year 2000 BC. These ancient sites became closely associated in John's mind with the golden age of his childhood, and this had important effects on his adult thinking.

In the meantime, as the leader of his brothers and sisters, John involved them in all kinds of imaginative pursuits; and when he was nine years old he created himself the commander-in-chief of the 'Volentiā Army': the last letter of 'Volentiā' being pronounced like the word 'aye'. Sitting in the half-boarded attic of Rothesay House, at a table with two lighted candles on it, he brandished two loaded 'cap' pistols at the house-maid, brought before him as a captive by the other children; and 'such was my hypnotic energy', he later wrote, that he forced his organisation upon every one of his fellow pupils at the Dame's school.

The Volentiā Army was a practical organisation; but John still had fancies about being a magician, like Merlin, and his powerful imagination played odd tricks on his mind: one night, for example, soon after moving into Rothesay House, John had a strange experience. Unable to sleep, he was looking out of his bedroom window across the South Walk: and it appeared to him that the passers-by were transformed into 'a fantastic procession of phantoms . . . ghosts who had the power of automaton-like progression, without a movement of legs or feet!' John was not particularly alarmed by this vision: his head was always full of strange fancies; and Charles Powys, who had more imagination than one might suppose, had encouraged these fancies[10] by inventing for his children a compelling and endless allegorical saga about the dangers which beset Giant Grumble and Fairy Sprightly as they used all their arts against the sinister activities of 'a scientific pedant, called by the narrator *"the Professor"'*.

In addition to this story-telling, their mother began to read to them the historical poems and romances of Sir Walter Scott, which led John to wish for:

> that kind of romantic struggle with things and people, things and people always yielding as I advanced, *but not too easily,* a

9

struggle which takes place in an ideal region, hewn out of reality and constantly touching but never quite identified with reality, such as might be most conveniently described by the expression *a Quest* . . . [and which] . . . had to take place in a world which was at once the real world and yet a world of marvels.

Before long, the Volentiā Army was only a part of this world, as John invented the complete mythology of an imaginary world, including the 'Dromonds': awesome creatures who lived in the prehistoric burial-mounds of Dorset; and the 'powerful but rather dwarfish' 'Escrawal-dons', the enemies of the Volentiā Army:

> The 'Volentiā Army' became in fact a sort of multiple Logos, standing midway between the visible and the invisible. In its realistic aspect it entered constantly into my daily life whereas in its ideal aspect it became part of an imaginary history that had no counterpart in reality. In this connection I can still feel the exact and identical thrill which I set to work, with several half-penny notebooks before me, to compose a language for the 'Volentiā Army'.

A good deal of this invention probably took place in the spring and summer of 1882, when John was still nine years old, and his brother Littleton was eight. They were still close friends, though John felt that Littleton had 'certain shrewd reservations' about the Volentiā Army; and while John was the undisputed leader in imaginative play, Little-ton was more intellectually acute, and also physically stronger. In his strength, Littleton was like their father: and on a certain long walk along the coast, the two of them would regularly watch 'with grave indulgence' when John stopped at the last moment, afraid of jumping across a stream which flowed into the sea, and which Littleton had cleared with ease. On another occasion that summer, John and Little-ton decided to emulate their father by walking the eight miles across the Downs from Weymouth to Dorchester. Having walked a good deal of the way, they were half-way up a high ridge when John was suddenly too exhausted to go any further:

> It was then that Littleton showed 'the rock from which he had been hewn and the pit from which he had been dug' by doing what anyone would have supposed absolutely impossible. He took the collapsed 'Johnny' upon his small unconquerable back

and actually staggered under this burden *up* the remaining portion of the ascent!

In this same summer of 1882 Theodore, who was now six and a half years old, began to take a more active part in the games of his two older brothers. Most relaxed with Littleton, with whom he exchanged 'an especial kind of badinage quaintly charged with all the little humorous details of their daily life', he was also strongly under the influence of John's imaginative world, and threw himself with great enthusiasm into the activities of the Volentiā Army. But he suffered from the excessive demands made upon him both by John and by their father. John misused the power he had over him, finding 'in his imagination a quick response to some of my most devilish games and some of my most scandalous experiments.'; and their father, overestimating his strength, took him on walks which were far too long for him, so that John later remembered 'little Theodore, white in the face and with great forlorn eyes like an over-driven animal, as he was dragged along some dusty road where the very flies joined forces to persecute him!' However, Theodore developed ways of protecting himself. At Weymouth he had often fainted during family prayers to secure some extra attention for himself; and now, in the garden of Rothesay House, beneath one of the newly planted shrubberies, he 'established, entirely for himself, a solitary retreat – a kind of infantile "Beth-Car" – to which he gave the name of "Bushes' Home".' In another way he asserted his independence: the Rev. Charles Powys expected all his children to be collectors, like himself: so John collected birds' eggs, and Littleton collected fossils and butterflies; but Theodore, as John put it, 'always so terrifyingly original, did actually collect nothing'.

Of the younger ones, Gertrude was now five years old, and Eleanor three; and the family had been enlarged twice more, by the birth in 1881 of Albert, and in 1882 of Marian: so that Mrs Powys now had seven children to look after. For another twelve months or so, everything continued more or less happily and uneventfully; though after a visit to Corfe Castle, John composed his first poem, a lurid effort which began:

> At Corfe Castle when the light
> Has vanished and the shades of night
> Steal o'er the ruins grey
> There is a dungeon from light of day
> Where now a grisly Spectre holds his sway.

Then, in 1883, their father decided that it was time for John and Littleton to be at boarding school, and he arranged for them to go some nineteen miles away to Westbury House, the preparatory school at Sherborne from which boys were expected to go on to Sherborne School itself. At the start of their first term, the Rev. Charles Powys accompanied his two eldest sons on their train journey northwards, sitting opposite them in the railway carriage as:

> they were now plunging, plunging indeed – as everyone knows who knows anything of school life – into stresses and tensions, shocks and endurances, the like of which, unless they went to war or became penniless outcasts, they would never again have to experience till the day of their death.

Some of these stresses and shocks were experienced almost immediately. At night, the brothers slept in a small bedroom under the authority of an older boy, who would take pleasure in hurling a heavy slipper at John's head whenever he made the slightest movement 'that could be interpreted as "sinful"'; and who generally ruled over them in a brutal and sadistic manner. During the day there was also some unpleasantness. On the very first afternoon, John proudly took out the new leather football which his father had given him, and carried it to the playing field. But it was round, and therefore the wrong shape for the rugby football which was played at Westbury House; and the other boys took his father's gift from him, and literally kicked it to pieces before his eyes.

This was a poor start for someone whose ability in games was, in any case, very limited. John disliked rugger and was a weak swimmer. He grew to hate the humiliation of afternoons spent playing cricket, when long hours of incompetent fielding on his part would be followed by a short innings in which he was invariably out for a duck. Nor did he enjoy cross-country runs, when he would see his headmaster, Mr Blake,

> waiting for us at some remote lane's turning, with his broad shoulders and military moustache, and that ubiquitous little dog at his feet.
> 'Well, Powys Ma.,' he would cry, as panting and breathless I trailed past him, bitterly envying that complacent poodle at his feet, 'Well, Powys Ma., no spurt left in you, I see!'

But although he did cane John and Littleton once, to punish them for drawing pictures of a caning in an art class, W. H. Blake was sympathetic as well as powerful. He had a feeling for literature, and, realising where John's talents and interests lay, he encouraged him with his prose writing, listened indulgently to his opinions on books, and very soon put him in charge of the 'Prep' library. This led to many happy hours of escapism for John, whose chief preoccupation had now become 'to live *as if I were at home and not at school'*. Sitting indoors, the key to the library in his pocket, he read his way indiscriminately not only through classics like Jules Verne's *Twenty Thousand Leagues under the Sea*, but through everything else which the library had to offer.

As well as the mental freedom to roam through the imaginary places of literature, John found that he had a surprising amount of physical freedom. Westbury House was in Station Road, at the southern end of the town; and each week there were two half-holidays when compulsory games were often cancelled, and the boys allowed to wander where they liked. On Saturdays they usually walked into Sherborne, where the fifteenth-century Abbey Church presided over a peaceful market town, with narrow lanes and old-fashioned shops where they could spend their pocket-money on the cakes and sweets for which John had developed an insatiable greed. On Sunday afternoons, which were always free, the Powys brothers would set off on long country walks. They both missed their home: 'Are the Volentias prospering? I hope they are',[11] John wrote rather sadly to Theodore during his first term away from home; and he later recalled that 'It was pathetic to see how our walks invariably showed a tendency to direct themselves towards that quarter of the horizon where our home was', a tendency which usually led them into the Park, the Long Burton Road, and Honeycombe Woods.

Littleton, more sociable and athletic than his brother, was in fact enjoying life at the Prep. But he was very loyal to his brother, not only going on walks with him, but playing games with him, and defending him from other people's attacks: in the swimming pool, for example, he made it his business to duck anyone who had ducked John. They also watched some of the Sherborne School matches together;[12] and John began to hero-worship the most distinguished of the Sherborne athletes and games-players.

John's closest friend at this time, apart from his brother, was 'a grave, rather womanish child', who lent him a copy of *The Three*

Musketeers by Dumas, and with whom he shared a 'kind of amorous romance'. Then the boy found a new friend, who:

> had picked up somewhere the piquant balladish expression, 'Tetine and Thomas Bedlam', and had promptly applied it to his friendship with my friend. This phrase enchanted me: and it gave me the most complicated pleasure to tease these two – for the drama of the situation robbed it of all jealous pangs – by repeating like an incantation 'Tetine and Thomas Bedlam' . . . till they were forced to flee from me in confusion. I seem to find in this 'Tetine and Thomas Bedlam' episode thus enjoyed vicariously, the clue to almost everything that I later became.

During the next two years Littleton continued to enjoy life, but John gradually became more and more unhappy. As he passed his eleventh and twelfth birthdays, John still enjoyed his reading, and his walks with his brother. But he could not read or be with Littleton all the time. Having lost the friendship of 'Tetine', he became increasingly isolated and a natural target for bullies, who twisted his arms, punched him, and even prodded billiard cues at his face. His spirit permanently scorched by the suppressed violence in his father's nature, John was especially frightened of violence, and could only cope with it by submitting to the bullies as meekly as possible, thereby suppressing his own violent impulses to retaliate. In time, like many children who are bullied, John himself became, in his own words, 'something of a bully'; and although he later recalled only one occasion on which he *'practised'* his 'sadistic tendency', when he deliberately got a boy into trouble with someone who slapped his face as a result, he appears to have been extremely unkind to his brother Theodore during the holidays.[13]

Theodore, eight and a half years old in the summer of 1884, had been attending a school in Dorchester; and attracted bullying in the family simply because he was so unlike everyone else, with his own ideas about what to do and where to go. Gertrude, already both capable and artistic, was seven; Nelly was a cheerful child of five; Bertie was three, and Marian two; and now, on 14 August 1884, an eighth child was born to Mary Powys, and named Llewelyn.

Within sixteen months of Llewelyn's birth, there were considerable changes, one of which affected the whole family. Early in 1885 the 'Prep.' was moved by Blake at his own expense from Westbury House to the new buildings of Acreman House, in the north-west of the town, and very much closer to Sherborne School;[14] later that year both John and Littleton moved on from the 'Prep.' to the 'Big School'; Theodore now began boarding at the 'Prep.'; and, most important of all, Charles Powys had been appointed vicar of the Somerset village of Montacute.

CHAPTER TWO

1885–1894

*John at Sherborne School, 1885–91, and at Corpus Christi College,
Cambridge, 1891–4.*
*Theodore at Sherborne 'Prep.', 1885–9, at school in Suffolk, 1889–91,
apprenticed to a farmer, 1891–3, then to his own farm at Sweffling in
Suffolk.*
Llewelyn a child at Montacute • their sister Nelly dies in 1893.

Montacute derives its name from the *Mons acutus*, the steep hill of St
Michael's which overlooks the village from the west; but its special
character comes from blocks of the rich yellow stone quarried from
nearby Ham Hill, and used for nearly all the buildings in Montacute:
the magnificent Elizabethan mansion Montacute House, which in 1885
was the home of William Phelips the squire; the shops and inns around
the main square, just to the south of Montacute House, and known as
'The Borough'; the houses which line the road as it runs westward from
The Borough along Middle Street, and then northward past the King's
Arms and along Bishopston; the fifteenth century church of St Catherine's, to the south of Middle Street, where Charles Francis Powys
was installed as vicar on 5 November 1885; and the remains of a mediaeval priory just beyond the church. 'Coming to Montacute from the
Roman remains of Dorchester', wrote John,

> was like plunging into the earth-mould of mediaeval romance.
> A portion of the Holy Rood itself had once been found on the
> top of Montacute Hill, and from the high ground above the
> village could clearly be seen the conical shape of Glastonbury
> Tor rising over the Sedgemoor marshes . . . into the rich soil of
> Montacute . . . that history-charged, mystical clay of Somerset,
> my mythological imagination sank at once like a plummet of
> privileged lead.

Outside the village, beyond Bishopston, lay the vicarage to which Charles Powys had removed his wife and eight children, together with their nurse, governess, cook, and two maids. The main building was a substantial one of yellow stone, with a 'slate roof and French shutters and jasmine, rose-muffled walls'.[1] Charles himself had a comfortable study just beside the front door; there were spacious dining and drawing rooms; and a considerable extension which provided the family with all the space they could require. Outside there were lawns and shrubberies, and a gravelled drive which curved pleasantly beneath overhanging trees to the Tintinhull road. When John was admiring this approach to their new house one day, Charles Powys, with his great capacity for 'intense . . . moments of happiness', was 'extremely gratified . . . and rubbing his hands together and protruding his upper lip, after his fashion when he suddenly felt happy, he replied with infinite pride: "I'm very glad, John, my boy, that you appreciate the home I have provided for you!"'

Mr Phelips welcomed the family very kindly, asking them over to Montacute House not long after their arrival to see his Christmas tree. He owned all the country round about, and allowed the children 'to go where we liked, and every nook and corner was known to us . . . Ham Hill with its quarries and grassy slopes . . . provided a wonderful playground.'[2] Mr Phelips was also one of the governors of Sherborne School; and there, after a short holiday, John and Littleton returned, together with Theodore, who was now bound for the 'Prep.'.

Most of the Sherborne School buildings were grouped immediately to the north of the abbey; but when they entered the 'Big School' together, John and Littleton had been placed in Wildman's House, some distance away in the south-west of the town. Mr Wildman himself, a bachelor and a classical scholar, was a good form-master, but a failure as a housemaster: so far as John could later remember, he 'just left us alone'. The headmaster, E. M. Young, seems to have given Wildman little support. Young had resigned a fellowship at Trinity College, Cambridge, to become a schoolmaster,[3] and was 'a cultural and liberal-minded gentleman', who wrote the excellent school song, beginning, *'Olim fuit monachorum/Schola nostra sedes'*, which John very much enjoyed. But he had tried to introduce a more civilised element into what had been an aggressively 'hearty' school; and, according to John, despite having been headmaster of Sherborne for seven years, Young was still being 'persecuted by all the bully boys of the place'; or, as the official record has it, he had 'somehow failed through fault or misfortune to secure the loyal cooperation of many of those with whom he had to deal.'[4] With such a weak headmaster, and an equally weak housemaster, Wildman's 'tended to get more and more into the hands of demagogues and gangsters.'

In this chaotic atmosphere, John found it very difficult to hold his own. He had begun at a severe disadvantage, as Littleton recognised, simply because he was 'so sensitive, imaginative and introspective and so full of his own importance'. Worse still, his arrival had been 'heralded by the news, "A poet is coming to the house next term,"' and this 'was enough to brand him as an oddity, one whom ordinary boys would find amusement in harrying.' He was teased for his appearance: 'Did you ever see such an ugly mug, in all your days, as Powys Ma.'s mug?'; for the way he ate: they said he chewed his food with his front teeth instead of the back ones; and for his lack of sporting ability. Indeed, his unpopularity 'grew and grew to such a pitch that it ended in what amounted to a Powys Ma. outlawing, a Powys Ma. baiting'; and he got it into his head that he was in many ways a complete fool.

In the circumstances, his scholarly progress was not rapid. A good examinee, he had started in the Lower Third, while Littleton began at the very bottom of the school. But in the Upper Third, Littleton passed him by, from then on was always at least one form ahead of his brother, and was even given a study before him. When John did at last qualify for a study, however, the two brothers shared one together; and Littleton redeemed what might have seemed an unforgiveable superiority in a younger brother by helping him a good deal with his work, even composing Greek verses for him to take into class as his own. For much of the time, John himself made very little effort; and in his first two years his favourite teacher was a Mr Whitehead: not because John learned anything, but because Mr Whitehead, while preserving good order, seemed to John to demand absolutely nothing, so that mathematical lessons with him were 'an oasis of peace and quiet in my tumultuous life', a time for John to sit quietly and dream. Later, he recalled that one morning, on realising that he was due to have a lesson with Mr Whitehead that day, he picked up his Euclid, and was filled with a wave of ecstasy, in which the book became:

> a sort of consecrated wafer, into which every lovely sensation I
> had ever had, had miraculously gathered itself. It is really
> possible that that moment was the most important of my whole
> life! . . . This tattered Euclid revealed to me that it is possible,

even when the bulk of your days and the larger number of your hours are full of discomfort, to embrace a thousand essences of life. The limbs of the loveliest women, the flanks of the noblest of hills, the mosses upon the most marbly rocks, the clearest waterfalls . . . our deepest pleasures strew behind them . . . leaves of delight [which can be] summoned up at will.

John was learning to enjoy whatever pleasures he could find, however solitary they might be. Changing before a swim, for example, he made sure of standing next to a very handsome boy, so that he could silently adore him; and, taking some interest in women as well as in other boys, he searched for images which satisfied his romantic feelings. Anything that was indecent, or bawdy, repelled him: what he liked was the 'daintily sketched outlines of the feminine form' which he could cut out from the pages of the comic *Ally Sloper*; and he would hunt through old editions of *Punch* to find drawings of 'delicate-limbed sylphs'.

At least John was able to discuss the horrors of school life with his brother Theodore, who was now at the 'Prep.', and hated it much more than John had done. In the past Theodore had always been closer to Littleton, who had treated him more kindly; but now he felt a good deal in common with his eldest brother, and the two of them managed to meet, deciding on one occasion that it would be 'far better to be a navvy on railway track than be at school'. Theodore joined both his brothers on their Sunday afternoon walks. He would wait for them at the top of the hill; and years later John recalled the hopeless sorrow of 'those mournful grey eyes, under that straw hat, that used to turn to us as we came hurrying up'. Theodore was desperately unhappy away from his home, in the company of people who never allowed him to have any of the privacy which he cherished. Luckily, his parents came to realise that a major change was necessary. Theodore's thirteenth birthday fell in December 1888; and the following spring, when it was time for him to leave the Sherborne Prep.,[5] he went on not to the senior school, but to a boarding school at Aldeburgh in Suffolk. Although this was even further from Montacute, it was a smaller school with a more friendly atmosphere; and it had the great advantage that the headmaster, the Rev. W. G. Wilkinson, was well known to Mary Powys: indeed, his wife was her best friend.[6]

John and Littleton continued their walks alone, tramping down lanes and across fields until they knew the countryside for miles around Sherborne, 'with the knowledge of poachers and game-keepers'. After the move from Dorchester to Montacute, their favourite walk was now to a wooded height above the small village of Trent, a height from which, in the distance, they could see the summit of Montacute Hill. When they grew older they discovered that there was just time, between two o'clock and six o'clock on a Sunday afternoon, to run the ten miles home, enjoy platefuls of strawberries, and run the ten miles back to school!

Seeing what a great effort the brothers were prepared to make to reach home for such a short time, it is easy to imagine how much they enjoyed their holidays. They did not always spend the entire time with their brothers and sisters: in the summer of 1888, for example, John and Littleton stayed in the heart of Dartmoor, with an old clergyman who had been their grandfather's curate at Stalbridge. But when they returned from Dartmoor, they were welcomed back into a large and happy family. John was now fifteen-and-a-half, and Littleton fourteen, and they had for company Theodore, aged twelve-and-a-half; Gertrude, eleven; and Nelly, nine. The younger children were Bertie, a shy child who spent his days in the nursery carefully piling up wooden building blocks; May, with her quick intelligence and her mass of curly brown hair; and Llewelyn, who had just enjoyed his fourth birthday. Then came Catherine, or 'Katie', born in 1886, 'the first Montacute baby, fair-haired with big grey eyes [and] an ardently affectionate nature'; and William, a baby only a few months old: so now there were ten children to be gathered round the great mahogany table in the dining room.

Llewelyn was one of those remarkable children who are not only good-looking, but who radiate happiness in a way which enriches the lives of all those around them. Described by Littleton as 'a lovely sunny child, always smiling and laughing, with a wealth of bright golden curly hair', he charmed family and friends alike. Away at Sherborne, John and Littleton thought of Llewelyn with particular affection, remembering for example the day on which he first learned to run, and then came up to them in the garden to say with happy pride: 'Watch I go!' He was a child for whom life was usually a joy: and now, at the age of four,

> as he stood to be measured for [a] velvet suit . . . he was 'so excited at being alive' that his mother had to be called to stop his jumping up and down and repeating, 'Happy me! Happy me!'

His brother John heard the same ecstatic cry from him as one bright day he danced up the garden path, between lawns and flower beds which seemed to him 'always held under a spell of golden grace.'

While the younger children played in the garden, John 'hypnotised Littleton and cajoled Theodore' into acting some Shakespeare plays. The Phelips children were easily persuaded to take part; one of the youngest of them was rather touchingly in love with John;[7] and the squire himself came to watch John play Hamlet, and as John thought, to gaze 'with wonder at the ancestral Welsh dragon painted in red and gold above the fireplace'. John had always enjoyed playing a part; but his new interest in acting stemmed from a visit to London. He had been taken to the theatre by one of his relatives, and had been lucky enough to watch several performances by one of the greatest Shakespearean actors of all time. So profoundly moved was he by the experience that when he was an old man he wrote to an admirer: 'If I were asked "what man had influenced your whole life the most" I should reply without a moment's hesitation HENRY IRVING.'[8] Besides acting, John continued to enjoy writing poems; and he was also trying his hand at stories. When Theodore was so desperately unhappy at the Sherborne Prep., for example, John had tried to cheer him up by reading out to him the first chapter of a dashing romance in which Theodore appeared, under another name, as the head of a band of smugglers.[9]

Part of the summer holidays was often spent at Weymouth, where their grandmother still lived at Penn House. It was here that John first held Llewelyn in his arms, as a very small baby; and it was while Llewelyn was still a small boy that John took him on an expedition to Portland which very nearly ended in tragedy: they were waiting for the train to take them back to Weymouth, when, as John later recalled:

> we were . . . pushed by the surging crowd to the platform's edge, and as the train came in Llewelyn was flung down upon the stepping board of one of the moving compartments and carried along with it as the train slowly drew up. I am sure he changed not a jot of his inquisitve serenity when someone who was sitting in the train lifted him up and lugged him in!

Had he missed the narrow stepping-board, of course, he would almost certainly have fallen beneath the wheels and been killed.

Their elderly Powys grandmother was now becoming an invalid, and a family of ten children was too large an invasion for her to manage. So one summer Theodore and Littleton went to stay in Norfolk with their grandfather Canon Johnson; while John stayed at Weymouth with the rest of his family, collecting seaweed, rowing in the harbour, or even on occasion gazing in ecstasy at the sun shining on the waters of the bay. Another summer it was John and Littleton who went to stay at Northwold. Their grandfather was sometimes rather severe; and their grandmother was always worrying that they had been drowned: Norfolk is full of waterways, and a navigable stream known to the family as 'little river' flowed through the back garden of the rectory itself. But their aunts entered into the spirit of things, especially their beloved aunt Dora; and it was a time of intense happiness for the brothers, who:

> bustled about in their small world, lively enough, threw their
> lines into Dye's Hole, watched the great salmon-trout in
> Harrod's Mill-pond, found greenfinches nests in the
> rose-garden with eggs in August, caught pike with their
> butterfly-nets and butterflies with their caps . . . got their boat
> from 'little river' into 'big river', found plums in unknown trees
> and dab-chicks where they looked for water-rats, learned to say
> 'Sir' to retired captains, 'How is my Joy?' to retiring maidens,
> carried live perch in fish-kettles and dead dace on withy-twigs,
> and even stole his handcuffs from the village policeman!

In the Christmas holidays, Charles Powys sometimes took his family to Oxford to visit his half-sister Pippa, now Mrs Walter Shirley, and John's Godmother. The youngest of Pippa's children, Ralph, was an undergraduate at New College: he took a kindly interest in his young cousins, and was especially friendly to John, reciting passages of Matthew Arnold to him, and giving him access to the Bodleian Library. John thoroughly enjoyed 'long snowy days of reading by warm fires'; and it was in Oxford on the River Isis that he learned to skate. Charles Powys was an excellent skater; and back home at Montacute he would sometimes take his children out skating on Vagg Pond, or the flooded fields towards Ilchester.

Charles did not often have time to accompany his children on their expeditions; but he was always interested in what they did, and gave them a measure of security by being always the same, both in character, and in the daily routine of his life. 'He had developed in him', wrote Littleton, a very strong sense of duty; and few, if any country parsons, ever fulfilled their task more conscientiously and thoroughly than he. Down in his study every morning at seven-thirty he would deal with his letters; family prayers at eight; breakfast immediately afterwards; then a brief space taken up in wandering round the garden; then work in his study . . . then to the school or the village . . . dinner at one-thirty; at two-thirty he invariably set out to visit the sick in the parish, or those who needed help in any way; back home again by five-forty-five; tea at six o'clock; then often to some meeting in the village; supper at nine and bed at ten o'clock.

The work of running the household, and of seeing to the day-to-day upbringing of their ten children, was left largely in the hands of Mary Powys. She gave them a good deal of freedom, but, as Littleton recalled, expected them to play their part as sons and daughters of the vicarage:[10]

We went to church morning and evening on Sundays; we went with our father to his prayer and missionary meetings: both John and Llewelyn [in later years] used to go to the men's class and talk to them; John also taught in the Sunday school. My two eldest sisters taught in the Sunday school and played the organ if the organist was away. We rarely missed morning and evening prayers at home; our mother did her best to teach all her children their catechism and Bible stories, and to interest them in missionary work.

She also made every effort to educate them in a broader sense, gathering them together in the evenings, and reading to them from the English classics. Her own chief pleasure seems to have been to read to herself for an hour after everyone else had gone to bed; but as the children grew older, even this was sometimes given up, and instead she would ask one of them to sit up with her to read out 'some selection of poetry or prose which particularly appealed'.

When the holidays ended Theodore returned to Aldeburgh alone; while John and Littleton were joined in their journey to Sherborne by Bertie, who had started at the Sherborne Prep. A child of 'massive and temperamental calm', Bertie coped with the pressures of boarding school life quite happily; and thought his eldest brother unnecessarily eccentric, regarding him on one occasion with 'faintly sardonic, indulgent disapproval'.

John now shared with Littleton a study which became a little corner of Montacute: their garden was a window box in which they grew blue cornflowers, and their house was a room in which they could heat up cocoa on a gas burner, and which included the miniature chest-of-drawers in which John kept his most secret possessions, their uncle Littleton's East Indian low chair, a heavily embroidered cushion from the drawing-room at home, pots of rhubarb jam made by their mother, and – in the autumn – a hamper full of walnuts and apples from their orchard. But although John could be happy in this study, his reputation within the school had unfortunately continued to decline. He was constantly teased and bullied, but still could not bring himself to fight back. However, he did not pity himself: on the contrary, he hated himself for not standing up to his persecutors. When his suppressed anger did break out, it was tragically misdirected: once against a whole nestful of unfledged birds, all of which he killed; and on another occasion he was brutally unkind to Littleton; though, afterwards, he was so remorseful that he handed over their autumn hamper to him complete, refusing to touch any of its contents himself.

Many evils bring some compensating good; and as an outsider John not only learned a good deal about human nature, but also learned how to survive: even if it meant, as it did on one occasion, that he had to pretend to be mad. The boys in his dormitory insisted that he should take a sponge, and go to another dormitory to throw it at a well-known bully. John felt sick with terror. If he obeyed, the bully would beat him; and if he disobeyed, the other boys in the dormitory would beat him. So he 'went mad', waving the sponge in the air, and dancing what he thought was a madman's dance, while he chanted the lines of his ballad on Corfe Castle. The trick worked: someone fetched the matron, and for a week he was allowed to sleep in a room on his own. After this success, he also 'went mad' when confronted in the gymnasium by either the horizontal bars or the trapeze: with similarly satisfactory results!

Sherborne was not a total disaster for John: in the senior part of the school he was taught by two men who genuinely inspired him. One of these was the Rev. King, 'profoundly English', and with ' Montaignesque zest for life'; and the other was Mr Wildman, a first-class teacher of whom John wrote: 'I can recall well a private lesson I had from him once in Greek grammar that turned the very tendons, fibres and bones of intricate language into things as lovely and provocative as coral or sea-shells.' Influenced by Mr Wildman's love for the classics, John proved his intellectual ability by winning the fifth-form prize with a Latin thesis modelled on the rhetorical declamations of Cicero.

But academic success did nothing to lessen the bullying. Nor was this surprising: Sherborne school as a whole was in a more unruly and divided condition than ever. The headmaster had been involved in a libel action brought against him by a member of staff whom he had dismissed on a question of discipline; the remainder of the staff were split into warring factions; and one housemaster had pulled out altogether, taking many boys with him.[11] In these circumstances the bullying increased, coming to a head in 1891, when John was eighteen and a half, and in his last year at Sherborne. Up to then, his study at least had been a secure refuge. But one Sunday, after tea, he heard sneers from outside the study door, and before long:

> our sacred study-door itself was thrown open; and the mob outside, full of both malice and fear began pushing one another in. To my everlasting disgrace . . . I became paralysed with terror . . . a contemptible scene followed . . . blows that were no blows, hits that were no hits, abuse that did not dare rise to effective vituperation, combined with a confused barging and hustling and jostling and threatening.

Eventually the head of the house intervened; and then it was time for chapel. As the service progressed, John, who was desperately upset by what had just happened, thought of a way in which he could retaliate. He could not defend himself with his fists, but he would do so with his tongue, in the Ciceronian manner. The housemaster was away, and the head of house agreed that, after supper, Powys Ma. should have a chance to speak. When the time came, he stood up, and the whole house listened in silence, spell-bound, as John:

> dragged in every single detail they derided me for, I exposed my lacerations, my shames, my idiocies . . . I referred to the great dilapidated umbrella I placed such stock in. I referred to my obscene fashion of chewing my food with my front teeth. I stripped myself naked before them . . . I had not failed. A hullabaloo of applause, puzzled, bewildered, stupefied, confounded, rose up around me.

His speech, though it was full of self-mockery, had at last shown the other boys in Wildman's that John had some spirit. For the first time, they respected him; and, as a token of this new respect, the boy who had led the attack on John's study brought a bunch of violets to the sickroom where John was laid up the following morning. After the stress and strain of the past twenty-four hours, John was in a state of general collapse. More particularly, he was suffering from an acute bout of stomach-ache, something which had troubled him before when he had been under pressure, but never so severely. Now he felt so unwell that he persuaded Littleton to carry a message all the way to Montacute saying that he must leave the school at once.

Charles Powys must have been concerned about his son's state of mind for some time; and the day after receiving John's message he arrived at Sherborne in a hired carriage to take him away to Montacute. In the peaceful surroundings of his home, John gradually recovered; though he probably saw no doctor, because Mary Powys believed in homeopathy, and had a large collection of natural remedies with which she dosed her children when they were ill.[12] John only returned to Sherborne once more, on the very last day of term, to recite the rather uninspiring verses on 'Corinth'[13] with which he had won the school verse prize. Years later, in *Wolf Solent*, he gave an unflattering portrait of Sherborne as Greylands school; but as a very old man he forgave or forgot the worst of his school experiences, and used to enjoy singing the Sherborne school song.

It had already been decided that, on leaving school, John should follow the family tradition and go up to Corpus Christi College, Cambridge. It was assumed that, like his father and grandfather, he would go on to be a clergyman; but in his own mind there were no strong commitments: merely a sense of peace at having left Sherborne permanently behind him. However, he was willing to fall in with his parents' plans, and so during the summer of 1891 he spent a great deal of time learning how to translate Euripedes for the 'Little Go', the first public examination for the History Tripos.

Although Theodore was still only fifteen and a half, his schooldays, like John's, had come to an end. He had enjoyed his Suffolk school much more than the Sherborne Prep; the Wilkinsons had often invited him round to their family quarters, and their daughter Christobel, some four years older than Theodore, and an intelligent sensitive young women who wrote poetry,[14] had treated him very kindly and completely won his heart.[15] Among his fellows, Theodore had learned to disguise his feelings: his 'inscrutable gravity'[16] made a great impression on Dr Wilkinson's small son Louis, later to become a close family friend; but although Theodore was in a very much healthier state of mind his parents still felt that his nerves would not stand the strain of a prolonged formal education. Instead of going to Cambridge and becoming a clergyman, he was to be a farmer; so he left school early, and was now working on a Suffolk farm, though he was allowed home in the holidays, like the rest of his family.[17]

Llewelyn was now just seven years old, and as lively and cheerful and engaging as ever. He had not yet gone away to join ten-year-old Bertie at the 'Prep.', so during John's long convalescence that summer the two brothers saw a good deal more of each other than usual, and a special friendship developed between them. John thoroughly enjoyed spending time with this radiant child, and played with him and told him long imaginative stories. Llewelyn found John like a second, much younger father: one who had the time to lie in the sun and talk to him; and John's views had a profound influence on him. Years later, for example, he recalled how:

> one summer morning on a woodland walk . . . he gambolled ahead and began beating off the heads of campions with the stick of his wooden hoop till John cought him in his arms and said, 'Llewelyn, you must never, never do that again, never in your whole life – for you must not forget that every tree, every leaf, every flower is alive *as we are alive* and it is only very stupid or very wicked people who can be indifferent to the destruction of their earth companions.'

When the holidays began, John naturally spent more time with Theodore, at that time still his closest friend in the family. Together they smoked tobacco, descended by a rope from the windows of Montacute to prowl through the woods in the middle of the night; and they even conspired together to buy a revolver and some ammunition. The revolver was John's idea: he intended to make certain that no one at Cambridge dared to invade his privacy as they had done at Sherborne, and felt quite prepared to shoot down anyone who tried. In fact there was a group of undergraduates who enjoyed wrecking the rooms of 'freshmen'; but, luckily for John as well as for them, when term did start, a mere glimpse of the revolver was enough to convince them that they had better look for other victims to 'rag'.

At the start of the autumn term, the Rev. Charles Powys had taken his eldest son to Cambridge, to interview the authorities, to introduce him to the wine-steward, whom he remembered from his own under-graduate days,[18] and to buy what was necessary to settle him in at Corpus. John's study at Sherborne had been like a corner of Monta-cute; but now he had the strange sensation that his rooms in Corpus were like a miniature of a household which he had never seen: his grandfather's Rectory at Stalbridge. No doubt the totally unfamiliar atmosphere of his new rooms, combined with the relief of having left Sherborne, gave John the feeling that he was starting life afresh. For the next three years he had a large measure of freedom to choose how he wished to live, to indulge his eccentric tastes, and to begin to learn what kind of person he really was. Very little pressure was placed on him or on his fellow undergraduates either by his tutors or by the rest of the college or university establishment: 'these wise and excellent men', he wrote admiringly, *'let us alone.'* He later added, rather unkindly, that the university as such had had no influence at all upon his taste, intelligence, philosophy or character. It is true that only one lecture, by Professor Seeley, seems to have made any lasting impres-sion upon him; but Cambridge provided John with a most satisfactory framework in which he could pursue his own interests. Not only did he lose his 'dread of facing people' during this period; but for three years he had complete relief from the sadistic images which had troubled him since he was a small child. He also lost interest for a while in sylph-like girls, after trying to seduce one of them, and finding that he had preferred to admire her from a distance. It may have been after this fiasco that he attempted homosexuality; but this too he rapidly aban-doned, finding it gave him no satisfaction whatever,[19] and he turned instead to what he believed was a life of virtue.

Somehow his sadism had been turned against himself, and con-verted into the most outrageous masochism. He knew that to others he appeared ascetic, but liked to think of his new way of life as chaste, idealistic, and aesthetic, and threw himself into it like a great actor, severely limiting his diet, being ruthlessly parsimonious, and deliber-ately cultivating the society of the most despised people in college. He certainly did not find in Corpus itself the intellectual society which he had expected: the college was divided into a 'fast' set, an evangelic set, and an athletic set; and for a while John found himself caught up in the rowing fraternity, on the strength of his father having once rowed for Corpus.

Despite this, John's first year at Cambridge was 'one grand out-pouring of seething, surging, whirling ideas'. Anyone who cared to come was invited to listen to his 'weird prophetic denunciation . . . entitled "Corpus Unveiled" '; and although he was dissatisfied with the quality of his formal poems,[20] and of the speeches which he began making at debates, he enjoyed indulging in 'crazy monologues': on one walk, for example, astonishing his comrade with an impromptu metaphysical dissertation defending the doctrine of the Trinity!

He made a few friends; though because of his habit of masochistic self-abasement they did not always take him very seriously. One of the strangest of them was the wealthy young G. P. Gooch, later a famous historian, and a man whose learning was, even then, quite remarkable. Hating the light, Gooch would sit in John's room in the darkness, his hand laid upon John's hand, 'discoursing at large on all the most subtle and difficult points in history, in philosophy, in politics, in political science.' Other friends included Thomas Henry Lyon, and Constantine Koeller. 'Harry' Lyon, as he was known, was a man utterly confident in the correctness of his own opinions; but he loved a discussion, and he was probably the friend with whom John was upon most equal terms. Koeller had been a tea-planter in India before returning to England with the idea of becoming a clergyman, and was ten years older than John. His knowledge of the world made him a respected figure among the undergraduates; and he responded to the idolatry of John's admiration in the most friendly way, acting as his intellectual mentor by introducing him to the work of writers such as Browning, and on one occasion visiting him at Montacute.[21]

In the summer of 1892, John joined the rest of the family for a summer holiday at Barmouth in Wales; and he spent as much time as he could in the company of Theodore, who was soon to have a small farm of his own at Sweffling in Suffolk. John suddenly decided that it was essential for Theodore to become a first-class rider, and after finding ponies, the two brothers set off into the mountains without more ado. Luckily John was not badly hurt when his pony fell down a waterfall; but this accident turned him against Wales for the time being. His father, who had been indulgently remaining silent while John insisted on eating nothing more than bread and treacle, as 'no one ought to eat what everyone could not get', now had to listen while John explained that he hated mountains, and was only really happy in Norfolk! In the circumstances, Charles's reply was a model of self-control: 'It's a pity you came with us then, John my son!' Soon after this, John, Littleton and Theodore went off alone for a few days to climb Snowdon; a trip spoiled for Littleton by John's meanness – or 'rigid economy', as he called it; and by the fact that John and Theodore were now such exclusive friends.

After the end of the summer holidays, the autumn and winter passed by uneventfully; but the spring of 1893 came so early that, in Llewelyn's words, 'it was as though the countryside was under some strange enchantment.'[22] Before the end of March, the cuckoos were calling, and the hedges were white with the delicate blossom of the blackthorn. With John away at Cambridge, Theodore in Suffolk, Littleton at Sherborne and Bertie at the Sherborne Prep., none of Llewelyn's older brothers were at home. Gertrude, now sixteen, spent much of her time helping their mother with the youngest children: Catherine, William, and Lucy. So at the beginning of April that year, Llewelyn, who was eight years old, roamed the countryside with his other two sisters, May and Nelly, savouring the smell of the yellow gorse in the sun, and hunting among the hedges for birds' nests. For some time, like all his brothers,[23] Llewelyn had been particularly fond of Nelly: a vivacious, attractive child of thirteen, full of romantic and poetic ideas.[24] She in her turn had enjoyed taking the lead with him – even managing to overcome his fear of heights as she 'daily pulled, pushed, lifted, scolded and coaxed' him 'to the topmost attic twigs of the walnut tree in the Montacute Glebe'.

This happy friendship was soon to end in tragedy. 'An evening came,' Llewelyn later recalled,[25]

> a spring evening full of the promise of summer, when, as we played at haymaking at the end of the tennis lawn, cutting the fresh long grass and setting it out in little heaps to dry, [Nelly] complained of a hurt in her side. She still played, she still laughed, but she was hurt all the same. Four days went by and she was dead. Those fatal hours can never be effaced from my memory . . . the flushed sunburnt face growing paler and paler, as she lay there stricken with fever in the great spare-room bed – my mother going about the house with a look first of anxiety, then of apprehension, then of mute despair . . .

For once, doctors were called in; but Nelly's appendix burst, and they could do nothing to help. The rest of the family were now home for the Easter holidays, and it was John who broke the news of Nelly's death to his brothers and sisters, telling them that she had been 'taken away by the angels'. Not long afterwards, when the summer term had begun, scarlet fever broke out at the vicarage, and one after another the younger children caught the disease. Amazingly, they all survived. For Llewelyn, however, the experience of watching his sister die, and of his own narrow escape from death, brought the realisation, at the early age of eight-and-a-half, that 'there is indeed so little time for any of us to play under the blackthorn'; and came as the 'first revelation, as to the outrageous nature of the terms upon which all human life rests'.[26] For the rest of his days his most fundamental belief was that one should enjoy life as much as possible while one still could.

Llewelyn had also seen his mother in a new and far from sympathetic light. When Nelly had realised that she was dying, she had called out to her mother asking her to say goodbye; but Mary Powys, who was perhaps still hoping for a miraculous cure, 'could not find it in her heart to satisfy the request'.[27] This appeared to Llewelyn to be an act of the greatest cruelty, and he never quite forgave her.

'God is love' is the text which can still be read upon Nelly's tombstone in the churchyard at Montacute; and the year after her death Llewelyn heard Charles Powys preach a sermon in which, talking about the harvest of God's people being gathered in, he declared: 'It will matter little *how* or *when* they have left this world', and reminded the congregation of God's promise to raise up his chosen people to everlasting life.[28] But it did not seem to Llewelyn that his sister's death could have been allowed by a loving God; and he was less impressed by his father's assurances about eternal life than by the lack of belief which he thought he had detected in John's voice when he said that Nelly had been 'taken away by the angels'. In time, Llewelyn came to believe that it is not in Christianity but in the natural world that the important truths about life are to be found. John had certainly been badly shaken by Nelly's death. Despite the seven years' difference between them, she was very mature for her age,[29] and he had felt strongly drawn to her, later recalling that:[30]

> My ideal future was to be a famous actor living with Nelly and always acting with Nelly for she and I were alike exactly in our mental life, our aesthetic or artistic life, our emotional life, our imaginative life, and our erotic life. We turned from one to another of these and kept them apart.

Theodore too had been very fond of Nelly; the news of her death was a shock which helped to confirm his melancholy view of life; and ever afterwards he had a special affection for young girls.[31] Meanwhile, the hard work of farming had not dulled his brain: at the end of each day he would settle down to read serious works of a kind which even a university student might find demanding. At this time, he was caught up in the grand spiritual melodrama of Nietzsche, and probably responded with sympathy to the lonely isolation of that philosopher, with his hatred for the mass of humanity. Theodore was himself very isolated: Sweffling is in the depths of the countryside, and it was some distance from the tiny hillside hamlet and church to Theodore's White House Farm.[32] The charming little white-washed farmhouse stood by a narrow lane, quite alone apart from the usual collection of barns; and a little further down the lane, a small row of farm-labourers' cottages. Theodore was capable, and, despite being only seventeen, he managed his labourers with authority; but a good deal of his farm-land was too low-lying and badly-drained to be very productive. It was very hard to make the farm pay; he had to go a long way to sell his produce; and it became for his brothers 'a sort of symbol of ultimate desolation . . . to think of Theodore, of a windy November afternoon, making his way, like Christian with his forlorn pack, to the weekly purgatory of Saxmundham market.'

When John came down for the summer vacation of 1893, less than three months after Nelly's death, there was still scarlet fever at Montacute. Gertrude, however, had recovered from the disease, and was no longer infectious; and rather than go home, John went on holiday with her, taking her to a farmhouse on the shores of Ullswater in the Lake District. From here they boated on the lake, visited places associated with Wordsworth and the other Lake poets, and walked out into the mountains in all weathers so that Gertrude could sketch, and John could write.[33] Miss Beales, the Montacute governess, wrote them a teasing letter on hearing of their activities:[34]

> What a model unworldly brother and sister you are, one sits in the pouring rain, and makes poetry, I suppose in praise of that fluid, and the other sketches the beauties of nature obscured by a veil of the same.

She also sent them news of their brothers and sisters:

> On Monday, May, Lulu & I had Bertie's birthday treat, a half holiday. . . . You would be amused to see the calm, patronising superiority of May and Lulu in the schoolroom, while Katie is there, I really can hardly help laughing outright, they look so funny at the end of the table; their benign, slightly

contemptuous smile, when Katie & I ecstatically embrace in the middle, is very fine.

After Nelly's death, life at Montacute seemed to be settling down to normal: when Gertrude returned, it would be to a Primrose League Fête, with 'a tennis tournament, lady palmist & café chantant . . . among the amusements'.

John went on to Weymouth to spend the rest of the summer vacation with Littleton, who had just left Sherborne, and was to join his brother at Corpus the following term. Their grandmother was now dead, so they stayed in lodgings known as Invicta House. It might have been an agreeable holiday, but Littleton soon found that John's Cambridge eccentricities were in full flood. He had recently become a vegetarian, in itself no bad thing; but, as usual, everything was taken to an extreme limit: he would spend half an hour in contemplative silence, before announcing out loud that he thought he might go on allowing himself *one egg* for breakfast. He had also become interested in Christian Socialism, and had developed his mania for being kind to impossible people to such a degree that one day he embarrassed a tramp by dragging him in to Invicta House to share their tea. The last straw came when Littleton had settled down in the sun to enjoy 'a summer afternoon's trance', and John angrily urged him not to sit down, but to keep on walking. Littleton rebelled, and in the wrestling which followed he trounced John and ended up by sitting on him.

After this, when Littleton and John went up to Corpus in the autumn, they saw little of each other. John did not believe that the atheletic Littleton would mix at all well with his intellectual friends; and although the two brothers occasionally went on walks, these were not a great success. Once, for example, John 'priggishly reproached [Littleton] for his absorbing interest in cricket', saying that he was afraid they might not meet in their next incarnation: 'Powys Ma., in this ascent, being likely to be promoted to some spiritual "Five A", while Powys Mi. was still in Three B."'

Although John still read lessons in church for his father, and had even attended some classes in Hebrew, he had now firmly decided against going into the church. Charles Powys accepted the news calmly: his eldest son would have made an eccentric sort of curate, and he allowed him to continue his studies at Corpus without a word of complaint.

John did not wish to be ordained; but he was very much preoccupied with religious, or other worldly experiences. From his first days at Cambridge, he had relished the 'mediaeval' experience of dining in Hall; and, looking at Corpus Old Court, he had compared it to 'some enchanted ruin in a fairy-like forest of old romance'. Later, roaming through the flatlands of Cambridgeshire, with the talismanic oak walking-stick which he had named 'Sacred' in his hand, his thoughts were lost in the sensation of a rapport between himself and the inanimate world about him: 'It was like a sudden recognition of some obscure link, some remote identity, between myself and these objects. Posts, palings, hedges, heaps of stones – they were part of my very soul.' In this state, he felt that he inhabited 'a sort of *half-eternity*, made up of a fusion of past and present, with the future, and all its wants and wishes, totally annihilated.' It was these 'rare magical feelings' which he came to regard as the 'secret within the secret' of his life: they were feelings about the past, somehow encapsulated in the present; and one, in particular, he later regarded as 'The greatest event in my life at Cambridge.'

He was walking along, not far from Trumpington Hall, on his way to visit a local novelist; when, looking at a stone wall as he passed by, he had 'a sort of Vision on the Road to Damascus':

> I observed, growing upon this wall, certain patches of grass and green moss and yellow stone-crop. Something about the look of these small growths, secluded there in a place seldom passed, and more seldom noticed, seized upon me and caught me up into a sort of Seventh Heaven . . . [in] this extraordinary moment . . . I felt a *beyond sensation* . . . to do with some secret underlying world of rich magic and strange romance. In fact I actually regarded it as a prophetic idea of the sort of stories that I myself might come to write.

In the summer of 1894, when John went down from Cambridge, he had little idea of how he was going to earn his living; but he had strong convictions about what was going to be most important in his life.

CHAPTER THREE

1894–1899

John lectures in Sussex 1894 onwards • his neurotic behaviour •
publishes Odes and Other Poems *and marries Margaret Alice Lyon,*
1896 • his circle of friends • lectures for Oxford University
Extension Authorities from 1898 • publishes Poems, *1899.*

Theodore farms at Sweffling.
Llewelyn at the Sherborne Prep., 1895–9.

Charles Powys treated all his children with the greatest generosity; and
when John left Cambridge, he promised him an immediate allowance
of £60 a year. Later, John regretted that he had not spent this money on
foreign travel, but even the abstemious A. E. Housman had only just
found it possible to live on £100 a year in the mid-1880s, and John
needed to find work in order to survive.

When he visited the offices of the well-known educational agents,
Gabbitas and Thring, last resort of so many would-be writers on
leaving university, they had just heard of the death of a professor who
lectured at a number of girls' schools on the Sussex coast. John caught
the next train to Brighton, trembling with excitement at the prospect of
'*Schools* of girls . . . like gleaming porpoises; shoals and shoals and
shoals of them'! The headmistresses who interviewed him were worried at first by his youthful appearance; but he talked his way into the
job, and was soon striding westward over the South Downs looking for
lodgings in the countryside. The little seaside town of Southwick
reminded him of Weymouth; and he settled there, paying a pound a
week for board and lodging with the family of Mr Pollard, the grocer.
On his lecturing days John walked into West Brighton[1] to give his two
lectures a week at each of the schools which employed him. It appeared
to be a highly satisfactory arrangement: his total annual income was

now somewhere in the region of £150 to £170; and he had a good deal of leisure in which to pursue his own interests.

At Montacute, Gertrude still busied herself with helping Mary Powys look after the younger children: Katie, with her love of animals; William, who had taken over Theodore's 'Bushes Home'; and the gentle little Lucy. Llewelyn, or Lulu as he was affectionately called, still spent much of his time playing with his twelve-year-old sister May; but now, whenever Bertie was home from school, they joined him to form an inseparable trio, giving their abbreviated names: 'May', 'Ber', 'Lulu', to the Mabelulu Castle, which became the centre of their activities.

The Mabelulu Castle had begun life as a lean-to shed, constructed by Theodore against the back of the kitchen garden wall at Montacute. Bertie had begun to make improvements to it, saving up all his pocket-money to buy the necessary materials; and Llewelyn, catching his elder brother's enthusiasm, spent his birthday money each August on 'pots and pans and crockery' to be used in it. In the summer of 1895, when Bertie was fourteen, and Llewelyn ten, they worked particularly hard, often getting up at three in the morning to carry on the work of sawing and nailing up; and then, later in the day:

> with May as chatelaine preparing food over a bonfire built by her brothers and presiding over the tea-table, the Three entertained visitors, who, while Bertie brandished a wooden dagger above their heads, were compelled to sign their names and write some verse in the visitors' book.

In September that year Llewelyn, now aged eleven, was sent away to the Sherborne Prep. He cried bitterly when the time came for him to leave home; but when he arrived at Sherborne, he was happier there than either John or Theodore. He was cheerful and good-looking, and admiration for his elder brother Littleton had inspired him with a great eagerness to be a successful games-player. So although he missed his home, writing passionately to his mother: 'I am loning to be home and see you stanting at the door and through myselve in your arms . . . It annoyes me to thinck I cant kiss you when I like',[2] he was also sociable, and he became popular.

John was leading a less happy existence; the girls whom he taught did nothing to satisfy one of his principal desires: with a solitary exception, they were too ordinary and human to be anything like the 'laughing and yielding sylphs' of his dreams. To attract him strongly, a woman had to be of 'a different sex altogether from the masculine and feminine that we know. It is of this sex, of this Saturnian sex, that I must think when in the secret chambers of my mind I utter the syllable "girl".'

Seeking such girls, John would stride up and down Brighton beach on summer days, eventually settling down to gaze in silent adoration at 'some soft, receptive feminine form whose ankles I could at least pretend belonged to a sylph-like body.' On these occasions, his feelings of erotic pleasure were acute. When he attempted to form a closer relationship, he found a curious 'romantic and sentimental' pleasure in the company of street-girls. Falling in love with them one by one, John sympathised with their superstitions, and admired the way in which, by never succumbing to genuine passion, they retained a 'strange, inhuman chastity'. But, as in Cambridge, he found that physical contact did not satisfy his erotic desires, and after a while he reverted to gazing at women from a distance. Once this led him to walk in from Southwick to attend every single performance of a pantomime in which he had:

> beheld at last, actually in the flesh, a real, living incarnation of my ideal sylph. . . . She was an extremely quiet girl, grave and self-possessed, and of a very dark complexion. She had praeternaturally long legs, very long slender thighs, narrow boyish hips, upright, rather square shoulders, and ankles of a ravishing perfection. . . . I made no attempt to speak to her or to approach nearer to her . . .

The pursuit of sylphs was only one of a number of manias from which John was now suffering. He later wrote that this was the beginning of a period in which he: 'came nearest to insanity . . . I gave complete rein to so many manias and aberrations that those who knew me best must often have wondered how far in the direction of a really unbalanced mind I was destined to go.' A certain inner determination, or, as he put it, 'nervous *power* . . . and the vitality of [his] constitution' prevented a breakdown; but there is no doubt that John was lonely, depressed and considerably disturbed. Sadistic and unpleasant images of all kinds troubled him even more than they had done when he was a child. Beautiful images, which comforted him, would suddenly be associated in his mind with something 'comic, grotesque, or revolting'. Like many depressed people, he began to suffer from neurotic dislikes and compulsions and fears of all kinds: for example, he loathed touching anything made of cotton, including handkerchieves and tablecloths, and was repelled by linen sheets; and he was compelled to wash his hands constantly, not even liking to touch a door-handle for fear of contamination. In his mental isolation and near-madness, he hated remembering that all children are born as the result of sexual relations; and when a casual acquaintance made a passing reference to this, John 'became so staggering sick' that he needed brandy to recover.

In his hatred of femininity he included the trees and flowers which had feminine organs; he could not even enjoy the singing of the birds, in case they were feminine birds; and his walks were ruined when he realised that the retriever presented to him by a friend was not a dog but a bitch! Worse was to follow:

> The thing went so far with me that I became panic-stricken lest I myself should develop feminine breasts with nipples, resembling the dugs of Thora. It was unpleasant to me even to encounter the harmless little hedge-flower that my father would never fail to remind me was named 'Nipple-Wort'. . . . Having come with such imaginative intensity to visualize my provocative sylphs as beings who yielded so completely to my embraces that there was no solidity left in them, I began to feel as if there were no longer any real solidity left in Nature, as if, whichever way I turned, the firm substance of the earth would 'go in.'

John Cowper Powys found considerable relief from these terrifying obsessions by escaping into books. He began to haunt second-hand book shops, though he was never a bibliophile, and would happily light his pipe with the aid of pages torn from whatever he was currently perusing! His tastes were broad; but he had a particular fondness for poetry, and was now reading 'with passionate delight' a volume of Yeats, strongly identifying himself with the romantic isolation of the lines:

> There was a man whom sorrow named his friend;
> And he, of his high comrade Sorrow dreaming,
> Went walking with slow steps along the gleaming
> And humming sands, where windy surges wend.

Writing was also a way of coming to terms with his experiences. In one unpublished play, written at Southwick in about 1894, John told the story of a man whose family at first condemned him for spending time with a prostitute, but later came to understand that she had saved him from becoming genuinely vicious.[3] John was also writing numerous poems, and in 1896 he showed them to his cousin Ralph Shirley, who visited him at Southwick. Ralph, realising how important it was for John to feel that he was having some success as a writer, obtained financial backing from Charles Powys, and then arranged for Rider and Company, a London firm, to publish John's first book: *Odes and Other Poems*.

Although john now regarded himself as 'a terrifyingly formidable genius', and was extremely excited to have some of his work in print, he was well aware how far short of the masters he fell. Most of his verses are pale imitations of Swinburne, Browning, Matthew Arnold and others; while occasionally John has lifted material almost word for word: 'That once with honey-dew was fed', for example, is clearly taken from Coleridge's *Kubla Khan*. However, *Odes and Other Poems* was recognised as important apprentice-work by the *Bookseller's Review*; and John was also pleased to hear from two of the poets to whom he had specifically addressed poems. From W. B. Yeats he received a long letter of advice and encouragement; and from Thomas Hardy a postcard inviting him to call at Max Gate, Dorchester.

John had regarded Thomas Hardy as the greatest living writer since reading a copy of *Far from the Madding Crowd*; and he had addressed lines to him which related how:[4]

> . . . there, in commune with thy mighty heart,
> I saw how life's light wreath of summer roses
> Remorseless Fate's inveterate frown discloses,
> And sullen Death's intolerable dart:

He was particularly struck by the way in which Hardy's characters are influenced by impersonal natural forces, and, when he had tea with Hardy on his lawn, he told him: 'how I detected in his work that same portentous and solemn power of dealing with those abstract-concrete phenomena, such as dawn, and noon, and twilight, and midnight, that Wordsworth displayed in his poetry.' Later that summer, Hardy travelled to Montacute to return John's visit; and Llewelyn took him down to the Mabelulu Castle, where he signed his name in the visitors' book as 'Thomas Hardy, *a Wayfarer*'.

Astonishingly enough, in view of his hatred of femininity, John was now planning to get married. The last set of verses in *Odes and Other Poems*, beginning:[5]

> Ah! Lady, deem not cold my lute
> Beneath thy Beauty's flame,

had been addressed to M. A. These initials stand for Margaret Alice, the sister of John's Cambridge friend, Harry Lyon. Harry was now established as an architect; but no doubt he returned occasionally to stay at his parents' estate in Devon, and John came to visit him there, and so met Margaret for the first time.

Margaret Alice Lyon often seems a shadowy figure in the background of John's life. In his autobiography, from which he did his best to exclude everything feminine, John never mentions her, and there are few clues about the nature of their early relationship in his letters: though he once wrote to Llewelyn about Margaret's 'soft sad beautiful eyes', so perhaps there was some hint of melancholy about her which reminded him of his mother. However, we know that John proposed to Margaret in a wild romantic setting, where the rocks of Haytor rise above the Devon moorland; and in further poems to 'M.A.' he identifies her closely with 'The very soul of nature',[6] compares her with the Goddess Diana, and tells of their first meeting:[7]

> Well I remember, O my sweet,
>   How first beside your native wood
> I found you, like a flower complete
>   In perfect flush of maidenhood
> Above your head the rocks looked down
>   With mystic meanings in their look;
> You loved their smile, you feared their frown,
>   And read their visage like a book,

The relationship described in these verses, between an adoring idealizing John, and a lovely natural Margaret, may well have been described and elaborated upon by John himself in his later novel *Wolf Solent*,[8] when he describes Wolf's relationship with Gerda Torp. Wolf, like John, worships nature; and Gerda, when she whistles, becomes 'the voice of those green pastures and those blackthorn-hedges.'[9] Wolf finds her 'maddeningly desirable'[10] and plans to marry her; though his emotions are so strange that 'he could not, properly speaking, be said to have fallen in love with her'.[11]

As soon as Margaret had agreed to marry him, John began planning for their future together. Charles Powys promised to raise his allowance to £100 a year from the date of the wedding; and John increased his income still further by finding additional lecturing work further along the Sussex coast at Eastbourne. Then he began searching for a house, helped by his brother Littleton, who had recently left Cambridge, and was about to become a schoolmaster. Eventually John decided on 'The Court House', a farmhouse which he was able to rent for £40 a year. It was agreeably and conveniently situated in a fold of the South Downs on the outskirts of the little village of Offham, not far from a railway station, and no more than ten miles from Brighton. Charles Powys gave his son £200 to furnish Court House; and John bought some excellent pieces early in the summer of 1896, while he was on holiday at Barmouth in Wales: he was staying there with Margaret, who was being chaperoned by her brother.[12]

In *Wolf Solent* it soon becomes apparent that Wolf and Gerda have very different temperaments, and are not really suited to each other: 'she and you will talk completely different languages!' Wolf is told.[13] And, as the day of his wedding approached, John seems to have wondered whether he was making a terrible mistake. He was being well looked after at Court House by a housekeeper; but his mental condition was still poor. Some of the money which his father had given him for furnishings was being spent in an Eastbourne shop, where John had found what amounted to a 'private lending library of fantastical "erotica"', which he took back to Court House to read at his leisure. He continued to be privately tormented by revolting images, and his housekeeper must have found him a considerable trial; he would eat no meat, subsisted largely on bread and milk, which he found suited his difficult stomach – it seems that he already had stomach ulcers – and he insisted on changing all his clothes every single day. A close family friend later believed that John's mother was instrumental in preventing him from backing out of the marriage;[14] and passed on the family story that on the eve of his wedding John was pacing up and down declaring: 'I can't go through with it! I can't go through with it!'[15]

There was certainly little chance of a complete sexual relationship drawing John and Margaret closer together. At their wedding ceremony the words 'With my body I thee worship' were left out 'for moral reasons';[16] and John had not only a distaste for complete sexual union, but a genuine fear of sexual intercourse with a virgin,[17] so it seems likely that their marriage remained unconsummated for many months. In the evenings, John would leave his wife alone, and wander out of Court House:[18]

> To pass whole hours looking at the ground
> Beneath me, at the darkening skies above,
> Until I lose myself and mix with them,
> And live the large life of untethered winds,

Margaret must have found him very difficult to cope with. His manias remained, and he developed now obsessions: his latest being that he would be killed in a railway accident. To counter it, he *'secretly always travelled first-class'*. But marriage did provide him with constant companionship, and with a pleasant home in which to entertain his friends.

His new brother-in-law, Harry Lyon, was a regular visitor, and the two men enjoyed debating philosophical problems as they had done in their undergraduate days. Another visitor was Alfred de Kantzow, an impoverished and somewhat eccentric Polish nobleman, whom John had met while he was still living at Southwick. De Kantzow, now in his seventies, wrote verses 'of a certain sombre and simple power', and had so powerful a belief in his own genius that he took it for granted that John's lectures must be exclusively devoted to his work!

As an indirect result of his marriage, John added two more friends to what he began self-consciously to think of as his 'circle'. One of these was Bernard Price O'Neill, a London doctor whom John met when he brought his family down to spend their holidays not far from Court House. 'Bernie' O'Neill was a well-read man with eclectic tastes, who combined in his 'slight but plump' frame a sympathetic interest in human nature with a whimsical sense of humour, and a 'microscopic interest in life' based upon the conviction that nothing existed which did not carry 'the occult signature of the Absolute'. In time he became a good friend to the whole Powys family, and John later wrote that:

> He supplied our Powysian life-cult – so rustic, so earth-bound –
> with overtones and undertones drawn from the erudition we
> suspected, the popular slang we avoided, the art we despised.
> He secretly fed his own fantastical imagination with revelations
> from the circus, the vaudeville, the argot of the market-place,
> the broad-sheets of the whole mad Beggar's Opera of the great
> city.

O'Neill also had a particular fondness for Rabelais, and introduced John to the outrageous humour of that great philosopher.

The other new friend was William John Williams, soon to be known in the Powys family as 'The Catholic'. He was a would-be priest who had never taken his final orders – presumably because of religious doubts – but who still dressed in clerical black, and devoted his formidable intellect to the task of crushing religious doubt in others: defending the church against heresies of all kinds, and attempting to bring every thing in the universe within the circle of the fundamental doctrines of the Roman Catholic Church. A strange but stimulating companion, with his eyes flashing black fire when he was excited, he had a small private income which enabled him to indulge his taste for sherry and port wine; and, after John had finished his lectures for the day, the two men would meet in one of the Eastbourne taverns to philosophise and exchange quotations from Shakespeare or Milton.

When John had been married for a year or two, Harry Lyon irritatingly told him that the routine of his life was becoming too comfortable, to which he replied in verse, saying:[19]

> You trouble me with your perpetual prayer,
> That I should leave this Lotus isle and float
> On the tremendous sea my puny boat,
> Steering against the winds of terror there.

However, he himself must have begun to feel that there was no future in lecturing to girls, for in the summer of 1898 he went up to Oxford to give a trial lecture for the University Extension authorities. He spoke on the Arthurian legend with such success that, before long he was travelling all over England giving 'the particular type of "Extension" lectures [on various literary subjects, but particularly on individual authors and poets] that were to prove so acceptable to the average intelligent public, and so contemptible to all conservative academicians.' John soon realised that his lectures, and later his published works of criticism, were despised by professional academics. He always felt that imagination and inspiration were more important than strict accuracy and orderliness, and he developed a unique lecture style modelled to a considerable extent upon his memories of the acting of Henry Irving.[20] Throwing himself into the character of the writer whose work he was discussing, John did not use carefully prepared notes, but 'imagination . . . the dramatic gestures of a born actor! My most spontaneous and childlike feelings, feelings that spring straight from my blood, my nerves, my soul.' Although he was soon branded as a charlatan in academic circles, and on one occasion received a stinging rebuke from his employers,[21] this did not prevent him from being applauded by enthusiastic audiences wherever he went.

From now on, John spent more and more of each year in a solitary peripatetic existence. Later, he felt that living so much of the time among strangers had 'helped to deepen my congenital ego-centric isolation'; but there were benefits: as a University Extension lecturer, he was entertained in private houses, and so came to be 'exceptionally familiar, not only with all parts of England, but with all manner of types of English family-life'. Also, his mind was stored with what he described as 'sunken treasures': impressions of 'various aspects of the Inanimate'.

Later, he was conscious that this was a period of his life when he behaved badly, selfishly taking what he needed from life and, on the whole, leaving his wife and friends to get on as well as they could. When he was at home, he would go off alone to walk up and down the mossy paths of the wood named Waringore; or, acquiring 'sinister cunning', would invent reasons for going to Brighton, so that he could spend the day hunting for 'anonymous ankles'; or he would travel to Weymouth, and deliberately swim out of his depth, so that he could savour the feeling that he had become part of the sea and the air and the sky, before deciding that, after all, he would swim back to the shore again.

Before he gave up teaching at his girls' schools, John took Margaret on a working holiday to Rome, where he was to earn some money by lecturing in a Roman hotel to 'an exhausted group of young ladies from Eastbourne'. There was one delightful afternoon, when they drank a bottle of wine 'in a deliciously sunny and secluded spot on the Palatine'; but it was not quite like a honeymoon: they took Bernie O'Neill's younger brother Willy with them and Margaret must often have been glad of his company, for her husband was bad-tempered and morose, and disappeared for hours at a time to follow his own pursuits. On another occasion, John left Margaret at Court House to be looked after by 'The Catholic', and set off for a fortnight to Paris with Bernie O'Neill, but he was so repelled by the brash sexuality of a Parisian night-spot that he retired to Rouen, where he had a bad attack of pain from his gastric ulcers before coming back to England.

John Cowper Powys was gathering sensations for a purpose: encouraged by William John Williams, he was busy composing a romance, in which the principal characters, under assumed names, were 'The Catholic' himself and Alfred de Kantzow. All his friends were gradually brought into the story, which became as interminable as the Rev. Charles Powys's endless romance about the Giant, the Fairy, and the Professor. It was never published – John described it as 'unpublishable' – but in 1899, helped once again by his father and his cousin Ralph, he published a second collection of verse, entitled simply *Poems*. The volume is dedicated to Bernie O'Neill, and contains verses written not only for his wife and brother-in-law, but for his brother Littleton, whom he envies for his easy kinship with nature. As in *Odes and Other Poems*, there is a good deal of imitative material, but there is also much more of his authentic feelings, as in these lines from *Earth Worship*:[22]

> Into the grass I fain would grow
>> And know
> What hidden powers, potent ministries,
> What endless hands and lips and tongues and eyes
>> What baffled ecstasies
> Struggle for utterance in the world below.
> Into the lives of leaves above the grass
>> I fain would pass,
> And find what sort of region'd angels there
>> Twine their entangled hair,
> What obscure nymphs, what dusky Dryades
>> Dwell in those ancient trees.

There are several less inspired fantasies, in one of which John imagines himself as the romantic poet on his death bed, exhorting his wife to plant 'one/Frail scentless violet'[23] on his grave, and lamenting that he has achieved so little. This lament is only one of a number of similar cries from the heart which suggest that John, at the age of twenty-seven, was very much more ambitious than he later pretended in his *Autobiography*. If so, the launching of his *Poems* was a severe disappointment: they were welcomed by some critics, but then sank without trace; and no further work of John's was to appear in print for another fifteen years.

CHAPTER FOUR

1899–1907

John and Margaret move to Burpham, Sussex, and their son Littleton Alfred is born, 1902 • *John visits America, 1904–5* • *writes* Lucifer, *1905* • *collapses at Worcester and has first stomach operation, 1907. Theodore gives up farming and moves to Studland, Dorset, 1901* • *he lectures in Sussex, 1902–3* • *moves to East Chaldon, Dorset, 1904, and marries Violet Rosalie Dodds, 1905* • *their son 'Dicky' is born, 1906* • *An interpretation of Genesis in print, 1907. Llewelyn to 'Big School' at Sherborne, 1899* • *to Cambridge 1903–6* • *becomes a school-master, 1907.*

In the January of 1899, Llewelyn Powys moved on from the 'Prep.' to the 'Big School' at Sherborne, at the somewhat advanced age of fourteen-and-a-half. He had secured his cricket cap and had been captain of football at the 'Prep.', but he was intellectually very backward, and entering the 'Big School' did not encourage him to work harder: 'For years', he wrote later, 'I remained in the lower school dreaming over my school books, my mind as dim and unlighted as the monk-haunted classrooms where I sat.'

Llewelyn was greatly missing the companionship of his brother Bertie, who had found the building of the Mabelulu Castle much more exciting than his school-work, and had left Sherborne early to become an architect. After going for a walk one Sunday with another boy, Llewelyn wrote sadly to Bertie: 'I thought of you all the way – I always do. Goodbye old Hedgehog I do love you so.' Llewelyn's other great friend in the family had been Marian, but she had a keen intelligence, enjoyed learning, and had outdistanced her brother for the time being. She was also far away from Montacute for most of the year, living with an aunt in Norwich so that she could attend the Norwich High School.[1]

Llewelyn was too sociable to be lonely for long: he threw himself into passionate friendships with other boys at school, particularly with one Lionel Myrlea; and in the holidays he spent more time with his youngest brother Willie, who was now eleven years old, and able to share in his activities. In the Easter of 1899 their friendship was strengthened when they spent a holiday together at Weymouth, where they had been sent to recover from whooping cough. They stayed in lodgings, and, as Llewelyn later wrote: 'Our coughs did not at all interfere with our freedom. I recall, for example, looking for birds' nests on Lodmoor before breakfast and carrying my brother on my back over many of its wide shallow lagoons, indifferent to wet boots and stockings.'[2] Nearly every day they went out on long walks, and once, on 'one of those supreme days of an English April that brings everything that lives an uncontrollable sense of well-being', they walked along the cliffs as far as White Nose:[3]

> The sky was clear and every coach-road shimmered at its far end with sun motes; the downs smelt of gorse, the meadows of daisies; and the whole earth fainted and danced, now enervated, now awakened by the breathless allure of a spring morning. Our walk along the cliff has never ceased to haunt my memory, as if we had been treading upon enchanted ground from celandine hedge to celandine hedge, from chattering stream to chattering stream, beneath the glancing flights of the newly arrived swallows.

Later that year, Llewelyn was delighted when Willie entered the Prep., and he was able to go out walking with him on Sunday afternoons, just as he used to do with Bertie.

Llewelyn saw little of Theodore or John at this stage in his life. Theodore was resolutely farming and reading Nietzsche in a remote corner of Suffolk; occasionally he was visited by Gertrude or John, but, since hearing of Christobel Wilkinson's death from tuberculosis at the early age of twenty-five,[4] Theodore was in a more profoundly melancholy state of mind than ever before. John himself was in such a poor mental state that when he was lecturing in Hamburg that winter, his morbid imagination seized on a picture in which a woman's breasts were somehow connected with blood, and, before long, the blood 'seemed to have the power of leaping from the page and splashing over my face. . . . It sank into me until it reached some deep-buried "loathing-nerve" that licked it up with frenzy.' Llewelyn saw more of Littleton who was now a classics teacher at nearby Bruton, but who devoted a great deal of time to his young brother, and gave up part of his holidays to take him on a special fishing trip to Exmoor. Once, during the summer of 1900, there was a remarkable meeting between five of the brothers:

> when John was staying a week-end with Littleton at Bruton . . .
> a meeting was arranged for Sunday afternoon at Cadbury
> Camp, the supposed site of King Arthur's Camelot, John and
> Littleton walked the eight miles from Bruton, Llewelyn and
> Willie six from Sherborne, and Bertie cycled twelve from
> Montacute.

The following summer John met Louis Wilkinson, the younger brother of Christobel, and now a tall and strikingly handsome Oxford undergraduate and a firm friend of Theodore's. Louis had admired Theodore since his schooldays, and had recently stayed at Sweffling with him, finding that his own undergraduate outrage against the establishment of the day mirrored some of Theodore's deeply held convictions: '"Church, Navy, Army, Bar," [Louis] had angrily declaimed. "Our only gentlemanly 'professions'!" "Liars, murderers and thieves," was Theodore's tranquil comment.' He told Theodore that after flirting with the Roman Catholic Church, he had just abandoned Christianity altogether; and on the strength of this Theodore at once named him 'The Archangel'. This nickname became still more ironic when, later that year, Louis was sent down from Oxford, for taking part, with his friends, in a series of 'Irreverent pantomimes, mock Masses and Confessions'; or, as the bishop described it, 'a long-protracted course of gross and outrageous blasphemies against the Christian Faith'. Oxford would not have him back again, but luckily for him, St John's College, Cambridge decided to give Louis a second chance, and he went up there in the autumn of 1902.

By this time, there had been three moves by members of the Powys family. Two of them were relatively undramatic: in January 1902, Littleton left Bruton, and moved to a larger school, Llandovery College in South Wales, much to the satisfaction of his father who thought of him as returning to the land of their ancestors. Not long afterwards, John and Margaret moved some miles westward, to the little village of Burpham near Arundel. Margaret's brother Harry was a friend of the curate of Burpham, and it was he who had first showed them Bankside – so called because a huge prehistoric earthwork formed the boundary on one side of its small garden. John was teaching full-time for the

University Extension Authorities, and no longer needed to be close to the girls' schools of Brighton and Eastbourne; while Margaret's heart was set on a move, perhaps because she was expecting their first child.

John later thought of Margaret's pregnancy as something of a miracle.[5] He had remained frightened by the prospect of sexual intercourse with a virgin,[6] and felt that he had never properly 'taken' even his wife, who had found that the only way to overcome his inhibitions was for her to go into hospital to be surgically 'deflowered'.[7]

Towards the end of August their son was born: 'A lively and lusty Boy', as John described him in a letter to Theodore, '[who] now makes the house resound with his crying. He is to be called Littleton Alfred, after dear Littleton and Margaret's Father: also Alfred de Kantzow who is to be his other Godfather – that is to say if he can be induced to enter a church.'[8] John's mother was staying at Burpham when the child was born, and enjoyed helping open the correspondence which followed;[9] and Littleton and Theodore were present at the christening.

However, a rift was beginning to appear between Margaret herself and some members of the Powys family. John's father had refused to lend them the money they needed to buy Bankside, no doubt regarding the move as an unjustifiable extravagance. The feeling that Margaret expected to live in too grand a style was reinforced when, after Littleton Alfred's birth, she insisted on having two servants to help her. Theodore at this time spoke rather gloomily to Louis Wilkinson about John's domestic arrangements: '"My brother John," he said. "He has those three women and he doesn't get very much from them."' But John wished Margaret to be happy during his long absences; and, as he wrote to Llewelyn, while negotiating for Bankside: 'Mag, when she first saw the place, long before we had any idea they would sell it cried, "That is the house I have been thinking of all my life!" So I have at any rate the satisfaction of feeling that she has what she likes best.'

A more dramatic move had been made by Theodore, who had decided to give up farming and become a writer. He was reticent about the precise reasons for his leaving Sweffling but years later a close friend believed that: 'there was some sort of crisis there, some plunge into the pit which left a black mark on him . . . he did once intimate that he had known an extreme melancholy there, as well as the mortification of being cheated by a bad bailiff.'[10] The reasons for becoming a writer go much further back: like his brother John, he was sensitive enough to have been profoundly affected by the tensions in their parents' relationship. John had enjoyed sadistic thoughts, and Theodore found that 'the contemplation of acts of violence' gave him 'a strange satisfaction'. Both brothers suffered from long periods of depression, and, to counter the unsatisfactory nature of their existence, they had begun to impose their own view of reality upon the world about them. While John's view was to some extent derived from ancient nature-mythologies, Theodore's was more disturbingly original. Louis felt that he inhabited a world 'set at [a] constant remove from reality': he had inherited some of his father's 'massive simplicity', and tended to divide people into 'good or bad, "honest cods" or "scurvy"'; while, after Christobel Wilkinson's death, 'Women were hardly allowed to be so much as that.' But there were unsettling depths both in himself, and his writing.

When Louis Wilkinson first visited Theodore at Sweffling, he found him looking, with his heavy moustache,

> astonishingly like Nietzsche. I remember him as a heavily built
> young man with grey melancholy eyes. His manners were
> courteous to the point of what seemed to me an ironic
> deference. Always he was a countryman . . . there was a brown
> and earthy soberness in Theodore's aspect. His talk was . . .
> slow, rather timid sometimes, but ripe and bearing authority.

On closer acquaintance, Louis detected a strange mixture of 'fantastic savagery and cruelty' together with 'deep benevolence', 'poetic sensitiveness to good and evil', and 'goblin humour'. To work out and describe his view of things had already become important to Theodore, and Louis records that:

> Already [he] was writing in the vein which was many years later
> to make his reputation, though not with the technique: already
> he was suffering his profound obsession with the ideas of God
> and Death. In those Sweffling days he wrote a dialogue between
> himself and God. 'Can you see everything?' 'I can.' 'Can you see
> Sally?' Details were given of Sally's girlish occupations from
> moment to moment, and then: 'I do not think you would like to
> see what she is doing now,' said God.

When he moved from Sweffling in September 1901, Theodore returned to Dorset, and by the early spring of 1902 he was well established in a cottage in Studland, a small seaside village at the edge of the lovely peninsula of the Isle of Purbeck. It seemed an ideal place in which to meditate and to write, and Theodore received considerable encouragement from John, who was arranging for some of de Kantzow's poems to be published, and promised that Theodore's writings would be his next concern. He told Theodore in March that de Kantzow had recognised 'originality and character' in his work, and added that, in his own view: 'self-confidence added to what you already possess, added, that is to say, to sensitiveness and tenderness and the affections of the heart and the taste for literary form which comes last but is most needful, would enable you to do almost anything.'[11] Then John apologised for seeming to lecture his brother, telling him that he only spoke because:

> I see my weaknesses in thee and thine in me . . . we are of the
> same mother . . . we are of the same blood . . . O my Theodore!
> Whatever dreariness befall you, whatever quagmires and
> quicksands await your feet, believe me, I have known them . . .
> you and I intellectually and nervously have been akin – you
> have more tenderness than I; I (perchance) more force than you;
> but when we have gone down into the house of shadows
> crowned or uncrowned with deathless bay, men will say after us
> they were of the same race, of the same suffering, of the same
> joys; They have gone to the same place.

Now that he lived in Studland, it was easier for Theodore to see his family, and once, when John and Bernie O'Neill were spending a few days at Weymouth, Theodore came over to visit them. On this occasion, the two brothers left Bernie watching the fishermen with their nets, and walked across the salt marshes of Lodmoor, their heads full of childhood memories; but before long, Bernie became as close to Theodore as he was to John, and inspired John with feelings of considerable jealousy when he accompanied Theodore on what was to be his only foreign excursion: a pilgrimage to Chinon in France, to visit the birthplace of Rabelais.[12]

Theodore's chief problem at Studland was lack of money: he was reduced to an allowance of £60 a year from Charles Powys, until John suggested that he should follow in his footsteps and become a lecturer. John introduced him to the Sussex headmistresses for whom he had once worked, suggested subjects for lectures, and by May 1903 was delighted to hear from several sources that Theodore's lectures had been extremely well received.[13] However, Theodore did not enjoy living in lodgings away from his cottage; and, apparently 'much disliking' the work of lecturing itself, he soon abandoned it.

Before he began his first course of lectures, in the autumn of 1902, [14] he had been visited at Studland by Bernie O'Neill; and they had been joined by Bertie and Llewelyn, who had set out from Montacute on bicycles, but had been forced to walk the last twenty-six miles of the journey after their cycles broke down at Mappowder in central Dorset.

Llewelyn was now eighteen, and had recently begun the painful process of awakening from a long period of intellectual slumber. After years in the lower school at Sherborne, he had suddenly been promoted to form Four A, where he was taught by the same Rev. King who had befriended John, and inspired him with his love for literature. 'In Four A,' wrote Llewelyn, 'I read for the first time passages from Homer and Horace and came to understand from punctilious translations the strange magic latent in books.'[15] When, in addition to this, John began sending him books of poetry, Llewelyn began to get 'glimpses of a wider and freer and more magnanimous world than that presented to me by the official schoolmaster and by the school chapel.'[16] At Studland, he was out in that freer world, able to read that he liked, to have long conversations with the widely-read O'Neill, and to learn from Theodore 'a healthy distaste for the work of the practical every-day world and an inveterate love of quaint and profound thinking.'[17] He was as warm-hearted as ever, and on this visit, rather to Theodore's dismay, Llewelyn fell in love with Angela, a young girl of only twelve or thirteen – much the same age as his sister Nelly had been when she died. It was a happily innocent relationship: they wrote loving letters to each other, and Llewelyn remained very attached to her for seven years or more. But the days of his innocence were coming to an end, and both his warm heart and his questioning of the established order led, later in 1902, to an emotional crisis.

Soon after the start of the autumn term, thoroughly depressed by losing his place in the House Rugger Fifteen, and worried by finding that, in the absence of Angela, he now had strong feelings for one of his fellow-pupils, Llewelyn began to be troubled by serious religious doubts. Until this time it had been supposed that he might follow his father into the church, but now he was reduced to asking himself: 'What is the good of struggling against lust when after death, there is the end, total annihilation, absolute dark-nothingness.' For several years he had relied heavily on Littleton's encouragement,[18] and now he wrote to him asking for advice. But Littleton, the most conventional member of the family, was engaged to be married, and could find nothing useful to say. He had already warned Llewelyn 'against the misconstruction apt to be imposed on affectionate intimacy between schoolboys, and also admonished him on the subject of sex'; now it seemed that his fears about his brother were being realised, and he was thoroughly alarmed.

In desperation, Llewelyn turned to John for help, and John wrote him two wise and affectionate letters. Accepting the fact that Llewelyn had lost his easy faith, and that he had a loving nature, he made no attempt to impose impossibly high standards. Instead, suggesting that his brother must find a new philosophy, and a new morality, he advised caution. A totally lustful life could not be a happy one, but:

> though the total repression that Christianity demands may be too hard for you, the moderation and self-control which the Stoic as well as Epicurean teach us to display, will stand you in good stead, and while not making you absolutely pure, will keep you from excess, from peril of shame and from remorse. The great thing is to keep your inner nature clear and strong. . . . Let us show that we Pagans have a religion and a morality which while it is less austere serves its purpose in saving us from excess as well as the Christian.

With his second letter, John sent Llewelyn some books which he thought would be of use to him: selections from Landor, and Carlyle's 'Sartor'; Llewelyn was greatly relieved by his eldest brother's practical and sympathetic response, and from this time transferred his allegiance in the family from Littleton to John. He had also received a friendly letter from Bernie O'Neill, who told him that he was being needlessly despondent, for:

> that which grown-up people and black-browed fogeys call religion and morality are usually nothing else but the ideas of the stupid and the hypocritical. All morality and religion are summed up in justice and charity, and I am quite sure you have gained in those two qualities since you first went to Sherborne.

Llewelyn still worried about the state of his soul, writing in his diary during February 1903:

> What would I give now to have the same innocence! and faith as I had when I was a little boy. How quickly all has changed. In the place of that curly-headed little rogue 'that other me' is now

> – a hardened liar! a licentious beast! a hipocrit, God knows what!
> I fear me of the consequences if I do not change. Let me try to
> live a pure, upright, kind, happy loving life.

But he was busy working and playing, falling in love with boys in the
term-time and girls in the holidays, and all the time reading the books
which John recommended to him; and the moment of real crisis had
passed.

Now it was John's turn to go through a period of religious questioning. His brother-in-law Harry Lyon had made a voyage to Australia,
and returned to England a practising Anglo-Catholic. Even in the past
Harry had often accused John – though not to his face – of being 'a man
without a soul'; and now the arguments between the two men became
less friendly and more acrimonious. A clever man guarding an intellectual position soon knows all the gaps in his defences better than his
opponent, and John began to have a secret distrust in his own security.
He would not give way to Harry Lyon, but he allowed himself to be
persuaded by 'The Catholic' to seek instruction in the doctrines of the
Roman Catholic Church, so that:

> Once, when . . . in his company, I actually left him reading
> Pascal in an out-of-the-way tavern, while I took the drastic and
> apparently fatal step of calling upon the local priest! . . . But the
> man was out; and I took his absence as a deciding omen.
> Theodore's laconic commentary upon this action of mine was a
> characteristic one. 'Of course,' he wrote, 'we know you do it to
> annoy your father.'

It is true that John did sometimes take a perverse delight in teasing the
Rev. Charles Powys. He finally relented from his plans to become a
Roman Catholic only when he had thoroughly worried his father with
the idea, so that he had turned to him, and asked pathetically: 'how can
you give me a blow like this, John, in my old age?'

Although he was ready to oppose his father, John fondly imagined
that his own son, Littleton Alfred, still less than a year old, would grow
up to 'take my side against the world'; and for a while parenthood
inspired him with notions of uprooting his family from Sussex, and
transplanting them to a Welsh valley, where he could 'send my
enemies to the Devil and possess my soul in peace.' He bought Welsh
dictionaries, devoured Welsh mythology, and was most disappointed
when he could find no mention of his ancestors in a Welsh genealogy.
However, Margaret was happy where she was; while John found

Welsh difficult to learn, and no doubt began to think that his plans were impractical. But although they remained at Burpham, the idea of Wales had become important to John; and as he continued with his endless lecture-tours, he often wondered whether they had made the right decision.

On these lecture-tours, John had now made another friend who became an important member of his circle: Tom Jones, a most unusual clerk in a Liverpool firm of cotton importers; a Welshman who possessed all the works of Nietzsche, and based his philosophy upon the poetry of Keats. He was a great womaniser, and after a day spent in cafés discussing philosophy, the two men would go out to the house where Tom had arranged to visit some of his girl-friends. Here John would entertain the company by reciting lines from Milton, before taking one of the girls on to his lap to caress her. Later, he recalled that:

> These periodic visits to Liverpool certainly remain among the happiest times of my whole life. And why? Because, for once I lived in a classic atmosphere of complete freedom as far as sex is concerned! . . . These Liverpool experiences were neither love affairs nor infatuations. They were, purely and simply, friendly erotic encounters between men and women . . . an eternal recurrence of the Golden Age.

No doubt these encounters were concealed from his wife; but John made no secret of his friendship with a prostitute called Lily. Later he was to describe her as 'by inclination . . . an old maid', and as 'The most innately chaste girl-friend I ever had.' She shared his 'passion for great clowns', and once, at her request,[19] they had 'visited together the grave of Dan Leno'.[20] Margaret very nobly allowed her to visit them for a few days at Burpham, perhaps believing that John was trying to reclaim Lily from her life of sin; but the visit was not a success: one of the servants, realising Lily's profession, was so outraged that she would not wait upon her.[21]

Llewelyn, to whom John had been recommending moderation in sexual affairs, might have been interested to learn of his married brother's escapades. Llewelyn himself left Sherborne at Easter 1903, and spent several months at Montacute being coached by his father for the 'Little Go'. Then he went up to Corpus as an undergraduate, to find himself in the same rooms once occupied by John: carved on one of the beams which supported the ceiling were the words: 'Pray for the soul of John Cowper Powys.'

One of Llewelyn's first concerns at Cambridge, far from praying for his brother's soul, was to call upon Louis Wilkinson, whom he had been warned against as a confirmed atheist by both John and Theodore. Louis was three years older than Llewelyn, but the two young men took to each other at once, the mature sophistication of Louis neatly balancing the natural zest for life of Llewelyn. It was a romantic friendship: Louis was dazzled by the 'sunlike look' of the young Llewelyn, with his 'crisp curly bright hair and fair complexion', and:

> From their first meeting the two were together almost every day, going for long walks, as far even as Ely, quarreling sometimes, when they would violently tussle and wrestle, each in anger inflicting on the other physical pain. For some while everyone but Llewelyn to [Louis], and everyone but [Louis] to Llewelyn, seemed irrelevant and dull.

Llewelyn's chief friends, apart from Louis, were among the college sportsmen: he enjoyed leading a 'rowdy' existence in their company, did very little work, and at the start of his second year founded the 'Club of the Honest Cods', which 'used to meet on Sunday evenings in the old court and drink hot punch and sing bawdy songs'.[22]

During the holidays, he returned to Montacute, often taking Louis or one of the 'Honest Cods' with him. Before long, Louis had met all twelve members of the Powys family. He made a particularly good impression on Mary Powys, though he felt that this had been because she saw him:

> shy and subdued. If she had seen me gay and self-assured I doubt if she would have liked me at all . . . Mrs Powys hated success. She hated, with secret intensity, well-constituted people, or even people whose health was too good. . . . John never gave any impression of success in the worldly sense. So she could love him without misgiving, as she loved Theodore . . . Theodore and she would sit in tragic communion, silent, with touching hands.

Louis was not always right about the Powyses, and Theodore would certainly have disputed the word 'tragic': in the privately circulated short story *The Child Queen*, written in 1902, Theodore wrote a moving description of how a mother's love for her child is gathered up and changed 'into a being more rare than anything upon earth . . . an angel.'[23] But Louis is often our only witness: and he has left a striking description of 'Powys solidarity' in the presence of their father, whom he describes as a man 'with the unwitting power of some dim pre-historic god'. Seated at the family dining-table, Louis felt like 'an alien invader without the ghost of a chance'.

Their talk, under Charles Powys's influence, was simple and direct: 'Any language but the simplest [being] to him an object of suspicion and contempt'; and Louis soon realised how inward-looking and how isolated from the every-day world the family had become. John, for example, had no idea about the workings of a thermometer, and was thoroughly bewildered when he asked Louis whether a room was warm enough, and was told that it was about sixty: 'Sixty what?' he inquired crossly, 'What the devil has sixty to do with it?' Theodore was particularly unworldly: he had never heard of the expression: 'You are pulling my leg'; and when impressed by the description 'plus-fours', forgot exactly what it was he had heard, and 'gravely informed me that he had just seen Mr Blank, who was "wearing all-fours"!'

The unity and comparative isolation from the world noticed by Louis Wilkinson had been increased by a number of incestuous attractions between brother and sister. Years later, one of their nephews was surprised by the strength of the sexual element in the relationship between some of his aunts and uncles;[24] while John Cowper Powys was prepared to admit in correspondence to having had such feelings for all but the eldest of his five sisters,[25] and declared on one occasion that:[26]

> Of all families in the world we Powyses ought to stand up
> fiercely in favour of Incest. What statue of all in the whole world
> is most famous? The Sphinx. And where is that? In Egypt. And
> whom did the Pharaoh Kings marry? Their sisters! O wise wise
> men!

From Montacute, Llewelyn often travelled down to stay with Theo-dore at Studland, which unfortunately was no longer the quiet, peaceful village in which Theodore had settled. Swanage, not far away, was suddenly becoming a popular seaside resort, and more and more visitors were pouring into Studland itself during the summer months. Together, Lulu and Theodore walked up and down Dorset looking for somewhere more to Theodore's liking; and at length, in the early summer of 1904, he moved into a terraced cottage in East Chaldon, a small village less than a dozen miles from Weymouth, but well off the beaten track. Theodore was relieved to be somewhere comparatively remote: he still suffered from bouts of depression, and, as John noticed, he would withdraw into himself when there were many people about and 'an expression of stricken, smitten, *terrible* melancholy would rise up, like an ice-cold film from the silt at the bottom of the sea and diffuse itself over his grey eyes.'

When he remained at Montacute during the vacations, Llewelyn was thrown mainly upon the company of his sisters: for after Littleton's marriage in the summer of 1904, Will was his only brother who was regularly at home. Gertrude, aged twenty-seven, had already given up thoughts of marriage, and settled down to looking after her elderly parents; but Llewelyn enjoyed playing tennis with Marian, who was determined on an independent career, and was busy learning typing and shorthand.[27] Llewelyn also went out riding with Katie, to whom he read poetry, and the two of them went on walks with their youngest sister, Lucy, who was still only fourteen. From time to time there were visits from other members of the family, and John in particular liked coming over from Burpham for short holidays. During the two years since John had helped Llewelyn through his emotional crisis at Sherborne, the brothers had become very close friends. John found Llewelyn:

> more full of the abounding magnetism of life than any human being I have ever known. He literally radiated the sun-born exultation that mounted up with immortal exuberance within him. Everything he touched turned to imaginative gold. His humour, his high spirits, seemed inexhaustible. He drank of Life till he reeled into the morning-mists of Creation.

Day after day, the two brothers would roam the countryside around Montacute, revelling in each other's company. On one memorable occasion, having walked as far as Ilchester, they took a boat on the river, and rowed along quoting poetry to each other, and felt 'so much in harmony', as John put it, 'that our souls within us broke in waves of happiness; each soul against the soul of the other.'

It was in the winter of 1904 to 1905 that John sailed to America for the first time, as the guest of the American Society for the Extension of University Teaching. Tom Jones saw him off from the Liverpool docks, and, as the *Ivernia* pulled away from the shore, John had the feeling that he was 'bound on some occult mysterious errand . . . a mouthpiece of Camelot and Carbonek and Stonehenge and Paladour, to the people on the further side of the ocean.' When the ship docked in New York, John was met by the president of the society, who took him for a ride in Central Park on a hired sledge with tinkling bells, before conveying him to their headquarters in Philadelphia. John found that his style of lecturing translated well to the United States, but during the next few weeks, his impressions of America itself were fleeting, as he was hurried from one audience to another. His chief discovery was the existence of slot machines which, for a nickel, promised to satisfy his voyeurism. In New York City, to his disappointment, the moving pictures of ladies undressing showed only 'extremely unsylph-like ladies, of plump and matronly aspect'; Philadelphia was more exciting: he could look through at real, live women; even if the effect was somewhat spoiled by hearing their mundane conversations.

In May 1905, a few months after his return from America, John went to Cambridge where he delivered a lecture on Catholic Modernism. It sounds a harmless enough title, but John had been dining at the High Table of his old college, and had been pressed to drink far too much port. He reached Louis Wilkinson's rooms in St John's College, where the lecture was to be given, without difficulty, but when he began to speak he had soon launched into a lengthy digression on the erotic element in religion! An Indian undergraduate passed a note to Louis saying that he was 'pained and grieved', and one of the Corpus Dons, who had accompanied John, was outraged. The incident was only closed when John apologised to the Corpus authorities, promising to clear up any 'misunderstandings' by giving a public lecture in due course. This he did some weeks later. Not many people arrived to hear him talk about 'The Religion of the Future', which may have been just as well, because what he had to say was scarcely less shocking than before. However, his brother Llewelyn and many close friends were present, including 'the Archangel', Bernie O'Neill, 'the Catholic', and Ralph Shirley: for a moment it almost seemed to John that an episode from the long-running saga about all his friends had come to life!

Since abandoning that saga, John had worked on a number of other romances. Sometimes one seems to detect in them the first highly distorted images of a later work: for example in the story of a reluctant prostitute who works during the day in a second-hand bookshop, where she is much coveted by the elderly proprietor.[28] But they were not very well written, and John laid them aside after, at most, a few chapters. To date his only published fiction, a weird short story called *The Hamadryad and the Demon*, had appeared in 1902 in a family monthly, the *Victoria Magazine*, edited by twenty-year-old Dorothy

Powys, a very distant cousin whose family John had met in Yorkshire.[29] However, he remained determined to succeed as a writer.

At Easter 1905 he had taken Margaret and their young child to Norfolk, and, while staying with his aunts, who now lived in The Close at Norwich Cathedral, John composed the bulk of *Lucifer*, a poem which runs to over three thousand lines. It was originally intended to be only the first part of a great epic entitled 'The Death of God', but it is valuable more for its philosophical thought than for the quality of its Miltonic–Tennysonian verse, and no one need lament that John did not spend more time on it. The theme of the poem is that the Christian God is the 'enemy of Youth, joy, love': 'Ice-cold sanctity/Alone he prizes'; and his priests are in league with the brutal capitalist system which supports them. Lucifer sympathises with the Red Flag of Socialism, and advocates revolution, being totally opposed to the Buddha's advice 'to struggle no more'. He is determined to overthrow God, even though he is aware that victory itself may be ultimately futile: 'Darkness may cover me;/Midnight may steal across my living veins;' but he is sustained by a fierce pride in the power of his will. From the Earth-Mother, with her 'placid wisdom' and 'sad knowledge' he learns that God can be destroyed with the help of Bacchus, the only one of the old Gods to retain his power; and after many wanderings, in the course of which he meets Pan and a Dryad – clearly one of John's sylphs, with her 'girlish thighs/And tender-moulded flanks' – Lucifer meets Bacchus, who gives him Thyrsus, the weapon with which God may be destroyed.[30]

After this poem had been laid aside, not to be published for more than fifty years, John also wrote a play; but it was never produced, and for several years, discouraged by his lack of success, he wrote nothing, concentrating instead on his University Extension lectures. Meanwhile, his marriage was becoming increasingly difficult. Margaret had begun to be a great deal less indulgent towards him, no doubt after listening to some of the highly personal attacks made upon him by her self-righteous brother Harry. John had been corresponding regularly with Llewelyn on religious and philosophical matters, but at this stage in their lives they never held to the same opinions for long, and John lamented that many of their friends, including not only Louis Wilkinson, but Harry Lyon, and Margaret herself,

> are right in the accusation they bring against us – you and I –
> (you 22 and I 34) that we don't do anything or stick to anything

or have any convictions but remain formless and stupidly
receptive and in our ridiculous affectations try to please
everyone out of cowardice and complacency.

Some of the tensions in the household at Burpham are encapsulated in
a memorable photograph taken during 1905 or 1906. John and Margaret were being visited by Bertie's new and attractive young wife
Dorothy, the distant cousin who had edited the *Victoria Magazine*.
Much to Margaret's fury, John had gone out rowing with Dorothy,
alone. The photograph was taken on their return: at its centre stands
Margaret, looking so tense and angry that she appears to have aged
twenty years; to her left stands Dorothy, looking nervous, as though
she fears that Margaret is about to strike her; to Margaret's right stands
John, his trouser-legs still rolled up after the rowing, and he gazes
truculently and defiantly into the camera, like a naughty child who has
been caught stealing apples, but who has every intention of repeating
the offence.[31]

Despite the difficulties of his home life, John did not return to
America for the winter of 1905–6. Instead, knowing that Louis Wilkinson had just come down from Cambridge, and was looking for
work, John arranged for him to be taken up by the Philadelphia
Society. From then on Louis lectured in America for six months each
year.

Unfortunately, Louis's absence did not encourage Llewelyn to work
any harder during his last year at Cambridge. In the summer of 1906 he
failed his Tripos, and had to be content with a Pass Degree in November. Earlier in the year, he had thought of becoming a lecturer, and
John strongly advised him to prepare a trial lecture for the Oxford
meeting the following summer. It was also suggested that he should go
out to the colonies, or into the church; but eventually, 'bowed down by
care and gloom' over the uncertainty about his future, he wrote to
Gabbitas and Thring asking them for a post as a private tutor. For some
while, he remained at Montacute, waiting for the postman to deliver
the 'queer little blue typed notices of academic vacancies' which his
father would 'very gravely' look over for him. Various interesting
possibilities, such as a schoolmastering job in Canada, came to
nothing; and then one morning in February 1907 there was some
very alarming news.

John's stomach ulcers had been growing steadily worse for some
time, and at last, 'Tortured with pain', as Llewelyn informed Louis

Wilkinson, 'for a week he lectured practically starving until at last he broke down.' Harry Lyon hurried down to Worcester, and took John back to London to see a specialist, who at once had him admitted to the London Hospital. After three weeks, he was allowed to leave, and Littleton arrived to escort him down to Burpham; but he was no better, and after an unpleasant bout of vomiting he was hurried back to London to be operated on.

After the operation, in which an ulcer was removed, John was visited in his London nursing-home by Llewelyn, who, profoundly concerned, tried to persuade him to abandon lecturing altogether. But John's brush with death had led him to a quite different conclusion: he felt that it was time to strike out more positively for his own happiness. To Llewelyn, he wrote that he planned to be more atheistical, more social revolutionary, and he decided that from now on America, where he could be far away from the frictions of his unhappy marriage, would play a much larger part in his life. It was a small thing which tilted the balance: the thought of the live women he had seen through slot machines in Philadelphia. In his autobiography he claimed that it was for this reason, *'and this alone'* that he decided 'to resume my lecture-work in America'!

Meanwhile Llewelyn had been appointed to a temporary post at a preparatory school in Broadstairs, and was reminded of his family's aristocratic connections when he learned that, 'Curiously enough I shall instruct Lord Lilford's heir in vulgar fractions.' He was the last of Charles Powys's sons to go out into the world. John was lecturing; Littleton teaching; Bertie practising architecture; and Willie, who had developed into a solid but not very sociable character, was happily farming near Montacute: it was an occupation which he enjoyed far more than Theodore had ever done.

Theodore himself was rarely idle. Neither John nor Louis had met with any success when trying to interest publishers in Theodore's stories, but he accepted this philosophically, telling Louis on one occasion: 'Keep the stories as long as you wish, and if they do not succeed this last time, I shall understand that they are either too wise or too foolish for this generation.' Curiously, his deep-seated melancholy was often expressed in brooding over something quite minor: 'He was like a tragic Prometheus', wrote John, 'whom the vulture that gnawed his liver forced to complain . . . to the pitying Oceanides about the gnats in the wild currant bushes up there.'

Then in February 1905, at the age of twenty-nine, Theodore proposed marriage to Violet Dodds, an uncultured village girl of eighteen, with raven-black hair. She could hardly have been more different from Christobel Wilkinson; but after Christobel's death Theodore had decided that: 'I don't want anything intellectual. I want little animals' roguery. I don't like ladies';[32] and Violet had her attractions. She was probably the original for Nelly Tibbitts in his story *God*, in which she is described as:[33]

> a girl of the earth, earthy; she had all the enticing and interesting
> ways of a little animal, and whatever she did or said delighted
> him. She was no thing of pretence; she had grown up in the
> village like a bluebell in a copse, and knew her own beauty
> because she often hung over the little brook. Her bulb was deep
> down in the soft earth, she drew her nourishment from the
> morning mists and the night dews.

Theodore adds that 'Her every movement showed a wedding wish', and in real life, he and Violet were married within three months. Although she had nothing in common with him intellectually, she was a cheerful, practical girl who gave him love and companionship, and also relieved his mind from the minor worries of running his own household. They had very little money, and there is some suggestion that he took up lecturing again for a short while, but if so, he soon abandoned it, and instead began 'writing notes upon the Bible'. In November 1906 his first son Charles, later known as 'Dicky' was born, and the work was laid aside for a while; but by June 1907 he had completed his *An Interpretation of Genesis*[34] which, though it had to be privately printed with the financial help of John and Louis, was the first important work by any member of his family, and is therefore a major landmark in our story.

An Interpretation, written in the Biblical style which, as his letters show, came naturally to Theodore, is an original, heretical, and at times profoundly moving attempt to distil the spiritual truth from the Book of Genesis. It conveys Theodore's own philosophy: man should enjoy life, as 'Full of poetry and loveliness is the Earth, and its longings are good'; but 'the true longing' of man is for his spiritual fatherland; and although death is the end of everything for the individual man he may still, while he is alive, live, as the prayer has it, in knowledge of the eternal truth. It also re-examines the old stories of Adam and Eve, of Noah, of Abraham and Isaac, and the others, and finds something original to say about each; and it contains some clearly autobiographical material – in discussing the story of Cain and Abel, for example, Theodore writes:

> And this is the law of the Truth, that knowledge in the body should be unknown, because by reason of Cain's pride in his knowledge he had slain his brother; so the wise are regarded as outcasts by all mankind. Mankind liveth only for the full life in the body; the wise live not for the body, and therefore the body despiseth the wise. And the wise, though they lead the body and show it wisdom, are not known by it; they are as slaves, being ever in want, and no one careth for them, save the Truth only; He careth for them.

Theodore had grown a beard while he was writing *An Interpretation*; the prophet of a world in which the life of the spirit has overcome the darkness in man, he now set out to explore still further into the truth, and wrote in April 1908 to Louis: 'In my work now I seem to be getting into the regions of much ice, where thoughts are few and bitterly cold, but there seems no other way, and what is beyond must be reached at last.'

CHAPTER FIVE

1907–1910

John resumes lecturing • to America in winters 1907–8, 1908–9 • ill summer 1909, resigns English lecturing, recuperates in Italy • takes Llewelyn to Switzerland, and sets out for America, December 1909.
Theodore moves to Beth-Car, another house in Chaldon, 1908 • his second son Francis Powys born 1909.
Llewelyn teaches at Broadstairs, 1907 • Bromsgrove, 1907–8 • is a private tutor, summer 1908 • to America with John, 1908–9 • at Sherborne Prep, May–June 1909 • looks after John, and in September 1909 meets Marion Linton at Shirley • returns to Sherborne • ill with tuberculosis, November • and goes to Clavadel, Switzerland, December 1909.

Llewelyn, who had taken up a temporary appointment at St Peter's Court, Broadstairs, soon found that he did not enjoy being a teacher, and later wrote: 'I don't suppose any young man who is worth anything would be content to spend his life as an undermaster in a Private Preparatory School, and no doubt this is the reason why one comes across such objectionable and imbecile types in such a position.' He found his colleagues 'petty and mean and wearisome'; while they called him 'Po face', and laughed at him for his serious interest in literature. The teaching involved Llewelyn in working at night with answer books and dictionaries to keep one step ahead of his pupils in maths and Latin; and there was added humiliation when a visiting teacher, discovering that his French was very poor, invited him to join her conversation classes:

A chair was placed for me at the end of the room and there I used to sit – like a great clownish dunce – while these clever children chattered to each other and to the lady. The mere possibility of being called upon to pronounce the simplest word made me literally sweat.

In his free time, he escaped to the sands of Margate or Ramsgate, glad to feel that he was part of 'the ebb and flow of the great world'; and occasionally he corresponded with John, who remained at Burpham recovering from his operation.

John's summer lectures had been cancelled; but he was fit enough to potter about the village, and told Llewelyn how he had been to tea at the vicarage with Margaret. At one point in the conversation, she had declared: 'would I have been born the only tomboy among the ladies of a hundred years ago!' to which a Mrs Mais, turning to John, perceptively added:

> 'You wish you had been born a hundred years hence!' 'Madam', cried I, 'by heaven, you read my very thought!' 'Why, what will it be like then?' she continued. 'Socialism will have opened up', I began. 'Enough, enough, I'm sick of the word', put in Madam, and the talk veered round to college servants.

John found himself out of sympathy with many of Margaret's friends; and he was certainly not faithful to his wife, though he was still fond of her. While he was at Burpham, he managed to sustain his relationship with his wife and his brother-in-law by what had now become for him a typically ironic self-abasement. Both his brother Theodore and his friend Louis Wilkinson were repelled by this. Louis was in any case annoyed with John, because he felt that he was being influenced unduly by what he called the 'spurious' emotions and the 'sentimentality' of Henry Lyon and his view of life; and so he was happy to translate into Latin a message which Theodore told him he wished sent to John: 'I do not wish to enter a house where a woman rules.' The message was Theodore's idea: he had a Biblical view of the position which women ought to hold in a family; but John blamed Louis, and for several months there was a serious rift in their friendship.

By the autumn of 1907, when John was well enough to resume his English lecture-tours, Llewelyn had spent a good deal of time at Montacute applying for jobs without success. Then, in November, he was summoned to Bromsgrove School, in Worcestershire. Less exclusive than St Peter's, it had an excellent headmaster, Mr Hendy,[1] who talked to Llewelyn in 'a friendly, intelligent way'; and, on accepting the appointment, he found that the masters were 'On the whole . . . a more dignified lot of men'. He also began to find teaching easier, and wrote to his sister May – who was herself teaching in Germany –

> I find on the whole I can cope with things better now; though the Egyptians in algebra and a clever youth in arithmetic have nearly extracted all the knowledge I have collected in these mysterious sciences . . . but I have learned to take the thing more calmly and even the possibility of exposure hardly ruffles the tranquillity of my mood.

Like A. E. Housman, Llewelyn was delighted by the surrounding countryside; with the approach of spring he felt 'moments of peculiar exultation', and he developed a lasting interest in wild flowers.[2] But although his fellow-teachers may have been dignified, he soon found that he did not care for them, and what he took to be their smug, self-satisfied point of view. Hendy, realising that Llewelyn was a misfit, first advised him to look for another teaching post; and then, when he was about to accept a job in Yorkshire, sensibly suggested that he should give up teaching altogether, and become a journalist.

This idea came as a great relief to Llewelyn. He had told May that 'The sight of fresh blackboards and new class-rooms filled me with horrible dismay, and yet I can't get out of it.' Now he wrote to Louis Wilkinson with a plan for going to live at Theodore's house on fifteen shillings a week:

> I mean to work frantically, desperately – sending articles and scraps again & again to the various editors.
> I shall try to get Theodore to lend me his back room.
> I shall have about £25 to start with – and will make one last effort to dodge the blackboard.

Rather to Llewelyn's surprise, his father was quite happy to fall in with this new plan; but by the same post as his father's approval came a letter offering him the post of private tutor to a fourteen-year-old boy at Calne in Wiltshire. The salary was good, and no doubt Llewelyn hoped that he would find time for his writing: at any rate, it was something certain; and, in a rather timorous fashion, he accepted, arriving at Calne on 6 May to take up his appointment. Almost immediately, he began to regret his decision. Not only was he 'unutterably depressed' by the sight of dull and familiar text-books; but he was rapidly made aware of his lowly social status. The servants were no more than 'ironically civil'; and his employers made him aware that they valued his company only in so far as he made himself useful: for example, they took him on a family picnic, so that he could look after their son; but then told him that there was no room in the car, and made him walk six miles home.

Llewelyn tried to console himself by reading a socialist journal *The Clarion*, and by escaping whenever he could to his lodgings, a mile away from the house. There he read Stevenson's essays, and, under the influence of their purity of style, practised writing essays of his own. But he was miserably unhappy; and when in July he came across a farmer from Somerset, Llewelyn 'longed to tell him to tell my brother that *he had seen me in Hell!*'

John had spent the first few months of 1908 on another American lecture tour. He had joined 'The Archangel' in Philadelphia; and the two men were now on better terms, though Louis found John's constant introspective worries about the state of his soul faintly ridiculous. John passed on a full account of these worries to Llewelyn; and when his lectures were so successful that he was invited to return the following year, he wrote to his brother:

> Again! and am I to go through these dreadful struggles all over again in this intoxicating climate? If only there were some open gate, some monkish habit, some talisman, some occult charm that could save me but no – Aged 35 – . . . If only I could really keep the vow I make never to deliberately pursue lechery again.

John had now discovered American burlesque, and would suffer the vulgarity and rather brutal humour of much of the entertainment for the sake of those 'cruelly brief' but 'heavenly interludes' when he could feast his eyes on the limbs of chorus girls. But his pleasure was clouded. As he later wrote in his autobiography: 'For the first time in my life this craving of mine for contemplating the limbs of women began to appear to my conscience as wicked.' John speculated that the presence of the almost wholly male audiences may have been partly responsible for this morbid awakening of his conscience. He despised them for enjoying the major part of the burlesque shows, with, for example, their 'sardonic and savage derision of tramps and hobos'; and yet he was a part of the audience himself: perhaps his own thoughts and desires were a good deal worse than the obvious brutality and coarseness of those around him?

Constantly John made good resolutions, and constantly he broke them, tormenting both himself and his friends with a catalogue of his 'sins'. But his confessions were highly selective and self-indulgent. In March, for example, when he admitted to Llewelyn that a clergyman's wife had fallen in love with him, and that as a result he had 'on . . . three occasions . . . lapsed from the path', he said nothing at all about something much more serious. Infatuated with Mabel Hattersley, a woman who was 'uncommon clever' and had 'a suspicion of the Hermaphrodite', he was arranging to pay her £150 a year if she would set up home in a flat in New York where he could easily visit her, instead of moving to Williamsburg as she proposed. He only told Louis about this when she had fleeced him of £50, decided not to stay in New York after all, and then vengefully exposed him to his American friends when he refused to pay what amounted to a blackmail of £80 a year from then on.

Despite all these excitements, John found time to think about Llewelyn's future. He realised that his brother was not happy as a teacher, and while he was still in America he arranged with the Philadelphia Society for Llewelyn to go out with him the following Christmas 'on a sort of trial trip'. The invitation actually reached Llewelyn shortly after he had begun his tutoring job: 'it is really serious', John wrote to him from Dresden, where in between lectures[3] he was buying pornographic books, reading them, and then throwing them into the river Elbe, 'it is really serious that you should be wasting your time like this.' At the beginning of August the tutoring came to an end; and Llewelyn began some hard work on the preparation of his trial lectures, later writing that 'It was now that I fell more completely than ever under the influence of my brother J. C. P. . . . the preparation for these lectures brought us much together.'

Several happy months followed for the two brothers. Llewelyn, secure in the arrangements which John had made for his future, was able to forget the humiliations and disappointments of the previous fifteen months. In John's stimulating company he began, as he later wrote, to take a renewed and lively interest in the world about him:

> We visited churches and peered curiously at the symbols and
> images that had meant so much to our race. We loitered and
> read the old weather-beaten inscriptions on the stones outside –
> we thought of Hardy and Shakespeare and of the still bones of
> the peasantry below in the earth. We stopped to watch village
> children dancing under the chequered shadows of old west

country elms. . . . And all the time the world unfolded itself
before my eyes, this world of sun and rain, of sea and river, of
churches and dead men's bones.

No doubt the two brothers also saw something of Theodore, who
moved in August from his cottage in the centre of Chaldon to a
red-brick house on the western edge of the same village. The house
looked up towards the hill known as High Chaldon; and because it
stood in the middle of grassland, Theodore named it 'Beth-Car', the
house of the pasture. It was in good repair, and, as he told Louis
Wilkinson, it was 'a little nearer the sea, and the garden is half an acre
. . . I shall be glad to let Babe have more room and sunlight.' Theodore
was now so poor that he gratefully accepted cast-off clothes from his
friends;⁴ but he was content with Violet and their children: the following year their second son Francis was born, and Theodore was to
recollect that this was one of the most enjoyable periods of his life.⁵

In the autumn, Llewelyn stayed at Montacute working hard on his
lectures; while John, touring England as usual, wrote him encouraging
letters: 'I long to hear your début on the New York platform', one letter
ran. 'How those girls in "pickaboo" blouses will sway and lean,
expand and melt; how they will "droop and wilter from adoring love".'
In December Lulu travelled up to the Midlands to watch John deliver
some of his lectures; on the eighteenth they stayed with Tom Jones
in Liverpool, and Llewelyn spent the night with a girl for the first time
in his life; and on the nineteenth they sailed for America.

Llewelyn's first lecture, on 5 January 1909, he himself described as
'not a failure, . . . [even if] not a great success'; but his début in New
York, three days later was little short of a disaster. One of the audience,
not unreasonably, called upon Llewelyn to 'take the first boat back to
England'; and Louis Wilkinson wrote of the lecture that:

> Listening to it was one of the most acutely embarrassing and
> distressing experiences I have ever had, and delivering it was an
> evident agony to Llewelyn. He stammered, paused, stammered
> again: one after another of his sentences crumbled and fell to
> pieces, and then, for many moments together, he would be, it
> seemed, struck dumb. He had notes; indeed, I think he had the
> whole lecture written out, but he was trying not to use the
> manuscript, and, when he did in desperation fall back on it, it
> completely bewildered him. . . . After the lecture I went back
> with him to our lodgings and slept with him there. He was in

extreme agitation, in real misery and despair. . . . He had
exaggerated, fantastically and beyond all measure, that
evening's misadventure.

In between his own lectures, and the bouts of gastric trouble which
were once again causing him pain, John coached Lulu, suggesting
ideas to him, and even on one occasion dictating the complete text of a
lecture for his brother to deliver. But even when Llewelyn simply read
from a prepared text, his lectures were often poorly received. Worrying
incessantly about the prospects of further failures, he worked harder
than ever on his preparation; and by the last week in February he was
so rundown and depressed that it only needed a bad cold to reduce
him, as he noted in his diary, to 'a suicidal mood . . . I am resigned,
even to death . . . Jack promises to carry my ashes to England in a
wonderful silver jar . . .' During March he felt that his lectures were a
little more successful; but his salary was reduced, and it seemed
unlikely that he would be asked to return to America the following
year.

However, in April 1909, when Llewelyn was back at Montacute, he
used the possibility of such a request to avoid coming to any definite
decision about his future. He hated the idea of office work, and this put
paid to a number of suggestions, including Ralph Shirley's, that he
should buy a junior directorship in a publishing house; and John's, that
he should go into the cotton business with Tom Jones. Nor would
Llewelyn apply for a permanent teaching post. At length he took a
temporary job at the Sherborne Prep, where his brother Littleton had
been headmaster for the past four years.[6] It was agreed that he should
teach only for the first half of the summer term, with an option to
return on a full-time basis in the autumn, if nothing else had offered
itself.

Llewelyn found the two months of teaching, in May and June, much
less disagreeable than he had feared; and he was then enjoying a
holiday in Devon with his brothers Bertie and Will, when he heard the
alarming news that John was once again seriously ill with stomach
ulcers: 'I hope I shall get thro'', John had written to him; 'but you will
not be surprised if you hear that I can't go on.'

Llewelyn immediately abandoned his holiday. Writing in his diary:
'Let me die – he belongs to the earth and has no soul', he travelled to
Burpham to be at John's bedside; and on 2 July, as John was then well
enough to travel, he returned to Devonshire with him, and took him to

Sidmouth, where his parents were on holiday. Llewelyn wanted their support in his efforts to persuade John to give up lecturing: on 3 July he wrote in his diary: '*I shall free Jack.*'; and he told Louis Wilkinson, 'we must get him out of lecturing, or he will be done for – he won't be able to stand another year's work like the last.' On 9 July, Llewelyn's view was confirmed by a London specialist, on whose advice John formally resigned as an Oxford University Extension lecturer, telling the authorities that he hoped Louis Wilkinson would take his place. The two brothers now planned that John should make money by writing poems, stories, and articles for the papers. He was already working on a book about Keats, and for a while had high hopes. However, towards the end of July, while Llewelyn was spending a few days away from Burpham, staying with Louis at Aldeburgh, John's first efforts were all rejected: these included a number of poems, and an article on Milton, about which John wrote crossly:

> Our darling Mr Orage of the *New Age* added insult to injury over the Milton by taking upon himself impertinent rascal! to criticize the production. 'Strong in passages' ran his graceful observation, 'but not sustained enough!'
>
> I enclose Philip Gibbs' sensible but not encouraging remarks. . . . How properly humiliating to the Powys Pride so often referred to!

By the time Llewelyn returned to Burpham, John was in much better health, and determined to resume his lecturing in America. Llewelyn was extremely disappointed at the failure of this second attempt to persuade his brother to lead a more peaceful life; but he tried to accept the situation philosophically: 'Jack will go to America. Women decay in misery, little children are dragged into lustful bondage, but it is still most unwise to take the world too seriously.' Acting as his brother's secretary for a while, he copied out two short stories for him: *The Incubus* – which Llewelyn renamed *Romer Mowl* – and *The Spot on the Wall*. Both the stories are work of a man with a powerful imagination; but though the ideas are clever, the execution is less than subtle: '"Dear God! What was that?" Every drop of blood in the Scholar's veins froze',[7] gives one some indication of the style of writing; and Llewelyn could find no home for them.

On 11 August the two brothers went to Montacute, where they were joined by Louis Wilkinson and Bernie O'Neill; and Theodore came over from East Chaldon. They were all very concerned about John's state of health; and Louis suggested that John should ask his father if he would pay for him to recuperate in Italy. To John's surprise and delight his father agreed, and it was arranged that John should travel out to Florence towards the end of September, with Gertrude as his companion.

In the meantime there was an angry scene between John and Llewelyn, who had begun to feel annoyed with his brother's apparent recklessness, and teased him mercilessly about wishing to return to America. John, aware that his motives would not bear close examination, lost his temper and shouted: 'Young man, I'll never forgive you for this'! But they were soon reconciled, and a few days later, in the churchyard at Tintinhull, they lay on tombstones while deciding quite amicably that 'there is no such thing as good and evil – everything is relative – and each situation must be dealt with differently. Discretion is to be the watchword.'

At the beginning of September, Llewelyn visited Derbyshire for the first time: his cousin Alice, Ralph Shirley's sister, was married to Mr Linton of Shirley rectory, and had invited him to spend a week in the house where five of his brothers and sisters had been born. While he was staying there he met Alice's nineteen-year-old daughter Marion; but on this occasion he took little notice of her, preferring an agreeable flirtation with one of her friends.

When he returned to Montacute, there had been no offer of another lecture-tour; and so at the start of the autumn term, Llewelyn set out for the Sherborne Prep. He had seen from John's unsuccessful efforts how difficult it was to earn a living from writing, and he was looking forward to working with his brother in a familiar setting. He had rooms of his own in Richmond Villa, so felt that he could preserve an independent life-style: 'Though a schoolmaster', he noted in his diary, 'I am still a Bohemian'; and after a happy week-end visit from Bertie, he recorded that 'Everything seemed to me to be the same. Am I privileged really to enjoy once again those happy far off days?' He would have been amused to hear that some of the family circle, thinking of characters for a masked ball, had decided that he should appear as King Charles II. Other choices included Littleton, a great fisherman, as Isaac Walton; Kate as Boadicea, Jack as Keats, and Gertrude as Queen Katharine of Berengaria.[8]

'Keats' and 'Queen Katharine' had found rooms in a small lodging house in Florence, and were living there very cheaply. During the day Gertrude sketched while John, his manias 'lulled to sleep' enjoyed the warmth of an Italian autumn, later writing that 'the feeling of the rose-scented, garlic-scented, grape-skin-scented, dust-scented sunshine, as I sat down on any sun-warmed stone or any fragment of marble . . . made the whole of human life seem in some mystic way *redeemed*.' Reacting in this direct, sensual way to the sun and stones of Florence, John began to ask himself how often he had genuine feelings of this kind, and how often his perception of reality was strained through his wide reading. He wrote to Louis Wilkinson about this, commenting: 'how hopelessly bookish – how *literary*! – I am – every impression seems made up of sentences out of books. Have I no really definite personality . . .' To counterbalance his bookishness and over-sophistication, he attended a Catholic service every day, hoping that he would 'get calmed and solidified and made a little more pagan'. John was also thinking about his writing: until recently, his great scheme had been for a book of poems 'more or less in the style of old Walt [Whitman]'; but now there was an important change. He began to feel that, instead of trying to go further along the lines of those stylists whom he most admired – at that time, Walt Whitman in poetry and Walter Pater in prose – he should be listening to 'the secret boy-maids' of his 'inner Self'. And at this time, reading Nietzsche's *Ecce Homo* in the Italian hills, he 'pretended . . . that I too, in my day and hour, would be a proclaimer of planetary secrets.' But pride in what he might one day achieve was combined with a great lack of self-confidence about his present abilities; and he wrote to Louis that, when he did try to listen to the voice of his own inspiration, he found that 'the Shrine of the Innermost is as empty as the Medici chapel'!

Towards the end of October John and Gertrude travelled on to Venice. Although it was now bitterly cold, John described the city to Louis as 'friendly and welcoming'; and far from being over-awed by St Mark's, like so many other travellers, he found it 'a darling little bedizened harlot of a church – a sort of Salome among the handmaids of the lord, so lavishly is she decorated with beguiling gold, so clasped with sapphires!' In November the two travellers set out for England; but they had only reached Paris when they received news that their brother Llewelyn had been taken seriously ill with tuberculosis, then usually fatal.

John felt that he was partly to blame for his brother's illness, believing that Llewelyn had caught the infection while he was worried, overtired, and facing hostile audiences in America. But the incubation period for tuberculosis is normally no longer than three or four months, and it is more probable that he was infected in May when, to help his father, he sat by the bed-side of a dying boy whose cough may well have been consumptive. In August Llewelyn had had an unpleasant premonition about the future: standing on the threshold of Beth-Car, and looking up at a yellow crescent moon with jagged horns, he remarked to Bernie O'Neill and to Theodore: 'You see that? It is God's claw and it will do me evil. I feel that it is a sign of harm to me.' In September he developed a persistent cough and cold which lasted through October and on into November. On the night of 3 November, he was lying awake, listening to the rain drumming against the window-panes, when: 'Suddenly, after a fit of coughing more violent than usual, an ugly conviction came over me that something was wrong. I lit a candle and discovered that my mouth was full of blood.' Half remembering Keats's words on a similar occasion, he wrote in his diary: 'That drop of blood is my death-warrant; I must die.'

The following morning he tried to continue with his teaching as usual; but was still coughing up blood, and, after informing Littleton, he arranged to see a doctor. 'You would like me to be Honest', the doctor told him. 'There is no time to be lost – you have consumption'; and Llewelyn 'Went to bed spitting out blood & blasphemies'. The windows of his bedroom in Richmond Villa were removed from their frames, with the idea that he should have as much fresh air as possible; and two days later he was visited by Littleton and May, with their father. To all of them, his death seemed inevitable; and after their visit Llewelyn wrote in his diary:

> I cried because Littleton cried: Father prayed – and I looked far away at the Honeycombe woods. The afternoon was very still. I saw Father's bowed head and my own hands transparent as I lay coughing in bed, & I thought myself dying. At first I grew alarmed (May said she saw 'the fear of death in my eyes') but afterwards quite resigned. I have lived twenty-five years, and can cry 'vixi' – there is no sensation unknown to me – I have experienced everything, and shall be found ready. I am at rest about Heaven – I shall die 'brimful of goodness' – with no remorse & no regrets, only a little piqued by God's impatience.

This mood of resignation was only one of the moods which, in his feverish mental state, he exploited for their dramatic possibilities. On other occasions, he cursed God; and he also wrote that, on another level, 'deep in my heart, I refused to realise how grave my sickness was. I liked to talk about dying, but I had no mind to die.' Then John arrived from Paris, and with an eccentric flourish offered Llewelyn ginger pop, after exclaiming: 'not Lulu ill, not Lulu ill . . . Jack's golden book is to be snatched from him.' Llewelyn, both amused and delighted, realised for the first time that his eldest brother loved him with precisely the same fierce and selfish love of which he himself was capable. Together, they talked of what might be done; and after staying only a single night at Sherborne, John hurried to Montacute, 'to urge Llewelyn's plea that an effort should be made to defeat "God's will" by sending him to Switzerland.'

John convinced his parents that they should provide the necessary money; though at first his father 'accused the doctors of exploiting the situation for professional profit'; and his mother was also opposed to the idea. Shortly afterwards, she visited Llewelyn at Richmond Villa; but he knew of her opposition to his plans, and the visit was not a success. Later, describing her as 'that strange woman who ever loved sorrow rather than joy', Llewelyn wrote that: 'my heart remained hard towards her. I knew that she resented my going to Switzerland and would have had me instead return quietly to Montacute to die peacefully there clinging to the Christian hope.'

Other visitors were more warmly received: especially Louis Wilkinson who had been prepared by John to fall in with Llewelyn's 'wishes that the humour and irony with which [his friends] treat the situation should be of the more intense and dramatic kind'. And after seeing Theodore, Llewelyn recorded in his diary: 'He loves me more than I had thought.' There was an amusing side to Theodore's visit: 'His chief preoccupation' wrote Llewelyn, 'seemed to be lest he himself should catch my complaint. He sat by the open window, inhaling the fresh air, and now and again drawing in his cheeks, as he uttered a thousand whimsical and fantastical observations.' A more sinister visitor was an old stone-mason from Montacute, who enjoyed telling Llewelyn that he had *'a churchyard cough'*.

Despite this sombre warning, the blood-spitting stopped, his temperature became normal, and in the first week of December he set out with John for Switzerland. Llewelyn felt fit enough to travel, and even to do some sight-seeing on the way, though

> he walked bent over, stooping forward like an extremely aged
> man, and as he walked he clutched with his fingers the bosom
> of his waistcoat just above his heart. He did this so constantly

that by degrees his waistcoat came to resemble one of those
tattered military flags that hang from the roofs of churches.

They arrived at the hospital of Clavadel, not far from Davos-Platz, on
the evening of 10 December. Llewelyn was warned that his fate was
doubtful, and wrote in his diary: 'am prepared for anything but intend
to put up a fight.' The following day, when John said goodbye to him,
he replied dramatically: 'Whatever happens, it is well that we two met.'
Then Llewelyn watched from his bed as his brother walked over to the
lift: 'My darling, my darling', [John] stammered out, then the sky-blue
lift took him down and I turned my face to the polished pitch-pine wall
and cried for the second time.' Llewelyn's lungs were in a very serious
condition, inflamed and spotted here and there by tubercula. Either
they would rapidly spread, and his lungs would soon be destroyed; or
they would begin to heal; but it was quite possible that the two brothers
would never meet again.

Fortunately, the first six weeks of his stay at Clavadel saw a considerable improvement, and Dr Huggard pronounced that Llewelyn had a
'good hope of recovery'. John was delighted by the news. He had
already arranged for Gertrude to go out to Clavadel to help nurse
Llewelyn, telling him 'You can't do much tarting when you're as bad as
you are now, and you can send her back as soon as you get up'; and
now he wrote in a further letter, from on board the ship in which he
was travelling across the Atlantic on the way to begin his fourth
American lecture tour, 'Hurrah once more, we rush into existence
again, all steam ahead!'

Llewelyn grew gradually better; he sent cheerful postcards to his
mother,[9] and Gertrude's company until the end of January did not
prevent him from losing his heart to Adele, a Jewess from Brussels. At
one time he even thought of marrying her, and noted in his diary: 'I
contemplate with astonishing equanimity the surrender of my Freedom. Why not *a little house* at Sherborne?' But when she treated him
unkindly he rapidly lost interest in her. The atmosphere in the hospital
was very like the atmosphere which gives rise to ship-board romances,
a product of separation from the restrictions of a customary circle,
enforced intimacy with strangers, and a sense of shared adventure – in
this case heightened by the fact that, for many of the patients, the end
of the voyage was death. Before long, Lulu was again in love: this time
with Lizzie, a girl from Newcastle whom he found not pretty, but 'very
amorous'. He visited her several times in her room; and instead of

teasing him, like Adele, 'Presently she pulled me towards her and I found myself eagerly embracing this pretty bundle of bones: inhaling the scent of her body, burying my head between the breasts, deliciously rounded, that protected her poor little wheezy chest.' He was conscious, as he wrote to Bertie, of the danger of 'kissing little consumptives'; but he found Lizzie wise, and 'very near to the ideal for which I have for so long sought'.

That spring, Llewelyn's father wrote to him:

> I hope now that you are stronger that you give some time
> regularly to reading & religious thought. Sometimes a season of
> forced rest from the things of the busy world becomes a time of
> distinct advance in our spiritual life – and I should like it to be so
> in your case.

Llewelyn certainly had time to read and to meditate; but he was not drawn back towards Christianity, as his father had hoped. Instead, he was very strongly influenced by one of his fellow-patients, a distinguished Hungarian gentleman called Dr Zsenda, whom Lulu described in his diary as 'the wisest of men, and a follower of Montaigne'. In the face of death, he remained 'mad to extract all he could from these last rare moments of intelligent consciousness'; and before he died he passed on to Llewelyn two important precepts which became the foundation of Llewelyn's mature philosophy:

> The position of a sceptic . . . is the only secure attitude to hold
> towards the Universe – that is, to remain *uncommitted* to the end.

and

> The art of living is to be fully aware of one's personal existence –
> to become a privileged spectator.

CHAPTER SIX

1910–1914

*John lectures in America each winter, under the auspices of Arnold
Shaw from 1911 • visits Clavadel, 1910 • his* Keats *rejected,
1910 • fetches Llewelyn from Clavadel, 1911 • meets Frances Gregg,
February 1912, and she marries Louis Wilkinson, April 1912 • with
Llewelyn, Frances and Louis to Venice, May 1912.*
Theodore writes Dialogues and short stories, but publishes nothing.
*Llewelyn seriously ill at Clavadel, July 1910 • returns to England,
1911 • to Venice, 1912 • writes short stories, 1912–13 • to
Switzerland, January 1913 •* The Stunner *published, 1913 •
engaged to Marion Linton, 1914.*
Katie's nervous breakdown, 1912, • death of Mary Powys, 1914.

On 14 April 1910, John Cowper Powys arrived at Clavadel, having
recently returned from America. His head was full of Nietzsche; and he
had brought with him some sadistic books from Paris, one of which,
with a look of 'shame and disgust', Lulu snatched from him and flung
into a mountain stream. Although Llewelyn still admired his brother,
he had maintained a more independent attitude since John had decided to return to lecturing against his advice, and now he urged him to
complete the *Life of Keats* on which he had been engaged for so long.
John replied defensively that he was convinced that 'the greatest
genuises have never written, but, like Bernie, have put their genius
into their lives'; however, he encouraged Llewelyn to go on writing his
diary; and the brothers also discussed Theodore's work, with John
reading out to Llewelyn a 'Dialogue' which Theodore had recently sent
to him.

After completing his *Interpretation of Genesis*, Theodore had continued to write dialogues in a Biblical style, and to live quietly at East
Chaldon with his wife and two sons. In one of these dialogues, he

imagines that he is being examined by his brothers. Bertie asks him 'Who can be happy with you Theodore? Old Jack alone can stay with you, Willie won't go near you, Lulu avoids you . . .'; and he replies:

> None of you know how dearly I love to see you, for often an angel carries me to a land of darkness, of black ice and past dead rocks, and I return home chilled, and a word from one of you, a kind hand grasp, would enliven again the dulled vitality, give me the warm sun again. I would hold you all very close . . . only you will not.

Soon it is John's turn to attack:

> You just sit outside [in] the sun, looking not reading, not writing, only looking into vacancy, running now and then after willful children, running for dish clouts, old kettles, foul pans, loafing through the days, filling them with a slut's labour and a rake's thought. We know you Theodore.

To which Theodore replies:

> Yea it is wonderful how I can believe and yet I do believe, that out of it all I shall become at last a true mother and give birth.

When Bertie complains that this is 'unutterable nonsense', and Lulu says 'You would starve were it not for our charity', Theodore explains that he is becoming willing to accept whatever the future may hold; and that his comments about 'becoming a mother' are part of his philosophy of spiritual growth through suffering. Man has within himself, says Theodore, a 'Father Spirit', whose suffering gives rise to a 'Mother'; and her creativity is expressed as the 'Father Spirit' dies, in the birth of the new life of the 'son of man'.[1]

John strongly advised Theodore to abandon this allegorical style: he and Lulu had both been impressed by the dialogue which John read out at Clavadel, but John said that he did not understand or appreciate[2]

> the part about Father Mother and Child. . . . As long as you describe in plain and simple language what you *feel* really and truly whether of inspired ecstasy and oneness with the hidden springs of life or of hopeless melancholy and lapsings into the caverns of gloom – I am sympathetic and ready to listen to all and perhaps even lift my materialism a little bit out of the way: but when you speak in parables all my interest dries up . . .

After spending ten days at Clavadel, days which were filled with discussions and long walks, John travelled back to England. He went straight to his family at Burpham; but although on one occasion he enjoyed bird-nesting with his son Littleton Alfred, now seven years old, it was not a happy summer. Worried by news that Lulu's health had taken a turn for the worse, and himself tortured by dyspepsia, so that he was 'not allowed tea or bread or rusks or butter or treacle or anything that I like', John was 'about as depressed by the ways of God as I have ever been in my life'. His relationship with his wife had also continued to deteriorate, and he added 'Margaret of course thinks that I care more for tea with sugar in it than for all the brothers in the world.' He could not talk freely at home: 'You know how subjects are barred, barred, barred'; there was an added irritation when Margaret became 'quite absorbingly and insanely devoted to playing 'Miss Milligan', a certain kind of Patience . . .'; and the situation was not helped by the bad feeling between Margaret and many of his family. Theodore in his less philosophical moments was convinced that Margaret felt he deserved to starve to death;[3] and in mid-May John persuaded Margaret to go to Montacute for a week with their son, but Bertie's wife Dorothy, that 'peevish bitch' as John called her in a letter to Lulu, refused to visit Margaret there.

Louis Wilkinson's description of the family as 'The Powys', Littleton's determination in his memoirs always to see them in the best possible light, and John's decision in his *Autobiography* to be frank about some areas of his life, but highly reticent about others, have led to the view that the Powys family was far more united than it really was.[4] At this time there was certainly a good deal of spiteful comment within the family, directed at various targets; and John himself was criticised with better cause than most. Mabel Hattersley, the woman who a few years earlier had fleeced him of £50 but had hoped for much more, wrote a vindictive letter to Margaret to tell her about John's payment. 'You can believe', John wrote to Lulu, 'that it was not a very nice July 5th when that letter to Margaret arrived – fifty pounds! . . . to Margaret at this moment I appear in the every exact situation of that well-known liar, Annanias.' Because his health was so much worse in England, John had already been thinking about staying in America for a greater part of each year, with only 'a short visit to Burpham and Montacute', and this unpleasant scene with his wife must have made the idea seem still more attractive.

In the meantime, Llewelyn's health had been deteriorating. In early

May, a cold kept him in bed for a few days, and he began losing weight. He could still describe Lizzie affectionately as 'very fresh and charming in her white muslin frock – warm cheeks, laughing eyes, fragrant hair – delicate white hands, frills, laces, and red, red roses'; but he began to worry that contact with her was endangering his health. When his sister Marian arrived towards the end of the month, he most unwisely accompanied her on long walks which further overtaxed his strength; and by 10 June he was writing that 'Dr Frey . . . heard the white ants busy at my lungs again. So I have fallen into the snare. . . . Will I be well ever again?' For twelve days he lay in bed; at the end of June he unkindly told Lizzie that she was 'a danger – a perilous delight'; and in his diary on 2 July he described her as looking 'pallid and unhealthy in the deepening twilight, and I shrank from her – this beautiful white-limbed vampire, whose purple lips had sucked the red life-blood from my veins.' For several days, he grew increasingly feverish:

> And then, one July midnight, a blood-vessel broke. I waked suddenly to feel that insufferable bubbling sensation in my chest, so familiar to consumptives. There was a rush of blood. I coughed and gasped for breath. Presently, with the pretty egotism of youth, I dipped my fountain-pen into the basin at my bedside and scratched a red cross on my diary, a cross such as a tramp might have made who could not sign his name, and yet who wished to record some important event in his wayfaring.

All night he lay motionless, while the doctors injected him with gelatine, and stood by his bedside. The immediate crisis passed; but it was more than four months before he was able to leave his bed again.

During these four months, he was visited by Littleton and Mabel, and by his aunt Dora; and John sent him letters full of family news: Lucy, their youngest sister, was engaged to be married to a farmer of whom Littleton and some other members of the family did not approve; May was working in 'An Old Curiosity Shop' in Cornwall; and John himself, before sailing for America in September, had completed his book about Keats. Unfortunately, both Methuen and Foulis rejected it, and many months of work came to nothing: perhaps, as John had feared, it was 'a little too intransigeantly unorthodox and Dionysic' to be acceptable. From America, John also wrote to Llewelyn about Theodore, saying that the whole family should treat Theodore's odd, stylised letters with respect, because his fantastic and to us irrelevant speculations are to him his expression – his art . . . they are his life-illusion! . . .

When you destroy a life-illusion you commit the one unpardonable sin. I have done it – I cannot be forgiven – I destroyed my wife's illusion of 'love'. Well – we must not destroy old [Theodore]'s.

When in November Llewelyn was able to leave his bed, he was much more cautious about his love affairs. He had lost all interest in Lizzie, though he had the grace to apologise to her for his unsympathetic behaviour; and when he began a new flirtation he would not even kiss the girl on her lips. In the meantime, he enjoyed a Christmas visit from Bertie; and in February 1911 Gertrude came out to Switzerland, and found him looking very much better.

Llewelyn had now befriended a dying scholar, Wilbraham, and was trying to convert him to his new philosophy that 'Learning and culture . . . are not ends but means – the end is Life itself.' They spent much time together, and in Wilbraham's company Llewelyn often went out to tea with two attractive young Swiss girls. Much to Llewelyn's pleasure, not only did Wilbraham eventually accept all his ideas; but one of the Swiss girls, Lisaly Gujer, fell in love with him, and was to remain strongly attached to him for the rest of his life.

By the middle of April, Llewelyn was well enough to think of leaving the sanatorium. John had returned to England that month, having cancelled the last fortnight of his lecture-tour as a result of acute dyspepsia; and, after attending Lucy's wedding, he agreed to travel on to Clavadel to collect his brother. He arrived there on 27 April; and two days later the brothers had set out for England and Montacute.

Gertrude had prepared a bed for Llewelyn in the nursery, a cheerful and sunny room which looked out across the fields towards St Michael's Mount and the distant remains of Montacute Abbey. At first Llewelyn spent most of each day reading or writing on a camp bed placed on the terrace; but sometimes he would walk in the garden with his mother, and he came to realise how far apart they had grown: one evening, as they saw the last rays of the sun transfigure an ordinary sow, Mary Powys commented: 'So the spirit of God will light up the most degraded soul.' At Clavadel, however, Llewelyn had finally concluded that there is no God, and no after-life. He was impervious to religious sentiments – visiting a scholarly priest later in the year he wrote: 'listened to his sly theology unconvinced' – and he concentrated on enjoying the surface of life. The most ordinary sounds: the slam of the back gate, or the voice of his father heard as he walked through the garden in the cool of the evening, assumed greater importance in his mind than the metaphysical theories which had once interested him, and which still intrigued his eldest brother.

During the summer months Llewelyn was visited by many of his friends and family. In July he walked with his brother John as far as Tintinhull, where he much preferred the tavern to the church:

> In a tavern one touches life at its centre. Here is the heart of the bee-hive. Here, at any rate, no spiritual treachery is tolerated; here, at any rate, no deceitful idealism stretches out tendrils white and sickly. . . . He who sits down on a tavern settle must even take the world as he finds it.

It was one of the hottest and driest summers of the century; and when Bernie O'Neill arrived for a nine-day holiday, he found Lulu 'wonderfully well . . . he walked with energy and talked on everything with interest and animation.' The two men managed to visit every public-house within walking distance of Montacute!

Early in the summer Llewelyn had been to stay with Littleton; and at the end of October he went down to East Chaldon to spend the autumn and early winter with Theodore at Beth-Car. On their first afternoon together, the brothers walked over the hills to Ringstead Bay, and Llewelyn was 'in high spirits to be near the sea again, and felt, as I inhaled the salt air of those lone beaches, that my cough, which had again been causing me anxiety, could not fail now to get better.' They were joined by their sister Katie, who, together with Lucy, had been helping Willie on the farm at Witcombe which he had been given by their father. Katie was a passionate highly-strung girl, later described by a nephew as living 'in another world from which she would not descend. More than any other Powys she would make sure whoever she was talking to would step out of the real world, and into another.'[5] In Llewelyn's words, she became transfigured when in close contact with nature: '"I am the hills," she cried, "The sea is my lover. . . . Yes, I am at ease and understood on these downlands. Once upon them, and all is forgotten."' Llewelyn spent many hours walking with Theodore and Katie; and once, with a typical access of daring, climbed up and down an extremely dangerous old smugglers' path on one of the chalk cliffs. He continued to observe himself, with a kind of artistic detachment: and for the first time noted the sadistic thrill which made him, in one unpleasant respect, a true brother of both John and Theodore. It happened when he was walking on the downs, and not far away from him a stoat caught a rabbit. He could hear the rabbit's cries, and later confessed that it had given him 'a sharp, attenuated refreshment to think of the tussle, down there below, between the mild-eyed, harmless, soft-furred creature and its lithe enemy, muscular and merciless.'

He also had time to observe Theodore, and once saw him:

> sunk in one of his worst moods of depression. His features had the same dreary look that was presented by the patient window-panes with the grey rain trickling down them. We talked together. 'In this life, all we can do,' he said, 'is each day so to tire out our limbs that rest is acceptable – and finally death.' I spoke of the blessedness of life, but he would have none of it. 'For a pint of honey a gallon of gall, for a dram of pleasure a pound of pain, for an inch of mirth an ell of moan. For as ivy doth encompass the oak, so do our miseries encompass our lives. Your philosophy is false,' he cried, with more emotion than I had ever known him to display, 'false, false, and again false. We must learn to welcome Death. Death is the great Father of all things; for without him there is no Life.'

On occasions like this, wrote Llewelyn, Theodore looked so dejected that one might have taken him for Judas Iscariot, rope in hand, on the way towards his alder tree. But there were other occasions when Theodore could be positively cheerful:

> when he has not seen too much of you, when he thinks he has enough money in his tea-chest to store his cellar with coal, when he thinks the common people regard him with a friendly eye, when he thinks his mattresses do not smell of old bones, as John once had the temerity to suggest, and when he knows that you are not making love to any *very young* girls, then he will have his days, his hours, his moments. On such occasions the most unexpected observations will come from his mouth, one after the other, like sparks from a Twelfth Night bonfire; his sardonic, dry quips, his double-tongued chirpings, jumping this way and that like crickets in a hot hay-field.

From Beth-Car, Llewelyn wrote regularly to John, who had now abandoned the Philadelphia Society, and was being managed by

G. Arnold Shaw, a humorous Yorkshireman whom he had first met on his original voyage to America in the *Ivernia*. Louis Wilkinson had persuaded Shaw to become a lecture-manager some time before this, and John had decided to join his two friends in what he described as their 'circus'. Louis was 'the stately and nostalgic Harlequin'; he himself was 'the clown . . . and Arnold was the ringmaster, the fellow with the smooth forehead, the bland smile, and the long whip. How roguishly he would crack this whip when his poor Cagliostro was despatched on a tour half across the Continent! "A *mean jump* for you, John!" he would say with a chuckle.' But John found that Arnold was kind and considerate to him in private life – far kinder than he was to Louis, whom he called 'Our Doc', and handled rather firmly – and on one occasion, when John was oppressed by all kinds of anxieties, he was immensely relieved when Arnold said to him: '*Put it all on me, John.*' The two men became firm friends; and John was glad to find that they both regarded lecturing not as an academic duty, but as a public entertainment: for he was reviving his early ambition of becoming an actor. As he wrote to Llewelyn, his present existence did not suit him:

> I whirl about from Ohio to Michigan, and from Michigan to Missouri, and as I travel to and fro I sometimes experience fear, fear of trains, of crowds, of hotels. . . . A mad, exposed, morbid person in America, that would be a bitter subject for a book. I act my rôle well enough; but oh, how tired I am of lecturing!

He had already considered a new form of entertainment, in which he would 'dress up as Nero, Heraclitus, Marlowe, Byron, Goethe, etc. etc. . . . and, as these actual people, returned to life, defend my historic loves and murders!' Now John wrote to Louis, who was temporarily lecturing in England, with the suggestion that he himself, Louis, and another friend of theirs, Maurice Browne, already known as a talented producer, should each write a play to be acted by three men – themselves – and three women, one to be the personal choice of each man. After three weeks of rehearsals, the plays would be taken on tour; with each author 'despotically' deciding on the cast for his own play. '*What a chance!*' wrote John, who was planning to choose as his acting companion a certain lady from Pittsburgh, 'What lovely situations! I shall certainly have a girl dressed up as a boy and – and all sorts of things – Only Maurice says that a majority vote must suppress anything *dangerous!*'

These plans came to nothing, and John had to be content with incorporating a degree of acting into his lectures. Later he recalled how Arnold Shaw was: 'delighted by my inspired "grotesqueries" and my wild prophetic incantations. Like Owen Glendower I "called up spirits"; and the more devilish and startling these denizens of the "vasty deep" were, the more Arnold chuckled.' His lectures were more successful than ever; by Christmas 1911 he had sent £410 home to Margaret, and he hoped to be able to send another £600 before the end of the season.

On New Year's Eve 1911, while John was in the States, Theodore, Katie, and Lulu were together at Beth-Car, where they read poems to each other and drank champagne before the two brothers set off for a walk over the Downs to an ancient stone circle. Llewelyn, who noted Theodore's 'inflexible loyalty to the poetic conception of the world which it has been his taste to create', was impressed by the sight of his brother entering the stone circle, with

> the shadow of his bowed figure – he had taken his old cloak about him – appearing, as it fell across the deep-sunken stones, like the shadow of . . . the prophet Amos! And with what curious, prophetic eyes he squinnied up at the sky during those still, frosty moments!

With their father's help, Llewelyn had arranged to be in Switzerland for the worst of the winter. January found him in the best hotel in Arosa, seducing a handsome young Englishwoman; the following month he was in poor health, and moved to a cheaper hotel where he lived more cautiously; but as soon as he felt a little better, caution gave way to reckless daring. He had realised that Clavadel was little more than fifteen miles away over the mountains, and he became obsessed with the idea of striding healthily down the slopes at which he had gazed when lying on his sick-bed the previous year. So on 29 February 1912, despite the fact that his temperature was once again climbing, Llewelyn walked over the snow-covered Furka Pass, and then traversed a high, desolate, and trackless mountain plateau before finding his way down into the Frauenkirch valley. He visited the sanatorium in triumph; but the effort had been too great, and that night there was once again blood in his mouth. For four days he lay in his lodgings in the village before being removed to Clavadel; and it was lucky for him that he was not more seriously ill. Although he wrote gloomily to John: 'my consumption does not get better, O I shall die', he was able to travel back to England on 19 March, less than three weeks after his crossing of the mountains.

On returning to Montacute, and picking up the threads of his rather dull existence there, Llewelyn suddenly found himself 'immerged in a great wave of apathy . . . the dead weight of the commonplace dragged me down and filled my spirit with lamentable misgivings'.[6] His usual good humour was further tested by strange fragments of news from America, which suggested that John and Louis were in the midst of all kinds of exciting experiences, and that Jack, in particular, had forgotten him for the time being. When John did write, it was not to sympathise with Llewelyn, but to hint at these 'exquisite and rare experiences to be related – new and unexpected and by the gods *impossible*'. Then came news of a girl called Frances, to whom John was passionately devoted. Since he could not marry her himself, he had engineered her marriage to one of his 'circle': 'I saw her first in Feb. . . . and Louis saw her exactly a fortnight ago to-day. They are going to be married on Easter Monday.'

Frances Gregg was a very beautiful woman of twenty-seven, with the large and appealing eyes of a star of the silent screen.[7] She worked as a teacher in Philadelphia, where her mother, a devout evangelical Christian, had founded a school for Italian immigrants, and made their home a centre for outcasts of all kinds, in particular ill-treated children and animals. Frances herself had no time for the church, though she very much admired the way in which, as she saw it, Christ had courageously launched a movement which challenged the established order of the entire universe. She thoroughly disliked the social and intellectual establishment on earth: she had a particular loathing for the police; and as a poet she was a member of the revolutionary Imagists of Philadelphia, and her closest friend was Hilda Doolittle, better known as H.D. Clearly aware of her own beauty, Frances appears in photographs as both sophisticated and provocative, though she was sexually inexperienced,[8] and when Ezra Pound had been in love with her, no more than a few kisses had been exchanged between them.

It was with Ezra Pound and Hilda Doolittle that Frances had attended John's lectures and when John met her he fell deeply in love with her. She was prepared to believe that his eccentricities were those of a typical Englishman;[9] and he was soon writing her a long poem which began:[10]

> Out of the depths have I caught thee, O my beloved!
> And never again

Though all the curses of all the heavens fall on us,
Drowning us, drowning us, drowning us both together,
Shall thou and I be torn from each other!

John swept her along with his plans: on 8 April 1912 Frances and Louis Wilkinson were married; and ten days later they were sailing for England with John and May. Llewelyn had already written a letter of congratulation to Louis, in which he commented: 'She must indeed be the ideal in whose quest we have trodden so many lustrous surfaces. . . . Even I feel some strange thrill as the lovely creature comes sailing eastward over the Atlantic water.' He had a personal interest in Frances: John had learned that Frances had attended one of Llewelyn's lectures in America, and had enjoyed it so much that she kept his photograph in the *Golden Treasury* next to a poem of Shelley's which he had read out.

John himself arrived home at Burpham to find a letter in which Llewelyn, in what he afterwards admitted was 'a curiously peevish tone',[11] accused his brother of deserting him. Three days later, John was at Montacute, where for several hours he endured Llewelyn's jealous complaints. 'Most of my reproaches', wrote Llewelyn, 'were infinitely mean and base: he offered no defence.' But then: '"Your apathy," he said, "I can soon dispel that. Already I see the great brazen doors swing back on silver hinges, for my youth has been renewed."' Under the influence of Frances, John had become convinced that 'this visible universe cannot be all – the very fact that we can review this one, and find it wanting, and conceive of others, proves that.' He told Llewelyn that his apathy was due to the fact that his pagan philosophy was not enough; and, to revive him, he intended to take Llewelyn to Venice, where they would meet Frances, who would be staying there with Louis. This was a generous proposal: Lulu 'positively cried aloud with joy'; and, despite opposition both from Llewelyn's doctor and from some members of the Powys family who feared that the journey and the excitement would be bad for Llewelyn's health, the two brothers travelled out to Venice in the third week of May.

On meeting Frances, Llewelyn wrote of her:

> The first impression she produces is of one walking in a trance, her head full of dreams, with the curious look of a person going on *a second errand*. . . . The next impression is of extraordinary timidity and shyness – more than shyness, a certain reluctance

> to step out into the world at all – precisely like the look of a
> Hamadryad standing waiting at the entrance of her hollow tree
> till the steps of some passing faun have died into silence. . . .
> She is tall and dark and very supple and slender . . . yet
> moulded with quite girlish and almost Tess-like contours.

Before long, he too was in love with her. Frances now had three
devoted men to worship her; and, entering into the romantic comedy
of the situation, she insisted, as John recalled:

> on dressing up as a boy; and we would accompany her in her
> gondola in this attire to the remotest possible spots where
> gondolas could be propelled! If Louis had not kept his
> East-Anglian sang-froid heaven knows into what wild events
> Llewelyn and I, in our mounting rivalry might have been
> led. . . . The feelings that this beautiful girl in boy's clothes
> excited in me rose like flames –

John had brought with him an introduction from his cousin Ralph
Shirley to the writer Francis Rolfe, or 'Baron Corvo' as he styled
himself; but the four lovers were so caught up in their own romantic
world that they soon ceased to be grateful for his liberal and assiduous
entertainment; and one day, parting from him at the foot of the
Campanile, John deliberately put an end to their association. Corvo –
in Louis's version of what happened:

> had asked when our next meeting was to be. 'To-morrow?' –
> 'We're engaged, I'm afraid, for to-morrow.' John, as the eldest,
> was our spokesman. – 'The day after?' – 'I'm afraid we're
> engaged then too.' – 'Well, perhaps Thursday?' At that point
> John lost his nerve. 'We're *engaged*!' he shouted. 'All the time!
> Up to the hilt! Engaged! *Up to the hilt*!' Corvo turned on his heel
> with one of the swiftest movements I have ever seen and shot
> away from us across the Piazza.

John's rudeness is understandable: Frances, with her 'boy-girl' appearance, was the very incarnation of one of his sylphs, and he was in a
highly over-excited state. Later, he wrote that he had been 'completely
enslaved' by her beauty; though he could not help masochistically
torturing himself at the same time, by imagining when he looked at her
lovely body that she was smeared 'from head to foot with some
grotesque sticky substance, such as marmalade or treacle!' In this

excited condition he had a strange experience. He had gone to the Ampitheatre at Verona, and found himself alone after flashes of lightning had driven away the usual crowd of tourists. Suddenly, his

> whole nature seemed transformed. . . . Alone in that Roman circle . . . the thaumaturgic element in my nature rose to such a pitch that I felt . . . the very thing I had been obscurely fumbling my way towards through all my lusts and my obsessions . . . that I really *was* endowed with some sort of supernatural power . . . a demonic formidableness . . . of which my enemies were well advised to beware!

Llewelyn had no such mystical experience: but the travelling and the excitement had had their effect. The brothers had only reached Milan on their return journey when he began coughing up blood, and was confined to bed for a number of weeks. In addition to this attack of tuberculosis, he began suffering from a kidney stone, and eventually sailed home from Genoa a very sick man. When they reached Dorset, John was ill with his usual gastric trouble, and Llewelyn suffered the excruciating pain of passing a kidney stone, and for the rest of his life had to take medicine to prevent the formation of further stones. When John left for Sussex, Llewelyn lay gloomily on his bed in the terrace walk, his mind dominated by thoughts of Frances. John tried to cheer him up with a letter suggesting that Frances would never settle down to be a good wife to Louis; and Louis himself told Llewelyn that he was not at all upset by Llewelyn's passion for Frances; and, far from trying to keep them apart, he brought her down to visit him at Montacute. John also saw Frances several times during the summer; but that autumn both he and Llewelyn had need of all their philosophy: not only was Ezra Pound in London, and seeing much of Frances; but something far more serious had happened: their sister Katie had suffered a nervous breakdown.

On holidays at Sidmouth, Katie had befriended two fishermen, the Woolleys; and she had met the man who lodged with them, Stephen Reynolds, a graduate of Manchester University some five years older than her. Reynolds was employed by the Ministry of Fisheries, but had also written the novel *A Poor Man's House*; and he was 'the first person [she] had encountered who would discuss politics and literature with her as if her opinion mattered.' She fell passionately in love with him; but although he was prepared to answer some of her letters, give her advice on what to read, and look over some of her own literary manuscripts, he did not return her love. Eventually,[12]

> so ungovernable did her infatuation become for this apparently self-centred young man that she was temporarily unbalanced and her parents were obliged to send her to a sanatorium in Bristol. 'I remember saying to myself' [she said later] 'they think I am mad, I *will* be mad.'

Llewelyn was at Montacute on the day of her collapse, and wrote at once to John, who replied: 'Poor Kate! . . . poor child! It is all a strange and tragic business – and in the future none of us will be altogether free from fear.' The brothers were well aware of the Cowper blood in their veins, and of the fact that the poet Cowper, though only a very distant connection, had suffered from melancholia which degenerated into madness. This knowledge reinforced the normal fears which inevitably arise in a family where there has been a breakdown: for many years to come, the possibility of his own manias degenerating into complete insanity became a regular feature of John's letters to Lulu; and Theodore, who was strongly attached to Katie, must have found that his own depressions were deepened by a similar fear. At the end of the year Katie was still in the sanatorium, but beginning to recover,[13] the following year she was sent to an agricultural college,[14] and at length she joined a women's cooperative farming in Sussex,[15] but she remained nervous, excitable, and a worry to the rest of her family.

In October 1912 John sailed for America; and the following month, sent Llewelyn a long and important letter in which he advised him that he should avoid feelings of depression about his own illness by taking up writing again, and heroically attempting to achieve something 'in spite of this crushing and evil destiny'. Llewelyn took John's advice, and this marked a major turning-point in his life. The apple-loft above the stables had been converted into his private den; and here, in the late autumn of 1912, he began to write short stories; continuing with the work, when he was well enough, throughout 1913. He was now twenty-nine years old; and far richer in experience and in human understanding than in the days when he had served his apprenticeship as a writer, turning out paragraphs in the style of Stevenson and others. May typed out some of the stories for him, and one of them, 'The Stunner' was accepted for publication in November 1913.

Llewelyn's stories were usually based firmly on real life, and this was no exception, as the hero was a well-known Montacute character, called 'The Stunner' because of his exceptional strength. As he lay on his death-bed, the power of the Stunner's love was such that one night he walked the three miles to the house of the woman he loved:[16]

> In the stillness of the night she had heard the noise of his coming a long way off. She ran out into the road to meet him. And there sure enough he was, advancing with deliberate steps, his bare feet sounding like an animal's pads on the August dust. With inarticulate moans he came up to her and a moment later she was holding in her arms the dead body of the Stunner, stiff and elongated and smelling of the earth.

As in most of Llewelyn's mature work, the writing is clear and direct, with similes drawn easily from the natural world which he loved; and it also contains a doctrinal element: in 'The Stunner', the moral to be drawn is that the power of love is the strongest force in the world, far exceeding the power of the Christian God. It was largely in the course of writing these stories that Llewelyn formulated his philosophy of life; but an important moment also came that autumn when, during a period of much better health, he went to stay for two nights with someone whom both he and Louis Wilkinson admired, Canon Stuckey Coles. One morning the old priest awakened him early, so that they could go up to look out of the attic window across the estuary of the River Axe, and watch the dawn breaking:[17]

> Over the flats of mud and shingle gulls were already uttering their first forlorn cries before winging their way inland for food. Soon the sky became streaked with red. I had a revelation. It came to me with conviction, with a certainty that has never since left me, that the true secret of life is braver, more happy than anything suggested by the punctilious altar at the back of this venerable old man's room.

John Cowper Powys, far away on the other side of the Atlantic for much of each year, had seen a great deal of Frances since the autumn of 1912. He had mild platonic love-affairs with other women, such as Nellie, the actress wife of Maurice Browne. John had made Chicago his headquarters in America; he had rooms in the Hotel del Prado alongside the Brownes, and enjoyed looking out over Lake Michigan with Nellie and quoting reams of poetry to her. Yet it was Frances with whom he was still passionately in love. He wrote after one meeting with her: 'I have my spring still – of rare piercing too sweet hours'; but their relationship was a difficult one. Frances teased him cruelly on occasion, and he wrote once: 'She is really wicked – beyond anything it is possible to imagine. . . . But I think I too am capable of depths of Satanism and cruelty – I think we suit each other very well.' He was also keenly aware of the ironies of a situation in which Frances had several men exactly where she wanted them, but was able to treat all of them badly if she felt like it; and John wondered whether she might not grow tired of Louis, and Ezra Pound, and himself, and 'start new campaigns in quite fresh directions'. But in the summer of 1913 when they were both back in England, he found himself 'more in love with her than ever', and bitterly regretting that he had encouraged her to marry Louis. 'Does it give you pleasure', he asked her in one letter,[18]

> to know that at this moment I am experiencing a suffering of a quite damnable kind because you belong to dear little Louis instead of me . . . I have been 'infatuated' as Louis will remind us before and I have idealized before – But may God swallow me if I have ever been in love before – Sadism is an insipid byplay to this . . .

In the meantime, his marriage to Margaret became more and more hollow; and he wrote to Llewelyn about her 'nervous irritability of temper', adding 'I pity this poor high-strung egoistic lady. . . . However! we may pity, but . . . we must strike out drastically for ourselves.' The only excitement came when there was to be a meeting between Margaret and Frances, and John wrote that:

> Messages and occult signs pass and repass between Frances and Margaret. Sometimes I almost fancy that they are in league, these two! And if so what can a poor strayed traveller do between such formidable planets – Pallas and Artemis in conjunction? What on earth will it be like when they are here and these two Critics of the Powys family actually side by side? . . . The whole situation is one that would make dear Henry James sweat with sweet perplexity.

John was now earning so much money as a lecturer that he could afford to renounce the allowance of £100 a year which his father had been making to him. He was also able to help some of his brothers and sisters: in particular Marian, who had returned to Montacute after trying a number of jobs, and finding nothing which really suited her. Charles and Mary Powys were pleased to have her at home, because

Gertrude had left Montacute to study painting, first in London and then, from the spring of 1913, in Paris.[19] But Marian was not at all happy with the prospect of looking after her ageing parents; and John promised to help her find work in America. Later she told a friend: 'I owe it entirely and only to Jack that I was able to go; it was he who persuaded our parents, he who paid for my passage, and they only agreed because he proposed to take me with him.'[20] When she arrived in New York in December 1913, John had found her a room, arranged for her to have meals at a nearby hotel, and was certain that she could 'get something at twelve dollars a week.' Soon she found work as a typist; and she settled permanently in New York State.

John also did his best for other members of his family: 'we eat a dinner at his expense once a week through the winter', Theodore told Louis. Theodore was not only supported by John, but by their father, who gave him £100 to pay off his mortgage, besides continuing his allowance; and Frances Wilkinson, very much impressed by Theodore's work, was trying to sell his short stories for him. Unfortunately she met with no success; and at the end of 1913 it was Llewelyn, with 'The Stunner' in print, who appeared to be the Powys brother with the most promising future in the literary world.

John was determined to emulate Llewelyn's success: 'We must really write now or we shall never write', he told him; and again:

> I must write – something – anything. Enormous visions stir the waters of my mind – huge, wavering, obscure. I would give pounds to be now permitted by Fate to retire with you to some place (even if it weren't sunny) and to write rapidly, feverishly – such amazing things!

But within a year they were separated by more than the Atlantic; and there had been other important changes within the family circle.

To begin with, early in 1914, Will Powys emigrated to British East Africa. Farming at Witcombe had proved too dull for someone of his adventurous nature; and he had successfully applied for the job of managing a farm at Gilgil.[21] Not many weeks after his ship had sailed the family were shocked to hear that Mary Powys was fatally ill with cancer. Llewelyn, so out of sympathy with her philosophy of suffering and resignation, still privately wrote of her as 'Wicked and mad'; but John reproached him for this, saying that 'There must be some daughters of darkness and the spirits of the night'; and that one should not 'prefer the firm, the capable, the wise, the sane . . . to such an Incarnation of the Eternal In Vain!'

When John reached Montacute in mid-April, his mother was still alive, though in considerable pain. Not wishing her to feel that he was waiting for her to die, he went on with what he had planned for the summer: a journey with Louis and Frances to Spain, where he annoyed them both by compulsively dipping his walking-stick into every historic stream they passed; and a brief stay in Rome, where he treated Bertie to a holiday. When he returned to England, feeling very unwell with stomach trouble, there was more family news: Lulu was engaged to their cousin Marion Linton.

The previous summer, Llewelyn had visited Marion Linton at Abingdon, where she was living with aunts after the death of both her parents. Llewelyn had never taken much notice of her in the past: although she was attractive, 'She had an intense rather intellectual face, with a touch of something neurotic and unhappy in the expression';[22] but now he was horrified to learn that she had fallen under the influence of a local priest, and was attending novitiate classes, with a view to entering the Roman Catholic Church as a nun. As he talked to this shy young woman, and tried to dissuade her from what he regarded as the pointless and frightful sacrifice of her life, Llewelyn, forgetting his declared passion for the unattainable Frances, began to fall in love with her. In May 1914 he had first told John that he was thinking of marriage; and in June, when Marion visited him at Montacute, he proposed to her by a stile in Marsh Lane: 'Sunshine and buttercups were everywhere . . . "If I get quite well," [he asked,] "would I have a chance of marrying you?"' At first Marion would not give him a direct answer, though she admitted: 'There is nobody else that I would marry but you'; and during the next few days they roamed the lanes and fields around Montacute, holding hands and exchanging confidences. Llewelyn was at his most radiant; and before long they were unofficially engaged.

Llewelyn had made it clear that their marriage would depend upon his being thoroughly cured of tuberculosis: but he was often far from well. Towards the end of June, when he had 'discolouration' again, a letter arrived from Willie, pointing out that Gilgil was an extremely healthy place, some eight thousand feet above sea-level, and proposing that Lulu should join him in the hope of a complete cure. A family conference decided that Llewelyn should go out to Africa; and soon a passage had been booked for 1 September, and he was making preparations for the journey 'in high spirits' at this 'new chance of getting quite well'.

Meanwhile Mary Powys began a rapid decline. On 28 July she was shivering uncontrollably, and saying as she sat on the terrace walk that she was 'afraid of the spirits'. On 29 July she told Llewelyn: 'it's not very nice going on living and always pain'; and when he cried, she looked at him 'quite coldly, with an expression of surprise, almost of contempt'. The following day she died. Jack travelled up from Burpham to lift the shroud from her coffin, and told his brother: 'I don't think I've ever seen anything so tragic and full of sorrow as that face.' Mary's death was a major landmark in the life of the Powys family; and her funeral on 4 August coincided with the end of an era in national and international life, for it was on that day in 1914 that Great Britain declared war on Germany.

CHAPTER SEVEN

1914–1915

John lectures in America, 1914–15 • meets Theodore Dreiser and publishes The War and Culture, *1915 • in England, summer 1915 • to America, and the publication of* Wood and Stone *autumn 1915.*
John, Theodore and Llewelyn prepare Confessions, *1915.*
Theodore at East Chaldon.
Llewelyn to Africa, and writes storis, 1914 • recovers health and becomes farm manager, 1915 • engagement to Marion Linton broken off, 1915.

Charles Francis Powys was still vicar of Montacute but he was now seventy-two years of age and with the death of his wife, and the outbreak of the Great War, he suddenly appeared to his family as an old man, whose feet shuffled as he walked, and whose hands shook as he spoke. At times, remembering Mary's death, he was miserably sad, and the tears ran down his cheeks; he was anxious about Katie's future, and Llewelyn's health,[1] and he must have feared that the approaching conflict would carry off more members of his family. At least there was no need to worry about Littleton, his favourite son,[2] who was more valuable to his country as a schoolmaster than as a soldier, and who was thoroughly happy in his work as headmaster of the Sherborne Prep. Nor did John have any intention of joining the fighting: he was too physically sick and mentally unbalanced to have made a good soldier, and so far as the war effort was concerned he was chiefly aware of a sense of general incapacity. It was his wife Margaret who threw herself into the struggle, posting up a notice in a local shop saying that England expected every man and woman to do their duty; and becoming secretary to the commandant of the Red Cross at Arundel.

Theodore had a strong sense of duty, and had decided to travel to

Dorchester to enlist as a volunteer, when an unpleasant incident changed his mind. He was bathing at Ringstead Bay with his eight- and six-year-old sons Dicky and Francis, when he was arrested as a spy! Francis was later able to recall that:[3]

> seeing us an officer and two soldiers came running down to the beach. They shouted and the officer waved his revolver. My father was pulled from the water at the bayonet's point and marched to the guardroom, stark naked as he was, with water dripping from his beard. (All men with beards were spies.) One soldier carried his clothes, the other walked behind pointing a bayonet. 'What a fine game!' we children thought and laughed and played on the beach until he presently returned. On the way home we would imitate the soldiers and that seemed to annoy him mightily; we could not understand why.

Theodore, not surprisingly, was furious, and wrote to Louis Wilkinson: 'Such a Corporal! God! I would like to see him prod his little stick into your belly. Anyhow I have kept at home ever since and leave the country to serve itself.'[4] Louis would have sympathised as he objected to fighting on principle, and remained abroad for most of the war to avoid any danger of being conscripted. By November 1914, however, Theodore's conscience was troubling him again: he felt that he should enlist, but no longer felt brave enough to do so, and in a black mood he wrote to John condemning himself as a disgrace both to his family and his country.

Bertie, a man of such strong convictions that he was nicknamed 'Brother Positive' by the rest of the family, was more determined than any of them to do his duty. Aged thirty-three, he was in excellent health, and tried to secure a commission, but besides being an architect, he had now become secretary of the Society for the Preservation of Ancient Buildings: the committee said that they could not spare him, and the military authorities advised him to continue with his work and look after his family.

There was no question of war service for someone in Llewelyn's state of health: so he continued with his plans for sailing to Africa to join Will. Their sisters were equally uninvolved in the war effort: though Gertrude, recalled from her artistic life to take her mother's place at Montacute, visited soldiers' wives as part of her parish duties. Marian had escaped to America just in time to avoid sharing the burden of those duties, while Lucy was fully occupied with her work as a farmer's wife. Katie, Charles Powys's favourite daughter,[5] was brought back to Montacute where she was given a small dairy farm close to the vicarage.[6]

Before sailing to America that autumn for another lecture tour, John Cowper Powys saw two of his oldest friends: 'The Catholic' visited him at Montacute, and as they sat in taverns they were entertained by the strange rumour then sweeping the countryside that the huge Russian army was secretly passing through England! Then, in Liverpool, he spent an evening with Tom Jones and some of his girls before setting off once more across the Atlantic. For various reasons, however, John was in exceptionally low spirits: not only was his mother dead, but his wife, boasting that there were eighteen Lyons in the war, had made him feel dreadfully incompetent; Lulu, his closest family friend, was on his way to an indefinite exile in Africa; and, worst of all, he had received a 'slaughtering attack' from Frances Wilkinson, the woman he loved best in the world. He had written one of his rambling, entertaining letters to her; and she had replied with a detailed criticism accusing him, in effect, of an almost total lack of sincerity. He answered her lightly, as he told Llewelyn he would, because he loved her so much, but his pride was deeply hurt.

The previous lecturing season had been a disappointing one, largely because Arnold Shaw had been too involved in a love-affair to drum up sufficient business: indeed, he had been acting 'so wildly and oddly' that John had thought him 'a little off his head'. So this autumn, when Powys arrived in New York, it was a great relief to find Shaw feeling so confident that he had 'suddenly decided, "overnight," as they say . . . after a happy supper at "Halloran's" . . . to be a publisher.' It was this decision, together with the outbreak of the War, which 'started [John] off at a break-neck pace writing books'. So keen was he that his first production, a long pamphlet entitled *The War and Culture*, appeared in print before Christmas.

The War and Culture was written in reply to *The War and America*, in which Professor Munsterberg of Harvard had sought to enlist American sympathy on the German side. Powys did not hesitate to praise the Germans and Austrians for their individual heroism but he condemned 'modern German culture' both for being provincial, in its rejection of the classical tradition, and for having a certain shallow cosmopolitanism. Contrasting the stultifying Teutonic ideal of the supremacy of the state with the Allied ideal of protecting the individual, he declared that it would be a major set-back for culture if Germany won the war, for:[7]

> Culture, in the deeper issues . . . is no carefully arranged
> system of rules and theories. It is the passionate and imaginative
> instinct for things that are distinguished, heroic and rare. It is
> the subtilising and deepening of the human spirit in the
> presence of the final mystery.

But John also condemned the narrow patriotism which forced men to fight or be thought cowards: the war, in his view, was of less importance than the coming struggle between Capital and Labour; and an Allied victory was chiefly to be desired because it would, in the long run, favour the cause of Socialism.

While John was writing *The War and Culture*, Llewelyn was on his way to Africa, and to an experience of life which had a far-reaching influence upon him. He had sailed from London on 4 September, and his engagement to Marion Linton did not prevent him from enjoying the company of the women passengers: though one of the most attractive was also extremely dull, and he wrote crossly in his diary: 'Some women are created for embraces alone – they should never be permitted out of bed.' Gradually they drew further and further away from England: on 19 September they sighted Ascension Island, and three days later they touched at St Helena; but all the time they were wondering whether an enemy ship would attack them if they crossed its path, and on 26 September Llewelyn wrote: 'I had my dinner by the light of the moon, as all the ship was darkened from fear of the Germans.'

Fortunately, they reached Capetown on 1 October without incident. The *Dunvegan Castle* continued round the coast of Africa, and on 16 October Llewelyn disembarked at Mombasa, and took the Uganda train:

> By the next morning we had left behind the dry scrub country
> and were crossing vast grass plains with the sun drenching
> down upon them. One saw many wild animals, hartbeests,
> giraffes, zebras and gazelles. From time to time the train
> stopped at stations and we looked out . . . at queer black men
> with decorated mangled ears, at tin-roofed houses and at
> burning hot earth.

On the 18th, Will met him at Gilgil station; and that night, 'too excited to sleep much', Llewelyn 'woke often and listened in terror to the sounds of the jungle'.

The last part of his long journey had over-tired him: he was soon spitting blood, and for six weeks he spent a good deal of the time lying on the verandah of Will's low stone house. During the day, he looked out across 'a garden full of coloured flowers' to the two hundred acres of ploughed land where peas, potatoes, flax and barley were grown, and to the enclosed fields where some fourteen thousand sheep were kept: and at night he slept on the verandah, which Will had to wire in to protect him from marauding leopards. Indeed, the farm seemed to Llewelyn to be unpleasantly insecure: to one side it was bordered by rough scrub country, and to the other by a thick and 'terrifying' forest which stretched away as far as the eye could see. 'One felt', he wrote, 'that oneself and one's handful of black servants were permitted a foothold here on sufferance only.'

In the mornings, Llewelyn began learning Swahili from 'a darling little black boy' who became a constant companion. Will had already picked up enough of the language to be able to control his ninety black workers, though on one occasion there was a misunderstanding among the Kikuyu after he had shot a bullock for them to eat, and this led to a minor riot in the course of which spears were thrown before he was able to restore order. In the afternoons, when Llewelyn's health improved, he was sometimes able to join his brother on a shooting expedition: they had only to cross a nearby stream to be in the thick of the forest, and when Will shot a bushbuck, 'what a clamour would arise! The green parrots would scream, the colobus monkeys would leap with chattering expostulations from branch to branch, and great white-winged turkey birds would circle above the tops of the trees.' Llewelyn absorbed other more powerful impressions of African life. For example, he had only been at the farm for two days when there was trouble over a dead Kikuyu boy: the tribe did not practise burial of the dead, and it would normally have been the father's duty to throw his body into the forest for the hyaenas, but the father was away, and when no-one else would touch the stinking corpse:

> Willie decided to burn the hut as he was told nobody would ever live in it again. He did so after dinner, I came out in my pyjamas and stood watching – all the natives disappeared. Presently we saw the body quite still in the middle of flames and all night the air was tainted with the smell of roasting flesh.

Llewelyn used this incident as the basis for one of the stories which he now wrote, and which he called 'Rubbish' in illustration of the uncivilised contempt with which many settlers regarded the native population. Most of the white men in the area had by now gone away to the war, and Llewelyn found that he had little in common with the six or seven who remained, and who certainly appeared to have no interest in philosophy or literature.

In writing stories like 'Rubbish', and in starting work on an autobiography, Llewelyn continued to transmute his experiences and sensations into literature. In so doing, he did not always keep precisely to the facts of what had happened: but nor did he make any effort to paint himself in a particularly favourable light. In his diaries, which became quarries for so much of his best work, he was ruthlessly honest with himself. In December 1914, for example, he recorded that he had shot at a hawk, but only wounded it. When it was brought to him, the natives begged him not to kill it, and so he left it with them; but when he returned some time later, he found them torturing the hawk by skinning it alive. Llewelyn was horrified, but also prepared to admit that 'A strange sadistic lust took possession of me, amazing in its intensity. I also could have lolled and laughed there in the sunshine and skinned it alive. With the utmost difficulty I got myself to hammer its head with the end of a hatchet.' By now Llewelyn was well aware that he was capable of sadistic impulses: this awareness had given him an important insight into one of the least pleasant aspects of human nature, and it became a corner-stone of his philosophy that: 'Evil is cruelty; there is no other evil.'

But now there was a change in his circumstances which made it impossible for Llewelyn to spend much time in writing or abstract thought. His health had improved enormously but the news from German East Africa was discouraging: the English settlers had been driven back, and some of Will's friends had been killed. Towards the end of January Will decided that he could safely leave the farm in Llewelyn's hands, and that he himself would volunteer to join the East African Mounted Rifles. 'His courage is amazing', Llewelyn wrote to John; 'he takes the whole matter with the same resolute cheerfulness as he used to display when he was dealing with the fierce animals of Witcombe.' And then, a few days later, on 6 February:

> Well, my dear Jack, Will has gone off and here I am alone. He was splendid! By God! it is not very nice to watch one's brother

ride off to the wars. I helped him saddle his mule, he might have
been a cavalier in the old days, so strange and alien an
occupation it seemed. . . . As for me I manage this farm for £8 a
month. . . . I pray I shall be guided to do what's right.

On the other side of the Atlantic, John had taken a flat with Marian
on 82 West 12th Street in New York. Rather to his surprise, he found
that his sister was not only 'powerful, capable and very high-spirited',
but that she had 'a perfect mania for "going into Society" of every and
any kind'. She soon moved them into an apartment on 12 West 12th
Street which she felt was more suitable; and partly because she was
very much attracted to him herself,[8] she encouraged John's new
friendship with Theodore Dreiser.

John had been introduced to Dreiser by Elaine, a Jewish actress of his
acquaintance who was now living with Dreiser in rooms not far from
the Powyses in Greenwich Village. All four were soon seeing a good
deal of each other, though John did not like Elaine and May was jealous
of her position with Theodore. John found Dreiser 'nobly and generously ugly', praised the 'Rabelaisian largeness of his good-nature', and
was amused by his habit of making remarks which might have come
from Theodore Powys's mouth: 'Always know for certain', he said to
John on one occasion, 'that with human beings the worst is true.' John
described the trials of strength in which the two men indulged, and
said that their friendship became so strong because: 'Dreiser and I are
both Magicians. We are two Lamas, who, while understanding black
magic and the ways of black magicians, prefer for reasons rather to be
concealed than revealed, to practice white magic.' John also greatly
admired Dreiser's single-minded dedication to his writing: his own
War and Culture ran into a second edition towards the end of October,
but before he could think seriously about starting another book, he
began a punishing schedule of lectures.

As a lecturer, John was now at the height of his powers. He himself
described how his hands, usually so 'inert, clumsy, helpless, heavy,
dead', became when lecturing totally altered so that 'my consciousness
flows through them to the tips of my fingers. They become sensitive
then, abnormally sensitive. I *feel* them as I speak; and between them
and the waves of my thought there is a direct magnetic connection.' He
related how he devoted himself so completely to the subject of his
lecture that he felt he became the author about whom he spoke. He
added:

the platform has been everything to me. It has been the bed of my erotic joys. It has been the battlefield of my fiercest struggles. . . . On the platform I have expressed by a whisper, by a silence, by a gesture, by a bow, by a leer, by a leap . . . certain inspirations concerning the secrets of life that, without any vain boasting, I do not think have been expressed very often in this world. . . . My 'lecturing' really was . . . a sort of focussing . . . of some special comic-tragic vein in the planetary consciousness.

He also found it an immensely stimulating experience: 'Instead of being vampirized by my audience, I vampirized *them*. . . . When I stopped . . . I felt light, airy, frivolous, gay and butterfly-like; whereas my audience . . . were like people who had spent a night of the extremest form of erotic debauch!' Maurice Browne, himself a frequent visitor to John's lectures, described his friend as 'Incomparably the finest public speaker whom I have heard', and wrote of him:[9]

When he spoke on a subject near his heart, he inspired his hearers. Once I heard him talk on Hardy for over two hours to an audience of over two thousand in a huge auditorium in the heart of Chicago's slums; throughout these one hundred and thirty odd minutes there was not a sound from his listeners save an occasional roar of applause or laughter; and when he had finished speaking we rose like one person to our feet, demanding more. The man was a great actor.

Powys stayed in Chicago for six or seven weeks at the beginning of 1915. There he flirted with Maurice Browne's latest 'discovery', Genefride, a lovely girl fresh from a convent, and he worked in a studio overlooking the lake, on *Visions and Revisions*, 'A book of literary devotions' in honour of Rabelais, Goethe, Keats, Thomas Hardy, Dostoievsky, Walt Whitman, and others. These essays are the closest that we can now come to the substance of John's literary lectures; they are both lively and original, and a wonderfully imaginative introduction to great literature. The characters in Hardy's Wessex novels are seen 'moving in tragic procession along the edge of the world'. The wine in Rabelais becomes 'the sap that rises in the world's recurrent spring . . . the ichor, the quintessence of the creative mystery . . . the blood of the sons of the morning . . . the dew upon the paradisic fields.' Powys writes with equal command of Keats's 'touch, ineffable, final, absolute, of the supreme Beauty', and of Dostoievsky's 'demonic power of revelation in regard to that twilight of the human brain, where lurk the phantoms of unsatisfied desire, and where unspoken lusts stretch forth pitiable hands'.[10]

Visions and Revisions was written by John at such speed that Arnold Shaw was able to publish it in February 1915; and, by then, the two men were already considering another book, to be called *Confessions by the Six Brothers Powys*. As John wrote to Llewelyn: 'I love the idea of us all going down to posterity together – even as we have lived!' In the event Llewelyn and Theodore were the only two brothers who showed any interest in his suggestion, but John was not deterred by this, and later that year he spent three weeks writing a detailed self-analysis. He was still depressed by the critical view which Frances took of him, and she seemed more than ever to belong to Louis when at the start of 1915 their first child, Oliver, was born. John's 'Confession' is highly self-critical; and it may be that in writing it he was attempting to win back Frances's respect, by laying bare his soul – or lack of it – just as he had once won over his House at Sherborne School by a similar revelation.

His life, he says, is given up to the pursuit of sensations – but this 'sensationalism' gives him little real pleasure. Instead of enjoying each moment of life to the full, as he advocates to others, he 'plunge[s] madly about, from hunting-ground to hunting-ground. I sink desperately into this obsession, into that vice. I let the most gracious moments go by utterly unremarked as I plan and plot the satisfaction of some absorbing desire, some ill-balanced greedy wish.' However, the purpose of his life is to turn his experiences into great literature: morality would corrupt him into becoming merely a good citizen; and in any case, one should enjoy what pleasures one can, for 'Our pleasures come and go, like swallows touching the surface of a stream, but the waters of unhappiness flow on without pause, swift, dark, and deadly.'

His only strong belief is in Fate, and he has a conscience only in so far as he loathes giving pain to animals and to other human beings. In other respects he maintains that he has no conscience at all, and is therefore a man without a soul; and he cannot blame those of his friends who become disillusioned with him when they find that there is no 'imaginative vision that should give these sensations coherence'. He adds that he sometimes feels that he has no real identity, except when he is lecturing: that he is 'a dead body', only really inspired with life by 'some great spirit from the past'. 'There seems to emerge from it all', he writes,

> for me at least, the image of a nervous, timid, morbid, but at the same time, reckless, figure; a figure full of quaint anxiety to be loved and admired, but utterly unable to love or admire itself; a figure troubled and perverted by strange obsessions; a figure blinded by obstinate pride, yet crippled by ridiculous humility; a figure grotesque and comic, but not devoid of elements of forlorn distinction; a figure struggling beneath the burden of its wretched contradictions, yet looking for no issue from its dilemma, save in the narcotic power of critical analysis, and the obliterating power of death.

As he lacerated himself with this complex and at times curiously moving 'Confession', John declared that he had 'No Philosophy; not even the Philosophy of having no Philosophy.'

In complete contrast Theodore had responded to John's request for a contribution to the proposed book of confessions by writing what was in effect a philosophy of solitude. Although he has never been ordained, Theodore finds that he can best describe himself as a priest. Most men, dominated by 'the getting mood' are bent only upon heaping up material possessions for themselves, and live from day to day as though they were immortal. But Theodore, as a 'priest', is set apart from these men. Instead of being dominated by a single mood, he is 'the soil in which God practises His divine moods'. Not all these moods are pleasant: some may induce in us a feeling of loving tolerance; but others may lead to hatred or despair, and the committing of fearful crimes. Theodore has vainly 'tried to hide amongst grassy hills; but the moods of God have hunted me out.' However, he has learned an important lesson: a philosopher need not act in accordance with the moods; instead, allowing them to pass freely through him, he may analyse them and in that way 'catch God in His own thought'.

Action, in any case, is usually wrong: the world is not made for work, says Theodore, but for joy, and 'the most pleasant and the most useful way that anyone can spend a day is to do nothing', for this may take a man 'a little way on the right road'. He realises that he himself has far to go: he still finds 'a curious pleasure in possessing a handful of bright gold coins'. But he wishes to live, not the simple life, but the deeper life: to get rich 'not by stealing from the poor, but by getting something more out of myself. . . . The cup I wish to drink is the cup of the earth's blood. I wish to drink deep of the silence, the deep mists, the growing corn and the movements of birds.'

He does not expect to be admired for this: such a life will bring 'from men . . . poverty and scorn, and from God, death.' But he is comforted by the love of Christ. In Theodore's interpretation, Jesus 'wished to create for a moment a state of vision with no earthly everlasting deadness about it . . . this new heaven, is life in a moment'. The effect of this vision upon Jesus himself was that 'all the signs of our immortal greed for life, in His life, are dead.' Jesus died to break the power of the moods of God; and it is by following His example that 'the old days of greed, of getting and keeping, will end.' Unfortunately, the church has perverted his teachings; hence the Great War:

> I see torn bodies, broken, buried in blood, that were a year ago
> very thoughtless young men; and I see the evil eye of our greed
> blinking and cruel. . . . Your little happy ways, your little
> business ways, your little rather long immortal ways, are a cause
> of all this, my brothers. . . . The moods of God have caused all
> this; they are causing it still. . . . And our feelings that go on for
> ever, – that we enjoy so much, – are they worth all this terror
> and horror and blood . . . ?

Theodore found the space in this powerful work to give an entertaining portrait of himself as he imagined he might appear to an outsider:

> Mr Thomas is married, and he digs in his garden. . . . [He is]
> what we call in the polite world 'a crank'. . . . He thought the
> raindrops beat with persistent spite upon him; and that the
> wind buffeted him as if it loved doing it. . . . Mr Thomas used
> . . . to brood in odd corners and try to hatch a little god out of
> his eggs – a little god that would save his type, the outcast monk
> type, from the well-deserved stones and jeers of the people.

Llewelyn was unable to make a similarly detailed response to John's request for a 'Confession'. In January 1915 *The New Age* had published extracts from the diaries recounting his journey from Montacute to Gilgil, but since Will had left to become a soldier Llewelyn was finding it increasingly difficult to do anything but farm. However, the previous autumn he had written eight or nine thousand words of autobiography, and he now sent this to John, together with extracts from his diaries which, carefully edited, and with some linking passages, give a vivid picture of Llewelyn as a private tutor, as a consumptive in

108

Switzerland, and as a newcomer to Africa. He also sent John his most recent diaries, in the hope that John would choose extracts from them to bring his life story up to date.

In the fragment of autobiography, which deals with his life up to the end of his teaching job at Bromsgrove, Llewelyn conveys his own distinctive philosophy from the very outset:

> To be suddenly born, to suddenly acquire consciousness on the surface of this unsteady and amazing planet, that is a chance indeed to justify everything.
>
> Life is a series of visions and sensations which by the wildest fortune it has been given us to experience . . .
>
> . . . it is for us merely to be irresponsible spectators of the drama of existence as it unrolls itself . . .
>
> nothing really matters

In Africa, says Llewelyn, the real nature of existence is 'brought home to one continually': there is 'Casualty, injustice,' and 'demoniac cruelty', and no evidence of a 'particular purpose in our corner of the universe'. It is 'death alone' which 'brings home . . . the fatal and exciting nature of our destiny, of the destiny of all living things who have each in their turn to go down into the pit.' What makes existence worthwhile is the capacity to appreciate and enjoy 'the continuous poetry of life'.

In his letters to Marion Linton, Llewelyn attempted to convert her to his pagan view of life: to wean her from the church, 'and make her gay and wicked'. Unfortunately, without the light and warmth of his physical presence, his arguments appeared to Marion to be genuinely diabolic, and in July 1915 she wrote breaking off their engagement, and saying that she had finally decided to enter a nunnery. Llewelyn tried to take this lightly, pursuing his own philosophy that 'nothing really matters', and he wrote to John: 'Marion I have let go without any very devastating emotion'; but he was more deeply hurt than he cared to admit, and within a month he was angrily attacking the church for what had happened, writing:

> Of course the direct origin of this is the moribund priest who from his deathbed has put out emaciated Catholic arms and ravaged her soul. If I had been there I do not think it would have turned out so. No circumstance will ever persuade me to forgive

the church after this. Let me get well and my craft and
wickedness will startle everyone I encounter.

John had returned to England for the summer, and it was at
Burpham that he heard news of the broken engagement. At first, like
Llewelyn, he blamed the priests for persuading Marion to become a
nun – and even suggested that their motive might be to lay their hands
on her inheritance. In the circumstances, he did what he could for his
brother, writing a long letter to Marion, and inviting her to come to
Burpham to discuss her decision with him. Rather to his surprise, she
agreed to a visit; and on 21 August John was able to begin a letter to
Lulu with the tantalising words: 'Well, my dear, Marion is here. I can
hear her undressing at this moment in the room next me. I told her I
would tell you she tore her skirt in our walk.' However, as he made it
clear in the rest of the letter, John was already convinced that Marion
would never marry Llewelyn. Indeed, he felt that she was not really a
suitable wife for his brother: 'she hasn't enough devilry or gall or gaiety
or amorousness', he protested. It was not, after all, the priests who
had influenced her, but 'a peculiar and wierd twist in her own cold little
head . . . I believe she is really made to be a Nun.' His attempt to make
this message less unpalatable, by adding 'I detect very unpleasing lines
in her face . . . a dry disagreeable sneering look' was not very successful. 'I know very well the aspects of her face which are unpleasing',
Llewelyn replied, but *'She was my choice.'*

Llewelyn's sense of loss was mingled with bitterness: he felt that he
had been made to look ridiculous. His very presence at Gilgil had been
part of his design for marrying the woman who had jilted him; now he
thought that he would never marry, and he fantasised that when his
father died he would buy an annuity with any money which he had,
and this would enable him to 'live a solitary and lively and selfish life in
Tangiers'. In the meantime he was trapped for the duration of the war
in a job which did not suit him, among men he did not admire. One
improvement came when the farm changed hands: the new owner, the
Hon. Galbraith Cole, took a personal interest in its day-to-day running,
and although Llewelyn found him a hard master, and was 'roundly
cursed' when he made a poor job of burning off lambs' tails, Cole had a
keen intellect, and could be a stimulating companion out of working
hours.

However, the last few months of 1915 were a depressing time for
Llewelyn. He was disappointed by the news that Arnold Shaw had
rejected both his and John's 'Confessions'; and John appeared to be

making few efforts to further his proposal that a selection of his short stories should be published. Now that Marion Linton was to become a nun, John had jokingly told Llewelyn that he would have to be 'content with the love of your Daddy Jack', and they were both hoping that John might travel to Africa the following spring. In the meantime, one of Llewelyn's few pleasures was in loving encounters with native girls. Earlier settlers had infected the tribes with syphilis, so Llewelyn restricted himself to kissing and cuddling, but the girls liked him, and he sometimes seemed to be acting out scenes from the Arabian Nights: 'she appeared and stood in the door way like a little slave girl', he wrote of one of his conquests:[11]

> I could not wait . . . I was so extraordinarily eager to see her when she lay bare on the bed. I kissed her ebony body – the smell of it was excellent, like the interior of some old & precious box found in the Sultan's attic at Zanzibar. She laughed a delicious cat-like laugh all the time. She kept begging me to have her . . .

There were other pleasant moments when Will was on leave for a few days, and the brothers walked through the forest, and bathed in hot springs; but it was not long before Will rode away, 'his white horse disappearing into the darkness', and Llewelyn was left alone with his work and his disappointments.

John Cowper Powys had been as disappointed as his brother when Arnold Shaw rejected their 'Confessions'; but he was delighted when in November 1915 Shaw published *Wood and Stone*, a long novel on which John had been working for much of the year. In the preface, John explained his reasons for writing a novel: every philosophical formula breaks down under the pressure of the actual complexity of human life, and the only way to approach the truth is 'indirectly, and by means of the imaginative mirror of art'.[12]

Wood and Stone, a large rambling novel, untidy as life itself, is concerned with a struggle between the mythology of power and pride, as symbolised by Stone, and as represented in particular by Mr Mortimer Romer, an unscrupulous quarry-owner; and the mythology of sacrifice and love, as symbolised by the Wood of Christ's Cross, and as represented in particular by Vennie Seldom, a young woman who intends to become a nun. The story is set in and around 'Nevilton' – in reality the Montacute of John's childhood, and it includes many characters drawn wholly or partly from life. Mr Taxater, for example, is clearly 'The Catholic', in Vennie Seldom there are elements of Marion Linton, and the description of Maurice Quincunx, the hermit, a man 'profoundly dependent on human sympathy' who does 'not like human *society*', who will mechanically saw faggots in his woodshed even when his mind is 'agitated to a point bordering upon despair', owes much to John's knowledge of his brother Theodore.

Still more interesting is John's description of the exceptionally warm relationship between James and Luke Anderson. James is pictured as morose and introverted; Luke, the younger by ten years, calls his elder brother 'Daddy Jim' just as Llewelyn called John 'Daddy Jack' – and is sunny, pagan, and a great womaniser. John Cowper Powys had so clearly modelled the Anderson brothers upon himself and Llewelyn that the latter, in his antimatrimonial frame of mind, was annoyed to find not only that Luke was married off at the end of the novel, but that he was married off to a girl who, though pretty, was extremely ordinary. 'Making Luke marry I am sure is a blunder', he wrote crossly to John, '– a blunder which hits me personally.'

Into the character of James were poured John's recurrent fears for his sanity, and part of the novel is a disturbing personal fantasy, which ends with James plunging to his death in a disused stone quarry, as he wrestles 'against the Forces that had . . . darkened his . . . days'. In real life John was depressed both by his unhappy marriage, and by his unsatisfactory relationship with Frances, and he was tired of finding distraction in the arms of Genefride and other women. But in his passion for writing he had found a way of securing himself against the pains of the real world, and he explained to Lulu:

> in this new mania for writing novels I have grown singularly independent of people and persons. I don't want to see anyone or make love to anyone. . . . You know I never really did have your power of enjoying life. I always was a bit mad, rushing here and there in this or that obsession. Well! writing's my obsession now and my heart hardens itself in its loneliness.

CHAPTER EIGHT

1916–1918

John in America to June 1918 • publishes Confessions of Two
Brothers, Wolf's Bane, One Hundred Best Books, Rodmoor, *&*
Suspended Judgments, *1916 • close to mental breakdown, 1916–17*
• physically ill from April 1917, and major operation September
1917 • Mandragora, *1917 • lectures in England on 'War Aims',*
summer 1918, and then back to America.
Theodore publishes The Soliloquy of a Hermit, *1916 •* Mr.
Tasker's Gods *rejected, 1916 • writes other works, none to be*
published, 1916–18 • rejected for military service 1916, 1917,
1918 • marriage under strain.
Llewelyn in Africa • rejected for military service, 1917.

Although Arnold Shaw had disliked John and Llewelyn's 'Confessions', he had been very pleased with Theodore's work, and published it in January 1916 as *The Soliloquy of a Hermit*. Theodore was delighted by a small payment of advance royalties, which enabled him to buy paper for his work, and clothes for his children;[1] and before long he received an excited letter from Llewelyn, telling him: 'This book at one stroke puts you beyond half the great ones of the earth.' By now Theodore had also completed a first novel, and after seeing part of it, Arnold Shaw had announced that he would publish *Mr. Tasker's Gods* in September. In the meantime, at John's suggestion, Theodore sent the complete manuscript to Louis and Frances Wilkinson, who agreed to edit and revise it for him.[2]

Throughout *Mr. Tasker's Gods*,[3] T. F. Powys is concerned with showing us the brutal reality behind the appearance of things. There is only a fleeting reference to the trenches, but he was writing in war-time, and the shadow of violence and cruelty is never far away. A village is less charming than it appears: the cows in the fields, looking 'the picture of content', still 'had their milk pulled from them, their calves taken away; they were fatted in stalls when old and struck down in pools of blood.' As for Mr Tasker: his gods are his pigs. Apparently a respectable farmer, and a God-fearing churchwarden, he is in reality 'a brute beast of the most foul nature': 'Too much live stock indoors', he says of his wife and family, and he devotes them most cruelly to the service of the pigs.

The church is under constant attack. It has curtained off and dimmed the light of Christ, and its services are no more than 'a sort of roll-call to enable authority to retain a proper hold upon the people'. The vicar of Shelton is a sadistic hypocrite, and two of his sons are as vicious and selfish as he, but a third son, Henry, is a simpleton with no desire to 'get on'. As the novel progresses, Henry is driven from the private Eden of his simplicity by an increasing awareness of what the world is really like. His evident goodness is a great offence to ordinary people, some of whom eventually incite an old tramp to kick him to death. There are other equally horrific scenes, and when in October Arnold Shaw was at last able to read the complete novel, he decided against publication.

This was an enormous disappointment for Theodore, but, after the initial excitement of seeing *The Soliloquy of a Hermit* in print, he had long ago relapsed into a state of misery. At times he had entertained thoughts of suicide[4] as he struggled with a second novel, *Amos Lear*; and although in June he avoided being called up for military service this was not, as he had planned, because of the letter which he had obtained from a Harley Street specialist saying that he was psychologically unfit to be a soldier,[5] but because an army doctor at Dorchester discovered that there was something wrong with his heart.[6] As a result, Theodore abandoned swimming,[7] one of his favourite forms of exercise, and an attempt in August to break out of his gloom by becoming clean-shaven and in that way radically altering his appearance, alarmed his wife, but did nothing to cheer him up.[8]

John Cowper Powys was just as depressed as his brother, and his unsuccessful efforts to find another publisher for Theodore's *Mr. Tasker's Gods* were only one disappointing element in what had turned out to be one of the worst years in his life. He had begun 1916 knowing that the sales of *Wood and Stone* were very poor; and he was then alarmed to hear from a specialist that at some time in the future a second operation would almost certainly be necessary to by-pass his duodenum. He also realised that the danger from submarines was such that it would be foolish to attempt his proposed journey to visit Llewelyn in Africa; a visit to England that summer would be almost equally dangerous, and carried the added risk that the authorities would not allow him to return to America, so he was compelled to spend a complete year away from home. The publication by Claude Bragdon of the Manas Press in February 1916 of the two 'Confessions' which Shaw had rejected, under the title *The Confessions of Two Brothers*, did not do much to lift his gloom, and an attack of influenza left him by the end of that month 'with a queer sense of unutterable depression and an indescribable loathing of my existence as a lecturer going about thro' these hideous cities.' The set-back to his hopes for success as a novelist had turned him back towards whatever consolation he could find in the arms of Genefride and other women; and he clung almost desperately to the friendship of Louis and Frances Wilkinson, despite their frequent critical attacks upon his work.

In January, to arouse interest in the Powys brothers, Arnold Shaw had published a pamphlet by Louis in which the merits of Theodore's *Soliloquy* were compared with those of John's *Wood and Stone*, very much to the detriment of *Wood and Stone*, which was dismissed 'as sounding brass and tinkling cymbal', a book without a clear philosophical centre. John accepted this criticism in his usual uncomplaining manner; and the fact that Louis and Frances also attacked his poetry 'as very bad' did not deter him from bringing out another volume of poems in March, under the title *Wolf's Bane*.[9] Indeed, in one of the poems, 'The Last Illusion', most probably intended for Frances herself, he wrote:

> On then with your deadly wit
> > And the darts of your glacial eyes!
> Mock love and slander it
> > Where under the dust it lies!
>
> For I, I can bear your scorn
> > As I follow wandering fires,
> Driven like all men born
> > By unredeemed desires;
>
> And you, you can bear my mild
> > Submission to your taunts;
> My pose of an injured child,
> > Mixed with unseemly vaunts.
>
> For we both know well, – though it stings,

> And we'll mock it to the last;
> That under these casual things
> Something holds us fast.

These were his best poems to date. They included a moving tribute to his mother, nostalgic poems about England, and two poems clearly based upon his feelings for his brother Llewelyn. In one of them he recalled miserably how he had once made Llewelyn suffer by telling him:

> 'I love not as you can love,'
> . . . .
> God help us! I see it now.
> To the darling of my soul
> Those words I said.

And in the other he recalled the occasion on which he had angrily declared 'I'll never forgive you!'; now, he records, his anger has dissolved:

> But between your hands and me –
> Hands that I hated so
> Because they were like a girl's! –
> Leagues of unfathomed sea
> Under the cold moon flow,
> Sprinkled with wrecks, not pearls.

Llewelyn himself was so delighted with *Wolf's Bane* that he wrote to John: 'your poems surpass anything that you have yet done.' But only a few weeks after the publication of *Wolf's Bane*, Knopf published *The Buffoon*,[10] in which the Wilkinsons – for apparently, although her name did not appear on the cover, Frances wrote a good deal of the book – had included an extremely unflattering portrait of John, in the character of Jack Welsh. John's outward appearance is described with considerable humour: Welsh gives:

> a sprawled effect . . . dressed in what looked like cast-off
> clothing. His coat and waistcoat, dark blue, were stained and
> spotted; some buttons were undone, others were missing. His
> trousers, equally negligent, were of a light grey, and quite filthy.

When asked to mount a pony-cart, he at once demonstrates his clumsiness:

Welsh grimaced, shooting out his lips and contorting his features. He waved his arms and spread his hands, holding them with a peculiar stiffness, as though they were made without joints. With manifest effort he placed one foot on the step, tried to balance himself, and then with a wilder wave of his arms collapsed on the road.

Later, the fun becomes less good-humoured. Ridicule is heaped on the way in which John has contrived his 'circle': Louis, as Edward Raynes, says to him: 'You heighten the character – abilities and vices – of everyone you meet, because that makes it more interesting and sensational for you. So you're aways moving among remarkable men: the plan works magnificently into the hands of your egoism.' This egoism is seen to extend into his family life: he admits that he treats his wife badly, and there is a long description of a night spent in Liverpool with Tom Jones – as Tom Fielding – and his girls. As if this were not damaging enough, his brother-in-law Henry Lyon, introduced into the plot as Reggie Tryers, declares that Jack Welsh 'has no soul, and his mission is to rob other people of theirs'. He then describes John's cerebral sadism, and suggests that he enjoys 'abominable vices' at second-hand, 'by getting other people to act them'. At this point the portrait becomes caricature: in Llewelyn's view malicious, and in Arnold Shaw's view professionally damaging to John's interests. Theodore believed that *The Buffoon* would not damage his brother, because despite everything he appeared in it as a great man, but he also advised John not to let it fall into the hands of his wife, and he admitted that he was astonished by the hatred which their old friend had exhibited.[11] John himself was extremely angry, and later told Frances that after reading *The Buffoon* for the first time, he had felt compelled to go out and sit under a tree to 'earth' his hatred.[12]

Amazingly, Louis had grown so used to John taking the most severe criticism without the slightest complaint, that he actually expected John to do all he could to promote sales. It is just possible that John might have done so, but by the time that Knopf began badgering him to publicise *The Buffoon* by mentioning it in all his lectures, John had learned how furious Llewelyn was about the book, and he 'struck – I wouldn't do it.'

By the end of April 1916, the lecture season was over, and John let their New York apartment and went out to a farm in Vermont with Marian, hoping to find peace for some serious writing. Unfortunately

Marian had fallen on the ice while skating, and injured the ligaments of her spine, so that she was for the time being an invalid, and exasperated John by suffering in the way he felt their mother would have done in the circumstances, with 'strained merriment . . . bowed head . . . [and], terrible irony'. Despite this domestic discord, John settled down to work and had soon completed a slim volume entitled *One Hundred Best Books*, which Arnold Shaw published in June. The choice was a highly personal one, ranging from Rabelais and Henry James to Vincent O'Sullivan's *The Good Girl*, from which Powys extracted a depressing passage about a married couple who would 'sit opposite one another silently, criticising with a drastic pitiless criticism'.[13] John then began work on his second novel, *Rodmoor*, but after a while he and his sister were joined in Vermont not only by Louis and Frances, but, as John wrote, by 'a dreadful person who imposed himself upon me'.

He fled with Marian to a cabin beside Lake Otsego in up-state New York; and from there he wrote an agonised letter to Llewelyn, telling him:

> I've never in my whole life since I was at school been more
> miserably wretched than I've been this summer . . . where I am
> now . . . is only just tolerable. I've been driven from pillar to
> post. I wasted a fortnight. Now I have to write as hard as I can –
> six or seven hours a day to make up for lost time. I leave this
> lake edge where our hateful hut is placed, and go in up to the
> hills to a tool shed in the middle of a field. There I keep a deck
> chair and ink and a coat and there I must now settle down to
> work and at all costs get this novel finished. I must not think of
> happiness – still less of pleasure. May is happy. Louis and
> Frances are happy and I must work.

In this 'miserably wretched' condition, John proceeded with his writing. He made Rodmoor a desolate, windswept village on the east coast, where the land is continually being encroached upon by the sea. The new novel was dedicated to the spirit of Emily Brontë, and the sea in *Rodmoor*,[14] constantly heard as it breaks upon the beach, provides the same kind of sinister, pervasive and palpable background as does the moorland in *Wuthering Heights* – which John had recently included among his *One Hundred Best Books*. In addition, two of the principal characters, Brand Renshaw and Linda Herrick, are drawn to the sea just as Heathcliff and Cathy are drawn to the moors; but there the similarity ends. The sea is more sinister than the moor: it is an image of the desolation of existence, and of the encroaching madness awaiting all those who take life too seriously. Brand uses Linda to distract himself from his unpleasant vision of reality. Other characters preserve themselves from insanity in other ways: the doctor with the help of his medicine-chest, the priest by saying his prayers, and Brand's mother, Mrs Renshaw, by Christian resignation and self-sacrifice.

Mrs Renshaw is an unmistakeable portrait of John's mother. She loves poetry and reading, and her face has the 'abnormally sensitive mouth . . . of a great tragic actress'. However, marriage has had a crushing effect upon her, and 'where religion or the opposite sex were concerned this strange being was diseased and perverted'. Disliking 'the complacent and contented ones of the earth', she feels that women are made 'to bear, to endure, to submit, to suffer'; and the death of a loved one is to be welcomed because it frees them 'from the evil of the world'.

Adrian Sorio, the central figure in *Rodmoor*, suffers from several of John's own anxieties. At the start of the novel, Sorio has just returned from 'the morbid sufferings of his years in America and his final mental collapse'. He meets the attractive but ordinary and practical Nance Herrick, and there is some chance that he may be happy with her. However, as he tells her, he has had a vision of a sylph: and when he meets Philippa Renshaw, with her 'slender equivocal figure', she is the incarnation of that vision. She may be perverse and malicious, but he is irresistibly attracted towards her. The central dilemma, similar to the one which John faced when torn between Frances Wilkinson and his wife Margaret, is clearly stated when Philippa tells Nance:

> 'It's women like you, without intelligence and without
> imagination, who are the ruin of men of genius. A lot *you* care
> for his work! A lot *you* understand of his thoughts! . . . what *you*
> are to him is a mere domestic drudge! . . . He'll never be able to
> write another line when once you've really got hold of him!'
> Nance had her answer to this. 'I'd sooner he never *did* write
> another line,' she cried, 'and remain in his sober senses, than be
> left to *your* influence, and be driven mad by you – you and your
> diseased, morbid, wicked imagination!'

There is no clear solution to this problem, and, under increasing strain, Sorio has another breakdown. All this time he has been working on a book in which he hopes to show that 'the essence of life is found in the instinct of destruction', and that beyond the 'absolute *white light*' of Nothingness aimed at by the saints, there is 'a relief, an escape, a refuge, a beyond-hope'. In death, Sorio finds his refuge; and in a highly personal fantasy John Cowper Powys watches as Sorio and Philippa Renshaw, versions of himself and Frances Wilkinson, are carried 'far from misery and madness. . . . Those two had sunk together; out of reach of humanity, out of reach of Rodmoor.'

With its morbid philosophy, its lack of a strong central plot, its unbalanced and generally unlikeable characters, Rodmoor is a thoroughly depressing novel, the work of a mind very close to breakdown. Theodore, who knew what it was to be so depressed that unpleasant visions began to flit across his mind, was highly alarmed by the letters which he received from John during that summer and autumn.[15] John admitted to terrifying hallucinations; and Theodore tried to comfort him by suggesting that it was only the insane who could understand the truth of things.[16] The reviews of *Rodmoor* were 'quite encouraging on the whole', as John told Llewelyn at the beginning of December, but he had to add that the book wasn't selling: 'It is too gloomy and melancholy for Americans.' He had completed the book during August in New York City, leaving Marian to the holiday-makers who had begun to make work difficult for him at Lake Otsego, and lodging with a doctor friend because their flat was let until the end of the summer. A fellow-lodger, curiously enough, was the Mabel Hattersley who had once tried to blackmail him. Rather surprisingly, they renewed their friendship, and by September Mabel was busily occupied reading the proofs of *Rodmoor*.

In the meantime John had begun work on a new book of essays, to be entitled *Suspended Judgments*.[17] He completed it in November, and it was published before the end of 1916: his fifth book that year. Written only two years after *Visions and Revisions*, *Suspended Judgments* is a considerably more profound and thoughtful work. John dedicated the volume to his friend, the highly individual Bernard Price O'Neill, and in it he makes a plea for the reader to follow the dictates of his own nature in everything, and so to be 'entirely personal and idiosyncratic' in his approach to literature. Criticism must be a 'genuine response, to the object criticised, of something reciprocal in us'; his own judgments, on Balzac, Conrad, Henry James and others, are 'suspended' because they are 'guarded from the impertinence of judicial decision by [their] confessed implication of radical subjectivity'. The formal, academic 'study of literature' is strongly to be condemned: anyone who meddles in it is a 'supreme fool'; and critical literature as a whole is 'a drug dulling one to all fine and fresh sensations'.

This does not deter John from stating his opinions forcefully. Wounded by Frances Wilkinson's attacks on his verse, he replied in two separate essays with salvos against modern poets in general, and the Imagists in particular: modern poets, forgetting that 'the essential nature of all great poetry' is 'the soul of music' in it, are condemned for treating 'the music of their works as quite subordinate to its intellectual or visual import'; and John congratulates 'people who feel the magic of music and the grandeur of imagination . . . without so much as ever having heard of "imagism".'

There are also a number of political asides in which he writes with passion of the failure of democracy, of 'the affiliation in revolt between the artist and the masses', and of the 'Utopian absence of any government . . . whereof all free spirits dream.'

Writing books was only a temporary escape from the real world, and as 1916 drew towards its close John remained fundamentally unhappy, writing gloomily to Llewelyn: 'Whether it is better to be alive than to be dead is a question.' His brother's absence did not become any easier to bear: in October John had declared: 'I think it is only half-living when I am not with you'; now he wrote to him: 'Aren't we like two sad Saturnians, picking out steps among the corpses, and signalling one another, over abysses and gulfs and chasms?' Llewelyn's friendship remained of enormous importance to John, partly because Llewelyn encouraged him and supported him in his work, and partly because they had an understanding that, although the world was an unhappy place, it was possible to withdraw to a 'translunar' region of Olympian detachment, in which it was clear that nothing really mattered. In *Suspended Judgments*, when John described this 'translunar empyrean'[18] he also wrote most warmly about 'the passion of friendship', saying that:

> Love, in the sexual sense, fails us in the bitterest crisis of our days because love, or the person loved, is the chief cause of the misery. Scourged and lacerated by Aphrodite it is of little avail to flee to Eros. But friendship – of the noble, rare, *absolute* kind . . . is . . . the only healing ointment . . . which can make it possible for us to endure without complete disintegration 'the pangs of despised love'.

Marian was once again able to be a help rather than a burden to her brother. While she was off work, she had occupied herself with lace-making, which she had once studied in Brussels. After a very short time, an example of her work received a gold medal in the Panama Pacific Exposition;[19] and on the strength of this she opened a lace shop in Washington Square. Each evening she returned to the flat which she shared with John at 12 West 12th Street; and he was grateful for all the attention that she could give him: for in the early months of 1917 the outlook appeared so gloomy that he became still more bitter and unbalanced. His books were not selling; Arnold Shaw had no resources to contemplate further publications; and without the incentive of knowing that his work would appear in print, John found it impossible to write. 'It is only writing that protects me from America', he wrote hysterically. 'I wish a tidal wave wd. drown the whole country and all its hundred millions.'

Then, in the early spring, there was another lecture tour to be endured. Shaw, full of hope, poured $400 or $500 into advance publicity. But on 21 April John wrote to Llewelyn from San Francisco, telling him that the tour had been a disaster: the war had killed the lectures, Arnold Shaw's money was wasted, and he himself was once again extremely ill – as ill as he had been before his first operation. Before leaving New York, he had enjoyed 'the happiest day I have had since Venice' in the company of two young actresses, but 'now the gods have swung me back to misery.'

The actresses were the ambitious but also highly feminine Margaret Mower, and the enchanting Helen Wylde. From his sick-bed in San Francisco John began 'desperately' writing poems for them, and when he struggled back East, to spend the early part of the summer living quietly with Marian in a country cottage near New York, he invited first Margaret and then Helen to stay.[20] Realising that another operation would almost certainly be necessary before long, he had decided to enjoy himself as much as possible before once again going 'under the knife', and while Marian spent most of each week working in her shop in the City, John amused himself by taking the two young women on his knee, writing more poems for them, and imagining that he was 'torn between' them.

The real passion of John Cowper Powys's life remained Frances Wilkinson. He visited her occasionally: she had recently had a second child, a girl, and was now living in New York. But he found her 'absolutely absorbed' in her children, and it seemed quite clear that he was to be denied a close physical relationship with her. There may be a clue to the way in which he came to terms with this, in a passage from *Suspended Judgments* where he wrote of:[21]

> that liberation of what we call love from the mere animalism of sexual passion. . . . It may be that a point can be reached – perhaps is already being reached in the lives of certain individuals – where sexual passion is thus surpassed and transcended by the burning of a flame more intense than any which lust can produce.

And he talked of humanity: 'plunging into the ice-cold waters of passions so keen and translunar as to have become chaste.' He had also begun to worry that sexual encounters might dissipate the energy which he needed for creative work, and no doubt this made it easier for him, during the summer of 1917, to 'escape from the napthalene river of lust', and, in what he later claimed was a symbolic act of self-sacrifice, to make a vow 'to give up all erotic pleasure – cerebral, voyeurish, or such as burlesque shows excited – until the War was over.'

Llewelyn pointed out quite rightly that the verses he had composed that year for his actresses, were lacking in vital passion, and in one particularly revealing poem, 'The Saturnian', John told how the search for ultimate truth had left him 'cold' to the 'human touch':[22]

> The wild-bird of my longing sings,
>   Always in the next hollow,
> And always, always it spreads its wings,
>   When I cross the hill to follow.
>   . . .
> Oh, I must follow it high and low,
>   Though it leave me cold to your human touch,
> Some starry sorcery made me so;
>   And from my birth have I been such.

In August, John's health improved enough for him to return to the City, and from 12 West 12th Street he sent Llewelyn entertaining accounts of friendships and love-affairs involving himself – presumably in a platonic role – Helen Wylde, Helen's friend Ralph, Margaret Mower, Maurice Browne, and Louis Wilkinson. He also went out to the suburbs to visit the Wilkinsons, and found Frances: 'more and more like our mother, and Louis more and more like our father. I suppose the fact of having two children clips her wings and ties her hands so that she has only energy enough left for ironical submission.' In fact, the Wilkinsons's marriage was in serious difficulties. Frances still loved Louis, but she thought that his behaviour in some respects was scandalous. She did not complain about his sexual infidelity, having agreed to his being allowed sexual freedom before they were married, at a time when she was so inexperienced that she had little idea what such freedom might entail. However, his general conduct did not always live up to her own high standards, and earlier in the year she had been particularly shocked by Louis's association with Aleister Crowley.[23] Louis, as John reckoned, enjoyed 'the perverted snobbishness of hobnobbing with so notorious [a] worshipper of devils', and was annoyed by his wife's attempts to restrain him. Crowley was also angry, and played on Frances's nerves until she was in such a wretched and terrified state of mind that he almost succeeded, with Louis's complicity,[24] in having her committed to an asylum. She avoided the trap, but only just; Louis was somehow brought to his senses, and the two of them had left New York for a while to escape Crowley's malign influence.[25] John made it clear that he had every sympathy with Frances over this unpleasant affair, and no doubt found himself a much more welcome visitor than he had been for some time.

In September John's latest collection of verse was published by Arnold Shaw as *Mandragora*. Theodore had suggested that John's insanity gave him power,[26] and in an important poem called 'The Ship' John described the creative process in which unpleasant impulses might be transmuted into something of artistic value. His 'cruelty' becomes a 'ship'; and then, inspired by a god who is both boy-like and girl-like, he sails away into heavenly regions, and urges others to do the same:[27]

> O Prince! make of your cruelty
>   A ship and not a sword.
> Give it masts of silver and ebony!
>   Give it bulwarks of carven ivory,
> And a figure-head of chalcedony;
>   And take on board a god!

That same month, John's health deteriorated sharply. He could eat little, was unable to work, and was soon so ill that he found it a great effort even to visit Frances. Until the very last moment he hoped to set

124

out on a lecture-tour to California, because his need for money was desperate; but commonsense prevailed, and with Arnold's promise of the $300 which he had borrowed to finance the tour, John made arrangements to go into hospital for a major operation.

Llewelyn had been convinced for some time that John's present illness was terminal, and on 21 October wrote a gloomy letter to him, saying that 'you may be dead or mad for aught I know'; but by then Theodore had already heard the excellent news that their brother had survived his operation, and was making good progress. His duodenum had been by-passed; for good measure his appendix had been removed, and although his nerves were in a poor state, and he declared that he would have been unable to 'get through' but for the daily visits of Helen Wylde, he was once again able to eat proper food.

John was also visited by a new friend, the dancer Isadora Duncan: she had admired his *Visions and Revisions* so much that she had sent him enough red roses to fill his flat, and he had written a poem for her in *Mandragora*. Later in the year, when John was out of hospital, he told Llewelyn that although he was not in love with Isadora, he was highly flattered by her respect for him, and added:

> She has been one of the most thrilling sensations – but that is a
> wretched word to express it – of my whole existence. She
> danced for me alone – with a beauty that makes the most
> beautiful young girls' dancing seem mere child's play. It was as
> though Demeter herself, the mater dolorosa of the ancient earth,
> rose and danced.

Two days after John had written this letter in Isadora's praise, he received a telegram which shows the strength of her feelings for him: 'FEELING TERRIBLY LONELY AND FORLORN I SEEK YOUR SPIRIT FOR COUR-AGE SEND ME SOMETIMES A WORD I SEND YOU INFINITE LOVE.' She was in California; and when he wrote to her as she had asked, a second telegram followed: 'YOUR SOUL DANCED WITH MINE TODAY AND GAVE ME WINGS AND NOW MY SPIRIT FLIES OVER THE MILES TO YOU REMEMBER I AM WAITING FOR YOU HERE DO NOT DISAPPOINT ME I SEND YOU INFINITE LOVE.'[28] John treasured the telegrams but Isadora's plea for him to follow her to California went unsatisfied.

Llewelyn and Theodore no longer feared for John's life, but their brother Bertie was in considerable danger: he had been conscripted, and was fighting in the trenches on the Western Front. Meanwhile Will had distinguished himself in some fierce engagements, delighting Llewelyn in August with the story of how he had personally captured six Germans, but after a spell in Nairobi hospital he had been detached from the main forces to make long treks in search of cattle to feed the troops.[29] Llewelyn himself had been examined for military service in April, but had been declared *'absolutely unfit'*, as there were still tuberculous bacilli in his expectoration. However, he also learned that there was no active disease in his lungs, that his other organs were free of infection, and that, if he remained in Africa for long enough, he might hope for a complete cure.

Although Llewelyn could not fight, he pointed out in a letter to John that it was not only the brave who lived, as it were, 'in the trenches'. Besides coping that year with a heavy burden of farm work, he had heard the disturbing news that a white settler had been speared to death three stations up the line, and he had also been troubled by a malevolent witch-doctor. Now 'pneumonic plague . . . *the black death kind'*, had broken out in East Africa. There were carts full of the dead to be seen each day in Nairobi; and Llewelyn's own house was alarmingly:

> overrun with plague-carrying rats. . . . Fleas that carry plague
> can only jump 2 inches, but since this scare I notice that not a
> few have had spring enough to reach my trousers where to my
> great content I have caught and killed no less than three of these
> naughty insects.

Theodore, like Llewelyn, was debarred from fighting. In May 1917 there was a review of men who had previously been exempted, and he once more visited the recruiting barracks at Dorchester, but no examination was made, because he was now past forty;[30] and he was told he would definitely be exempt from military service until the conscription age was raised to fifty. He returned to Beth-Car, to a household which was very much less contented than it had once been. Thanks to Littleton's generosity, Dicky was now at the Sherborne Prep.,[31] and Francis was shortly to follow him there; but Violet was tired of making personal sacrifices because of their poverty, and she had begun to nag Theodore so mercilessly for his lack of success[32] that Theodore was driven to ask bitterly about the Almighty's motives for implanting such unpleasantness![33] It was in these circumstances that Theodore transferred some of his affection from Violet to her half-sister 'Georgie', who lived in East Chaldon with their mother and Violet's 'hated step-father', Jack Jacobs.[34] Theodore had made Georgie a central character in his unpublished *Amos Lear*, completed the previous autumn; in his letters to John he sympathised with his brother's romances, and confided his own amorous feelings[35] and his fear that Georgie might run away with a soldier;[36] while by the autumn of 1917 he was reaching the last part of a new novel in which he had used Georgie's name in the title: *Georgina, a Lady*.

John had made an excellent recovery from his operation: before the end of 1917 he was once again lecturing, and his financial position, which had been a great worry to him, immediately improved. Soon he was able to repay a loan from Harry Lyon, and to tell Charles Powys that it would no longer be necessary to dole out money to Margaret at Burpham. However, lecturing was an exhausting way to earn money, and he began to wish that he could secure a permanent lectureship which would give him both a reasonable income and enough time and energy for his writing. Even 'some potty provincial university' in England would do: but he realised that this was out of the question: as he told Llewelyn, 'the university circle suspect me as a dangerous radical, and I cannot see any of them either in England or America giving me a job'.

As he grew physically stronger, he became determined to return to England. Margaret tried to dissuade him: if he was unable to return to America for some reason connected with the war, there would be no money available to complete their son's education at Sherborne. John decided to take the risk: indeed, he was beginning to hope that he *could* play some part in the war. On hearing in April that his brother Bertie was a prisoner-of-war in German hands, he wrote: 'things are getting a bit too crucial with these spiked helmets so near the Wessex lanes. I cannot, I really cannot, eat ice-creams and drink grape-juice in California, while these barbarians overrun the earth.'

In May 1918 the conscription age was raised to fifty. Theodore was once again exempted because of his weak heart, but John, who was now eligible to be called up, believed that if he himself resisted the 'beckoning and calling' which he now felt, he would be 'betraying something more important to me even than Margaret's happiness and my son's education'. He was very nervous about becoming a soldier, or of doing ambulance work if he was not required for active service, but he wrote to Llewelyn:

in my heart of hearts I have an old desire to have my little
adventure and to risk something, and not to be so confoundedly
protected to the end of my days! Am I, or am I not, really afraid
of anything that can happen to me? I tell you not for nothing am
I the son of Mary Cowper. Do I want to Live Forever?

So John visited the British Recruiting Office in New York. Much to
his surprise, he was rejected not because of his poor stomach, but
because the examining doctor discovered an old tubercular scar on his
lungs, a scar from some attack so mild that he had known nothing
about it. After a few more weeks of lecturing, John decided to travel to
England in any case, and in June he sailed across 'in a regular fleet of
eleven great liners'. His plan was 'to visit various war-preparations so
as to be able to lecture on the war in America'; but he also made a
second attempt to become a soldier. This came to nothing when
another doctor found the scar on his lungs, and sent him to a specialist
for further examination. Still determined to make some contribution,
John secured a job touring up and down the country lecturing on 'War
Aims', and while engaged in this patriotic task he managed to fit in a
number of visits to friends and family.

Thomas Hardy received him in the most friendly manner at Dorchester, and John stayed with Bernie O'Neill in London, and with Tom
Jones in Liverpool. John also visited his father, who had recently
resigned as vicar of Montacute and gone to live with Gertrude in
Weymouth; and he travelled to Ringstead Bay to meet Theodore: 'We
walked slowly towards one another', John recorded; 'We were like two
ghosts meeting after centuries.'

Theodore had now completed *Georgina, a Lady*, and another book
called *Hindcliff Tales*, but although interest from a publisher had
recently given him some encouragement, he had still published nothing since his *Soliloquy*. John found him looking: 'tortured . . . terrible
. . . rugged . . . earthy . . . tragic', and commented to Llewelyn: 'What
a life he leads, alone with his little wife and the gentle Francis, and
always thinking about how to deal with the question of "Georgie".' In
another letter, on his return that autumn to America, John told
Llewelyn: 'I think we shall meet again – I think so. But meanwhile
neither of our lots is as bad as Bertie's in a German prison, or of
Theodore's in the prison of his own depression, or of L.C.P. in the
prison of (and that is the worst!) a bourgeois marriage.'

Llewelyn had certainly come to enjoy some hours of his African sojourn, particularly on Sundays, when he would spend the mornings reading, and the afternoons walking 'up to the forest, or by the side of the stream that wound its way down to Elmenteita lake.' But the summer and autumn months of 1918 were a terrible time for him: there was drought, famine, and a forest fire; dysentery broke out among the natives, and disease among the cattle. Llewelyn spent his days amid alien scenes of terrible desolation, 'going from sick man to sick beast. . . . Great funeral pyres could be seen in all directions and each of these smouldering bonfires of animal flesh was surrounded by hosts of marabou storks.' Then in November, quite suddenly and unexpectedly it seemed to him, the Great War was over. Sometimes, as Llewelyn wrote to Gertrude, he felt 'exhausted mentally beyond expression', but he had survived the worst that Africa had offered him, and at last he could see an end to his years of exile.

CHAPTER NINE

1919–1921

John lectures in America, 1919–21, but in England, May to August
1920 • attempt to live with Frances Wilkinson in San Francisco,
summer 1919 • writes After My Fashion, *1919–20(?) • publishes*
The Complex Vision, *1920 • with Llewelyn to California, summer*
1921.
Llewelyn returns from Africa to England, summer 1919 • writes near
Weymouth, 1919–20 • work accepted, spring 1920 • to America
with John, August 1920 • late in 1920, work accepted by New York
Evening Post • *and meets Edna St Vincent Millay, 1920 • to*
California, summer 1921 • 'cured' of TB for two years.
Theodore remains in East Chaldon • writes Black Bryony,
1919–20 • Plays, *1920 •* Hester Dominy, *1920–1 • in touch with*
Sylvia Townsend Warner, 1921.

Llewelyn Powys was obliged to remain at Gilgil for some months after
the end of the war: it was not until January 1919 that Will secured his
discharge from the army, and it was then arranged that Llewelyn's
place as farm manager should be taken by his brother with effect from 1
March. In the meantime, Llewelyn was content to let Will take the
decisions, and the two brothers spent some weeks driving the sheep
and cattle to healthier pastures nearly a hundred miles to the north. At
last, towards the end of May, Llewelyn received his passage papers
home; and the very next day he left for Mombasa. He need not have
hurried: the sailing of the SS *Rufus Castle* was delayed for sixteen days,
and all the hotels were full. However, he spent an interesting week
living in an attic room in the native quarter, with a mosque opposite,
brothels all around, and a lively market not far away; and then he
moved to a hotel outside the main town, with palm-thatched huts for
bedrooms. While he was there, his cabin box was rifled, and many of

his African mementoes stolen, but he had kept his money and his passport under his pillow, and two days later, on 19 June, he set sail for England.[1]

Llewelyn had spent nearly five years in Africa, and sometimes felt that he had been brutalised by the experience. He had not hesitated to ride down a native whom he suspected of sheep-stealing, cut at him with a whip, and then kick him;[2] and earlier in the year he had complained to Theodore that: 'The sun, naked as it was born, sucks out one's life blood, and nourishes savagery long since made dormant by the pious lives of our ancestors. Teeth here grow sharp and claws grow long.' He had certainly become tougher both physically and spiritually: not only was his health improved, but he had endured separation from family and friends, and had been compelled to self-reliance in the heart of a natural world which he had come to see as beautiful, savage, and indifferent, like some cruel mistress. His mind was stored with vivid impressions, the raw material for literature; and his wallet contained a credit note for over £300, on which he hoped to be able to live until he could support himself by writing. He arrived at Southampton on 2 August in an optimistic mood, and travelled directly to his father's house in Weymouth.

John Cowper Powys had returned to America in the autumn of 1918, planning to write a third novel: it was to be 'more quiet and less mad' than *Rodmoor*, to 'have Sussex for its background and I think Nature must obtrude itself less.' But he had written no more than a hundred pages of his new book – probably a first draft of *After My Fashion* – when he became convinced that his work was valueless, and in mid-November he sent a despairing letter to Theodore lamenting his failure.

Theodore replied that John should continue cheerfully: his own situation was very much worse. Mr Melrose, the publisher who had been taking an interest in his work, had rejected *Georgina, a Lady* and remained undecided about *Mr. Tasker's Gods*; and Theodore would have to continue to rely upon Littleton's generosity to keep Dicky and Francis at the Sherborne Prep.[3] At Christmas he was cheered up a little by a present of 10s. from Bertie; but his generally pessimistic view of human nature was reinforced when Bertie and Dorothy visited East Chaldon, and he learned from his brother that Dorothy was becoming shrewish, and that she constantly and quite unfairly complained that Bertie was chasing after young women.

Theodore's own family life remained soured by poverty: at the beginning of 1919, when Francis was extremely ill, Theodore and Violet found to their horror that their worries about him dying were being overtaken by what seemed a still greater anxiety: how on earth would they manage the funeral expenses? Once it had only been Violet who was embittered, but now Theodore became jealous of those more fortunate than himself, and wrote angrily about the amount of money which an ordinary infantryman could happily dissipate in a single drinking session.[4] He continued to write every day, though it was not long before *Mr. Tasker's Gods* was again rejected. Theodore deduced from this rejection that the Almighty must be an idiot: for it was He who had made Theodore, and caused him to write his idiotic books![5]

Although John wrote frequently to Theodore, he could not afford to return to England for the summer of 1919. Lectures were hard to come by, and it would have been difficult enough to earn a living for himself, without the added responsibility of paying for his wife to live in style, and his son to have a private education. Instead he went westward to California, where he found lecturing work in San Francisco, and spent his spare time on a philosophical treatise; but he was soon very much distracted from this by a surprising development in his correspondence with Frances Wilkinson.

Ever since her conflict with Aleister Crowley, Frances had been ill with heart trouble, and on at least one occasion she actually collapsed, her lips turning blue in a painful and terrifying bout of angina; but Louis appeared to be no support. Their son Oliver recalls that their marriage had by then degenerated 'into a series of vicious domestic arguments'.[6] Knowing that John had been in love with her for seven years, Frances finally decided to place herself entirely in his hands, as much for the children's sake as for her own. This was astonishing news for John, who had grown accustomed to their existing relationship, and 'after the reluctances and agitations of a man too suddenly presented with his heart's desire', he sent Frances:

> letter after letter of ambiguous encouragement and passionate doubts. He wrote that he would welcome Frances to California with a whole heart, if only he could think of a way to support her, her son, her daughter, her mother, and – Good God, he had forgotten – her mother's dog; of course he would have to continue to support his own wife, whom he hardly ever saw but could not divorce, and his son; and other dependants. Finally he [wrote] . . . that, together they would overcome all difficulties.

These difficulties certainly included Frances's state of health: she was now so unwell that tuberculosis was suspected,[7] quite apart from her recurrent heart trouble, and it was clear that she needed hospital treatment. Following John's detailed instructions she travelled out to California accompanied only by her four-year-old son Oliver, who was John's godson. The rest of her family remained with Louis in Philadelphia, there to wait upon events.

John met the travellers at the railway station near the Golden Gate, and took them to the small house which he had rented in Sausalito. But although he now had Frances under his own roof, he was far from happy. His usual worries about lack of money and the problems of supporting his family were reinforced by a sense of sexual inadequacy as he contemplated living with a woman who might require more than 'translunar' passion; and it was also clear that Frances was not prepared to moderate the force of her intellectual convictions. Talking about literary matters over their evening meal, John and Frances accidentally alarmed Oliver as:

> their voices became more and more emphatic; their tones grew
> higher, creating an alarming tension, bringing a dangerous,
> intellectually murderous stridency into the room. Every
> evening, they reached that point of argument – argument that
> was the more frightening for seeming to me to be meaningless,
> almost mechanical: my mother advocated A; Jack countered
> with B; which my mother displaced by an emphatic A; which
> Jack countered with an indignant B; which was cut to pieces by a
> sharp A; and so on, progressively.

At length, one evening, Oliver 'rapped out, "Stop talking!"', and there were no more of these arguments in his presence. Some days later, Frances went into hospital; from where she returned, after treatment, with the pronouncement of the doctors 'that she would, with care, recover.'

In addition to looking after Frances and Oliver, and giving an occasional lecture, John was now hard at work on the philosophical treatise which he eventually called *The Complex Vision*. This was a remarkable undertaking for a man, who, only two years before this, had written that he had 'No Philosophy; not even the Philosophy of having no Philosophy';[8] and it must have owed a good deal to the influence of Frances, who had always strongly expressed her wishes that John should commit himself to a point of view.[9]

As his starting-point, John declared that all previous interpretations of the universe were utterly remote from human experience; and he added:[10]

> What we have come to demand is that the centre of gravity in our interpretation of life should be restored to its natural point of vantage, namely, to the actual living consciousness of an actual living human being.

His philosophy is therefore to have as 'its central assumption and implication . . . the concrete basis of personality which we call "the soul".'

He goes on to say that every living thing has a soul, or 'complex vision', seen in imaginative terms as 'a pyramidal arrow of fire, moving from darkness to darkness . . . from mystery to mystery . . . keep[ing] its apex-point directed to the mystery in front of it.' When the elements of the complex vision are perfectly co-ordinated, something which may happen only once or twice in a life-time, the 'apex-thought' of our soul allows us insight into the mysteries of the universe, and we receive 'whatever measure of permanent illumination adds dignity and courage to our days.'

Powys then describes his own illumination: an illumination of enormous interest because it contains many of the ideas and beliefs which give such a highly individual colour and such a remarkable philosophical depth to the best of his subsequent novels. He finds that there is not one universe, but many, each one half-discovered and half-created 'by the encounter of various individual souls with that one "objective mystery" which confronts them all'. By an act of faith the complex vision assumes that all the various universes are aspects of one universe; an act of faith which seems justified when we realise that in dealing with others we all appeal to the same ultimate standards which are the product of some vision greater than our own. Since there can be no vision without personality, it makes sense to talk about 'the invisible companions', conscious and living souls which are free from the laws of the physical world, and can therefore 'remain in perpetual contact with every living soul born into the world'. Beside these 'immortal children of Nature' is the figure of Christ, a personification of all the love in the universe, and not to be confused with the historical figure of Jesus.

Finally, 'The secret of the Universe . . . turns out to be personality'; the universe consists of souls, and there is no such thing as 'dead matter'. Not only animals and vegetables, but rocks, mountains and stars have souls, and the apparent deadness of matter is 'one of the ghastly illusions with which the sinister side of the eternal duality undermines the magic of life.' For at the heart of all things, there is a duality: not between flesh and spirit, or between love and hate, but between love and malice, defined as *'that which resists creation'*; and it is the struggle between love and malice which provides the fundamental motivating force of the universe.

This strange and powerful vision, with a strong mythological element in the figures of 'the immortals', was weakened in the concluding sections of the book by an attempt to make everything subservient to John's dream of a communistic state. Such a state, he hoped, would provide a framework within which the 'evil . . . possessive instinct', spawned by malice, would be overcome; and instead creative energy would 'expand and dilate'.

Frances, who had once caricatured John's eccentricities in *The Buffoon*, was highly impressed by this vision of the future. John's superstitious nature was still clearly revealed by the golden seals and amulets and other talismen that hung from his watch-chain;[11] but now he was flattered and considerably influenced by Frances's new view of him as a creative thinker whose writings might foretell the future development of mankind.[12] Besides advocating the overthrow of society – he considered calling his new book *The Philosophy of the Revolution* – he had also written about the future of women who, when economically independent, might be 'able to present, in philosophy and art, the peculiar and especial reaction to the universe which women possess as women'.

Frances had given John important encouragement, and he had given her a home at a critical stage of her life; but their time together was short. A normal sex-life of the kind which Frances had once enjoyed with Louis might have drawn them closer to each other, but there was no chance of that; and John, realising that Frances's first loyalty was to her children, could not help regarding Oliver as a rival for her love. Things became still more difficult when the household at Sausalito was increased by the arrival of the children's Italian nurse, together with Frances's two-year-old daughter Betty, her mother, and her mother's Newfoundland dog which, as Oliver recalled, 'bit everyone at first sight'![13]

They all lived together for a while, but they were very short of money. Even if a publisher could be found for it, a philosophical work such as *The Complex Vision* was unlikely to generate much income. In the meantime John tried working for the newspapers, but could only earn $10 a week for an article on a book page, and by mid-November he was 'desperately' writing short stories. Frances had high hopes for these, but none of the twenty which he wrote were ever published.

At last, realising that her children would never have a secure future if she stayed with John, Frances decided to return to her husband. Louis Wilkinson must have felt some jealousy and resentment at losing his wife and children to John, but he would have considered such feelings to be unpardonably old-fashioned,[14] and had let them go without complaint. Now, in the same 'modern' spirit, he was prepared to have them back again without any recrimination: he was living in England, and told Frances that she and the rest of her menage could follow him there if they wished.

At the beginning of November, having left Frances in Philadelphia[15] preparing for the transatlantic journey, John set off alone for New York. Marian had given up their flat and moved into an apartment which was only large enough for one, so John was to share rooms with an acquaintance: 'I don't know', he wrote to Llewelyn, 'that in my present rather morose mood I shall be able to be genial enough.' He was very upset by his failure to provide for Frances, and very anxious about her future: 'Her lung is reported just healed by the X-rays', he told Llewelyn,

> but she still ha[s] a nasty cough and the Thyroid trouble in her neck affects her heart. I do pray and hope Louis will secure for her a nice little house near London with a garden where she can really feel at 'home' . . . for me it's either Frances or nothing as far as female butterflies are concerned . . . if only she gets safe to England and Louis looks after her nicely

Towards the end of November Frances and her family sailed from New York, and John was at the quayside to wave goodbye. Long after her ship had vanished over the horizon, he was haunted by her presence: 'There is certainly a ghost', he wrote to her. 'It scolds. It laughs disdainfully. It covers its head. It stands at the window. I do not vex it. I give it bits of things to amuse it while I am away.'[16] More practically, John had written to Llewelyn asking him to help Frances if he had the chance, and making it clear that: 'Anything you may be able to achieve in that direction is for me.'

Llewelyn had been in excellent spirits ever since his return from

Africa. For a time it was enough to be back in England. Bertie visited him at Weymouth, where he lived with Gertrude and their father, and within a few weeks he had also seen Theodore, Ralph Shirley, Louis Wilkinson, and Bernie O'Neill. His chief desire was to achieve 'some literary success', and soon he had settled down to work: 'I write all the morning', he told John, 'after lunch read Gaston de la Tour in the little garden, after that at 3 o'clock go a walk with Father, over Lodmoor and the downs behind Preston.' At night he slept out on the verandah; and by mid-October[17] he had bought a revolving shelter, which he set up in the deserted walled garden of a ruined cottage above the coastguard station overlooking Weymouth: 'Sometimes', he wrote,

> I wake looking towards the White Nore and those familiar cliffs with the sun coming out of the sea. Sometimes towards Portland and a glimpse of glimmering water beyond Chickerel where an opening in the land allows a view of the West Bay. Sometimes towards Hardy's monument with the bare outlines of the Dorset downs, and those long low white lines of Dorset water. Sometimes towards the White Horse and Sutton Poyntz. . . . Gertrude comes sometimes to paint and Father to see me now and again. . . . My days are deliciously long and I let them pass into oblivion with reluctance.

He was too busy writing to worry about being sociable, or about his health: even 'a bad bout of discolouration' early in November did not alarm him unduly, as his temperature remained normal. He had kept a diary during his journey home, and sent this to J. C. Squire at the *New Statesman* for his opinion; while by Christmas 1919 he had also written a number of short stories and essays. These included 'How it Happens', the nightmarish account of a young Englishman who commits suicide after travelling to Africa and contracting syphilis from a native girl; and 'Black Gods', a remarkable essay in which he reflects upon 'the secret of Africa' – that all the religions of Asia and Europe are illusions, for:[18]

> Africa, like one of her own black-maned lions, laps up the life-blood of all the delicate illusions that have for so long danced before the eyes of men and made them happy. Truth alone is left alive. What was suspected in Europe is made plain here: *at the bottom of the well of life there is no hope.* Under Scorpio, under the Southern Cross, and in the clear light of this passionless, tropical sunshine, the hollow emptiness of the

world's soul is made certain: *the surface is everything, below there is nothing.*

Atheism did not make Llewelyn at all despondent: 'the surface' of life was all that he required, and he was in supremely cheerful and self-confident mood. He regularly walked the ten miles to East Chaldon, where he felt able to comment authoritatively on Theodore's unpublished novels, considering himself much more helpful than their brother John: 'perfectly useless your shouting "genius, genius"', he told him, 'and being too lazy or foolish to give [Theodore] honest criticism. Of course he becomes melancholy – what a fool you are!'

Theodore thrived on a little practical encouragement, and told Louis Wilkinson: 'Lulu has certainly cheered me with his merry jesting, and as a critic I regard him as very wise.' Louis too offered help, saying in mid-November that he would try to make alterations to *Georgina, a Lady* which would fit it for publication; and he interviewed Mr Melrose, who was then wondering whether to publish one of Theodore's other novels, *Amos Lear*. But Mr Melrose could not make up his mind; and in December he announced that Theodore's genius might not be recognised until after his death. This brought back Theodore's gloom: in a letter to John he fantasised about being dead, imagining that someone called out his name and received no answer; and he informed his brother that he would write no more novels once he had completed *Black Bryony*.[19]

The black bryony of the title is a poisonous plant, symbolic of the evil in human nature, and although he tells this story of village life with his usual dry wit, Theodore makes clear, as he describes all kinds of unpleasant behaviour, the futility of attempts by the rector or the schoolteacher to make the villagers into better people. Mary Crowle, the central character, is a Salvation Army preacher who can be inspired by religious ecstasy, but who is also capable of theft and seduction. One of the most complex and vital of Theodore's creations, she is possessed by what Theodore had once described as 'the moods of God'; and the tragedy of her existence becomes the tragedy of any mortal driven by conflicting passions which can neither be understood nor controlled.

There was a happy interlude from work on *Black Bryony* on New Year's Eve. Theodore invited Llewelyn to spend the evening with him, and, as Llewelyn wrote: 'we saw the old night out, we read Charles Lamb's essay, and sang songs and ate nuts and drank white port and made merry.' Afterwards, Theodore returned to his writing, encouraged by the news that Frances Wilkinson had taken over from Louis the job of correcting *Georgina, a Lady*, and that she had promised to call on Curtis Brown to inquire about the contract for *Amos Lear* which he was expecting from Mr Melrose. Llewelyn, too, returned to his writing, but soon abandoned it in a state of depression. He had depended on his savings to support himself while he became established as a writer, but, on Louis Wilkinson's advice, he had invested heavily in German marks. The collapse of the mark meant that his savings were virtually wiped out. 'You are a b . . . , and where is my money?' he wrote to Louis in January 1920. 'The only good thing about you is your wife and I haven't money to come up to London to see her.' None of his work had yet been accepted for publication, and soon he would 'feel completely ruined'.

Desperately seeking inspiration, he went to visit Thomas Hardy at his home in Dorchester only to find, in his own words: 'a very old, dapper country gentleman moving about quickly, jerkily like a sparrow or Tom Tit, unaware that I had ever seen him before or was in any way connected with literature.'[20] Sensing the futility of his own existence, Llewelyn wrote to John:

> You talk of my producing a formidable novel about Africa, but I tell you I find this impossible. It was a natural instinct that led me to waste my time with these futile little sketches and short stories. I did it because I could do nothing else . . . this idea that I could write is an illusion.

His depression had been deepened by feelings of sexual frustration. He described how:

> I used to lie on my bed in torment, and during these midnight vigils it would seem to me that amorous dalliance was the one thing that mattered in life, that the complete and utter gratification of one's most lively whim was, in truth, the only real and abiding good to be found on earth.

Now well into his thirty-sixth year, Llewelyn started worrying about grey hairs and getting old. The restrictions of middle-class respectability, which he blamed for his unhappiness, were firmly associated in his mind with his father's household, and he began to hate 'the click of the fiendish little front gate . . . the movement of people going to hold communion, and Father always there on these bright afternoons ready

and waiting to sally out for a walk like some large harmless impor-
tunate dog.' He enjoyed Gertrude's company, finding her 'inexpressibly sweet . . . indulgent and sympathetic'; but their father was sinking
slowly into mental senility, and it seemed dreadful to Llewelyn that her
life should be 'spoilt' by the burden of caring for him.

At the beginning of February Llewelyn's gloom was deepened when
J. C. Squire, literary editor of the *New Statesman* returned 'A Sheepman's Diary', rejecting it and making no comment upon 'Black Gods'
or the other stories Llewelyn had sent him. Three weeks later,
Llewelyn heard that the *New Age* was to publish his 'As It Happens',
but since no payment was involved, this did not impress him as much
as it might have done. He went to see Theodore less often, perhaps
depressed by the contrast between Theodore's persistence and his
own apparent lack of staying-power; and he wrote more depressed
letters to John, telling him on one occasion: 'Nobody can help me,
nobody can give me confidence except you.'

John too had been finding it difficult to earn a living, and began 1920
in a thoroughly dejected frame of mind. He had completed a drama-
tised version of Dostoievsky's *The Idiot*, but was not hopeful that
anyone would accept it; and his major work for the previous year, *The
Complex Vision*, had been rejected by Liveright. Furthermore, he had
'lamentably few' lectures to look forward to; he had to ask Littleton for
money 'to keep Margaret going for a bit', and he told Theodore it was
unlikely he could return to England that year.

But then, towards the end of January, things began to improve: a
lecture tour in the Middle West, which had seemed unpromising, was
hugely successful; and Arnold's office, which had been in one of its
periodic states of disarray, was transformed into a place of hard work
and careful planning by a new clerk, who at the beginning of February
was already arranging John's lectures for the following season.

Letters still took up to a month to cross the Atlantic, and it was not
until 26 February that John received a 'letter of dilapidated mental
collapse' written by Llewelyn on 24 January. He at once replied with a
long letter full of helpful advice, but by the time his letter reached
England, Llewelyn's affairs had also taken a dramatic turn for the
better.

In March, while Gertrude enjoyed a brief holiday in Paris,[21] Llewelyn
had broken the monotony of his own existence by a long round of
visits. He began by crossing over to Jersey, where he had the alarming
experience of visiting an old friend whose nerves had been shattered

by the war: he was now an habitual drunkard, and lived alone in a vast, decaying windswept mansion at the sea's edge. Returning to England, Llewelyn visited several members of his family, and was offered a teaching job by his brother Littleton; he was seriously tempted by the prospect of financial security, but he had now heard some very exciting news about his writing: in New York the editor of *The Dial* had accepted 'A Sheepman's Diary', and sent him a cheque for £13; while in London J. C. Squire, who had earlier rejected 'A Sheepman's Diary', accepted 'Black Gods'. Llewelyn began to feel, once again, that he had some future as a writer, and he wrote to John on 7 April: 'I am passing through a critical time of my life, evidently I am once more mounting to the crest of this bloody wave of fate.' John soon had some more excellent news for his brother: the staff of *The Dial* were 'thrilled' by Llewelyn's work, and he had become 'a cult to them'.

Towards the end of April,[22] John Cowper Powys sailed for England. Llewelyn was waiting for him on the quayside: his increasing optimism had led him to shave off his beard, and John wrote to their sister Marian:

> He looks so much older that he was waving to me for quite a long time and I looked straight at him and did not recognise him. . . . We talked of his coming [to America] and he has made up his mind to housekeep and cook for us, taking it as seriously as his writing, until he can help us to keep a servant.

Llewelyn had definitely decided that his future lay in New York, and it was arranged that he should cross the Atlantic with John later in the year. For the time being, however, he returned to Weymouth to write the African novel which John had been urging him to attempt for so long; while John himself travelled on to Burpham, where he spent much of the next three months with Margaret, and resumed work on his own novel, *After My Fashion*.[23]

John's previous novels had both contained strongly autobiographical elements, and *After My Fashion*, dealing at some length with the problems of loyalty and deception in a modern marriage, relates still more closely to John's private life: which may well be the reason why he made few, if any efforts to publish it during his lifetime. The central character, Richard Storm, a man very much like himself, wishes to be a great poet but can only make a living from criticism. He is torn between his love for two women: Nelly, a charming product of the Sussex countryside, and Elise Angel, whom we meet for the first time in New

York. Nelly is not simply a portrait of John's wife Margaret, but they have much in common, and John could well be attacking his wife when he describes Nelly's 'fierce claim . . . for absolute loyalty' as 'a wild demand of insane possessiveness that no human soul had a right to make upon another.' Elise Angel is in most respects a clear portrait of the great dancer Isadora Duncan, but in her relationship with Richard Storm there are constant echoes of the relationship between Frances and John: Elise is Richard's great obsession; she is not afraid to tell him that his poetry is imitative and second-rate, and when they try living together for a while they both realise that, despite the strong attraction which binds them together, they are temperamentally incompatible.

Overall, John's new novel was one of self-doubt, and was rarely transformed by the mysterious personal vision of the universe which he had elaborated in *The Complex Vision*, but at least his characters live. Llewelyn had only written the first part of *Aliens in Africa* when he lost all impetus, and turned to his eldest brother for help: 'How the Hell you make your characters talk intelligently', he complained to John, 'I can't conceive – mine become quite dumb when they are together.' The ease with which John wrote back, making a great number of helpful suggestions, only underlined the limitations of Llewelyn's talent. When describing what he had seen himself, he was an excellent writer, but he did not have the ability to imagine original characters and bring them to life on the printed page. It may have been something of a relief when Littleton asked him to fill a temporary vacancy on his teaching staff: in any case, by the time John's letter arrived, Llewelyn was working at the Sherborne Prep, and *Aliens in Africa* had been permanently laid to one side.

Soon after the end of the summer term, Llewelyn began preparing for the voyage to America, but first he joined John and Bertie for what was to be a depressing visit to East Chaldon. They found that Theodore was enduring yet another year of poverty and disappointment: a contract for *Amos Lear* had never been signed, and for months there had been no news from Frances about her corrections to *Georgina, a Lady*. Theodore was worried that this was his fault for not having invited her to stay:[24] the real truth was that Frances had worries of her own. She and Louis were desperately short of money, and their new plan was for Louis to remain alone in London, while Frances and the children lived as cheaply as possible in a French cottage.[25]

Llewelyn himself was so short of money that Gertrude had to lend him the fare for his passage to New York; and then on 14 August, the day after Llewelyn's thirty-sixth birthday, he and John sailed from Southampton.

John and Llewelyn shared with Marian an apartment which she had found at 439 West 21st Street. It was only a small apartment, but for the sake of his health Llewelyn usually slept on the roof: after a day in the crowded city, he found it a 'liberating' experience to 'emerge through a little trap-door to find myself alone with fresh night-wandering clouds, alone with the cozening moon and a myriad isolated stars . . .' Unfortunately, the arrangement of living together was not a great success. None of the men with whom Marian flirted meant half so much to her as her eldest brother: she had built up a very close relationship with him since moving to New York,[26] and she was profoundly jealous when Llewelyn's arrival meant that John was no longer able to give her his undivided attention. Soon there were all sorts of minor conflicts between Marian and Llewelyn: she complained that he did not take proper care of his health; she declared that it was a great shame that he 'could not live indefinitely on tea and eggs', as she and John had always done; and the conflicts continued even after John's departure on a lecture-tour.

For some weeks, Llewelyn Powys hunted vainly for a job. He wanted literary work, but his experience lay chiefly in managing sheep and cattle, and when he went despairingly to an employment agency they could find nothing for him: stock-ranchers were not in great demand in New York City! One political journalist to whom he betrayed his total ignorance of contemporary politics strongly advised Llewelyn to abandon his literary hopes and go West; and at one point Llewelyn even considered becoming an undertaker's assistant. His luck changed for the better when he secured a letter of introduction to Mr Dounce of the *New York Evening Post*: Dounce asked him for some essays on African life, and paid him $3.75 for his first production, 'A Porcupine in a Kitchen'.

This was the beginning of Llewelyn's literary success: his articles, with their clear, direct descriptions of his African experiences were immensely popular, and became a regular feature of the *Evening Post*. Soon he was earning his living, and paying his share of household expenses; while by the end of November he felt so well established that he returned £32 of the money which he had borrowed from Gertrude.

Although Llewelyn sometimes felt uneasy in sophisticated New York Society, he began to meet other people in the literary world, and formed a long-lasting friendship with the writer Van Wyck Brooks when they discovered that they shared a low opinion of Amy Lowell's poetry! Edna St Vincent Millay also became a life-long friend. Llewelyn had been greatly impressed by her poems, which seemed to him 'to express a spirit at once daring and sensitive, and to possess a beauty which, however slight, was separate and authentic as only true poetry can be.' Nor was he disappointed when, armed with an introduction, he called on this highly attractive young woman at her lodgings in Twelfth Street. He detected a 'shadow of vanity', but wrote that 'below her laces and ribbons there will always remain a barefoot poet, doomed yet redeemed, under the shadow of Eternity.' Some weeks later, after a Christmas Eve party at which Llewelyn had 'felt sullen and out of it', he was pleased to find that Edna accepted his offer to escort her home. They were very much attracted to each other, but the enduring basis of their friendship was not so much physical attraction as a shared poetic vision: it is beauty 'under the shadow of Eternity' which informs the best of Edna St Vincent Millay's poetry, just as it does the best of Llewelyn Powys's prose.

John was still away from New York on his lecture-tour. In September, not long after he had left, Dodd Mead and Company published *The Complex Vision*, which was given a favourable review by Edgar Lee Masters. John was based in Chicago for much of the autumn, and was able to see a good deal of this erudite lawyer, with his granite chin and genial, bespectacled eyes. He had first met him five years previously, and they were now close friends: Masters thoroughly appreciated John's lectures, while John found in Masters 'an original poet of first-rate philosophic weight and power'. Besides lecturing and visiting his friends, John found time to read: he told Llewelyn how 'I go constantly to my favourite book-shop and read Psycho-Analysis from the expensive shelf'; and after discovering that the celebrated 'Oedipus Complex' was 'the clue to everything', he dreamed about their mother: 'so vividly, so very vividly . . . I love her. I am in love with her. I am Oedipus – and she is dead'!

John also wrote to Theodore each week, enclosing a cheque for £1 with every letter. Theodore was touchingly grateful for this money[27]: without it they would have suffered real hardship, but with it Violet was able to afford warm clothes and new shoes for the children,[28] and Theodore could buy not only coal[29] but the occasional luxury: sugar, and even a bottle of gin: though he kept this hidden, having got into his head the curious idea that it would be taken away from him if their brother Bertie heard about it![30]

Bertie was in fact being extremely helpful and business-like on Theodore's behalf. There was still nothing but disappointment over *Amos Lear*[31] and the other novels, but Bertie took three pieces which his brother had written for the newspapers, and sent them all round London until at least one was accepted by the *Sphere*.[32] In the meantime, Theodore had completed three country plays: *Blind Bartimaeus*,[33] *Father Adam*, and *The Hawk's Nest*,[34] which he sent to Marian to be typed.[35] Unfortunately he seems to have had little or no idea of what would work on stage: one of the directions in *The Hawk's Nest* reads: 'Under the tree a pheasant is walking. A rabbit runs by and nibbles the grass and hops merrily away'![36] Then at the very end of 1920, Theodore resumed work upon a short novel, *Hester Dominy*.[37]

In this neatly constructed story, Hester Dominy is an attractive Sunday-school teacher whose life has been dominated and blighted by the church. Her own attempt to break away and find happiness ends in failure, but she inspires happiness in others. Three men escape from the spiritual deadness of their own existence when they fall in love with her; and although two of them soon return to their old ways, a tailor, Mr Antony Dine, is more fortunate. Love for Hester permanently breaks the power which greed has always exercised over him. Abandoning his endless labour and his grasping wife, he lives in a shepherd's hut where he experiences moments of eternal happiness; and when his savings run out, he bravely refuses to make any compromises, and is contemplating suicide when death mercifully intervenes.

Theodore Powys, very like his character Mr Dine, sometimes wondered whether he had already experienced the happiest moments of his life, and whether, therefore, suicide might not be the best solution to his problems. In January 1921, after a nightmare in which he 'learned' that Llewelyn loathed him, he was in a particularly depressed state; and he was further distressed by the news that John's *The Complex Vision*, which he had very much admired, had sold extremely badly.[38] Other financial and professional anxieties surfaced in a bitter letter to Louis Wilkinson, in which he wrote:

> I am very glad that Frances is happy in France. I would go there too – if I could. My rates have gone up 4 times. . . . Coal is four times as much too.
>
> I write very little now. I have had influenza – and it's in my

bones now. But Lord I am too great a coward to put a pistol to my ear. Lulu makes out it's so easy. So it may be to him.

After so many months of failure in 1919 and 1920, Llewelyn enjoyed giving the impression that everything was now easy for him. Writing to Louis in March 1921, he admitted that his health was by no means perfect; but he boasted shamelessly that he was writing 'a great deal for the Evening Post and the Freeman, also for the Dial, Metropolitan, and other Journals'; and he also claimed – no doubt hoping to make Louis envious – that he was 'having girls all day long'. In fact, only the previous month he had written to John lamenting that: 'I don't have the number of girls I anticipated, I don't have any at all'; and his only brief romance during this period was with an old friend of John's, which did not please John very much when he heard about it!

In March, Llewelyn had flu, but the tedium of lying in bed was relieved by the 'enchanting' discovery that he could look directly into the windows of some boarding houses opposite, see 'pretty young ladies' undressing after a day at the office, and catch' glimpses . . . of their slim, white, naked figures moving to and fro in their bedrooms'. When he recovered, it was decided that he should spend the summer in California with John, who had lecturing engagements out there. In April he joined his brother in Chicago, and they travelled by train through Arizona, across the Colorado river, and on to San Francisco.

The next few months were a happy time for the brothers. They shared rooms in boarding-houses, first at the Alta Mira, and then at the Holly Oaks. Lewelyn went to nearly all John's lectures, and was invited with him into some of the most fashionable homes in San Francisco. He also met John's great friend Theodore Dreiser, who wrote about the brothers:

> When they both walked into the room, it was as though
> between the two of them, all that was beautiful, intelligent and
> worthwhile contemplating in the way of thought and spirit
> suddenly swept into the room. Jack with his profound
> knowledge of philosophy, poetry, literature, along with the
> magic common touch which he has never lost, – Llewelyn with
> his great child-like beauty – physical as well as spiritual – his
> massive head of golden curls, his beauty-loving eye lit up by a
> smile that contained all the sunshine in the world. . . . Once
> seen together, one can hardly separate one from the other.

However one morning both brothers were thoroughly alarmed when Llewelyn spat blood. On the advice of the poet George Sterling, Llewelyn placed himself in the hands of a mysterious Dr Abrams, who used 'some dangling plummet of his own contrivance' to find where the tuberculosis was active. Then he painted Llewelyn's right shoulder-blade with a bright yellow substance, set him in front of an 'electrical machine', and attached 'a round-shaped battery, causing my flesh to tingle as if the fin of a seal had been placed against it.' After ten such treatments, Llewelyn 'was pronounced cured': he declared that he believed in the doctor's quackery, and, amazingly enough, he had no further trouble from tuberculosis for two years.

The most important result of his 'cure' was that Llewelyn's self-confidence was greatly increased, and this led to more frequent success with women. Such success had its attendant dangers: once Llewelyn was afraid that he had contracted syphilis; and he had an unpleasant quarter of an hour when he learned that a married woman had confessed her affair with him to her husband! However, he survived both these alarms, and for a while he settled down to enjoy the company of his favourite, Lydia Gibson,[39] a rich and beautiful creature of whom he wrote:

> She was an extraordinarily sweet-natured girl and suffered from
> no inhibitions whatever. To this day the memory of her gay
> laughter fills me with joy. A few hours of her company had the
> effect of ridding my own mind of I know not how many mean
> moralities.

Llewelyn had not been on the West Coast for long when the *New York Evening Post* began taking very much less of his work; and although his friend Van Wyck Brooks accepted 'The Stunner' for publication in the *Freeman*, he soon realised that he was 'too far from the centre of things' for his literary career to prosper. At the beginning of October, therefore, despite Marian's protests about the danger to his health, Llewelyn decided to return with John to New York. Marian had moved into a smaller apartment, not wishing to repeat the experience of sharing with both brothers; and so they found a room not far from Washington Square at 148 Waverley Place. But their first night back in the city was spent at the Seville Hotel, where, having signed the register, Llewelyn was delighted to be asked by the clerk whether he was 'the Llewelyn Powys who writes about Africa'.

It was now more than a year since Theodore's brothers had left

England; and he himself was regularly spending the larger part of each week at Weymouth, sharing with Gertrude the burden of caring for their elderly father. The Rev. Charles Powys's mind had practically failed, but he was sometimes happy sitting with a book; and John was touched to hear that this father who 'in old days . . . had such a contempt for dear John's wild ideas', would now sit perpetually turning the pages of *The Complex Vision*. Although Charles read without understanding, he was still physically fit, and needed careful watching. On one occasion Gertrude lost him while out picking blackberries; on another occasion he disappeared completely for most of the day. The full story of where he had gone and what he had done was never discovered, but he was found twenty-five miles away at Milborne Port,[40] not far from his childhood home at Stalbridge; and Llewelyn later wrote that his father had actually reached Stalbridge Rectory, perhaps wishing:[41]

> to revive in his mind old memories of his childhood, to remind himself for the last time through the sense of sight, before he entered the realm of dust and darkness, of the exact look of the mulberry tree, of the chestnut-tree whose every bough he knew from climbing them as a boy.

With Charles Powys living in dreams and silence, and with Gertrude watching with a mixture of bitterness and resignation as her life passed by with all her artistic ambitions unfulfilled, Greenhill House must have been a dispiriting household for Theodore to visit; but at least it made a change from his own home where he had to endure humiliating poverty, the nagging of an embittered wife, and the daily task of writing what no one else wanted to publish. In October 1921 his royalties for the previous half year were precisely 7d. All his letters for this year and the previous one have a miserably wounded feel about them: 'Lulu and Jack dance naked on the sands of California but so do not I', he had written enviously to Louis Wilkinson; and one wonders how much longer he could have struggled on without some form of wider recognition.

Fortunately, the seeds for such recognition were already being sown. In the summer of 1921 the sculptor Stephen Tomlin, known to his friends as 'Tommy', took lodgings in East Chaldon. Liking the village, and very much impressed by Theodore, whom he described as 'a most remarkable man . . . a sort of hermit, and he has a very fine head', he decided to live there for a while. When he returned to

London in September to pack up his sculptures, he interested one of his friends, Sylvia Townsend Warner, in Theodore's work. Sylvia, who was then an unpublished author in her late twenties, bought and read the *Soliloquy*, and admired it so much that she sent Theodore some of her own writing. He liked the 'little ironic touches' in her work, and in turn sent her a typescript copy of *Mr. Tasker's Gods*.[42]

Although the blackness and ferocity of this novel alarmed and shocked Sylvia, Theodore reassured her with a sane and friendly letter. He had recognised from the first that they had something important in common:

'Do you ever find the evenings dark!' he had written to her, 'From certain thoughts that you express in your play I should imagine that you do sometimes.' Tommy Tomlin, who had also read *Mr. Tasker's Gods*, told Sylvia that he himself had been puzzled by Theodore's apparent identification of sex with lust, but that Theodore was 'not in the least Puritanical, in fact just the reverse. He has a distinct streak of Rabelaisian lewd laughter and loves to surround himself with all the prettiest girls in the village.'[43]

Although Theodore did not actually meet Sylvia until early in 1922, he was now in touch with someone who was to do more than any other woman to encourage him and to help him to get his work into print. By a remarkable coincidence, it was while Theodore and Sylvia were exchanging their first letters that Theodore's literary brothers fell in love with women who were to be of equal or even greater importance in their own lives.

CHAPTER TEN

1921–1923

John lectures in America • falls in love with Phyllis Playter, autumn 1921 • sees her again in August 1922 and spring 1923 • holidays in England, summer 1922 • on west coast, August 1922 to May 1923 • published Samphire, *1922,* Psychoanalysis and Morality, *1923. Theodore in England • meets Sylvia Townsend Warner, March 1922 • David Garnett impressed • New Leader* accepts stories, *October 1922 • Chatto accepts* Black Bryony, *1923. Llewelyn in America • falls in love with Alyse Gregory, autumn 1921 • lives with her in Patchin Place from 1922 • quarrels with John over Phyllis, January 1923 • publishes* Ebony and Ivory,*1923. Peter Powys Grey born, summer 1922 • Charles Powys dies, August 1923.*

In March 1921, before spending the summer with Llewelyn, John Cowper Powys had made a visit to the small town of Joplin which was to have a profound influence upon his future happiness. Franklin Playter, one of the most interesting of the townsfolk, was already his friend;[1] and when John arrived to give a lecture, it was natural that they should meet. Playter was an adventurous Canadian, a real frontiersman at heart, who had lived a rugged life in New Zealand and Australia before starting a coal-mining business in Pennsylvania.[2] It was his mining interests which had brought him to Joplin, but he also took a keen interest in the literary world, and had built up a substantial library. His daughter Phyllis, a girl in her late twenties, no longer lived at home, but on this occasion she was visiting her parents, and she went with them to John's lecture. When the lecture was over, she was introduced to John; and she later recalled that 'they liked one another immediately.'[3]

Phyllis lived independently in Kansas City, her birthplace and the home of her mother's family. Her childhood had been rather too lonely and bookish, though her father, whom she very much admired,[4] had paid for her to have an excellent private education in Boston. Eighteen years old when her parents moved west to Joplin, she liked the new country but felt that her life had no purpose there, and fell into a state of mild depression.[5] She had inherited her father's literary interests, and might have been happy if she could have written a novel, but unfortunately she set herself such high standards that she could never complete anything to her satisfaction, and it was after one such failure that she had moved away from her parents to take up secretarial work in Kansas City.

John's lecture-tour had soon carried him away from Joplin and eventually back to New York. Although Phyllis was no great beauty, he had been very much struck by the originality of her mind and was eager to see her again. His chance came in November, when another lecture-tour brought him back to the mid-West. Visiting Phyllis a second time, he realised to his surprise and delight that he was falling in love with her, and she with him. He was now in his fiftieth year, and she was not yet thirty, but the difference in their ages was never of much importance, for their relationship rapidly developed into that rare wonder, a marriage of true minds. Continuing with his tour, John spent the evenings in lonely hotel rooms in Memphis and other cities, writing some of the verses which appeared the following year as *Samphire*: they were written at Llewelyn's request, and some of them bear the marks of forced composition, but among them is one simple and direct poem entitled 'November', and, since that was the month of their second meeting, John probably wrote it with Phyllis in mind:[6]

I will come back to you and you to me;
When the poplar-trees blow white and the rooks fly home,
And the fishermen draw their nets out of the sea;
I will come back to you and you to me.

When across the flooded weirs the wild-fowl fly,
When the dead leaves fall from each remembered tree,
When over the withered grass the plovers cry,
I will come back to you and you to me.

Llewelyn, in New York, was once more selling stories and articles, though not with any great regularity: 'Sometimes all seems to be going well', he wrote to Gertrude, 'and then suddenly I feel I shall never be able to struggle through.' At night he slept on the roof of 148

Waverly Place, wrapped in blankets and red baize curtains which had come from Montacute; in the mornings, if it was fine, he sat and wrote in Washington Square, and in the afternoons and evenings he put on his 'polite clothes' and went out visiting. Without these clothes, which included a 'magnificent over-coat', his social life would have been impossible, and he was so frightened about losing them that he had long ago protected his room, which was otherwise 'bare as a barn', with a massive police-lock, 'the most ingenious contrivance ever invented by man's brain'! Now lack of money compelled Llewelyn to move to a smaller room in the same building, and when he was feeling depressed he would consult a short-story writer who lived on the floor below 'as to the secrets of the trade we followed', and 'would spend hour upon hour studying a little paper called "How to Write!"' For some time it was only the *Freeman* which really kept his career alive: Van Wyck Brooks gave him books to review; and fortunately Llewelyn's writing 'hit the fancy' of the editor of the *Freeman*, Mr Nock. 'My paper on Nicholas Culpeper,' wrote Llewelyn, 'which had gone to every magazine in the city, won from him the greatest commendation, and was followed by several other literary appreciations of old-fashioned, out-of-the-way English writers.'

Llewelyn's writing had also attracted the interest of Alyse Gregory, who was closely associated with *The Dial*,[7] and she invited him to tea in her rooms on the ground floor of 4, Patchin Place. This building was one of a small number of three-storey terraced houses, set about with ailanthus trees, and lining both sides of a blind-alleyway opening on to West 10th Street, and only yards away from the roar of traffic on Sixth Avenue. A far less salubrious quarter of New York than it appears today, it was shaken by the rumble of an elevated railway, and the 'Howls of prisoners' could sometimes be heard from the Old Market Prison nearby.[8] Patchin Place was not far from Llewelyn's lodgings, and on the afternoon appointed, after walking up Christopher Street and crossing Greenwich Avenue, he soon found himself:

> sitting down to tea before a bright fire in a lamp-lit room filled
> with delightful old-fashioned furniture. These rooms suggested
> to my mind my rooms in the Old Court of Corpus, and were
> entirely different from anything I had seen elsewhere in New
> York, as, indeed, was the poise, the intellectual intensity, the

freedom from preconceptions, as of a child uncontaminated by
the world, of my grave, delicately ironic hostess, whose round,
white arms seemed to me then, as I looked at them in the
flickering light . . . as delectable as dairy junket.

Llewelyn was immediately attracted to Alyse, a beautiful woman
almost exactly his own age, with 'corn-gold hair' and 'eyes of speed-
well blue, with their glance as direct as an arrow-shaft'.[9]

Alyse had spent her childhood not far from New York in Norwalk,
Connecticut, where her father was a doctor, a melancholy man of
humane and liberal principles. Her mother, from a scholarly background, had artistic leanings and was 'a rebel and an agnostic'. Alyse
had inherited her father's melancholy and her mother's rebelliousness,
but was distinguished from her parents by a remarkably fine singing
voice, said to resemble that of the great opera singer Melba. She
completed her training as a singer in Paris, where she received enthusiastic notices before abruptly abandoning a promising career. Returning to America she first dedicated herself to social reform, and
to the women's suffrage movement, and then undertook a succession
of jobs in New York, including journalism, 'work for the Carnegie
Foundation, a long spell in advertising . . . and running a tea-shop'.[10]

In Paris, her beauty had made her the centre of masculine attention
wherever she went, and she had received more than one proposal of
marriage, but she was tragically unfortunate in her love-affairs. Her
first lover had deserted her, and the second was crushed to death in a
road accident. In New York, she was constantly seen during the war
years in the company of a brilliant young writer, Randolph Bourne, but
she rejected him in favour of a Franco-Spanish poet who told her after
Bourne's untimely death that he himself was married, and intended to
leave her. His desertion brought Alyse to the brink of suicide, but she
was saved 'by the honest matter-of-fact humour of an English soldier',
and she threw herself into literary work, writing reviews and articles
for Van Wyck Brooks and others. Her tea-shop had been forced out of
business, but not before she had won the friendship and admiration of
two of her regular customers who were the owners of *The Dial*:
Schofield Thayer, who became her lover for a while;[11] and Dr Sibley
Watson. When they discussed manuscripts with her, they were forcefully impressed by her literary judgment, and although Alyse refused
any official post on *The Dial*, she soon became closely associated with
its editorial policy.

In addition to sharing her literary interests, Llewelyn was extremely handsome; while she belonged to what she was to describe as 'that amiable sex one of whose merits it is not to refuse a delight offered with an equal mixture of *finesse*, daring, gallantry and circumspection'.[12] Within a few weeks they had become lovers. Many girls found Llewelyn attractive, and he had been leading a busy social life: in particular, he was still seeing a great deal of Lydia Gibson,[13] who had followed him from California to New York, and when he first met Alyse, he told her: 'If you want me to have dinner with you this week, you had better tell me, as I am booked up for every night.'[14] However, Alyse Gregory soon occupied a very special place in his affections: not only was she beautiful and intelligent, but she loved him with the unselfish devotion of his mother, and he began to feel that his real home was by her side, writing later:

> I fell more and more under the influence of the sweet security of Patchin Place, until all my other familiar haunts seemed, one by one, to grow dull – until, indeed, I felt no contentment of spirit unless I knew that I was on that very day to find myself knocking on the darkened door of that particular sanctuary of civilisation.

When John returned from his lecture-tour he found that Llewelyn 'used to make me curse by slipping off to tea with her & leaving me to go to some tea place alone.' Llewelyn was generally with Alyse at weekends also: sometimes they would go alone to a deserted beach on Staten Island, or for a walk along the New Jersey canal at Newark; and if they were feeling more sociable, they visited Van Wyck Brooks and his wife, or travelled out to Connecticut to spend a week-end with Alyse's parents.

In the early spring, John returned to California. On one memorable occasion he and his west coast manager, Jessica Colbert,[15] visited the studio in Hollywood where Charlie Chaplin was 'directing and re-hearsing "The Pilgrim"'. The comedian impressed John so much that he later described him, along with Thomas Hardy and Augustus John, as being one of the three greatest men he had ever met. Chaplin described to him 'Most eloquently . . . a certain ideal performance, at once profoundly humorous and profoundly tragic, that at intervals kept teasing his imagination'; and Powys wrote: 'I learnt [from him] to have some – clear, definite, & easily grasped by my will-power to follow – ideal of life for myself independent of everybody else.'

When John returned to New York, on his way to England, he found that his sister Marian was in need of help. He and Llewelyn had continued to see her from time to time, and no doubt she attended with them one of the performances of John's adaptation of Dostoievsky's *The Idiot*, which was put on several times for charity during April and May;[16] but she had found that Llewelyn was so involved with Alyse, and that John's head was so full of thoughts about Phyllis, that she was rather lonely and isolated. Her own love-affairs had been unlucky, and her current lover, the lawyer Ernest Angell, was not free to marry her. Despite this, Marian deliberately set out to become pregnant by him, determined to have a child, even if she could not have a husband. When she explained this to John some months later, and asked for his help in avoiding a scandal, he kindly told her that the situation was 'neither absolutely black, nor absolutely white, but *grey*'. Using this colour for a surname, they then invented a journalist called 'Grey' who was said to have married Marian, and to be the father of her unborn child![17] Llewelyn entered into this deception, announcing in July when Marian's son was born that he had been named Peter 'after his father'. Before long, they had invented a further twist to the plot: Marian's imaginary husband was despatched to Italy, where John had decided that he should die of malaria before too many awkward questions could be asked.[18]

John himself was in England at the time of the birth, spending an unusually happy summer at Burpham, where his remittances had created a comparatively sheltered world very different from the one which he usually inhabited. Margaret appeared to be 'altogether more flexible' in her attitudes, and John attributed this to the benevolent influence of their son, Littleton Alfred, who had inherited 'none of [the Powys] "malice" and none of the Lyon vindictiveness'. Littleton, enjoying his time at Cambridge, mixed easily in good society, and had been invited to go grouse-shooting later in the year. But John found him 'simply constructed', and was pleased to think that he could 'grow and be happy in these backwaters for a bit'. Perhaps because he never put any pressure on him, leaving his upbringing entirely to Margaret, John was more of a close friend than a father to Littleton: they commented on each other's poems, and even discussed their respective sexual predilections without shame or embarrassment.[19] Littleton, for example, talked freely about his romantic friendships with other young men, and on walks pointed out unselfconsciously to John the places 'where live the beautifullest lads'.

During the summer, John saw many of his friends and family, and had tea with Thomas Hardy in Dorchester, but his most memorable visit was to East Chaldon: he particularly liked Theodore's eldest son Dicky, with his 'sturdy originality' and unfailing wit; and he told Llewelyn that he had:

> never left Theodore himself in better spirits or better health, largely due to Mr Tom Tomlin the Sculptor, a bewitching gipsy-like young William Blake, with the most caressing respect for Theodore, who he calls 'Theo' and makes the old rogue laugh and chuckle till he's red in the face.

Tommy Tomlin had been acting as Theodore's literary adviser; and a few months before this, on a Friday evening in March, when Sylvia Townsend Warner had arrived to spend a long week-end with him, he had taken her over to Beth-Car. They arrived in pouring rain; and, as Sylvia later recalled:[20]

> It was Violet who came to open the door, Violet who I loved at first sight; and while she was helping me off with my coat Theo came and stood in the parlour doorway and I heard for the first time that soft deferring voice.
> 'Is this Sylvia? Tommy, how very kind of you to bring her so soon. But I hope it will not harm her, bringing her out in the rain. Her hands are rather cold . . .'

Violet made tea and they sat and talked in a hot, rather overcrowded room; while Sylvia, looking at her host, was struck by the fact that 'his beauty was of a pagan and classical kind, and that instead of a hermit or a prophet I was looking at a rather weather-beaten Zeus.' The following day Sylvia walked again to Beth-Car; and on Sunday she went to Evening Service at Chaldon Church, to hear Theodore read the lessons. The Old Testament lesson, with its words about 'the latter rain that refresheth the earth', had been deliberately chosen to celebrate her arrival; and before Sylvia left East Chaldon both Theodore and Violet were encouraging her plans for moving into a deserted cottage about a mile from the centre of the village.

A few weeks later, towards the end of April, Tommy travelled up to London to hand over to Sylvia the typescript of Theodore's *Hester Dominy*. After talking for some time about how best to find a publisher, Tomlin recalled that he had once met the author David Garnett, who might possibly be persuaded to give them some advice. So, in June,

Miss Warner tracked down Garnett in the rare bookshop which he ran in Taviton Street near the British Museum, and rather nervously presented him with the typescript, which he agreed to read. While awaiting his verdict and advice, Sylvia revisited East Chaldon, where on Midsummer's Day Tommy began reading to her Theodore's latest work, a short novel which he had entitled *The Left Leg*.

There is not a single character in *The Left Leg* who is so well drawn as Mary Crowle in *Black Bryony*, or so innately interesting as Mr Anthony Dine in *Hester Dominy*. But although Theodore has abandoned any attempt to make his characters three-dimensional, they are firmly rooted in his experience of village life: the portrait of the warm-hearted Minnie Cuddy, for example, must owe something to the existence of Nelly Trim, the East Chaldon dairymaid 'who, it was said, would yield herself to any wanderer who chanced to come to her lonely dwelling.'[21] Luckily, the fact that the characters in *The Left Leg* are more representational than real is perfectly suitable for the kind of extended parable which Theodore had now written, a parable in which the lessons to be learned about spiritual and moral relations are securely based upon the philosophical doctrines of Theodore's own *The Soliloquy of a Hermit*. At the centre of the plot are the grasping and lustful Farmer Mew, a personification of the 'getting' mood, who amasses great wealth without finding true satisfaction; and the saintly James Gillett, whose search for wisdom brings him worldly ruin but spiritual riches. The novel also includes the first appearance of Mr Jar the Tinker, a predictably unorthodox representation of Jesus, who soon announces that 'I never go near a church.'[22]

Sylvia Townsend Warner was very much impressed by *The Left Leg*, regarding it as greatly superior to any other work of Theodore's which she had seen; so it is not surprising that Theodore was in such excellent spirits when John visited him towards the end of July. Later in the summer Tommy Tomlin brought David Garnett to visit Theodore, and Garnett announced that he had enjoyed *Hester Dominy*, and suggested that an approach be made to the publishing firm of Chatto & Windus. With Tomlin's encouragement, Theodore was already in the process of extracting a number of his manuscripts from the dilatory Mr Melrose, and he was delighted to think of making a fresh start elsewhere. On 22 September he wrote to Chatto enclosing *The Left Leg*, and Garnett smoothed his path by lunching with Charles Prentice of Chatto, and trying to interest him in Theodore's work. Prentice was soon asking to see further stories, and before long he had received typescripts of

Tadnol, Black Bryony, and *Hester Dominy*. Theodore also sent him *Abraham Men*,[23] a novel of similar length to *The Left Leg*, but instead of another extended parable, he had now written a surrealistic story with autobiographical undertones.

In *Abraham Men*, a vision compels Luke Bird, the central character, to give up his clerical work in the town, and to come to Little Dodder to preach salvation to the villagers. However, he finds that they can hardly be touched by conventional religion. Instead, they live in a strange and brilliantly evoked world of 'pure country magic',[24] but they do have a clear understanding about the terms upon which life is to be lived, and they think of God as a sinister and unpredictable being in the background of their everyday lives. Luke himself has a moment of illumination, in which he begins to understand the way in which everything that happens, whether good or bad, is accepted as part of the book of village life, but eventually he returns to the more comfortable certainties of the town.

David Garnett had not been favourably impressed by his first sight of Beth-Car, which he described as 'a hideous red-brick box with ugly windows', surrounded by 'a space filled with long tussocky couch grass with a few dwindling fruit trees and a disused run for some fowls', but he had found Theodore impressive if somewhat eccentric:[25]

> a grey-haired, elderly, heavily-built man with a big head and powerful rugged features. His very sharp eyes under bushy eyebrows summed one up; he was a moralist and a shrewd critic of men. The grey eyes were those of a relentless and severe judge. But . . . he was exaggeratedly polite and spoke with an excessive humility and gentleness, as though he were an unarmed man addressing gunmen ready to shoot on sight.

Garnett's work on Powys's behalf included showing his stories to Virginia Woolf, who was kinder when she wrote to Theodore than she was behind his back,[26] and Garnett also recommended Theodore's work to the editor of the *New Leader*, who by mid-October had accepted several of his short stories for publication. Theodore wrote to John with the good news that he no longer needed any financial help, and he was now so much more optimistic that there was a marked change in his handwriting: the crabbed and wounded look of previous years suddenly vanished, to be replaced by a more flowing and confident script.[27]

John had returned to America in the third week of August, his chief desire being to see Phyllis again as soon as possible. There had been some chance that she might be in New York, and, thinking it unlikely that Marian would allow the two of them to stay in her house, John had asked Llewelyn to 'just keep in your mind the problem of how it may be perhaps conceivably worked out that I could get a night – actually that – with my friend!' Phyllis was not in New York, but John contacted her immediately, and within a week or ten days they were both staying in Joplin at her parents' house. John was very happy to be with her again, though unfortunately he was not feeling very well, and the heat was so intense that, as he wrote to Llewelyn, 'Phyllis and I could do nothing but sit side by side on dead logs with our feet in a river, day after day.' Then, after moving on to Denver to deliver some lectures, he had to travel to San Francisco, at the urgent request of Jessica Colbert.

When John arrived there, he was irritated to find that there was no reason for Jessica's urgency. She seemed to be devoting all her time to a local theatre, and although she talked of producing his Ibsenesque play *Paddock Calls*, this never came to anything, and she had arranged very few lectures. This was a source of considerable embarrassment to John, who had to ask for advances from Jessica to meet his various commitments, including Margaret's allowance of £50 a month, and £100 for their son's autumn term at Cambridge. Although Jessica paid what he asked for, she did so with a very bad grace, and made little effort to find him more work. Llewelyn was annoyed to hear of this, and told John that he should take a firmer line with his manager, but John could only reply:

> Lulu, do you think I like you to tell me to take my affairs in hand etc etc etc. It's like telling one of those Tadpoles in that pond to exert itself and walk on its tail down to the Farm for a bottle of milk. I can no more see myself having that kind of drastic competent conversation with Jessica than I can see myself in an aeroplane.

Llewelyn no doubt felt justified in giving his brother some rather fierce advice, because it was he who was responsible for the one encouraging feature in John's professional life that autumn: the publication of *Samphire* by Thomas Selzer of New York.

Llewelyn was having a good deal of work accepted by the *Freeman*, and John had written to him in October congratulating him on his 'immense successes'. But Llewelyn's experiences with the *New York Evening Post* had shown him how ephemeral such successes could be, and for some time he had been hoping to consolidate his reputation by persuading someone to publish in hard covers a number of stories and autobiographical essays about his life in Africa and England, which he had collected under the title *Ebony and Ivory*. In the spring of 1921 Llewelyn had read one of the essays, 'Black Gods', to Theodore Dreiser, who liked it so much that he had promised to write an introduction to *Ebony and Ivory*, and he introduced Llewelyn to the firm of Boni and Liveright. This introduction merely wasted six months, because Mr Liveright, unwilling to offend Theodore Dreiser, but equally unwilling to risk publishing Llewelyn Powys, promised everything and performed nothing. By October 1922 four more publishers, including Selzer, had turned it down.

Now Llewelyn turned to Mr Symon Gould, the young Jewish director of the American Liberty Service, who was already an admirer of John Cowper Powys's work. Gould promptly accepted *Ebony and Ivory*, and soon persuaded the brothers to put all the works of 'The Two Domes' as they now jokingly called each other, into his hands. When Llewelyn wrote to Louis Wilkinson in December, he told him some of Gould's plans: *Ebony and Ivory* was to be published early in 1923, with the flattering introduction which Dreiser had written, and it was to be followed some months later by a selection of Llewelyn's biographical essays to be called *Thirteen Worthies*. With his letter Llewelyn enclosed a cheque for £11, as partial repayment of a loan Louis had made him a year or two earlier. Remembering that Louis's advice had caused him to lose £300 on his return from Africa, he repaid the money most ungraciously, writing: 'I am just making a bare living out of writing and the surplus I send to a friend in Chiswick, the pox take him'; but his future looked more secure than it had ever done, and he was personally happy. The departure of one of Alyse Gregory's fellow-tenants had meant that Llewelyn had been able to leave Waverly Place, and he was now sharing the whole of the ground floor of 4, Patchin Place, with his mistress. 'It is cold over here now,' he wrote to Louis, 'but I have a warm bed to sleep in these nights and am as merry between the sheets as a young orange-throated cuckoo in a hedge-sparrow's nest.'

In the mornings, once Alyse had left for the office, Llewelyn spent his time writing in the small back-yard at 4, Patchin Place; and in the afternoons he called on his friends, who now included the writer Arthur Ficke – introduced to him by John – and the poet Padraic Colum. It was on his way to a tea-party in Washington Square one afternoon that Llewelyn had one of the most nightmarish experiences of his life. Looking into the face of a total stranger, he found himself affected

> in a most startling manner. The tattered great-coat, with little
> heaps of melting snow peaked up on both shoulders, might
> have sheltered the walking corpse of some enemy of mine,
> green from the grave, *who recognised me and whom I recognised*.
> Never in my life had I seen such evil features as those that
> looked up at me out of the mist, and yet it seemed to me that I
> knew them.

Hurrying on, Llewelyn discovered to his horror that the sinister stranger had turned and was following him. Walking still faster, and then breaking into a run, Llewelyn reached his friend's locked door, rang the bell, and moved aside into a darkened recess, hoping that it would look as though he had already entered the house. But the stranger had seen him, and in another moment was climbing up the steps towards him. Just as he came close, and was threatening to rip open Llewelyn's belly with a knife, Llewelyn heard the jangle which meant that the door could now be opened. He slipped inside; but that was not quite the end of the story. When he announced what had happened, and looked out of the window, there was no trace of the man who had threatened him. 'Even to myself', Llewelyn wrote later, 'my story seemed the most utter folly, and my friends went back to their chairs and resumed their conversation.'

Alyse helped Llewelyn to prosper by publishing more of his work in *The Dial*; and during the course of 1923 the successful publication of *Ebony and Ivory* and *Thirteen Worthies* further enhanced his reputation, and made it easier for him to get his stories and essays accepted elsewhere. Alyse was also responsible for Llewelyn meeting many distinguished literary figures, some of whom they entertained at Patchin Place, and some of whom went with them to the dinners arranged by Thayer and Dr Watson, the owners of *The Dial*. Llewelyn did not admire everyone whom he met, and took a real dislike both to Hugh Walpole, with his 'too agreeable tea-party manners'; and to Rebecca West, whom he described as 'abusing her talent and originality for the satisfaction of obtaining a reputation for "smartness"'. Llewelyn also met the notorious Frank Harris, and he was present at a party arranged by Theodore Dreiser when, bottle in hand, 'there entered upon us a youth a little the worse for drink, whom everybody called Scotty, and who, I learnt afterwards, was the novelist Scott Fitzgerald.'

Unfortunately, Llewelyn's generally happy and interesting life did not prevent him from becoming jealous about his brother John's devotion to Phyllis Playter. Phyllis herself was strongly attracted to the world of publishing, and in November 1922 had taken a job with the Haldeman–Julius company of Girard, Texas. Curiously enough, one of her first tasks was to proof-read some of John's work, since Haldeman–Julius had come to an arrangement with Symon Gould, and were serialising John's *One Hundred Best Books* in a weekly paper. John, still away in California, longed for her company, and towards the end of December he wrote to Llewelyn saying: 'I get lonely sometimes – I miss Lulu and I want Phyllis. Do you know I haven't 'made love' to any person since I left her in August – not one!' Llewelyn had long understood that women were to be no more than a pleasant distraction from the important business of his friendship with John, but now his brother appeared to have stronger feelings for Phyllis than for himself and he was deeply offended. John did his best to smooth things over with a further letter:

> Lulu, I wish it were lawful for me to send you a vast package of the letters I have received from Girard, Kansas! So that you should recognise, really and truly, that my little funny-face is a noble and distinguished Intelligence! . . . if you saw these letters you would not find it in you to scold me as though I made too great a fuss – for really the girl is an astonishing little wise-head. . . . I am in love with her Mind, brother; with her Mind.

There the matter might have rested. But John wished to have someone to whom he could confide his feelings about Phyllis, and, realising that Llewelyn was unlikely to be sympathetic, he wrote instead to Marian, feeling that he could trust a sister with whom he had been 'pretty intimate . . . in times past'. He was wrong. Marian was even more jealous than Llewelyn; and when in January 1923 she received a letter from John detailing not only how much he loved Phyllis, but also the cerebral nature of his affections, she took her revenge by passing the letter on to Llewelyn, knowing that he would be infuriated both by its content, and by the fact that John had chosen to confide in her instead of him. Llewelyn immediately sent John a typewritten letter of denunciation.

John did not reply at once; but then, when pressed to do so, wrote no less than three long letters of self-defence. In the first he told Llewelyn that he had no intention of writing about Phyllis 'to the Maberlulu *en masse!*' but that

> On general grounds . . . girls as girls are very thrilling and very exciting, and if my reactions to such excitement take a cerebral and sentimental . . . form rather than a 'rogering' honest cod form, I can only plead that nature has made me so . . .
>
> . . . I am just as unappealed to by your light o'loves as you are by my proceedings. But I shall never change . . . I loathe the other method. I shrink from it. It destroys my life-illusion. I have to love my particular girl, while she is my girl, just in this way, as a mad unbalanced almost Lesbian clinging to her. . . . I have in place of a soul a maniacal idolatry of the feminine young girl which only – and please note that! – has in all other cases been brought to an end not by anything I have done or by my unfaithfulness, but by their turning against me in natural malicious or righteous fury.
>
> But my present one won't do that – you will see!

Within a day or two John had written a second letter to Llewelyn, in which he accused his brother of being mean and unsympathetic, and he commented sharply both on his '*Smart Set* sarcasm' and his immature attitude to women: 'It appears it's all right to "talk" as long as you talk a little contemptuously of the girl, but the moment you grow serious and make an idol or fetish of the girl – why then it becomes "aesthetically unpleasing".' He added that: 'So far from my "talk" about Phyllis being superficial, it is my bold front to the world that is superficial. The silly thing about me is that when I get a pen in my hand, all the seething suppressions of my inner life come pouring forth.' In his third letter, he once again asked Llewelyn to question his attitude to women, suggesting that Llewelyn preferred Alyse's company to that of some men, not merely because she was his 'gentle companion'; but because she had 'a more interesting intellect'. He also stated that Llewelyn's attack had been just as unfair as the attacks made on Oscar Wilde for his homosexuality, and declared:

> Nature puts her seal on what is best for each of us by the mystery of happiness that such things bring. And if I feel very happy in my onanistic abandonments; if I feel absolutely thrilled

with delicious magical secret lovely happiness when I 'talk' of themselves to my girls and make idols and fetishes and funny little worshipped sticks and stones out of them and find all the mystery of Nature in them – well! who can blame?

I refuse to obey any aesthetic rules or moral rules or philosophic rules as to my life.

By this time John had moved on from San Francisco to Hollywood; while Phyllis remained at Girard. She was writing articles as well as editing and proof-reading: but although the work was interesting, she found it 'awfully hard and exhausting', and had more than once 'been on the edge of "breaking down"'. Sadly, John's own position was worse than ever. Jessica Colbert's theatrical ventures had been a disastrous waste of time and money, and although she talked grandly of lecture-tours in Australia or China, she never organised them, and John wrote on 24 January that he had been idle for three weeks. Lectures were at last arranged for February and March, but his income remained too low to satisfy his wife's demands, and on 17 March he wrote to Theodore:[28]

I get terrible letters of desperate appeals for more money from Burpham – I can't think how I manage to have any happy moments at all with such debts – up to £100 – accumulating there and tradesmen not paid.

But really its getting so far beyond me – the whole situation – that I just go on from day to day living in the present and putting it out of my mind. I have not the least intention of shooting myself as some financial failures seem to do so quickly!

The shortage of lectures had at least given John time to write. Towards the end of January he was engaged upon *The Art of Happiness*, a short book which he described to Llewelyn as 'a kind of breviary of furtive fantastic self-culture', and in which he attempted to show sensitive people how they could enjoy life. He told them that they had no moral duty to 'face up to reality'. Dogmatic materialism presented a view of the universe which was either a lie, or deserved to be treated like one; and they should deliberately choose to live in a dream world of their own creation, using whatever devices helped them to protect, prolong and restore their moments of happiness. John did not immediately find a publisher for *The Art of Happiness*, but another short book, *Psychoanalysis and Morality*, was published in the early spring by

Jessica Colbert. In this work, 'peering down from some Saturnian observatory', John noted how curious it was that 'sex-sensation' had become associated with 'sin'.[29] Psychoanalysis, he hoped, would teach us instead that sex-pleasure was 'something to be taken humorously, indulgently, ironically'. John also wrote *James Joyce's Ulysses – An Appreciation*, an essay in which he praised what he described as Joyce's 'savage fury', a fury based upon pity, and expressing: 'the most significant of all pities, the pity of a man for the womb that bore him, for the paps which he hath sucked.'[30] Llewelyn failed to find a home for this essay in New York, but Haldeman–Julius, who had told John via Phyllis that they 'wd. dearly like a volume of critical essays from me' published it in their occasional miscellany, *Life and letters*; and during the course of 1923 they also republished the essays included in John's *Suspended Judgments*.

In March Phyllis Playter left her job in Kansas, and set out on a journey to Paris which had been delayed since the previous autumn, but first she visited John in California.[31] One of John's greatest friends on the west coast, Colonel Charles Wood, an elderly man with something of a literary circle, 'could make nothing of her'; but when she travelled to New York, and stayed with Llewelyn and Alyse for several nights before sailing for France, she made a highly favourable impression. In May Llewelyn wrote a warm letter to John suggesting that when he had returned from California, and Phyllis from France, they should all live with Alyse under the same roof in Patchin Place. This marked the end of the quarrel between the two brothers, and John replied:

> Lulu, my darling,
> I am so sorry I said horrid things to you. I kiss your corrugated forehead – and I kiss your beautiful curved mouth. You know I was only fighting fiercely for the thing I value most in the world, which is the love of Lulu. I was afraid if I didn't justify my weakness . . . all would be lost.
> . . . I cannot tell you how the idea of coming at last to New York and being there with my girl and with Lulu thrills me with happiness when I think of it.

It was Jessica Colbert who had planned the return to New York, where she hoped to 'run' John in some kind of partnership with his former manager, Arnold Shaw. John would now have preferred to be free of both of them; but he had Margaret's needs and wishes to consider. She had only paid her bills in April by borrowing £100 from her brother Harry Lyon; and now she begged John 'not to take any new untried and unknown person', telling him that she needed £200 to last her until the end of September. When John arrived in New York in the second week of June, he had 'an enormous poisoned knee', and had to wire ahead to ask Llewelyn to meet him at the station with a wheel-chair. Llewelyn found him 'frail and sick', and wrote an angry letter to Littleton denouncing the wife and son whom he considered were ruining John's health by their selfishness:[32]

> Words cannot express the bitterness I feel towards Margaret. She has had £650 in nine months. . . . She should have let Burpham while Littleton was at Cambridge and lived in a cottage. . . . I feel slightly indignant with Littleton Alfred . . . is he also blind to what Jack is?

John was now in his fiftieth year, and although his knee soon recovered, the strain of trying to support his family in a style of living far superior to his own, and of trying to satisfy the conflicting wishes of his two managers, was too great. On a visit to his sister Marian's house at Sneedon's Landing, he had gone for a solitary walk, when a fit of unconsciousness came over him:

> when, so to speak, I woke up, and I must have walked at least a mile and a half in total unconsciousness, I found myself in that house by the river from which I had started. And I awoke to consciousness to discover myself caked in mud from head to foot, as if I had been rolling in a ditch, while I was dismayed to discover that the worst part of the mud was my own excrement.

Once he had cleaned himself up, John seemed none the worse for this unpleasant experience; he had suffered twice before from 'queer fits of unconsciousness': once when changing trains in England not long before his collapse at Worcester; and once when walking on the prehistoric embankment at Burpham. There was to be one more of these collapses, in 1925 or 1926, but when he was eventually able to give up lecturing and live quietly with Phyllis, they came to an end.

The present crisis was resolved for John when his brother Littleton cabled 'that he was going to take matters in hand', and presumably relieve him from the responsibility of Margaret and Littleton Alfred for the time being. This was 'an enormous relief',[33] and John began to enjoy life once again: he joined Llewelyn and Alyse on some of their excursions, and he was delighted to find out how many New York book-shops were prominently displaying Llewelyn's two books.[34] There was also good news from Theodore.

In February, Theodore had agreed to a suggestion from Chatto and Windus that *The Left Leg* should be the title story of a volume which would also include *Hester Dominy* and *Abraham Men*. In March he corrected the proofs, and dedicated the three stories individually to those who had given him so much help and encouragement: Sylvia Townsend Warner, David Garnett, and Stephen Tomlin – or 'the God head', 'the Dove', and 'the Son of Man', as he described them in a letter to Sylvia.[35] In April, advance copies were ready, and Louis Wilkinson found that London critics were already talking favourably about Theodore's book, and in mid-May *The Left Leg* was published, to considerable critical acclaim. Later in the year an edition was published by Mr Knopf in New York, and although *The Left Leg* did not have large sales in either England or America, it established a small but devoted following for Theodore's work. His brothers were particularly pleased: 'It is well & deeply worthy of you', wrote John; '. . . The *Left Leg* is the most original & metaphysical, *Hester Dominy* is the most touching & poignant & exciting to read . . . And *Abraham Men* is the best as a work of art.'[36] And Llewelyn wrote to their brother Littleton:[37] 'I keep hearing references to it made in literary circles. What a chance beyond all chances if a little good fortune were really to surround that white, melancholy head of East Chaldon before it is finally put under the chalk downs!'

During the first part of the year, Theodore had completed a new novel. This he called by the name of its principal character, a man who begins life with the misfortune of being christened: not Mark, as his mother intended, but *Mark Only*. From then on, his mother rejects him, and his life becomes little more than a catalogue of misery. For once, Theodore offers little or no philosophy to reconcile us to the grimness of his vision. There is humour in the book, and some happiness: Mrs Tite reels drunkenly around the vicarage, and Emmie Paine the maid is allowed to settle down with Mr Thomas the chimney-sweep. But the overall picture has become so black that it cries out for parody.

In July, Theodore enjoyed a visit from Louis Wilkinson, who was seeking a divorce from Frances, and had brought with him 'Nan' Reid, the woman who was to be his second wife. Louis still earned his living as a lecturer, but was now turning his attention once again to writing: he had just submitted an article to *The Dial*, and he talked to Theodore about a new novel, the first he had begun to write since working with Frances on *The Buffoon*. Shortly after this visit, Theodore was working on the proofs of *Black Bryony*, which Chatto had decided to publish in the autumn, and, remembering that Louis had introduced him to a mixture of beer and stout, he wrote to him: 'I hope "Black Bryony" will pay well enough so that I can afford a little more of this new drink.'

Within a week of writing this letter, Theodore was in a position to forget such small-scale financial worries. On 5 August 1923, the Rev. Charles Francis Powys died, leaving each of his ten surviving children £3,000, then a substantial sum. All of them found the money helpful; and for some of them it made a very considerable difference.

Lucy, the youngest, lived with her husband Hounsell Penny and their daughter Mary in the village of Horsebridge, Hampshire. Lucy herself had no extravagant tastes. 'Books', wrote her brother Littleton, 'Books and nature, shared with her daughter, were everything to her.'[38] But Hounsell had a mill on the banks of the River Test, and no doubt the money was a useful injection of capital into the family business.

After the Great War, William had been awarded the Croix de Guerre de Leopold II for his services in driving cattle from the Belgian Congo to our troops in the east.[39] More important, as a soldier himself he had also been awarded a grant of land by the colonial administration; and now he was able to use his inheritance to build up the farm which he owned at Kisima, to the north-west of Nairobi, and not far from the shores of Lake Victoria.

Katie had given up farming at Montacute earlier in the year, and had spent the summer on holiday first with Theodore, and then with Lucy.[40] Now she began to think in terms of living permanently at East Chaldon in a cottage of her own, while she tried to write like three of her brothers. At the same time, she intended to use some of her money to travel, and made plans to go over to New York in the autumn.

Llewelyn was happy living in New York with the two people who meant most to him in the world. His fortieth birthday came only eight days after his father's death, and on it he told Alyse that he was 'made to be loved'.[41] But despite his happiness, and the success of *Ebony and Ivory* and *Thirteen Worthies*, his professional affairs had recently received a set-back; Symon Gould's American Library Service was going out of business,[42] and although Llewelyn was planning a new book about his African experiences, to be called *Black Laughter*, he had no contract with a publisher, and overtures to Knopf proved abortive. In these circumstances, it was both useful and reassuring to have a large sum of money in the bank: where it probably remained. Llewelyn's experience of investment had not been a happy one, and when he went downtown to visit some stockbrokers, the sight of their 'denaturalised, inhuman faces' made him so nervous for the safety of his patrimony that he 'bolted' without a word to anyone.

In another part of the city, Marian was hard at work trying to build up business in her third lace shop. The first, in Washington Square, had been a great success, but her move in 1920 to 'grand' premises in the Gotham quarter had been over-ambitious, and in 1922, not long after the birth of her son, she had been forced to move to a smaller shop on Lexington Avenue. Some of her stock was extremely expensive, so extra capital would have been an enormous help.

Across the Atlantic her brother Bertie was forty-two years old, an established architect with a growing reputation. The quality of his life in London with Dorothy and their daughter Isobel was little changed by his inheritance: what chiefly affected his happiness, or lack of it, was Dorothy's sharp tongue, and he was becoming increasingly ill-at-ease in her company.

Although Gertrude had loved and cared for her father, she must have regarded his death as a welcome release for both of them. Charles Powys had died peacefully with a 'wonderful look' on his face.[43] She herself was free at last, at the age of forty-six, to pursue her career as a painter, and within three months of her father's death she had travelled to Paris,[44] where she intended to resume her artistic studies.

Theodore, aged forty-eight, no longer had to worry whether he could afford beer mixed with stout, and there was no need for much more expenditure on his elder son Dicky, who had been learning Swahili[45] and intended to travel out to Africa in December to join Will at Kisima. But Theodore felt that he should give Francis the chance of a public school education, and sent him to Bruton,[46] where Littleton had once been an assistant master. Uncertain what to do with the rest of his inheritance, he loaned £500 to Louis at interest; and this caused him new worries: 'if you were hanged', he wrote to Louis, 'or lost one of your members, (which prevented your earning money by your books or lectures or playing bridge) would I still receive my money? Would my interest & principal be protected against your total dismemberment?' Some of the remaining money was invested in National Savings Certificates, but the rest was simply left in the bank after Theodore, rather like Llewelyn, lost his nerve about investing in stocks and shares: 'one of these days', he wrote to Louis, 'they will all burst like a bubble . . .'

In the same month that his father died, Littleton retired from teaching at the early age of forty-nine. A conscientious headmaster of the Sherborne Prep., he had worked himself too hard during the difficult years of the war and the period immediately following, and in early 1923, as he later recalled:[47]

> after some weeks spent in bed, my doctor told me that if I wanted to fulfil the normal span of life allotted to man, I must surrender and hand over the school to others. The joy of being alive had always meant so much to me that I did not hesitate in coming to a decision.

By the end of April, arrangements had been made for the school to be handed on, and these arrangements left Littleton financially secure. The doctor had told him to spend the summer and autumn resting, but as the principal executor of his father's will he was unable to do so. First he organised the funeral, and Charles Powys was laid to rest with his wife in the churchyard at Montacute, beside their daughter Nelly. Afterwards Littleton, Theodore, Bertie, Gertrude, Katie and Lucy 'gathered once again at the Vicarage, and after tea sat together on the terrace walk, where in old days so many important family plans had been discussed and decisions taken.' Then Littleton and his wife Mabel went on with Gertrude to Weymouth, where it took them until November to divide up the estate, before setting off for a six months' holiday in Italy.[48]

Earlier in 1923, Littleton had been able to take John's financial affairs in hand by loaning him a substantial sum of money, on the understanding that John need not repay him until their father died. Now John was able to clear this and other outstanding debts, and still have some money in hand. At the age of fifty, he could look forward to a happier and more productive period of his life.

CHAPTER ELEVEN

1923–1925

*John lectures in America, 1923–5 • with Phyllis in Patchin
Place • signs for five years with Keedick, February 1925 • in
England, summer 1924 • publishes* Ducdame, *1925,* The Art of
Happiness, *1925,* The Religion of a Sceptic, *1925 • begins* Wolf
Solent, *February 1925.*
*Theodore writing in East Chaldon • journey to London, and son Dicky
to Africa, November 1923 • wastes 1924 on* The Market
Bell *• publishes* Black Bryony, *1923,* Mark Only, *1924,* Mr.
Tasker's Gods, *1925.*
*Llewelyn writing in America • very ill after expedition to the Rockies,
1924 • with Alyse Gregory in the Catskills, September 1924 – April
1925, and marries her October 1924 • affair with Betty,
1924–5 • publishes* Thirteen Worthies, *1923,* Honey and Gall,
1924, Cup Bearers of Wine and Hellebore, *1924,* Black Laughter,
1924, Skin for Skin, *1925 • leaves with Alyse for England, May
1925.*
Katie's visit to America, 1923–4.

Theodore Francis Powys had been writing regularly for more than
fifteen years, and his new friend, Sylvia Townsend Warner, who was
now working on a novel of her own, was fascinated to see how his:[1]

> books grew like stalactites and stalagmites. He deposited them,
> secretively and methodically – a process taking place in a cave.
> After breakfasting, rather late, and leisurely, he went off to the
> parlour, sat down before a large solid table, read for half an hour
> (usually in the Bible) and then set to work. He wrote
> uninterruptedly for three hours or so, put his work back in the
> table drawer, and began again, where he left off, on the
> following morning. . . . When I happened to pass the window,

I saw the same grave, dispassionate countenance, pen moving
over the paper, dipping at regular intervals into the inkpot.

Theodore's working day was invariably the same. After lunch, as
Sylvia observed, he would set out for a walk, deciding on a particular
gate or telegraph post which he must tap with his walking-stick before
returning home. Then there would be tea, and later, sometimes after
dark, a second walk: 'I remember him', wrote Sylvia, 'coming back
from one such walk, but sooner than usual, and looking troubled. "I
heard a noise in the hedge. I said to myself, It's only a rat. But then I
thought, Who made that rat?"'[2]

Like his brother John, Theodore had a powerful imagination which
transformed the world about him into the strange and occasionally
sinister world of his books. Sometimes he wrote directly from his own
'transformed' experiences: for example, Edward Garnett guessed quite
correctly that the ghostly hounds heard in *Mark Only* before someone's
death, derived from the Scotty dogs of a certain Mrs Ashburnham. This
irritating woman, who rented the rectory in East Chaldon, used to
waylay Theodore on his walks in order to engage him in conversation.
On one occasion, seeing her in the distance, Theodore hid from her,
lying face downwards in a field of stubble. But the Scotties discovered
him:[3]

> He remained motionless as the Scotties scampered up and
> sniffed at him, then he heard a footstep, then silence. At last
> Mrs Ashburnham asked brightly: 'Communing with Nature, Mr
> Powys?' She had been standing beside him for a full minute.

Sylvia Warner reckoned that, had it not been for Violet, Theodore's
'bent towards theology and contemplation would have kept him
writing about God and Theodore Francis Powys'. She observed again
and again how Violet, with her constant chatter which many people
found annoying, brought the world of village life into Theodore's
hearing:[4]

> Violet, returning from the village post-office, or from a journey
> to Dorchester in the bus, or reading bits of local news aloud
> from *The Dorset Echo*. . . . Observant, speculative, credulous,
> unaffectedly interested in her neighbours, naturally talking the
> local dialect yet just enough removed from it to have an ear for
> its idioms, and with a memory ramifying into every local

pedigree and bygone event and oddity, she was an inestimably good purveyor.

Theodore spent the spring and summer of 1923 writing one of his lightest and most entertaining novels. East Chaldon has been transformed into *Mockery Gap*;[5] and, in a generally amiable fantasy, Theodore makes us smile at the illusions and pretensions of his characters. Mr Gulliver, for example, has very probably never travelled outside the county, but because he retails an ironic comment about his name, the villagers come to regard him as 'a traveller to far countries and as a viewer of strange fowls and creatures in them'; and Mrs Topple, the schoolmistress, is wrongly believed to be good at controlling naughty children, so that 'When any child in the village performed some doughty act more than usually atrocious, such as spitting at or kicking his own parent, Mrs Topple would be sent for. And when she came she would take a cup of tea and complain about her bad leg . . .' Illusions can have serious consequences, and there is a darker side to the book. Under the illusion that he is doing good, Mr James Tarr from Weyminster interferes in the lives of the villagers, and indirectly causes the death of four of them, and the serious injury of a fifth. But the arrival of a Christ-like fisherman casts a spell of unusual contentment over the village. The children become less cruel; Mr Gulliver welcomes the birth of a child to his unmarried daughter, instead of turning her out of the house, and the local vicar finally consummates his five-year-old marriage.

As soon as he had completed *Mockery Gap*, Theodore started on a more serious piece of work. *Innocent Birds* begins badly with nine rather self-indulgent chapters of scene-setting, but then it develops into a tragic and moving drama of considerable importance. The title of the new novel refers directly to the maidens of the village of God's Madder, and ironically to large black birds which fly in from the sea, and are portents of evil. A newcomer to the village, Mr Solly, has learned that God has promised a gift to God's Madder, and the chief aim of his life is to discover what that gift may be, and who will receive it. He discovers that the recipients of the gift will be Fred Pim and Polly Wimpole, who are in love, but whose plans to marry are thwarted by Polly's cruel employer Miss Pettifer. Evil is also at work in the shape of Mr Bugby, the landlord of the Madder Inn, who plans to rape as many 'innocent birds' as possible, and manages to throw some suspicion for his crimes on to the Rev. Thomas Tucker, an excellent if unorthodox priest, who shares Theodore's own habit of climbing out of windows to escape people he does not wish to see, and is always reading out of a book with a plain cover which is said to be full of wicked tales!

Much suffering is caused by Miss Pettifer and Mr Bugby, and Fred and Polly are eventually driven to commit suicide, but we are largely reconciled to all that has happened by the strength of Theodore's underlying philosophy. Death, he says, is the gift which God has promised to the young lovers, and they have received it gladly, not as a tragedy, but as a happy release from tragedy. Nor is the remainder of the picture wholly black: Miss Pettifer, for example, is unable to find a maid to replace Polly, and is forced to light her own fires, and when she manages to get hold of Thomas Tucker's book, intending to expose him by sending it to the bishop, she finds to her fury that it is – the Bible!

In November 1923 *Black Bryony* was published by Chatto, and generally well received, and at the beginning of December, although he was still busily engaged on the final chapters of *Innocent Birds*, Theodore took a few days' holiday, so that he and Violet could see their elder son depart for Africa. They travelled to London, where they stayed with Bertie and his family in Hammersmith, and they watched Dicky set sail in *The Gloucester Castle* on the morning of 6 December. Tommy Tomlin then took them to lunch in a Soho restaurant, to a picture show, and finally on to Sylvia Townsend Warner's flat for tea. Sylvia later remembered it as 'a rather painful afternoon'; Theodore, very sad about his son's departure, drank tea, but would eat nothing, and did not even remove his large overcoat. Violet, on the other hand, was determined to enjoy her visit to London, and chatted away about the Underground, and double-decker buses.[6] They visited many of their friends, and one evening they had dinner in Sylvia's flat, with Tommy Tomlin, David Garnett and his wife Ray. Sylvia had made it 'a rather solemn affair, with such splendours as I could afford', and she felt that the marrons glacés on the table totally altered Theodore's view of her. He liked to 'make a legend' out of people he knew:[7]

> Thus, on first meeting me he had elected to find me a Learned Lady. Now the marrons glacés had given him a hint for a new reading of my character. Hebrew, astronomy, and all the other lendings were allowed to slide off my protesting limbs, and in a twinkling he had put plumes in my hair and a fan in my hand and was enjoying me as a pampered jade of Asia.

Theodore himself had been transformed into a minor literary celebrity; and had to endure parties given in his honour. He managed to derive some amusement from a luncheon party given by Douglas Goldring, at which it was noted that Theodore's 'behaviour . . . was inlaid with an irony so delicately figured that to most it was imperceptible.' But on his final evening in the capital, he arrived with Violet, Bertie, Dorothy and Isobel at a huge party being given in Tommy Tomlin's studio, to discover that most of the guests did not know each other, and were waiting around in uncomfortable solitude, while Tommy himself had not arrived! Theodore rose to the occasion, appearing 'perfectly and unaffectedly at his ease', and soon the party was under way. Later in the evening, when Tommy had at last arrived, Theodore even agreed to cut with a nib (the pen being mightier than the sword) the first slice of 'a home-made cake of vast size . . . iced and emblazoned with a Left Leg in sugar of natural colourings'. The following day he awoke feeling ill and exhausted, and, as Sylvia records: 'having thanked us all with the handsomest acknowledgements for such an enjoyable visit, he left London, unassailably determined never to come back to it.'[8]

On the other side of the Atlantic, John, Phyllis, Llewelyn and Alyse had spent the summer and early autumn of 1923 living amicably together in the same house in Patchin Place. Then in November, while John was away lecturing,[9] Katie Powys arrived in New York to begin a five months' visit.

Llewelyn usually spent the mornings working in the New York Public Library. He had now established a connection with the publishers Harcourt Brace & Co.; and, besides writing Black Laughter, he was busy selecting and arranging material for two collections of his work which they were to publish the following year: Honey and Gall, with a dozen informal essays on subjects such as 'The Moods of March'; and Cup-Bearers of Wine and Hellebore, with essays on six authors, including the poet Cowper, and Llewelyn's friend Padraic Colum. Katie, who was herself hoping for some success as a poet and a novelist, worked at his side; and in the afternoons they went for walks, sometimes going:

> eastward along Tenth Street, till we came to the river, and there,
> on a bleak wharf, with the gasworks behind us making
> periodical explosions, we would sit for hours together looking
> over the grey waters of the East River . . . at gulls and sailboats
> and free, ocean-travelling ships.

Llewelyn was pleased to hear from Katie that Lucy enjoyed his writing, and wrote to her: 'I adore you for that especially as Bertie thinks my writing is affected and Littleton still has the audacity to regard my best periods in the light of second best Prep. Essays, while Theodore gives them all to the devil.' He added: 'I think Katie is happy over here. . . . It is lovely to feel her arms like iron bands round me again.' Katie was indeed happy: she was being treated as an interesting and worthwhile person in her own right, and, as Alyse saw it, her time in America was 'a great liberating experience'.[10] That winter, it was Katie who took an interest in 'the famous prophet and magician, Gurdjieff', and who persuaded Llewelyn and Alyse to attend one of his performances; no doubt she was also responsible for inviting Gurdjieff's apostle, Mr Orage, to come to tea in Patchin Place to discuss the new cult which had grown up around his spiritual master.

Gertrude was having a less successful time in Paris: she had found that total freedom to pursue her artistic career was too great a responsibility, and she was suffering from a loss of nerve.[11] When in March 1924 her Aunt Dora's last illness gave her the excuse to hurry back to England, she was glad to do so. There had been some talk during the winter about Gertrude living with Katie,[12] and when Katie returned from America in April, the two sisters moved into Chydyok, an isolated farmhouse in a fold of the downs between East Chaldon and the sea. Their relationship was not an easy one, but Gertrude was happier for once again having someone to look after.

Missing Katie, and feeling once again the lure of the Dorset countryside, Llewelyn wrote to Littleton telling him that he too might leave America in about a year, as he was becoming tired of 'the clatter & barbarism of it all'.[13] In the meantime Alyse had been persuaded to become managing editor of *The Dial*: this was largely an administrative post,[14] but it brought her, as she later wrote, 'In touch with minds original and imaginative – the pick of all Europe and America – what higher fortune could I desire?'[15] Llewelyn himself completed *Black Laughter*, which was published later in 1924 by Harcourt Brace; and at the end of May he accepted an invitation from Dr Watson of *The Dial* 'to join him on an expedition into the Rocky Mountains'.

After a long train journey west, the two men hired ponies, guides, and a string of mules, and began 'heading for the wilderness'. While Dr Watson hunted unsuccessfully for grizzly bears, Llewelyn walked through the forests, a pistol on his hip, and saw elk, moose, grey geese and eagles. Unfortunately, when they reached the Rockies, Llewelyn became over-ambitious: one day he managed to reach 'the top of the highest of all the mountains', but then came a terrifying experience. Trying to discover a short cut, he followed a stream down the mountainside, only to find himself on the edge of 'a shocking precipice . . . with the water racing past my boots toward the treacherous crevice'. Overcoming dizziness and shaking knees, he climbed back through a thunderstorm to the top of the mountain, and eventually reached camp 'Exhausted, and soaked to the skin'.

The first hint that he had seriously overstrained himself came to Llewelyn in the form of a dream, in which he and his brother Willie saw that there were fresh gaps among the rows of apple trees in the orchard at Montacute: 'my heart sank with unutterable dismay', wrote Llewelyn, 'at this new evidence of life's fatal instability.' As he and Dr Watson retreated from the Rockies, Llewelyn began to feel unwell, and gradually became 'convinced that the bacilli put to sleep by Abrams' magic had come awake again'.

By the end of July, Llewelyn was back in New York. He had a good growth of red beard to show for his weeks in the wilderness, but he looked ill; and Alyse, who during his absence had lived 'in a nightmare of ceaseless dread and anxiety', was shocked by his appearance, 'so thin and so changed'. She added: 'He does love me with his whole heart. Perhaps we shall never again be separated until one of us dies.' The day after Llewelyn's return, he accompanied his brother John to the offices of Doubleday, Page & Company, the publishers who were taking an interest in John's new book, *Ducdame*.

John Cowper Powys had been working since the summer of 1923 on this novel, the first he had written since discarding *After My Fashion* some three years before. *After My Fashion* had marked a temporary lack of confidence by Powys in the philosophical ideas which he had set out in *The Complex Vision*. The very process of expressing his beliefs at such length and in such detail had compelled John, as his brother Theodore noticed, to doubt their truth.[16] By the beginning of 1923 however, he had regained enough confidence to declare in *The Art of Happiness* that belief in the strangest set of one's own ideas is wiser than facing up to life as it is seen by materialists. Now, in *Ducdame*, a book whose title promises something magical, and a little sinister, with its Shakespearian gloss of 'calling fools into a circle',[17] John turned away from the domestic themes of *After My Fashion* to a grand metaphysical conflict of the kind which he had written about in *Wood and Stone* and *Rodmoor*. In *Ducdame*, he takes up the theme of the struggle between the creative and destructive forces in the universe, or, as he had expressed it in *The Complex Vision*, the struggle between love and malice, the two sides of the eternal duality at the heart of everything. At the centre of the conflict is Rook Ashover, the squire of a small Dorset village. He is living with his mistress Netta Page, whom he loves, but who cannot bear him children. Since Rook's only brother, Lexie, is ill and will also have no children, it seems likely that the ancient line of Ashover will become extinct. The local vicar, William Hastings, is delighted by this, since he wishes for the extinction of everything, and, rather like Adrian Sorio in *Rodmoor*, he is writing a book which he hopes will contain the secrets of unravelling the universe. However, the creative forces are determined to make a battle of it, and they have on their side not only the wishes and hopes of the dead generations of Ashovers who are buried locally, but also Rook's mother, a formidable old lady who has devoted her life to the Ashover family; and Rook's cousin, the Lady Ann Wentworth Gore, who means to marry him and have his child.

As in John's earlier novels, there is a great deal of autobiographical material. Even one comparatively trivial incident, when a maid refuses to take morning tea up to the bedroom of Rook's mistress, is clearly based upon the occasion when a maid at Burpham had refused to serve John's friend Lily.[18] Once again, there are clear portraits of himself and of Llewelyn – this time as Rook and Lexie Ashover: Llewelyn is drawn with great love and skill; but John's self-portrait is rather more interesting, because he has allowed Rook Ashover to entertain many of his own philosophical ideas. From the very beginning of *Ducdame*[19] we find Rook wondering whether: 'there really did exist something corresponding to the old Platonic idea of a universe composed of mind-stuff, of mind-forms, rarer and more beautiful than the visible world.' Equally strange ideas are carried into the body of the book, as the Dorset landscape, nostalgically described, becomes a living presence, with some parts of it able to respond 'in some particularly intense way to the influence of moonlight'. Later, we are taken beyond the known universe, when Rook, after looking into a gipsy's crystal ball which is called the Cimmery stone, hears of Cimmery Land:

> some Elysian Fourth Dimension – out of Space and out of Time
> . . . where large and liberating thoughts moved to and fro over
> cool, wet grass like enormous swallows . . . thoughts that were
> made of memories and of hopes, and never of logic or of reason;
> thoughts that came and went under a thin, fine, incessant rain

that itself was composed of the essence of memory, the memory of old, defeated, long-forgotten gods whose only immortality was in this gray, cool, silent, sadly driven mist! . . . it came over him that this Cimmery Land . . . was the very thing that he had so often vaguely dreamed of.

Stranger still, Rook finds in a moment of despair that the normal laws of space and time no longer apply, and he is allowed to talk to his unborn son, who appears as a young man riding by on a horse, giving him the love and recognition that he needs, and not expecting him to be different from the man that he is.

In real life, John was now a much more contented man than the highly self-critical Rook Ashover. He had discovered in Phyllis Playter a woman who gave him happiness, without being upset by his lack of passion. However, John still felt some responsibility for his wife and son, and shortly after visiting Doubleday with Llewelyn to discuss *Ducdame*, he sailed for England to spend August and September at Burpham.

Littleton Alfred, who came over to Burpham to visit John and Margaret, had literary ambitions like his father, and was spending his spare time on a '"study" of his own sensations', but he was also training to be an architect under the supervision of his uncle Harry Lyon, with whom he now lived, and whose Dartmoor home, 'Middle-cot', was already willed to him. In the circumstances, there was no real need to retain the large house at Burpham; but because it had been Margaret's home for twenty-two years, and because he knew how devoted she was to every inch of the house and garden, John felt that it would be cruel to insist that she should move somewhere small and less expensive to maintain. The sad but inevitable result of his kindness was that he ran through the inheritance he had received on his father's death at great speed.

Later in the summer John fitted in a visit to Frances Wilkinson, who was now living in England again, and writing an autobiographical novel, and he also went over to see Theodore. The brothers exchanged news: John had received his contract for *Ducdame*, together 'with a very friendly letter from Russell Doubleday', and Theodore's *Mark Only* had been published in the spring. Theodore was also working on a new novel, *The Market Bell*, and he showed John the manuscript of his *Mockery Gap*.[20]

Although everything seemed to be going quite well for Theodore and John, the news from America about Llewelyn had been highly disturbing. One morning, soon after John's departure from New York, Llewelyn had felt 'a sudden sharp stabbing pain', under his right shoulder. In his own words: 'It was the kind of pain that demands attention, that cannot be ignored, and when I reached Patchin Place, I found that I had a high fever. I left New York for the country that very afternoon.' Alyse had already insisted that they should spend a few days with her parents at Norwalk, hoping that Llewelyn would be better away from the oppressive heat of the city, but on the train, some twenty minutes from their destination Llewelyn:

> realised by a certain familiar impediment in my breathing that I
> was going to have a haemorrhage. I sat as still as I could,
> 'freezing'. It availed me nothing. Every few seconds I could feel
> my lungs filling with blood; and to breathe at all it was necessary
> for me to cough little, short, choking coughs. . . . The mere
> suspicion that I was really *this time* going to die put me into a
> state of deepest misery. I could not bear that my hour should be
> yet.

He reached Dr Gregory's house in a dangerous condition, and on 12 August John received a letter from Alyse telling him that his brother was seriously ill. Then, on 13 August, there was another letter from Alyse and a cable from Llewelyn himself: it was his birthday, and he wished John to know 'that I had at any rate reached forty years'; but he was still a very sick man, and he had to stay with Alyse's parents for more than a month and a half, lying in the open air, while gradually his fevers subsided, and his strength returned. By 1 September, Alyse could write in her diary:

> Llewelyn is working on his paper for the *Atlantic*. Now his
> temperature is steady, but I feel the same anxiety for his health.
> I go down every day to New York to my office and return. Now
> we are together on this little balcony and he cherishes me
> dearly, and our hearts are inseparably knit.

Fearing the consequences of a return to New York, Alyse and Llewelyn decided to find some really healthy place to live, close enough to New York for Alyse to continue as managing editor of *The Dial*. On the banks of the Hudson, fifty miles from the city, the town of Kingston looks westward to the Catskill mountains, and near the village of Montoma, in that wild and beautiful land, Alyse discovered a farmhouse to rent: it was 'situated on the top of a winding mountain road', not far from the home of their friend, the author Richard Le Gallienne. As soon as Llewelyn was fit enough to travel, he and Alyse were driven over; and on 13 September, after spending a moonlit night on the verandah of their new home, they woke to the beauty of 'The branches of the pine trees with freshly fallen snow', and 'the rising sun over the fir trees'.

On their arrival at Montoma, Llewelyn and Alyse had felt it necessary to pretend to be married,[21] but Llewelyn was extremely embarrassed by this deception, and soon decided that it would make life much easier if they turned the pretence into a reality. He did not intend that the open nature of their relationship should change: it had always been understood between them that neither was to burden the other's life with suspicion or jealousy, and Alyse was well aware that Llewelyn had recently been enjoying an affair with Betty, an artist and sculptor[22] whom Alyse described as 'so young, so beautiful, and [she] loves him so passionately.'[23] Alyse did not complain about this, for she believed that it was her moral duty to give Llewelyn his freedom, and now that there was talk of marriage, her chief difficulty lay in agreeing to take marriage vows which might compromise her own integrity as an avowed feminist. Eventually, somewhat against her better judgment, she sacrificed her doubts to Llewelyn's wishes; and 31 October, when John was due to arrive in New York, was chosen as their wedding day.

That morning, Marian met her brother's ship, and the two of them caught the next train to Kingston, where they were welcomed at the station by Llewelyn, Alyse, Richard Le Gallienne, and their cousin Father Hamilton Cowper Johnson, who had travelled from Boston to conduct the wedding ceremony. The marriage then took place at a small church in Kingston: Le Gallienne acting as best man, and John adding his own dramatic touch to the proceedings by formally joining Llewelyn's and Alyse's hands.[24] The following day, Alyse wrote of her wedding: 'It is what Llewelyn wanted, but some cloud lies upon my spirit as if I had betrayed something in myself.'

John stayed at their farmhouse for a few days after the wedding, keeping Llewelyn company while Alyse returned to her work in New York. She planned to be with Llewelyn as much as possible,[25] but once John was gone, Llewelyn was often left for several days at a time with no company besides that of the servant who came in during the mornings. During the second week of October he again spat blood, which made Alyse very anxious about leaving him at all; but the mountain air was excellent, and after this set-back Llewelyn continued to improve. His recent sufferings had reminded him of his first attack of tuberculosis, fifteen years earlier when he had been teaching at the Sherborne Prep.; and he began to write a first draft of *Skin for Skin*, a remarkable volume of autobiography, certainly one of the finest of Llewelyn's mature works and probably his masterpiece, in which he records, both philosophically and poetically, his determined attempt to enjoy life to the full.

On leaving Llewelyn in Montoma, John spent a night at Marian's home in the Palisades before returning to Patchin Place. Phyllis had spent the summer with her parents, and he now sent her money to make the journey to New York. John was busy looking for a new manager, and, rather to his surprise he found that several of the most well-known ones were keen to have him on their books. He tended to favour 'the great Lee Keedick – the most formidable of all the managers – the one who ran Chesterton', but he would not commit himself to any long-term contract until he had been able to take advice from everyone, and in the meantime he accepted a few individual lectures. Towards the end of October, Phyllis arrived, and he played chess with her on the evenings when he was free, telling Llewelyn that 'it is as like C.F.P. and M.C.P. [their parents] playing chess as anything you can imagine.'

Phyllis also typed out articles for him; and in mid-November, when the page proofs of *Ducdame* arrived, she helped him to go through them. Their life together was not without some anxieties: John was visited rather early one morning by Dr Watson of *The Dial*, when Phyllis had only just got dressed, and John's own washing things still littered the floor. This made John worried that his close association with Phyllis would be detected, and give rise to unfavourable comment. However, they remained in Patchin Place, and when Bertie arrived in New York at the beginning of December, Phyllis prepared a special 'Volentia tea'[26] complete with an English plum pudding, for herself, Alyse, Marian, Bertie, and John.

John had arranged for Bertie to give a number of architectural lectures in New York, but Bertie had come over to America at Llewelyn's expense, and immediately after the first lecture he hurried out to spend a few days at Montoma. This was the first of several visits, and Llewelyn was particularly pleased when both John and Bertie spent the New Year with him and Alyse. 'In the evenings', Llewelyn wrote to Lucy, 'we would gather round a wood fire which Bertie would build with extreme care and deliberation. We would talk and sometimes he and I would play draughts.' The news from England was that Gertrude had decided to live permanently with Katie, and was soon to break up the household at Weymouth. Llewelyn, who had now completed *Skin for Skin*, and intended to remain in Montoma for at least another year for the sake of his health, wrote to Gertrude on 10 January 1925, asking her to destroy none of his papers, and informing her that Bertie had promised to see to his share of the furniture. A week later, after making a particularly successful speech at an architectural dinner in New York, Bertie sailed for England, where he arrived to find Theodore in very low spirits.

Until quite recently, Theodore had been in a comparatively cheerful frame of mind: his income had been sufficient for his needs;[27] Augustus John had visited him, and talked of returning to draw him when the days were longer;[28] and he had completed his latest novel, *The Market Bell*. Then, at the beginning of January, Theodore's mood changed abruptly when he learned that Sylvia Townsend Warner thought that *The Market Bell* was unpublishable. He wrote her a very mild letter, thanking her for speaking out, and adding:[29]

> I am glad that the Market Bell hasn't turned all I have done into ashes in your mind. I shall try once more – with Mr Weston's Good Wine – a short novel. And then I shall rest. As long as I get over 1926, Francis's last year at school, I am very well content.

In fact, her comments had made him very depressed, and he revealed his true feelings in a letter to John. Pointing out that it was several months since any of his short stories had been accepted, and that a complete year's work on *The Market Bell* had been a total waste of time, Theodore speculated gloomily about his days as a creative writer being over.[30]

The publication in mid-February of *Mr. Tasker's Gods* did not bring an immediate return of self-confidence, as it was greeted by a number of extremely hostile reviews,[31] especially from those who were outraged by Theodore's attacks on the clergy. But in spite of these reviews more than 700 copies of *Mr. Tasker's Gods* were sold before the end of March. Chattos were encouraged by this to publish *Mockery Gap* later in the year, with *Innocent Birds* to follow in 1926; and there no longer seemed any immediate danger that Theodore would once again be reduced to poverty.[32]

In the meantime, his celebrity in certain circles was on the increase; and early in 1925 he was visited by T. E. Lawrence, famous as

Lawrence of Arabia, but now working under the name of T. E. Shaw as a private soldier in the Tank Corps. Lawrence was stationed at Bovington Camp, less than ten miles away from East Chaldon;[33] and when he arrived on his motor-bike for the first of several visits, both Theodore and Violet were won over by his easy charm, and his evident admiration for Theodore's writing.[34]

John Cowper Powys had met few people so remarkable as Lawrence, but while he was in New York during the winter of 1924 to 1925, he and Phyllis were visited by the poet E. E. Cummings, and saw something of Theodore Dreiser, who was living in Brooklyn in a 'neat suburban *ménage*' with his mistress Helen.

John had now been lecturing under the auspices of the 'Lee Keedick Bureau' for several months. He had been favourably impressed when Keedick agreed to find a job for John's former manager Arnold Shaw, now somewhat broken down in health; and on Llewelyn's advice he signed up with Keedick for five years, and also agreed to give him 10 per cent of all his earnings as an author: at which Keedick, 'both surprised and pleased . . . said "Your confidence in me shall not be misplaced."'

At this time, two of John's books were about to be published. One of them, *The Religion of a Sceptic*, had been commissioned by Dodd, Mead & Co., publishers of *The Complex Vision*. A very short book, dedicated to 'The Catholic', it was based upon a lecture which John had delivered the previous October, and contained the argument that the true secret of religion is to be found in regarding it as mythology. The other book was *Ducdame*, published in New York at much the same time that *Mr. Tasker's Gods* was published in London, but although John's novel was very much better reviewed than Theodore's, and he had enthusiastic letters from Arthur Ficke[35] and others, the sales were disappointing.

However, he was already working on his fifth novel,[36] to be set at Bradford Abbas in Dorset, and eventually to be called *Wolf Solent*. He had begun this book in February, on a lecture tour which took him from Chicago down to New Orleans,[37] while Phyllis remained in New York, trying to make progress with a novel of her own. Llewelyn and Alyse also had novels in mind: Llewelyn was intending to work on the manuscript of the African book which he had abandoned five years previously, and Alyse was writing *She Shall Have Music*, an autobiographical work in which the heroine, 'Delicate and intractable . . . built her own inner life apart'.[38]

Llewelyn and Alyse appeared to be happily established at Montoma, but as the winter began to pass away, and the first signs of spring appeared, Llewelyn was filled with an overwhelming desire to return to England. It would mean Alyse giving up *The Dial*, which in normal circumstances would have made her extremely unhappy. But there were other considerations: Llewelyn had been corresponding with Betty, and towards the end of January had actually asked Alyse if Betty could stay with them at their farmhouse. Alyse recognised how passionately Betty loved her husband; but, true to her principles, she resolved 'to show no feeling. It is, after all,' she wrote in her diary, 'what I have been expecting.'[39] In fact Llewelyn was more in love with Alyse than with Betty, whom he advised to find happiness by marrying another artist. But even when Betty had taken his advice, and become Mrs Reginald Marsh, she still attempted to become pregnant by Llewelyn, hoping that a child could be passed off as her new husband's,[40] and Alyse felt quite certain that Betty would take Llewelyn away from her if she could.[41] By the beginning of March, therefore, Alyse had agreed to leave America.

Llewelyn immediately wrote to Gertrude asking her to look for a suitable home for him and Alyse somewhere near East Chaldon, and to take good care of his share of the family furniture: 'I want *everything* I can lay hands on', he wrote firmly. 'Let nothing be lost. I am going to set up house now. . . . My PURSE IS DEEP. -. . . We'll all be as snug as rabbits in a moment.' Llewelyn also wrote to John, telling him: 'It's awful to me the idea of leaving you, my darling Jack, but you know what it is – *I want to go home*.' John might have been annoyed: he had been looking forward to seeing a good deal of Llewelyn, and had only recently been persuaded by his brother to commit himself to a further five years of lecturing in America, but he replied in the most friendly manner, saying that Llewelyn's decision could not affect the love between them. Later in the month the two brothers saw each other briefly in New York,[42] and at the beginning of April, having read the manuscript copy of *Skin for Skin*, John wrote again to compliment Llewelyn on its excellence.[43]

Llewelyn and Alyse left Montoma to spend the last two weeks of April in New York, where Llewelyn corrected the proofs of *Skin for Skin* and renewed his friendship with Arthur Ficke and Edna St Vincent Millay. Then at the beginning of May they visited Alyse's family at Norwalk, where Llewelyn wrote a letter to his sister-in-law containing a warm tribute to Alyse:

I cannot tell you how happy I always am with [her]. I had no
idea that I should ever find anyone I could love and honour so
much. . . . She is certainly the most distinguished woman I
have ever met in my wanderings . . . I can hardly imagine
anyone who seems to me further removed from the vulgarity of
the everyday world.

The following week he and Alyse sailed for England.

CHAPTER TWELVE

1925–1928

John lectures in America and works on Wolf Solent, *1925–8* • *in England, summer 1926* • *publishes* The Secret of Self-Development, *1926.*
Theodore in England, publishes Mockery Gap, *1925,* Innocent Birds, *1926,* Mr. Weston's Good Wine, *1927.*
Llewelyn in England, 1925–7 • *quarrel with John, spring 1926* • *affair with Betty Marsh, summer 1926;* • *publishes* The Verdict of Bridlegoose, *1926,* Henry Hudson, *1927* • *to America for* New York Herald Tribune, *and begins his romance with Gamel Woolsey, 1927–8.*

Early on the morning of Friday, 15 May 1925, as they neared the end of their voyage across the Atlantic, Llewelyn and Alyse woke and looked out of their port-hole 'at a half moon and a smooth sea and the green fields of Devonshire with the gorse on them white in the moonlight'. Disembarking at Plymouth, they continued their journey by train, and had soon arrived in Sherborne, where they were met at the station by Littleton and Mabel. To Littleton's embarrassment, Llewelyn greeted him with unreserved affection: 'I gave him a kiss', Llewelyn told John with some amusement, 'but he looked rather nervously at the ticket collector.' Later in the morning, after a brief visit to Littleton and Mabel's 'Quarry House', all four of them motored down to East Chaldon where they lunched at Beth-Car with Theodore and Violet.

That afternoon, Alyse met still more members of her husband's family for the first time when she and Llewelyn walked over the Downs to have tea with Katie and Gertrude at Chydyok. Here they stayed for several days, until they were ready to move into a home of their own. Before leaving America, Llewelyn had arranged to rent one of the coastguard cottages about a mile and a half from Chydyok on the cliffs above the White Nose; and on Monday he and Alyse 'went up to see our little cottage which looked very well – sunshine and larks and sparkling gorze, and sea and adders in the gorze, and a meadow-pippin's nest which we found with eggs hard "set".' They were quite alone: the other cottages were empty during the holiday season, and even then Llewelyn and Alyse actually slept a hundred yards away in Llewelyn's old revolving shelter, which was pegged into the ground 'in a little dale sheltered from the wind but about twenty yards from the edge of the Headland.'

They spent their mornings writing. Llewelyn had soon produced a number of reviews, essays and articles, including the atheistical *A Butterfly Secret*, and then, encouraged both by the success of *Skin for Skin* in the United States, and by John's suggestion that he should write a series of sequels,[1] Llewelyn began a further slim volume of auto-biography describing his five years in America. He intended to call it *The American Jungle*, and it was actually advertised under that name by the New York firm of Harcourt Brace, who had done so well with *Skin for Skin*, but John persuaded him to change it to *The Verdict of Bridlegoose*,[2] a less offensive title which recalled the down-to-earth wit of Judge Bridlegoose in Rabelais's *Gargantua and Pantagruel*. By the end of 1925, when Llewelyn had completed *The Verdict of Bridlegoose*, Alyse had finished her autobiographical novel, *She Shall Have Laughter*. This too was taken by Harcourt Brace, and both works were scheduled for publication the following spring.

In the afternoons, Llewelyn and Alyse went out walking or visiting. Their arrival affected family relationships in a way that was not always welcomed: on one occasion, for example, Gertrude was most offended when she arrived at Beth-Car for tea to find that Llewelyn, an unin-vited guest, was already there and had usurped her place.[3] Theodore was always especially pleased to see Llewelyn, and wrote to John praising their brother for remaining cheerful even when suffering from rheumatic trouble, and Alyse for looking after her husband so well.[4] Alyse herself noted:[5]

> There was no-one whose company Llewelyn relished more than
> that of Theodore when in one of his good moods . . . they used
> to walk through the lanes and meadows of East Chaldon
> conversing on matters close to the earth and far removed from it
> – one defending life, the other praising death. Then they would
> return to Beth-Car for one of . . . Violet's famous teas.

Llewelyn and Alyse were soon drawn into the circle of Theodore's literary friends, and when David Garnett's first novel, *The Sailor's Return* was published that year, Llewelyn reviewed it favourably. Visitors to East Chaldon that summer also included some of Llewelyn's oldest friends: Louis Wilkinson arrived with his second wife, Nan; and Bernie O'Neill and his family came down from London for a short holiday. 'We went to Weymouth one day,' Llewelyn wrote to John,

> and came upon Theodore and Violet and Francis seated on corporation chairs in the most crowded part of the front. Theodore looked very benevolent, though he was eager to dissociate himself from 'our party,' saying to Bernie when he met him in St Mary's 'there go your friends', and a little later told Alyse that he had just seen 'her husband.'

Bertie stayed with them for a fortnight in August, and the following month Llewelyn and Alyse went travelling themselves: they motored all the way over to Suffolk to see Hamilton Rivers Pollock, one of Llewelyn's friends from Cambridge days, and now a rather melancholy country squire; they revisited Cambridge with Pollock, and then went up to London for three days. When they returned to the White Nose, they heard the important news that Llewelyn's nephew, Littleton Alfred, had decided to take Holy Orders. Llewelyn tried to accept this philosophically, but was unable to do so: 'Think of this Golden youth of whom I am so proud becoming a mincing Priest', he burst out; '. . . I would rather he had been a beggar on the road to Framlingham.' John felt that it was vital to allow his son to take his own decisions; but he begged him to be prepared to withdraw from the priesthood if he discovered that it did not suit him,[6] and, on hearing how Llewelyn felt, he wrote asking his brother to be as sympathetic as possible, and saying that it would be a tragedy for Littleton Alfred to be denied Llewelyn's friendship at this important stage in his life.[7]

John himself had been uncomfortably isolated for much of the summer. In June Phyllis had gone to stay with her parents, while he himself set out on a lecture-tour of the mid-west;[8] and despite interesting experiences, such as meeting a number of Red Indians,[9] the excitement of travelling had lost much of its savour; and not long after this John told Llewelyn that he would willingly give up lecturing and settle down to lead a peaceful domestic life with Phyllis.[10] At least he had been able to join her at Joplin for a few days at the beginning of

August,[11] and a week or so later they were together again in New York.[12]

John had no more lectures until the beginning of October, so for six weeks they were able to lead the life of their choice. They wrote, went to a nearby restaurant to enjoy simple Italian meals washed down by glasses of ale,[13] and had long agreeable discussions about literature and philosophy.[14] Where Frances Wilkinson had constantly disagreed with John, poured scorn on ideas which were important to him but alien to her, and tried to change him for what she considered to be the better, Phyllis Playter was prepared to accept him for the man that he was.[15] She was also a constructive critic of his work,[16] and with her love and support he was making excellent progress on *Wolf Solent*,[17] the novel which at long last was to establish his reputation.

Like his earlier books, *Wolf Solent* contains strongly autobiographical elements: it had been set in Bradford Abbas because it was there, in his mother's womb, that Powys believed he must have experienced the first stirrings of consciousness;[18] moreover, many of its pages were written in hotel rooms on lonely lecture tours, and Powys described how:

> travelling through all the states of the United States except two, I became more and more intensely aware of the hills and valleys, the trees and various flowers, the lanes and hedges and ponds and ditches, of the country round Sherborne . . .
> *Wolf Solent* is a book of Nostalgia, written in a foreign country with the pen of a traveller and the ink-blood of his home.

Wolf Solent himself is a 35-year-old teacher who has lost his job in London after making a wild outburst against every aspect of modern civilisation, and who is now returning to his native Dorset to be the secretary of Squire Urquhart of King's Barton. Because of disturbing incidents in his early life, Wolf has taken refuge in a mythological world of his own invention; and at the heart of his 'mythology' there is a struggle between good and evil, seen in the black and white terms of conventional morality. Dorset appears to him to be a beautiful but strange and sometimes extremely sinister world: his predecessor as Urquhart's secretary has died in what appear to have been mysterious circumstances, and there are dark hints of homosexuality, lesbianism, incest and even necrophilia. When Wolf Solent discovers that Urquhart wishes him to help with the writing of a history about the darker side of Dorsetshire life, he believes that he has become directly involved in the contest between good and evil which means so much to him.

Wolf is also strongly attracted to Gerda Torp, a beautiful eighteen-year-old who whistles like a blackbird and seems to be in touch with powerful natural forces: by marrying her, by finding work as a teacher, and by eventually throwing up his connection with Urquhart's 'evil' book, he appears to have chosen the right path. But the marriage is a disaster: Wolf and Gerda have little in common, and Wolf realises that he has confused love with 'a mixture of lust and romance'. The woman whom he should have married is Christie Malakite, a fragile-looking girl in her early twenties whose figure, as one might have guessed, is 'slight', 'sexless', and 'androgynous'. There is between Wolf and Christie, as perhaps there was between John Cowper Powys and Phyllis Playter,

> no barrier of any sort . . . to talk to Christie was like talking to himself or thinking aloud. . . . The slender little figure before him, with those thin hands and those touchingly thin legs, drew into her personality, at that moment, every secret of girlhood that had ever troubled him. . . . He felt as if he could share with this elfin creature a thousand feelings that no other person could possibly understand – share with her all those profoundly physical sensations – and yet mystical, too – that made up the real undercurrent of his whole life.

In the novel, Wolf Solent recognises that any closer involvement with Christie or with Squire Urquhart would destroy his 'mythology', as he would no longer be able to see himself as 'taking the side of Good against Evil in the great occult struggle'. When his desire for Christie and his need for money push him towards such involvements, his last minute efforts to preserve his integrity only succeed in alienating both Gerda and Christie; and with his 'mythology' destroyed he sinks into the state of suicidal despair which has haunted him ever since looking into the face of a despairing man on the steps of Waterloo Station. When Wolf becomes aware that he himself has the very same homosexual tendencies which he has previously thought of as 'evil' when he noted them in others, the process of disintegration is almost complete, and he begins to walk towards Lenty Pond, knowing that before long he may drown himself, and morbidly fascinated by the probable instrument of his destruction.

After all this, the novel ends in a surprisingly minor key. Powys was aware 'that with a terrific gathering up of my forces, the general situation of the book . . . might have been made to mount up . . . and finally break in a great crashing catastrophic . . . finale'; but he explained in a letter to one of his family that he took his characters 'so seriously that I can't bring myself to sacrifice them in cold blood to an artistic finale, unless I were heroic enough to be prepared . . . for such a suicide or for such a tragic end myself.'[19] So Wolf Solent comes to see that traditional morality is too simple, but there is certainly more than the visible universe, which is 'merely a filmy, phantasmal screen separating him from an indrawn reality'; and Wolf has a kind of vision, in which a field of golden buttercups becomes 'a symbol, a mystery, an initiation . . . the magnetic heart of the world rendered visible!' He has not yet learned how to synthesise this new vision with what was best in his former 'mythology', but he has learned that he can still get pleasure out of life, that his soul is capable of 'stoical resolution', and that, if things go wrong, one is *allowed to forget*': for the future, his talisman will be the words: '*Endure or escape.*'

Towards the end of 1925, John Cowper Powys was at his happiest when writing *Wolf Solent*, because then he could forget that lectures were hard to come by, and money was short.[20] He had made a little money from an article which he had written about himself, Theodore, Bertie and Llewelyn under the title *Four Brothers: a family confession*; and from the publication of *The Art of Happiness*. But the American edition of *Ducdame*, in John's view inadequately advertised by Doubleday, brought in far less than he had hoped;[21] while royalties on the English edition were swallowed up by the financial incompetence and eventual bankruptcy of the publisher Grant Richards. At the beginning of December, John reckoned that his income had fallen by almost two-thirds, and although what remained would have been enough for Phyllis and himself, the duty of maintaining Margaret at Burpham meant that the situation had become serious. Phyllis might have added to their income by proof-reading, but John wanted her energies to be directed exclusively towards *Wolf Solent*, and, in the meantime, he was touchingly grateful to Phyllis's father for giving him a new lining for his old overcoat.[22]

However, later in the month John was considerably cheered by receiving a typescript copy of Llewelyn's *The Verdict of Bridlegoose*, sent to him for corrections: he thought it excellent. To bring it luck, he called out his brother's name several times in the street as he walked past a financial institution, and a little later, when a lady looked at him oddly, he affirmed his belief in the book's success by giving several of the loud cries with which he sometimes terrified people who had irritated him![23]

Theodore had done little writing since the autumn, when *Mockery Gap* was published, and *Mr. Weston's Good Wine* completed. Writing *Mr. Weston's Good Wine* had occupied him for most of 1925. It is the book for which he is best known, and on completing it, Theodore wrote a letter to John telling him that he now had enough work to present to the Almighty on Judgment Day, and if the Almighty disliked it, that simply could not be helped![24]

Mr. Weston's Good Wine[25] is a daring and strikingly original allegory in which mankind, principally represented by the inhabitants of the village of Folly Down, is visited by God and an Archangel – who appear as Mr Weston, a travelling salesman in wine, and his assistant Michael. When they arrive at Folly Down in their Ford car, a thoroughly sinister atmosphere develops. Time stops, and Mr Weston mysteriously knows all about the villagers without previously having met them. He is capable of great severity: the Lion of Destruction is unleashed to frighten two sinners into repentance, and to cause the death of Mrs Vosper, an evil woman whose chief delight lies in bringing about the ruin of young girls.

The general question of whether God or man is to blame for the evil and suffering in the world is frequently asked in *Mr. Weston's Good Wine*, but never satisfactorily answered. The truth appears to be that God is sadly aware not only that the Bible has some imperfections, but that the whole of His creation is imperfect. Mr Weston's pity for mankind leads him to do everything he can to ease man's burden; and this he achieves by selling him some of his 'good wine'. But since drinking wine blurs our sense of reality – the title of the novel is taken from a scene in Jane Austen's *Emma* in which Mr Elton makes violent and ridiculous love to the heroine under the influence of too much of Mr Weston's good wine – illusion rather than illumination is seen to be at the centre of God's plans for us.

The first of Mr Weston's wines is the light wine of love, which enables Luke Bird to be happy with the beautiful Jenny Bunce, but love is not a permanent solution to the troubles of life, as we see when we meet the Rev. Nicholas Grobe. The tragic death of his wife has led him to abandon his faith, and he is a most unhappy man. When he is supplied with the light wine, his heart warms, and he begins to believe that he will one day rejoin his dead wife in Paradise; but he knows that when the effects of the wine wear off, he will once again be miserable.

He prefers to die happily in his illusions, and so he becomes a willing customer for the second of Mr Weston's wines, the dark wine of death.

T. F. Powys retained strong prejudices against women throughout his life, and sometimes openly asserted that their place was in the kitchen; but when he was writing *Mr. Weston's Good Wine* his anti-feminism had been modified a little by his friendship with Sylvia Townsend Warner: Mr Weston admits that he may have been unfair to women in the Bible, and that 'it may still be possible to teach some of the younger [women] the right and proper use of our good wine.' However, despite this modification in Powys's views, the way in which he treats sexual relations in this novel often suggest the fantasies of a man who is fundamentally alarmed by women's sexuality. Nicholas Grobe's daughter, for example, enjoys her wedding night with the Archangel Michael, but is then struck by lightning; and Nicholas Grobe's wife is recalled just as oddly: child-like and sexually provocative, she aroused in her husband feelings of fear and guilt as well as of desire: '"My dear," he would say nervously, "perhaps I might – would you think me too horrible? – but you know how lovely you are." . . . and she would draw his head nearer to her heated lips, and force his hands to fondle her.'

After completing *Mr. Weston's Good Wine*, Theodore remained in a state of creative exhaustion for almost a year, during which *Innocent Birds* was published and he tried to sell a few short stories, but otherwise he did little but worry about his younger son's future.[26] There was still pleasure to be gained from the company of his friends: towards the end of November 1925 he visited Thomas Hardy at Dorchester, and he also met Llewelyn several times each week.[27] The brothers spent Christmas together at Theodore's house, and saw in the New Year at Llewelyn's cottage.

The peaceful routine of life at the White Nose was disturbed when on 17 January 1926 Alyse received a telegram from Vienna. For some time the eccentric behaviour of her former lover, Scofield Thayer of *The Dial* had given rise to comment,[28] and now he had become seriously deranged: though not too deranged to beg for help.[29] Llewelyn and Alyse travelled to Vienna at an hour's notice, and found Thayer:

> with 'a persecution complex' amounting to madness. . . . The
> whimsies that filled his mind were infinite beginning with
> imagining dictaphones down to the very beggars in the streets
> who mock him with their blind eyes.

In their efforts to help Thayer, the Powyses twice consulted Freud. Llewelyn later described the great psycho-analyst as having 'the demeanour of a sagacious country doctor', but he spoke excellent English, and they were:

> vastly taken with him. He treated us with great courtesy. He was, I think, very much taken with Alyse as though her firm dorian glances restored him in a world of crooked complexes.

Sadly, Thayer proved to be past hope of rescue, but before Llewelyn and Alyse left Vienna, they were able to admire the Breughels in the picture galleries, and make an excursion up the Danube to the little village of Durnstein. On their way back to Dorset, they spent several days in Paris, where they visited Balzac's grave; and in London, where Llewelyn accepted an invitation to write a biography of Henry Hudson, as one of the 'Golden Hind' lives of the great explorers. When they reached the White Nose, they found two more telegrams from the unfortunate Thayer, and Llewelyn wrote to John:

> At the very moment I open a telegram from Austria signed Richard Clayfoot while Alyse has one signed Tolstoy and this after *suspecting* me in Vienna and duping us into thinking he would return in our company to the White Nose only to have luggage and valet thrown out on the platform at the last moment.

Some weeks after receiving Llewelyn's letter, John and Phyllis were visited by Thayer's partner Dr Watson, who brought the welcome news that portions of Alyse's forthcoming book were to be published in *The Dial* – which had also accepted a long article by John on Theodore Dreiser. The poet E. E. Cummings was now living in the room next to theirs, and although occasionally an unpleasant smell of ether drifted from his doorway, John and Phyllis were pleased to have a neighbour upon whose discretion they could rely: for they still did not like it to be generally known that they were living together, and occasionally the unexpected arrival of an acquaintance would compel Phyllis to pretend that she was just leaving, after which she had to wander the streets for an hour or two until the coast was clear. Other embarrassments at this time included an angry letter from a young lady who had fallen in love with John, and was furious when she discovered that her feelings were not reciprocated; and the troublesome visits of Patrick, an Irish parasite who had been befriended by Alyse and then by Llewelyn, and whose demands severely tested even John's almost limitless capacity to propitiate.[30]

However, the Lee Keedick Bureau had been finding John plenty of lectures, and although he had been making little progress with *Wolf Solent*, his tract on *The Secret of Self-Development* was published; and he had earned enough money to be able to spend the summer in England, while Phyllis visited her parents. He intended to be kind to his wife, and to see as much as possible of his son, and he wrote to Llewelyn begging him not to be angry if he went straight to Burpham, and remained there until the start of the term at Littleton Alfred's theological college at Oxford.[31]

But when John arrived at Bankside at the beginning of April, he found an angry letter from Llewelyn waiting for him: 'You need have no fear', Llewelyn wrote, 'of my expecting or demanding any of your time over here. . . . I have hardened my heart and expect nothing of you.' It seemed ridiculous to Llewelyn that John should devote so much time to a wife he disliked, and he was also annoyed with him for making some unflattering remarks about Alyse's novel.[32] John replied that he felt a duty to be kind to his wife, that his affection for Llewelyn was no less because he wished to see his son, and that he would have invited Llewelyn and Alyse to Sussex but for the probability that Llewelyn and Margaret would have dreadful quarrels. This letter reassured Llewelyn, who answered: 'I meant that I hardened my heart not towards you, but towards the prospect of seeing little of you. . . . You know how I cherish you and how I love you.'

Soon after Littleton Alfred's return to Oxford, John and Margaret went there to see him. Unfortunately their visit coincided with the start of the famous General Strike of May 1926: the trains stopped running, and they were marooned in Oxford for about a week longer than they had intended. They might have been able to leave earlier than they did, but John had a great deal of sympathy for the strikers, and felt that renting an automobile would make him a black-leg,[33] while Margaret rather tiresomely only felt able to travel by train, and to travel when normal service had been resumed.[34] Eventually, leaving her to wait for such service, John set out on his own, and travelled in a guard's van down to Dorset, where he was met at Wool Station by Theodore.

Theodore was feeling particularly gloomy after being cheated out of some interest on one of his investments;[35] and when John asked him: '"I hope you haven't minded being [here] so long?"', he replied very grimly: '"I might just as well wait here as anywhere else. The end is bound to come if we wait long enough.'''![36] After staying with Theodore, John went on to visit Llewelyn, who was working hard on his life of Hudson, but who found time to join John and Alyse on many walks and excursions. On one memorable occasion, the three of them arranged to be driven over to Montacute: Llewelyn's imagination had transformed the village into an enchanted world, and he radiated happiness as he led his companions through the scenes of his well-remembered childhood.

At the beginning of June, John continued his round of visits: he travelled on to Cambridge, where he saw Harry Lyon, and stayed at Corpus with Margaret's brother-in-law Ted Pearce, who was now the Master;[37] then he went to Suffolk to see Frances Wilkinson,[38] who was in financial difficulties, and in very bad health: later in the year she was operated on for cancer in the London Hospital, and had both breasts removed;[39] he also went to London to stay with Bertie;[40] he visited Arnold Bennett;[41] and he went to see his old friend William John Williams: there had been alarming reports about 'The Catholic's health;[42] but he had now given up drinking spirits, and had bizarre stories to tell about a sojourn in Spain, where he had mingled with military men and prostitutes, only returning to England after an unpleasant incident which had left him with one of his fingers missing![43]

By the end of the month, this whirlwind of visits was over, and John had sailed back across the Atlantic to New York. From there he wrote enthusiastically about *The Verdict of Bridlegoose*, whose publication appeared to have confirmed Llewelyn's reputation as an author.[44]

Llewelyn was delighted by this good news. In America, he was now the most highly acclaimed of the Powys brothers, while in England he must often have felt overshadowed by Theodore, who was visited each summer by a stream of admirers. Llewelyn had to be content with the attentions of Reginald and Betty Marsh, who took a cottage in a nearby hamlet for a few weeks in June. Betty was still passionately in love with Llewelyn, and to Alyse's knowledge she slept with him, still hoping to bear his child and pass it off as her husband's.[45] Her attempts to become pregnant were once again unsuccessful, and Reginald Marsh, not knowing what was going on behind his back, was touched by Llewelyn's kindness, and wrote admiringly about his 'measured majestic sentences', adding: 'In his whole being there was something god-like, dramatic.' Certainly, Llewelyn at the age of forty-two was a strikingly handsome man whose experiences had taught him much. In the face of illness and under the constant threat of death, he had developed a pagan and poetic philosophy of such wholesomeness and sanity that he was almost 'god-like' in his influence on some of those around him. Just as much of an evangelist as his father, he was glad to find that young people, in particular, turned to him for help during major crises in their lives; and to such a one he wrote at about this time:

> All deep natures have suffered from despondency and
> especially at your age when the crudeness and futility of life
> become suddenly more apparent than its hidden secrets. But life
> is deep and mysterious and beautiful as well as cruel and
> shallow and hideous, and in the few years each one of us has to
> live it is worth our while to cultivate our taste and discrimination
> and imagination for our own happiness alone. . . . Read
> everything you can lay hands on. Escape through your troubles,
> through your own *lonely* mind.

Llewelyn had been revising *Skin for Skin* for an English edition to be published by Jonathan Cape; and during much of October and November he and Alyse were up in London, where he had more research to do for his life of Hudson. They also met Arnold Bennett, who very much liked Alyse; and they saw a good deal of Louis Wilkinson, and invited him to the White Nose for Christmas. He accepted the invitation, and came down with his wife, but although the visit was, generally speaking, a success, Louis was so disgusted with the sweet wines which Llewelyn offered him to drink that he gave him written instructions about how to educate his palate. Llewelyn's taste must have been atrocious, for after carrying out one of the suggested procedures, he wrote to Louis: 'I could detect no difference in the Burgundy after it had been opened one day, two days, three days, seven days – all exactly the same, the same, the same!'

His brother John's taste was, apparently, equally bad, 'vitiated by bootlegger's whisky in prohibitionist America', but at this time John could hardly have afforded even such modest luxuries as an occasional bottle of wine at the dinner table. Since his return to America at the end of June 1926, there had been few if any lectures arranged for him; and when in October Llewelyn offered to help, John replied that if he did receive a large sum of money he would feel compelled to send it on to his wife Margaret, which was not at all what Llewelyn had in mind. Although Phyllis's own health was fragile, and her weight had fallen to around seven and a half stone, she determined to apply for a job as a waitress. Very much to John's relief, she was rejected on interview. He regarded her practical help and moral support as far more important than a little more income;[46] and the lack of lectures was enabling him to make good progress on *Wolf Solent*.[47] Luckily, on the very day of Phyllis's unsuccessful interview, John received a down-payment for three lectures; and the immediate financial crisis was brought to an end.[48]

There followed a period of relative calm, but early in 1927, John was separated from Phyllis for a while, and was lonely and miserable as a result. Towards the end of January, Phyllis's 86-year-old father, Franklin Playter, became very ill, and she was summoned to Kansas.[49] By the time her father began to recover, John was about to set out on a lecture tour, so Phyllis remained with her parents until the end of March.[50]

In contrast, Llewelyn and Alyse were leading a happy and romantic life at the White Nose. Alyse's diary entry for 26 January gives the flavour of the time:

> To Dorchester, whipped and buffeted by the wind, the heifers
> scampering down the hills like buffaloes, Llewelyn so tender, so
> charming – always so aware of each other, so natural, one to the
> other. The walk back by sunset, the sky a pale yellow with
> purple floating clouds, then the sea and our solitary home, and
> tea before the fire and always the wind.

And the following month Llewelyn wrote: 'We are very happy together and I often wonder at the good chance that led me, wayward and wanton, to the discovery of her personality, so cool and deep and sensitive and rare.' He was in better health than usual, both the frequency of his headaches and the severity of pain in his kidney being reduced by a plain diet that Alyse had devised for him; and he was hard at work on the final chapters of his *Henry Hudson*, which was completed in the second week of March, and published in England later in the year. As a biography, it is rather disappointing. The background to Hudson's voyages is described in tiresome detail; there is little or no attempt to describe Hudson's character or to analyse his motives; and there are a number of largely irrelevant asides about the fate of the whales and other matters. But Llewelyn was an excellent story-teller: the voyages of the *Hopewell*, the *Half Moon* and the *Discovery* among the mists and ice of uncharted northern seas are vividly described; and John Cowper Powys, who read the manuscript in April, told Llewelyn that he and Phyllis felt as though they had travelled with Hudson on his perilous ventures.[51]

In May, John heard that Llewelyn had been asked to travel to New York at the end of the year as a visiting critic for the *New York Herald Tribune* books section. The invitation had come from Irita van Doren herself; and since Llewelyn had no immediate plans besides writing for the papers, and it would be a great opportunity for him and Alyse to see John, Phyllis and their American friends, he had gladly accepted. There was other news of greater importance to John: Littleton Alfred had passed his final theological examinations; and Margaret, deciding to live with her son, had determined to put a tenant in at Bankside: so at last the years of having to support her in that grand establishment were over.[52]

The remainder of the summer and the early autumn passed by uneventfully enough for John and Theodore: John worked on *Wolf Solent*, lectured in New Mexico,[53] and in September entertained Bertie's beautiful daughter Isobel, who had come to New York for an extended holiday,[54] while Theodore wrote short stories, and awaited the November publication of *Mr. Weston's Good Wine*; but Llewelyn's summer was clouded by the accidental death of an American friend who came to stay with them, and who fell to his death from the cliffs not far from the White Nose.

On 1 November, Llewelyn and Alyse set sail from England in the *Leviathan*, but it was not an agreeable voyage: Llewelyn felt unwell, remaining in his cabin except at meal-times; and when he first arrived in New York he was coughing up traces of blood.[55] Fortunately, a short period of rest revived him; and John, who had been away lecturing, returned to New York in December to find him leading a very busy life. He was working for the *Herald Tribune*, attending various literary functions – at one Rotary Club luncheon, John told him not to mind having his name pinned to his lapel, saying: 'just imagine you are a ram at Dorchester market'; and entertaining at Patchin Place such celebrities as Ford Madox Ford, and '"Big Chief White Horse Eagle," the surviving king of all the Red Indians'.

Phyllis Playter had found rooms for Llewelyn and Alyse just across the way at 5, Patchin Place; with the result that Llewelyn had also begun to see a great deal of Gamel Woolsey, a 28-year-old woman with 'dark hair' and 'calm grey eyes'[56] who had been living there since the previous year, and who was described by John as 'the little poetess'. The daughter of a cotton planter from South Carolina, Gamel was both strikingly attractive and keenly intellectual, and Phyllis had taken to her and begun inviting her round.[57] At the age of sixteen, Gamel had been reading both Latin and French with ease, and was:

> already absorbed in poetry. Then came a series of misfortunes that developed a morbid tendency in her mind and character which was reflected in a prevailing melancholy of expression, lending her dark beauty an appealing pathos that proved moving to both sexes. First, she became a victim of tuberculosis and spent a year or more in a sanatorium. Then she became attached to a young homosexual who committed suicide. Driven to leave home by her mother's alcoholism, she went to New York with the intention of becoming an actress, but instead of going on the stage she became the mistress of a handsome young journalist.

When Gamel became pregnant, the journalist dutifully married her, but she made a mockery of his decision by having an abortion, on the grounds of her tubercular history. After this she became 'afraid . . . of living with him'; and they were now either separated or about to separate.

Llewelyn Powys and Gamel Woolsey had much in common, including their tubercular sufferings and their love of literature, and Llewelyn found in Gamel's poems romantic themes and images of a kind which very much appealed to him. In an original and surprisingly neglected voice, she could write movingly of Roland, of Charlemagne, and other heroes; or, in a more private poem, describe how:[58]

> In the house of the moon where I was born
> They fed a silver unicorn
> On golden flowers of the sun . . .

Gamel shared Llewelyn's sense of wonder but lacked his strength of will, and, as she seems to have recognised, this made her in some respects curiously passive and child-like:[59]

> In all but face I am the same
> The child who watched the tulips grow,
> The child to whom they gave this name.
>
> I wandered through the changing world,
> Seasons passed by me, summer bloomed
> Upon bare boughs, dry leaves were furled.

It was not I who made the change;
Somehow the landscape darker grew
The clouds became a mountain range.

. . .

Yet through each shift and change the same;
Though the mind changing changes all;
I am the child they gave this name.

This vulnerability was not the whole story by any means: in 'Immutable' she writes:[60]

You twist and shape me to your will,
I bend to all the moods that pass;
But I am proud and secret still,
And but more truly what I was.

There was something in her spirit mysterious, hidden, and inviolable, that gave her wistful beauty an especially haunting quality. At the same time, she was physically warm and uninhibited, writing about sexual pleasures:[61]

Feeling this passion in the flesh
Is beautiful beyond the dust,
And men have toiled long lives apart
For things not half so fair as lust.

The combination in a woman of spiritual mystery and physical warmth has always been devastating; and for Llewelyn there was the added attraction that Gamel was fifteen years younger than his wife. One day, when he and Alyse were preparing to set off for Norwalk to visit her parents, he found himself grumbling 'that it was a long time since he had made love to a girl and that he was growing old, [and Alyse] replied in pique, "Why don't you stay in New York then and see the poetess?"' Once these words had been uttered, Alyse was too proud to recall them. Llewelyn remained behind in Patchin Place, and, during the two nights that Alyse was away, he and Gamel became lovers.

1 Montacute Vicarage, home of the Powys family from 1885–1918

2 The Powys brothers at Montacute Vicarage: from left to right, John Cowper, Littleton, Theodore, Bertie, Llewelyn, and Will

3 Dr Bernard Price O'Neill, the close friend of both John and Theodore, with Violet and Theodore Powys

4 Thomas Hardy, who encouraged John Cowper Powys and visited him at Montacute

5 Llewelyn Powys, taken while he was at Cambridge

6 Louis Wilkinson, Llewelyn's friend at Cambridge, who became an important member of the Powys circle

7 The Sherborne Preparatory School: taken when Littleton Powys [2nd adult from left] was Headmaster, and was being assisted by Llewelyn Powys [4th adult from left]

8 Family and friends at Montacute, c. 1911: Back row from left to right: Dorothy Powys, her husband A. R. [Bertie] Powys, John Cowper Powys, the Rev. Charles Francis Powys, Louis Wilkinson, and Will Powys

Middle row, from left to right: Marian Powys, Margaret [Mrs J. C.] Powys, Mary Cowper Powys, Frances Wilkinson [nee Gregg], Katie Powys, and Gertrude Powys

Seated on the ground, from left to right: Littleton Alfred Powys [JCP's son], Isobel Powys [ARP's daughter] and Llewelyn Powys

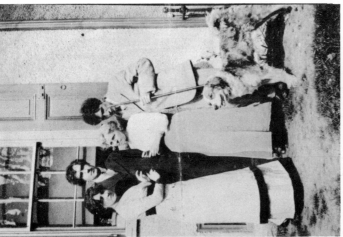

11 Louis Wilkinson standing between his wife Frances and his mother-in-law. John Cowper Powys [seen holding walking-stick] for a short time was to take responsibility for the two women, not to mention Frances's two children, their Italian nurse, and the dog!

10 Isadora Duncan, who once filled John's room with flowers, and asked him to come away with her

9 Frances Wilkinson, who as Frances Gregg married Louis Wilkinson, but was adored by John Cowper Powys

13 Sylvia Townsend Warner, who gave important encouragement and practical help to Theodore Powys

12 Edna St Vincent Millay, the poet and devoted friend of Llewelyn Powys

16 Llewelyn Powys in 1924 during his ill-fated expedition to the Rockies

15 Phyllis Playter wearing Breton national dress on a visit to France in 1923

14 Phyllis Playter standing by some hollyhocks. She lived with John Cowper Powys for forty years, and gave him the calm companionship which enabled him to produce his masterpieces

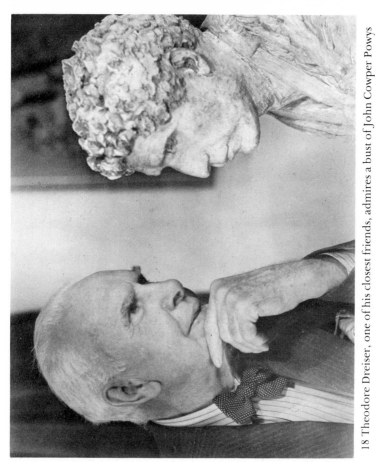

18 Theodore Dreiser, one of his closest friends, admires a bust of John Cowper Powys

17 Alyse Gregory on the day of her wedding to Llewelyn Powys in October 1924

19 Gertrude Powys in 1926, when she was living with Katie Powys at Chydyok

20 A portrait of Gamel Woolsey, the American poet with whom Llewelyn Powys fell so passionately in love

21 Gamel Woolsey and Llewelyn Powys

22 Phudd Bottom, John Cowper Powys's and Phyllis Playter's home in Up-state New York

23 Theodore Powys with David Garnett, who did so much to promote his work, and David's son Richard

24 John Cowper Powys's wife Margaret with their son Littleton Alfred

25 John Cowper Powys

26 Llewelyn Powys at Chydyok, not long before leaving for Switzerland for the last time. In his left hand he holds an 'Ankh', the Egyptian symbol of enduring life and generative energy which he adopted as his own, often incorporating it into the design of his books

27 Theodore Francis Powys

28 Alyse Gregory as an older woman

29 Littleton Powys and his wife Mabel at the Quarry House, Sherborne

30 John Cowper Powys in bardic costume in North Wales

CHAPTER THIRTEEN

1928–1930

John lectures in America, 1928–9 • in England, and visits
Glastonbury, summer 1929 • ill in America, and moves to upstate
New York with Phyllis • publishes The Art of Forgetting the
Unpleasant, *1928,* Wolf Solent, *1929,* The Meaning of Culture,
1929, In Defence of Sensuality, *1930,* Debate! Is Modern
Marriage a Failure, *1930,* The Owl The Duck and – Miss Rowe!
Miss Rowe! *1930 • begins* A Glastonbury Romance, *1930.*
Theodore publishes The House with the Echo, *1928,* Fables, *1929,*
Kindness in a Corner, *1930.*
Llewelyn with Alyse to England, April 1928 • to Holland, Betty
Marsh, and news of Gamel's pregnancy, July 1928 • writes Apples
Be Ripe *in France, August 1928 • on to Palestine, news of Gamel's*
miscarriage, and illness at Jerusalem, October–November
1928 • writes The Cradle of God *in Capri, winter 1928–9 • to*
Dorset with Alyse and Gamel, summer 1929 • Gamel's abortion,
August 1929 • Gerald Brenan in love with Gamel, Llewelyn and
Alyse to America, 1930 • Llewelyn publishes The Cradle of God,
1929, The Pathetic Fallacy, *1930,* Apples Be Ripe, *1930.*
Death of Tom Jones and 'The Catholic' 1929.
Alyse publishes King Log and Lady Lea, *1929 • Katie publishes*
The Blackthorn Winter, *1930.*

When Alyse Gregory returned to New York there was no outward
change in her relationship with her husband. Llewelyn Powys returned to the room which they shared, assuring her that he regarded
her with just as much love and affection as before, and he saw little of
Gamel Woolsey, who was enduring a long and final series of visits
from her own husband. Together, Llewelyn and Alyse spent a few
days in the country as the guests of the Van Wyck Brookses, and

together, they planned an exciting expedition overseas: Llewelyn had secured a contract with Harcourt Brace for a book about the Holy Land, and it was intended that he and Alyse should leave America before Easter, 1928, and travel first to England and then to Palestine.

But, inevitably, there was an inward change. Llewelyn's brief affair with Gamel had frightened Alyse much more than the attentions paid to him by Betty Marsh, and while Llewelyn was spending a few days with Edna St Vincent Millay and her wealthy husband Eugen Boissevain in upstate New York, Alyse confided in her diary:

> It is just as it used to be – the sound of the city coming up in waves and dying away – the sirens, a flute playing, the soft spring air coming in at the windows, even the chairs are the same, yet I am another person. . . . It is fear that eats at my heart, my fear that at some time in our lives there will come a moment when his glance will have lost the ardour that is the fount of all my joy.

Alyse was now working on her second novel, *King Log and Lady Lea*, and she was planning to dedicate it to Llewelyn with the lines:[1]

> Those pretty wrongs that liberty commits
> When I am sometimes absent from thy heart,
> Thy beauty and thy years full well befits
> For still temptation follows where thou art.

In this way, she told Llewelyn that she accepted his 'pretty wrongs', while secretly she adjured herself to 'Let no betrayal of his trust in me ever divide us.' Psychologists might plausibly suggest that she subconsciously connived at Llewelyn's infidelity, from the same profoundly masochistic streak which had led her into so many disastrous relationships in the past, but the only certain thing is that Alyse suffered dreadfully for her feminist convictions. She was almost unnaturally ready to see the virtues of a rival, and in Gamel's case the situation was complicated by the fact that Alyse was attracted to her almost as strongly as was Llewelyn. In her *King Log and Lady Lea*, a highly autobiographical novel which deals with the difficulties for a married woman of maintaining 'her inner life', Alyse imagines that the heroine, after hinting that her husband should have an affair, then deserts him and lives with the other woman herself in a covertly lesbian relationship.[2]

Towards the end of April, Llewelyn and Alyse sailed from New

York. Alyse's health gave cause for some concern during the voyage to Plymouth, but she was consoled by Llewelyn's reaction which showed that he still cared for her:

> I saw in my illness when that attack came upon me a look of frenzied anxiety in Llewelyn's eyes that drew me back to life, happy even in my illness in his love. To be together in England again, what happiness! And the ride on the train, the country like a vast flower garden . . .

When she was examined in an English hospital, there was no trace of anything seriously wrong,[3] and so they were able to settle down once again to a peaceful existence at the White Nose. Llewelyn resumed his walks with Theodore, who was able to tell him the East Chaldon news: his son Francis had been ill, but was now better and back at work; Katie had written a play, and a novel which Louis Wilkinson's second wife Nan was trying to get published;[4] and Theodore himself had been delighted when a specially bound limited edition of 600 copies of *Mr. Weston's Good Wine* had sold out, bringing him nearly £70 in royalties.[5] He had also been collecting some of his published short stories for a volume to appear later in 1928 under the title *The House with the Echo*.

After spending a peaceful month in Dorset, Alyse recovered; but Llewelyn had a 'slight temperature', and he wrote to Gamel telling her that the 'adventure to Palestine' would probably have to be postponed. In the meantime there were numerous visits to and from family and friends, the most notable occasion being when Mrs Hardy and John Middleton Murry came to tea, and talked about Thomas Hardy's death. In June Llewelyn received a letter from Gamel, saying that she was writing an autobiographical novel, and she enclosed a book into which she had written a selection of her poems. After reading through them, Llewelyn replied:

> They left me with the feeling of old gardens – sad, wistful, rain-drenched and belonging to a far-off time. They are proud and yet desolate and made me wish that I had the power of setting you safe and sound between two Unicorn stallions. . . .
> May I really keep this little book of poems, the central petal of so lovely and cherished a flower.

The following month, Llewelyn and Alyse decided that it was time to set out for Palestine, but they wished to avoid the hottest and unhealthiest weeks of the middle-eastern summer, so they planned to travel in easy stages, and spend some time together on the Continent. On 18 July they travelled up to London, where they stayed with Bertie for a few days, and on the 22nd they crossed over to Holland.

They had arranged to stay in Antwerp with Reginald Marsh, who showed them 'some fine Rubens pictures' in the art galleries while his wife Betty, who was still in love with Llewelyn, made plans to be alone with him so that she might still have a chance of bearing his child. However, Llewelyn received momentous news from across the Atlantic which made him feel little inclined for further extra-marital adventures: a letter arrived from Gamel Woolsey announcing that she was pregnant by him! He did not reply immediately, and said nothing to Alyse, but he refused to go away with Betty for 'a secret weekend', and told her all about Gamel and the child she was expecting. Not surprisingly, Betty felt rejected and betrayed, and from that moment she turned against Llewelyn, and made no more attempts to seduce him.[6] On 26 July Llewelyn and Alyse moved on to The Hague, and from there, still hiding the news of Gamel's pregnancy from Alyse, Llewelyn wrote to his mistress: 'My dear Gamel, Thank you for your last very exciting letter. I await the next mail from you with eager anxiety. You must be very careful of yourself. Your letter was a lovely one . . .'

From The Hague Llewelyn and Alyse went on expeditions to Delft and to Amsterdam, where Llewelyn achieved the principal aim of his visit to Holland: he saw for himself the relics of an event that he had described in his *Henry Hudson* biography, William Barents's 'wintering in Ice Haven at the end of the sixteenth century . . . [after which] . . . the rude furniture of his famous shelter had remained in its nest of atomic matter until its discovery practically in our own lifetime.' The relics included shoes, ropes, pots and pans, tallow candles, and a flute; and for Llewelyn, since an argument with his brother John two years previously, in which John had asserted that: 'The nature of things is wilder than most of us suspect. . . . There are whispers of veracity in every religion. . . . All is permeated with the essence of mind', these relics, and indeed any tangible evidence of man's historical past, now appeared to be an important practical proof of his common-sense view of the nature of existence. Men lived out their 'fragment of time' in the light; and then the darkness covered them, and they were gone. 'For all intents and purposes', declared Llewelyn, 'the world is what it appears to be.' With this belief strongly reinforced by what he had seen in Holland, Llewelyn's original purpose in travelling to Palestine, which had been simply to record his impressions as a traveller, gradually widened out into an attempt to reassess the truth of Christianity in the light of whatever tangible evidence could still be examined.

On 30 July, Llewelyn and Alyse set out for Paris, and from there, Llewelyn wrote to John asking him 'to look with a benevolent eye on the little poetess when you see her entering Patchin Place with her peculiar stooping gait half concealed under her goat skin coat.' After some time in Paris, the travellers moved on to Belley, an agreeable country town set between Lyons and the Swiss border in a hilly land of 'vineyards and . . . shady woods and meadows'. Here they were to 'spend six weeks quietly and inexpensively awaiting our Crusade'. Llewelyn had still said nothing about Gamel's pregnancy to Alyse, and she, very happy and very much in love, wrote in her diary on 20 August:

> Let me never be unaware of my fortune! A day is like one of our walks when one wayside scent follows another – now the walnut leaf, now the sap of freshly cut wood, now water mint, now hedge parsley – so one mood melts into the other, but always beside me, so that I can turn and look at his beautiful head, is my love with his swift imagination, his heart open to my every word.

But it was probably that very evening that Llewelyn broke the news: for the next day's entry strikes a tortured note:

> My walk to the village down the white road; the shutters tightly closed from the glaring sun. When I walk alone I am freed of this desperate preoccupation. I nurture Llewelyn's confidence and he robs me little by little of mine – he, who is so charming to me, so good, so blind. I think of Gamel and my failure to have Llewelyn's child. How can any man see into this kind of pain? I try to build up my courage for the future. I can say nothing to Llewelyn because he thinks my fear a disloyalty to him, and this struggle between life and death goes on in my heart. If I were ten years younger, then Llewelyn and I would be equal, but we are of the same age. But I must engrave into my heart *never for one moment to be forgotten* not in any way to limit his freedom. She is a brave girl.

'The little poetess' remained in Patchin Place. For most of the summer she had seen little of Phyllis and John: Phyllis had spent two or three months with her parents while John, sustained by a flask of bootlegger's whiskey, had been lecturing in the south-west; but by mid-August they were both back in Patchin Place, and one evening early in September Gamel prepared a meal for them.[7] Their only news of interest was that John had visited in New Mexico a distant cousin, Warwick Powys, who had memorised long passages from Llewelyn's books, and felt as proud as Charles Powys had done about being descended from ancient Welsh princes![8] Gamel's evident suffering made a considerable impression on them, and John wrote to Llewelyn the following day, in reply to his letter from Paris: 'I doubt if I should ever be myself what you might call *thick* with the poetess, but we do both admire her and shall do our best, you may depend on it, under the circumstances to be especially sympathetic.'

During the six or seven weeks that Llewelyn and Alyse stayed at Belley there were few local distractions: though one September morning they came across that remarkable American writer, 'Miss Gertrude Stein scratching her head like a school boy in the middle of Belley Square'; and Llewelyn was able to complete the first draft of his autobiographical novel, *Apples Be Ripe*.[9] The title is taken from a bawdy country rhyme:

> Apples be ripe
> And nuts be brown,
> Petticoats up
> And trowzers down.

This is highly appropriate because, after some introductory chapters in which Llewelyn vividly recalls his early life – the one significant difference being that Chris Holbech, his hero, is an only child – the novel develops into a sustained attack on middle-class morality. Departing from strict autobiography, Powys describes Holbech marrying the conventional Adela. Horrified to discover that Adela thinks sex is 'nasty', Holbech is forced to ask himself 'What did society and modern education do to girls to subvert their natures at this rate?' Adela, a 'disciplined, lady-like woman', who would like to 'impose her tiresome second-rate values upon everyone living' looks very much like Llewelyn's idea of his sister-in-law Margaret; and when Chris finally runs away from Adela, he is made to pass by what is clearly John Cowper Powys's home in Burpham; looking in through the window he sees John getting ready for a journey, and asks himself 'Was that figure . . . also preparing for an escape?' A further scene of some autobiographical interest is included: Holbech dies, mourned by several pretty women; and Powys describes one of them being very jealous when she learns that another woman is expecting the dead man's child.

Towards the end of September, Llewelyn and Alyse left Belley for Venice. It was sixteen years since Llewelyn had stayed in Venice with John, Louis and Frances; and he wrote to John, 'I remembered it all so well – the well heads where Frances sat, the streets where we bought red currants . . . St Mark's with the very same red-coated priests mumbling their benedictions. . . . It was as if I had died and come alive again.'[10]

From Venice they sailed down the Adriatic and through the Gulf of Corinth until they harboured at Piraeus, the port of Athens. Warned to remain aboard, because of a raging fever which had killed more than one hundred thousand during the last few months, they nevertheless went by train to Athens, and made their way to the Acropolis where, as Llewelyn recorded:

> We now went up to the Parthenon. Because of the pestilence in
> the city we were absolutely alone on the hill. It was
> extraordinary! It was as though the Greeks had only recently
> gone, had only yesterday stolen away, leaving their white
> temples to the butterflies and to the little lych-owl of Pallas
> Athene. The mute inscriptions on the fallen fragments of marble
> were like moving lips.

From Athens they took ship for the Holy Land. While they travelled along the coast of Asia Minor Llewelyn was:

> reading the Bible in preparation for my book on Palestine. Lying
> in my bunk at night, and upon the deck during the day, I dug
> deep into the body of the noble volume. The breathing living
> poetry of its pages bore me along as upon eagle's wings.

When they reached Haifa in Palestine, Llewelyn and Alyse went ashore; and that night, after being driven to an Austrian hospice on Mount Carmel, they went out and walked upon the mountain. Llewelyn, with the story of Elijah's contest against the priests of Baal firmly in his mind, realised:

> With suppressed emotion . . . that I was actually present in the
> body on ground where the Prophet had trod. All the romance

and violence, all the poetry of the ancient story, drifted into my consciousness as though I were in actual fact close upon the footsteps of the obsessed holy man, with his cloak and his staff and his wallet of parched barley.

Llewelyn was not in perfect health; but several days after their arrival in the Holy Land, he and Alyse set out very early in the morning for a long and tiring journey to the monastery which marked the site of Elijah's sacrifice. From the roof of the monastery, they could look out over 'Mount Tabor and Gilboa and the hills about Nazareth and Little Hermon', and see 'the plain of Jezreel and the brown dusty sun-absorbing hills of Samaria'; but the heat was intense. On coming down from the roof Llewelyn felt ill and giddy, and had to rest for three hours in one of the rooms of the monastery. In the cool of the evening they returned to the hospice, but Llewelyn was now running a high fever, and was forced to stay in bed for ten days. Alyse, worried that the sickness might be consumptive, or that Llewelyn had caught the Athenian fever, wrote in her diary:

> a deep misgiving fills my heart. The chirping of the birds and a flute playing despairing Arabic notes come through the window and I look over on Llewelyn's flushed face, and long for deliverance from this crushing anxiety. If he is spared this time never let me squander a second.

Before long, she too was lying ill, but the fever was not a serious one, and as soon as they were able to travel, they moved on to Nazareth and to Lake Galilee. Then at last they came to Jerusalem where one evening at sunset they walked through the Jaffa gate, and Llewelyn:

> was aware of a trembling down my spine and through the marrow of my thigh-bones. Even to me this high reward had been granted. In swift procession the pageantry of the city's past swept through my brain . . . I heard its street cries come down the centuries – the canticles of Solomon, the lamentations of Jeremiah, the voice of the priest and the voice of the prisoner.

When they collected their mail in Jerusalem, they received distressing news from America: Gamel Woolsey had suffered a miscarriage after being 'involved in an accident to a taxi'. John Cowper Powys was very upset by Gamel's unhappiness over losing Llewelyn's child, and wrote to his brother on 28 October asking him: 'Do give, O great master, the wench *another chance*. Console her with some such words, I beg you, for it was a bitter blow to her.' No doubt Llewelyn wrote a consoling letter to Gamel; but evidently John felt that something more definite was needed to restore Gamel's spirits, and he sent Llewelyn a further letter asking that she should be allowed to live close to him and Alyse when they finally returned to the White Nose. Alyse unselfishly consented to this singular request from her brother-in-law,[11] but it was a painful decision, and she wrote in her journal:

> now once more the future closes before me and I am without light. But I must not let him see. . . . It is not so much that a child will separate us as that she, like B[etty Marsh], is so passionately in love with him, and that she is a generous, sensitive, deep-natured girl. . . . I must build up my life apart. . . . Let me see her as I know her to be – one who is lonely, poetic, generous, proud, one who craves love as all creatures must. Let me not by word or thought deprive her or Llewelyn.

She added philosophically: 'It is my scourge and my deliverance, the means by which I relinquish life and regain it – this seed of flowering insight.'

Despite the bad news about Gamel's miscarriage, Llewelyn had decided that he must continue collecting material for his book, and he and Alyse remained at Jerusalem for several weeks. They made excursions to Bethany and Hebron, and in Jerusalem itself they visited many places of interest, including the Wailing Wall and the Dome of the Rock; and on their second visit to the Church of the Holy Sepulchre, which Llewelyn described as 'a nesting-place for masquerading rogues', he 'entered the inner cavern . . . with Alyse striking matches, and lay down in the grave of Joseph of Arimathea which was shaped like an oven, and which I found fitted me well.' Several days later, after an exhausting walk round the walls of Jerusalem, Llewelyn was taken ill at the breakfast table, after which he 'lay in bed for many days and yet never spat white'. When he was well enough to travel, he and Alyse decided to leave Palestine at once: they spent the rest of the winter on the island of Capri, where by 22 November they were established in a room in Anacapri, 'a small room with flowered mats, a kettle simmering on a stove burning olive roots, vases regularly replenished with flowers picked on their walks, and the table piled high with books which they read and discussed together.'

Meanwhile John Cowper Powys had spent the early part of the autumn lecturing in Tennessee; but before leaving New York he had cut *Wolf Solent* to Schuster's satisfaction, replacing one section of three hundred pages with a new chapter of some seventy-five pages.[12] *Wolf Solent* was due to be published the following spring, and John, pleased with his achievement, told Gertrude that he would now like to abandon the lecturing life, and become a full-time author;[13] but although he and Phyllis frequently discussed the idea,[14] he knew that he would have to wait till his present agreement with Keedick ran out before coming to a final decision.[15] In the meantime, there was mixed news from England: Margaret was living happily at Folkestone with Littleton Alfred,[16] and Frances Wilkinson had made a good recovery from her cancer operation,[17] but in December a despairing letter arrived from his old friend Tom Jones: because of the recession, his firm had collapsed, and he was living in great poverty and hoping to hear of an opening in the United States for an experienced accountant.[18] Later, John was to ask himself:

> Why didn't I wire him the means to sail at once? If I hadn't the cash I could surely have borrowed it. He must in his time have spent double the cost of such a voyage on me. No! I put down plenty of sympathetic words – little black marks on white paper signed 'Jack' – but I did not wire him his passage money.

The sequel was a sad one. After spending Christmas in London with the O'Neills, Tom remarked to Louis Wilkinson 'that he had had enough of his life on the terms offered him then by destiny', and not long afterwards he was found dead. In 1933 John was to write that 'With a single exception' – presumably the death of his mother – 'the death of Tom Jones affected me more than any death I have as yet known.'

During the eight weeks that Llewelyn and Alyse remained in Anacapri, Llewelyn wrote *The Cradle of God*[19] in which, with occasional references to his own experiences in the Holy Land, he traced the origins of Christianity, and, as he recounted Biblical stories, he showed how the idea of God had evolved in the Jewish mind from the primitive to the more advanced. However, Jesus was a great teacher and not God Himself; and even his 'illumination' had been 'perverted' into an 'absurd and exaggerated superstition' which was 'the product of the mind of St Paul'. Powys did not deny that the Bible contains spiritual truth, writing: 'The yearnings of the human heart have created a religious poetry, pure and primitive, and it would be unbecoming to mock at the expression of so much authentic feeling . . . the voice of deep-hidden longings, the child of tears.' But he believed that the church imposed false values on society, and he urged young people to 'Give no heed to these false teachers, but with emancipated hearts make your escape sure. Your heathen loyalties shall be deeper and truer than their loyalties. . . . Even now your hour passes. . . . Lift up your eyes and behold the sun.'

By January 1929, when Llewelyn and Alyse had moved to the Hotel Weber at Capri, the rough draft of *The Cradle of God* had been completed, and Alyse began to type it out. Beginning to doubt the value of what he had written, Llewelyn sent a copy to John, telling him: 'I am inclined to think I have failed in this book. I fear it is dull – a tedious paraphrase of the Book of Books.' But John replied that it was excellent, though he did suggest ways in which a few passages could be made more lively.[20] This seal of approval was of tremendous importance for Llewelyn, who wrote from Capri on 21 March: 'Your long letter seemed to me the most important that I had ever received and I was relieved. I had waited in suspense. It was like passing the Tripos. I really trembled before I broke the envelope. . . . It was a day of joy.' His pleasure was increased by John's news that Gamel had also read and generally approved of his work.[21]

John and Phyllis had been keeping a friendly eye on Gamel Woolsey, who by mid-December 1928 seemed to have completely recovered her spirits. They found her one evening happily choosing poems for publication in a magazine,[22] and they entertained her from time to time. In January 1929 they also entertained Edgar Lee Masters, and took Theodore Dreiser to hear one of John's lectures.[23] John was able to tell Dreiser that work on the proofs of his new book was at an advanced stage, and before long John heard the excellent news that when *Wolf Solent* was published in May, it would appear not only in America but in England, where it had been taken up by Jonathan Cape. This news did a good deal to relieve John of a number of worries: he was behind-hand with a work entitled *The Meaning of Culture*,[24] and there was some confusion about underpayment of taxes.[25] Shortly after receiving news of Tom Jones's death, he also heard that 'The Catholic' had died suddenly while on holiday in France.[26] However, John was sustained by the loving companionship of Phyllis Playter, and in one of his letters to Llewelyn, letters full of praise for the way in which Phyllis had brought him contentment, he was able to tell his brother that their dream of finding a quiet retreat in the country had suddenly been realised. Arthur Ficke had bought on their behalf a small house in upstate New York, not far from his own country property.[27]

In the second week of April, Llewelyn and Alyse began the journey home from Capri. Travelling via Naples, they visited the ruins of Pompeii, and the crater of Solfatera: the paintings at Pompeii made Llewelyn reflect that a life of 'unredeemed sensuality' was almost as depressing a spectacle as a life of strict obedience to the church; and at Solfatera, looking into the bubbling mass at the centre of the crater, Llewelyn felt that he had been allowed 'a glimpse into the fundamental substance of the earth . . . the accidental irrelevance of human life became plain.' But influenced by Gamel, to whom poetry was more important than the real world, he wrote: 'Shame and suffering and horror there are, but there is also a whispering in the wind. All is not lost. From the beginning to the end of life there is poetry.'

From Naples, they travelled to Rome, where Llewelyn visited the catacombs, 'eloquent of the incipient hours of [the Christian] fantasy'; and from Rome they went on to Florence and Paris before returning on 10 May 1929 to their Dorset cottage. They were 'excited and happy' to be back at the White Nose, though at first Llewelyn's pleasure was clouded a little when he discovered that their new neighbours were 'two girls . . . with a gramophone and cars'. However, as he told Rivers Pollock, he could not 'be as splenetic as I wish to be', for one of the girls was 'attractive. . . . She hangs up on the line little silken meshes for supporting her little breasts which are as pleasantly shaped as any William pears on your garden wall'! But Alyse herself, knowing that Gamel would shortly be arriving, was never free from anxiety and wrote in her diary: 'My mind looks forward with anguish to the future. Where can I fly, where hide, who confide in, where bury myself?' Llewelyn will never know this kind of suffering.'

Lodgings had been found for Gamel Woolsey in a small house about twelve minutes' walk from the White Nose. She arrived in mid-May, and her first meeting with Llewelyn and Alyse must have been a difficult one, for it was understood that she had come to England to have Llewelyn's child, and she must have expected Alyse to be hostile. But seeing her that first evening looking 'pale, tired and ill; at supper she ate nothing, and [there were] . . . tears in her eyes', Alyse felt not hostility, but 'protective pity'. Later, when Gamel had returned to her cottage, Llewelyn wondered aloud whether Gamel's visit was a mistake; but, as Alyse realised, 'His heart . . . [was] set on her having his baby', and 'during the following weeks he visited her daily, often he took Alyse to tea with her at her cottage rooms, more often she came to them for the day and Llewelyn escorted her home after supper.' Often Alyse would be

> preparing supper in the kitchen, while Gamel lay on a couch listening to Llewelyn's reading poetry. On her side Gamel devoted herself wholly to Llewelyn's interests: she mended his clothes, pasted photographs into his albums, searched for worked flints to give him, and read the books he chose for her.

Alyse found the situation surprisingly easy to deal with, and wrote later in the year: 'I accepted it all with resignation not untempered with happiness. So I thought of his spirit not dying, that eager spirit I loved, so I accepted her with tenderness too, this brave and beautiful girl who accepted *me* with such generosity.' John had returned to England that summer to visit his family, and he wrote to Llewelyn on 11 June telling him that Alyse would come to believe that he could love Gamel without loving her any less;[28] and indeed by 3 August Alyse was writing in her diary: 'The summer has been a happy one when I have seen all my fears as false, and I love and appreciate Gamel.'

However, in one respect, John Cowper Powys may have understood Gamel Woolsey better than either Llewelyn or Alyse. Llewelyn had fallen in love with Gamel's beauty, with her mystery, and with her intensely imaginative reaction to the world; but it became evident that her most singular characteristic was her ability to live in a strange world of dreams and myths, and this was always slightly alien to him. As her lover, he liked to share in the private world which she called 'middle earth'; poetry was an important part of this world, and she brought him to believe that true poetry is a distillation of philosophical wisdom; but the real world, even if regarded in a somewhat personal way, was always Llewelyn's province. Nor was 'middle earth' the natural home for Alyse, with her keen analytical mind, although she was drawn to her rival precisely because she recognised so clearly her virtues and her vulnerability. John, on the other hand, had begun to see in Gamel's poems and dreamy preoccupations the evidence of contact with a deeper reality, a reality to which ancient myths and legends could furnish important clues.

John spent the first week of his English summer living in lodgings near his wife and son at Folkestone, and working on *The Meaning of Culture* which had been promised to W. W. Norton for July. He was

also considering writing another novel: this was to be set at Glastonbury, and to be concerned in some way with the legend of the Holy
Grail; and John wrote to Llewelyn inquiring after Gamel's health, and
pointing out that it was she who knew more than any of them about
legends of this kind.[29]

In mid-June, John went up to London where Frances Wilkinson was
working as a journalist on the staff of the *News Chronicle*, in charge of a
special children's section to which she contributed occasional stories of
her own.[30] John's *Wolf Solent* had recently been published, and now he
found that Bertie – who had at last divorced his tiresome first wife, and
married the delightful Faith Oliver – was about to make his own
contribution to the family bookshelf, with the publication of two clear
and authoritative works on architecture: *The English House* and *Repair of
Ancient Buildings*.

There had also been a considerable revival in Theodore's literary
energies. Since the publication of *The House with the Echo* the previous
year, he had completed nineteen new short stories which appeared in
print in the autumn of 1929 as *Fables*. These *Fables*[31] are an uneven
collection of tales, by turns ironic, whimsical, macabre and philosophical, in which unpalatable truths about human experience are
pointed by the comments of animals, or inanimate objects, or even
abstract ideas. An old pan on a rubbish heap notices that even a good
wife may be 'sustained and comforted' after her husband's death 'by
the simple things that need not be done, now he is gone'; a grave-stone
argues that he is more important than 'Mr Thomas' – Theodore's
pseudonym for himself in 'Soliloquies of a Hermit' – because after Mr
Thomas has been buried for fifty years, he has been forgotten, and his
skull, which has worked its way to the surface, will be crushed and
used to manure spring onions, while the grave-stone endures; and in
'Darkness and Nathaniel' a former optimist comes to realise that he is:

> an old man, entirely forsaken and miserable, who had all his life
> cheated himself into believing that Light was his friend.
>
> As soon as Nathaniel Crow knew himself and knew what he
> was, a presence entered the room. Darkness was come . . .
>
> 'Dear Darkness, have you anything to give?'
>
> 'I give eternal longings,' replied Darkness, 'And after that true
> happiness.'
>
> 'And what is true happiness?' asked Nathaniel.
>
> 'Death,' replied Darkness.

Theodore had written more about the delights of death in a new novel, *Kindness in a Corner*,[32] the more serious pages of which contain a rustic paean in honour of burial, delivered by Truggin, the sexton of Tadnol, who tells a couple afraid to die:

> Thee do begin to die when thee be born. Life be only a death-bed, and our pulse do ring out our own passing bell, that do stop only when we be gone.
>
> Thee mid fancy, maybe, that the poor body of a man, ready for burial, be a sad sight to see, but 'tis then that 'is happiness do begin, and the winds do sing, and the smallest clod do whisper a word of gladness, when a man be taken out of sin into joy.

It is only in the corner of a grave, Powys declares, that God becomes pure kindness; but this message is delivered with great good humour in what is essentially a gentle rural comedy, with a plot worthy of Wodehouse. The title, *Kindness in a Corner* also refers to the life of the central character, the Rev. Silas Dottery, most affectionately portrayed, who sighs when beset by troubles: 'In this corner where I live . . . I have tried to be kind.'

Dottery, created very much in Theodore's own image, is unduly perturbed by the slightest domestic upheaval, and likes to spend his days reading, writing, walking and meditating. His troubles begin when he forgets the day on which the Bishop of Ashbourne is due to arrive at Tadnol to hold a Confirmation. Dottery can find only one candidate to present to him: seventeen-year-old Lottie Truggin, the sexton's grand-daughter, who has already been confirmed several times before! The bishop is too preoccupied with his own recent and disastrous marriage to the abominable Miss Pettifer to notice anything strange, but Canon Dibben, who has accompanied him to Tadnol, is very much aggrieved, and is soon listening with interest to his wife's fantastic suggestion that Mr Dottery 'keeps a girl . . . for his pleasure . . . In the study cupboard'. In one hilarious scene the Canon, announcing loudly that 'The hour has come to discover the whore of Tadnol', plunges into the cupboard: only to become hopelessly entangled in some fishing gear! Eventually Mr Dottery is restored to favour, with the agreeable prospect of marriage to Lottie Truggin, who favours older men, and especially clergymen, since their highly-developed sense of sin makes love-making more exciting.

Theodore's sister Katie, who had become increasingly independent of Gertrude, and was shortly to buy a cottage of her own at Sidmouth,[33] had also been busy writing: she had drawn on her farming experiences for 'Vagaries of the Milkmaid', a romantic novel about a nineteen-year-old girl with a passionate nature who runs away with a handsome but worthless gypsy, and by so doing nearly forfeits her chance of happiness with the village blacksmith. The plot is melodramatic, but the novel contains a lovingly observed portrait of country life as it was actually experienced early in the twentieth century. Littleton, who revised the manuscript, was highly impressed,[34] and so was David Garnett's father Edward, who recommended it to Jonathan Cape. When Cape turned it down, Katie enlisted the help of Nan Wilkinson, now her close friend, and she took it to Constable,[35] by whom it was accepted for publication in 1930 under a new title: *The Blackthorn Winter*.

John had come down from London to stay with Katie and Gertrude at Chydyok;[36] and he then spent the last week in June and the beginning of July 1929 with Llewelyn and Alyse at the White Nose. While he was there, Constable published Alyse Gregory's second novel, *King Log and Lady Lea*. Cape had accepted Llewelyn's *The Cradle of God* for publication in the autumn, although they rejected *Apples Be Ripe*, and meanwhile he had begun work on *The Pathetic Fallacy*, a kind of sequel to *The Cradle of God*, for it tells in some detail how, in the centuries after the crucifixion, the spiritual wisdom of Jesus came to be forgotten by a church which perverted his teachings and destroyed freedom of thought, inventing strange dogmas which all must believe or be eternally damned. Llewelyn looked forward to a time when such dogmatic accretions could be torn away from Christianity, writing:[37]

> The compassion inherent in it will then be absorbed in the culture of the race so that the poetry at the centre of this childish neurosis will for ever continue to play a part in man's spiritual evolution. A certain tenderness, rare and disinterested, will owe its origin to Jesus.

John was thinking a great deal about his own new work; and he persuaded Llewelyn, Alyse and Gamel to go with him for several days to Glastonbury. They were happy together, and imagined a perfect society in which the four of them were joined by Phyllis and Will Powys.[38] Alyse enjoyed more of Llewelyn's undivided attention than usual, for John and Gamel spent their time walking round Glastonbury and its ruins together,[39] while John learned all that Gamel could teach him about the legends which cluster thickly in and around that haunted town.

Then, after spending a fortnight with his wife and son, who were on holiday near their old home at Burpham,[40] John handed the completed manuscript of *The Meaning of Culture* to his publisher,[41] and went on to Norfolk where he had arranged to meet his brother Littleton, and they spent a week there, aged fifty-six and fifty-four, as 'sole lords' of their grandfather's Northwold Rectory. It was a nostalgic experience which made them, in John's words,

> unspeakably happy. . . . Over the gulf of . . . forty years the now white-headed Littleton and the now invalidish Johnny exchanged wordless signals with those two little boys whose whole life in those enchanting purlieus with those incomparable people had been one scarce broken paradise; and in a sense it was our farewell to those little boys! Back together they receded from this momentary re-incarnation, back hand-in-hand, little Johnny and little Littleton, till they faded into the branches of the cedar on the lawn, into the bushes by the fish-pond, into the poplars along the river, into the alders of Alder Dyke.

In the second week of August, John went on to Suffolk where Frances Wilkinson[42] and her children were holidaying at the Old Rectory, Badingham. Oliver, then fourteen, later recalled seeing something 'astounding and frightening and marvellous': his sister was lying ill in bed, and John went up to amuse her. Spying on them unobserved, Oliver watched as John played with some dolls:[43]

> The dolls were talking. I was certain, for a moment, that they were alive. . . . [They] had distinct characters, different voices, interrupting each other, overlapping each other's voices in their preoccupations. . . . Jack was *watching* . . . the voices came from his mouth, but they were not remotely like his . . . It was as though the dolls were making *him* speak. . . . I had never seen the inanimate given such life.

Later, before beginning his long return journey to America, John spent a night at Bertie's house in London,[44] where he was to witness part of a highly unpleasant episode in the lives of Gamel, Llewelyn and Alyse.

The summer of 1929 had been an enchanted time of increasing love and happiness for Gamel and Llewelyn, who later reminded his mistress of a midsummer night when:

> you told me you would love me forever until you were dead *and as I looked at you I knew I could never love anyone as I loved you*. I got some sacks out of the gardener's house and you were alarmed because I upset and broke a flower pot, and yet glad when we made a nest between the rows of sweet peas in the flower bed near the cedar tree. I can feel now your hair upon my face – and how bright your eyes were! I kissed your eyelids, I gave you butterfly kisses, I felt such strange longings . . .

In July, Gamel discovered that she was pregnant once again. Everything was happening as she and Llewelyn had hoped. Alyse was still content: on 3 August she wrote of her fears about losing Llewelyn being false; and on 13 August, Llewelyn's forty-fifth birthday, she bathed with him in the sea and wrote afterwards in her diary: 'He is so kind to me, so devoted.' But within a day or two came what Alyse described as 'the great shock'; Llewelyn and Alyse were having supper with Gamel when she announced to them both that she had consulted a doctor, who had advised an immediate abortion, 'as she had signs of consumption, with a temperature and night sweats. . . . As she spoke, she wept; "she always cried easily", said Alyse, who at that moment while Llewelyn held Gamel in his arms to comfort her felt for her "a tenderness very like his own".'

The three of them travelled up to London, where they stayed at Bertie's house in Hammersmith Terrace while arrangements were made for Gamel to enter a nursing home. John joined them on 18 August, for a Sunday which he afterwards described to Llewelyn as 'the most agitating I seem ever to have remembered passing with you'. Gamel was miserable enough, but Llewelyn appeared to be even more unhappy, while Alyse was dismayed to find that she could do nothing to comfort him: 'the child had to be sacrificed', she wrote, 'and I saw Llewelyn struck down as I had never seen him, far from me for the first time, out of the reach of my love, alone with his sorrow, unheedful of my love. We are sundered.'

Shortly afterwards, Gamel was admitted to the nursing home, and operated on. Llewelyn, thinking not only of the danger to Gamel, but of the certain death of their second unborn child, had tears streaming down his face as he waited for news. When he heard that it was all over, and that Gamel was in no danger, he immediately telegraphed John, who was on the SS *Olympic* bound for New York, and was roused from his sleep at dead of night to receive his brother's message.[45]

Gamel came back from the nursing home to Bertie's house where, as Alyse later recalled, she 'convalesced comfortably . . . in a ground-floor room with windows opening upon the river. As she gathered strength, she gained in beauty, with pathos in her large grey eyes and a pale transparency of complexion beneath her blue-black hair.' In mid-September they returned to Dorset, where Llewelyn and Alyse settled in again at the White Nose, and Gamel took rooms further away than before, at a cottage in East Chaldon.

Although this made it a longer walk for Llewelyn to reach her, Alyse saw it as 'a device to lure him into spending longer hours with her while avoiding the dangerous time of late evening when he had to be on his way home'. Alyse was bitterly unhappy, but dared not betray her feelings for fear of making Llewelyn ill, while at the same time she hated herself for having any hostile feelings towards Gamel, writing: 'I can see into her loneliness and uncertainty. So if I reject her I beat down myself . . .' But it was hard to see Gamel:

> making herself more and more essential to Llewelyn's life;
> learning his little ways that I know as I know my own pulse
> beats; immolating herself to please him, mending his clothes,
> correcting his manuscripts, studying the things that interest
> him; and as I see him never willing to let a day pass without
> seeing her I draw back from the future. We are inextricably
> bound together.

Alyse remained utterly devoted to Llewelyn, writing later in the year when Llewelyn looked pale and had gone to bed feeling faint, 'my whole world shakes and rocks, and nothing matters to me but his health, nothing, nothing –'. It was a wild winter of rainstorms and violent gales: windows were broken in their cottage, and on one occasion their shelter was completely overturned.[46] Llewelyn later wrote of it as a time when his love for Gamel had grown more ardent, and in a letter to her he recalled with pleasure:

> the passionate love we felt for instance in the barn they call
> Shotts that winter morning when we sheltered from the hail and
> still had half an hour before we had to be at White Nose. I
> remember so well the look of the walls green with dampness,
> and the look of the farm machines, such discreet and sober
> witnesses of our delight. It was like making love in a Cathedral,
> and although I made wild love, forgetting all modesty in my
> intentions, yet I think that half hour was blessed . . .

Alyse, seeing how her husband and his mistress drew together, began to think of suicide, and in mid-December wrote in her diary: 'If I could rid my mind of this haunting desire for death. . . . Only my death can free us – all three.'

Towards the end of the year Llewelyn himself became despondent: *The Cradle of God* was given an extremely hostile reception by the conservative British press, and sales were negligible. On New Year's Eve, as he sat in Gamel's cottage taking tea with her and Alyse, he commented gloomily on the loss of the baby and the failure of his book. He had now virtually completed *The Pathetic Fallacy*, which must also have seemed doomed to failure, for it was a much stronger and therefore more offensive attack on the established church than his previous work.

They had all spent Christmas with Theodore, whose household was also rather subdued. Only two months previously it had been suspected that Francis had tuberculosis. This suspicion was fortunately unfounded, but Francis still had to return to Beth-Car to live with his parents, because his nerves had been over-strained, and he needed a long period of peace and quiet to recover his health. He occupied himself by composing poetry,[47] and when Llewelyn and Alyse had tea at Beth-Car on 3 January Theodore announced that he himself had now completed his major work of the previous year, a novel with the strange title of *Unclay*, and that he would 'never write another book'.

Unclay[48] was indeed to be the last of T. F. Powys's novels, and in it he gives some explanation for this. Novel-writing, he says, is a generally thankless and ill-rewarded task because God's taste in literature is unsound, and 'He often prefers any fool or charlatan to a good writer.' Furthermore, a writer should know when to stop, despite God's foolishness in allowing authors 'to write on, when, for the sake of posterity, their lives, as well as their works, had much better have been shortened'. 'Unclay' itself is a word invented by Powys to describe how Death ends a man's life; and in the story Death himself visits the village of Dodder, armed with his scythe, and carrying a parchment with God's written orders to unclay both Joseph Bridle and the girl he loves, Susie Dawe. But Death has a bad memory, and on losing the parchment, which is found and hidden by Joseph, he forgets his orders; after seducing a number of the village women, he falls in love with Susie himself, and plans to die with her, leaving the rest of mankind to 'the horror of everlasting life'. As in *The Left Leg*, God appears as Tinker Jar, mending kettles and weeping for the trouble which He has caused in the world; and there is a rich gallery of other characters, including Joseph's aunt Sarah Bridle, who thinks she is a camel; Joseph's friend Mr Solly, who tries to protect himself from the dangers of love by thinking of all women as vegetables; Daisy Huddy the prostitute, who after listening to the book of Joshua hangs a scarlet thread from her window as a sign of her trade; an unworldly vicar; a sadistic farmer; and the master of the hunt, Lord Bullman, who wishes to revive the *droit de seigneur*! There are also descriptive passages of great beauty, strange philosophical speculations such as 'will the last enemy destroy Him too? Will God die?'; and two very dark scenes, in one of which a pond becomes 'a charnel-yard, full of cadavers, all visible', and in the other of which the drinkers in the village pub, drinking to Death, see each other as corpses:

> Those who in life were ugly were worse now. Out of the rotting eye of Mr Mere, a worm crawled, and yet the farmer drank each cup with renewed relish. Old Huddy raised his mug to his lips that were but blackened gums, and drank to Death, who eases every labourer's task, laying him down in a bed from whence no farm cock can hurry him at dawn. Landlord Titball, moving in a ghastly manner, had the appearance of a ten years' burial, that filled the cups dexterously with mouldy hands. Mr Dady looked even more horrible.

Unclay, the seventh of T. F. Powys's full length novels to be published, concerns itself with Death just as *Mr. Weston's Good Wine* concerns itself with God. Having dealt so fully with his principal preoccupations, Theodore found himself left with nothing further to say which could not be said most aptly in a short story. So by January 1930, at the age of fifty-four, he had completed his work as a novelist.[49] Looking over that work some fifty years after Theodore's last novel was published, *Mark Only*, ambitiously conceived and once highly praised, now appears to be the least successful novel, with its excesses deservedly parodied by Stella Gibbons in her *Cold Comfort Farm* – an attack on the writings of Powys as well as those of Mary Webb. The black humour of *Mr. Tasker's Gods*, the fantasy of *Mockery Gap*, and the poetical philosophy of *Innocent Birds* will all find their admirers. A little above these novels stands *Black Bryony*, with its highly personal inquiry into the workings of the feminine psyche. Finally, at the summit of Powys's achievement as a novelist, can be seen the remarkable trinity of *Mr. Weston's Good Wine, Unclay,* and the good-humoured *Kindness in a Corner.*

John Cowper Powys, at the more advanced age of fifty-seven, still had many novels to write: of the half-dozen which were later to be acknowledged as his major works he had only completed *Wolf Solent;* though he was already doing a good deal of reading for the novel which became famous as *A Glastonbury Romance.*[50] However, in the autumn of 1929, the unexpected success of his *The Meaning of Culture*[51] encouraged him to believe that it would be financially possible for him to abandon the lecture platform and to become a full-time author. In *The Meaning of Culture* Powys described how he felt that a cultured man should approach philosophy, literature, poetry, painting and religion, and he argued that 'Culture aims at producing a free spirit, in the deepest sense: free, that is to say, from the fanaticisms of religion, the fanaticisms of science, and from the fanaticisms of the mob.' He also suggested ways in which any individual might live with heightened awareness and happiness, choosing his own path, but tolerant of the paths others have chosen; profoundly sceptical, yet ready to believe in 'the boundless polytheism of the universe'. Before the end of 1929, *The Meaning of Culture* had been reprinted at least eleven times; and the following year it was taken up by Jonathan Cape for an English edition which was itself reprinted no fewer than six times.[52]

But when John made it clear to Lee Keedick that he wished to give up lecturing, he was referred to a clause in his contract by which Keedick was enabled to sign him up for a second term of five years. Seeing how enraged John was to learn of this, Keedick agreed that he would no longer take a fixed percentage of John's earnings as an author – a percentage which, as they both knew, he had done absolutely nothing to earn; but he remained adamant about keeping John on his books as a lecturer.[53] John was encouraged to resist Keedick by his principal New York publisher, Mr Schuster, who suggested the wording of the letters which John now wrote making it clear that he was prepared to take legal proceedings to recover his freedom.[54] Keedick eventually capitulated, but it was probably the deteriorating state of John's health rather than any legal argument which made him release John from his obligations.

John had been suffering from mild dyspepsia during his visit to England in the summer of 1929; and that autumn he 'began to realise that my gastric ulcers had moved from the pit of my stomach and pitched their tents in my "duodenum". From this new position they proceeded to carry on a series of virulent attacks on my peace and comfort.' Dr Thomas prescribed various palliatives,[55] but by February 1930 John was frequently in such pain that he could not even sit up when he wanted to write a letter; and he was suffering from disturbed nights, during which Phyllis nursed him with sympathy and milky drinks.[56] Dr Thomas finally sent him to the stomach-specialist Dr Einhorn, and by the beginning of March John had decided that he would somehow get through his lectures until the end of the month, and would then move with Phyllis to the house which Arthur Ficke had purchased for them in upstate New York.[57] In the meantime, while continuing to read for his Glastonbury novel, John also began a new philosophical work[58] to which he later gave the striking title *In Defence of Sensuality*.[59]

Declaring that 'Our Western civilisation at the present moment requires nothing so much as a John the Baptist of sensuousness, a Prophet of simple, primeval, innocent sensuality', John Cowper Powys attacked 'certain gregarious elements in our modern life . . . such as seem to me to be slowly assassinating all calm ecstatic happiness', and dreamed of 'a new "culture" ', which would be 'a return to a remote past whose magical secrets have been almost lost amid the vulgarities of civilisation.' Many of the ideas which he had already written about in *The Complex Vision*, such as the duality at the heart of the universe, make their reappearance in this highly discursive but much more readable work, but greater importance is ascribed to the philosopher, seen as 'the seer, the sorcerer, the medicine-man'; and Powys's occult speculations, usually so plausible and full of insight into the nature of the human condition, occasionally lapse into the merely fanciful, as when an ideal love is said to be 'the blending of two eternal dialogues in a five-fold eternal dialogue . . . an absolute living quincuncx – the number which, according to Sir Thomas Browne, is the most lucky of all . . . the cumulative voice of the *Number Five*.'

When *In Defence of Sensuality* was published later in 1930, it was one among many publications by the children of Charles and Mary Powys in what was a remarkable year even for that prolific family. Llewelyn's book on the history of Christianity appeared as *An Hour on Christianity* in America, and as *The Pathetic Fallacy* in England; while the English publisher Longman, who had been at Cambridge with Llewelyn and visited him twice at the White Nose, brought out his novel *Apples Be Ripe*. Constable published Katie's novel *The Blackthorn Winter,* and a selection of her passionate but unpolished poems appeared as *Drift-*

wood. Bertie's book, *The English Parish Church*, quickly established itself as a standard work. Chatto published Theodore's *Kindness in a Corner*, and also *The White Paternoster*, a collection of his short stories. In *Debate! Is Modern Marriage a Failure?* the text was published of a debate in 1929 between John Cowper Powys and Bertrand Russell. John argued that marriage was 'a success in that it is one of the surviving fortresses against the mechanisation, industrialisation, commercialisation of human life',[60] and he also painted a picture of the kind of fruitful relationship which he enjoyed with Miss Playter, though never with his own wife. John's other publication in 1930 was a limited edition of the short story: *The Owl The Duck and – Miss Rowe! Miss Rowe!* This fantasy about an old couple who are magically helped to die before the authorities can take them away to a Home, is dedicated to Phyllis Playter, and is also a loving farewell to their life together in the rooms at 4, Patchin Place, where the story is set.

At the beginning of April 1930, John and Phyllis left Patchin Place and New York City, and travelled by train to Philmont, a small town more than a hundred miles to the north, in the foothills of the Catskill mountains. From Philmont they were driven in a hired carriage to the little village of Harlemville, and then along a narrow winding lane which runs through wooded hills and cultivated valleys to the small and remote hamlet of 'Phudd': a few farms and cottages inhabited by the descendants of Dutch settlers, with nothing to mark its centre but a church and a graveyard where three 'dirt roads' met. Edna St Vincent Millay lived not many miles away near the village of Austerlitz with her husband Eugen Boissevain, and Arthur Ficke's home was also nearby.

The traditional timber-frame cottage which Ficke had purchased for John and Phyllis, and which they named 'Phudd Bottom', stood at the foot of a long, gently-sloping hillside. Separated by a low stone wall and a small front garden from one of the lanes,[61] it looked southward across a small stream and an orchard to open farmland and the encircling hills. The local farmers were friendly, and accepted John and Phyllis without question as man and wife, but the nearest shop was a mile away, and it was difficult to buy fresh vegetables.[62] They also had to contend with a garden that was badly overgrown, a cottage in need of decorating, and toilet facilities that were primitive in the extreme. They cleared a little of the garden themselves, and Phyllis planted vegetable seeds and later made jam from some of the fruit bushes. After three months they managed to find a man to help them with the decorating, with the heavier work in the garden, and with renovating the outside lavatory;[63] and since they were lucky enough to have electricity laid on, they bought a number of modern aids such as a fridge and a hoover which reduced the work-load considerably.[64] A mains supply of water could not have been hoped for, and did not exist, but they had an excellent well of water whose purity and sweet taste more than repaid the effort of pumping.[65]

Within a few weeks John Cowper Powys had begun work on *A Glastonbury Romance*, writing while lying down to ease the pain from his dyspepsia, as he had learned to do in Patchin Place, and before very long there were a number of visitors. First, in June, came his sister Marian, and his nephew Peter Powys Grey,[66] now a sensitive, intelligent child of eight; then, in July, Edgar Lee Masters stayed at a nearby farm with his wife and child,[67] and one memorable weekend the two men were visited by Arthur Ficke, Edna St Vincent Millay, and another young poet, Witter Bynner.[68] In August, John's cousin Warwick Powys stayed with him[69] while Phyllis was away in Kansas; and finally at the very end of that month, Llewelyn arrived at his brother's cottage alone and in a very unhappy state of mind.

Llewelyn had almost travelled to America eight months before this, in December 1929, when he was feeling despondent about the failure of *The Cradle of God*, but he and Alyse had decided to remain at the White Nose. Alyse's novel *King Log and Lady Lea* had also been a commercial failure, but by the beginning of 1930 she had completed her third book, *Hester Craddock*, in which Hester, the heroine, loses the handsome artist whom she loves to a more beautiful rival, and then, faced with a choice between 'nothingness or torment, torment or nothingness', commits suicide.[70] Alyse herself thought frequently about suicide. Determined not to stand in the way of Llewelyn's happiness, she positively encouraged him to see Gamel alone for lunches and walks, but on 2 February 1930, while her husband and his mistress were lunching together, she wrote despairingly:

> She is never out of his thoughts. . . . When all is well with her
> his heart turns to me but . . . our old true intimacy has
> vanished. If she has his child, his very bones will melt with love
> and gratitude . . . he thinks I should welcome this, and I do . . .
> but in my own thoughts it is always accompanied by the hope of
> my own death.

But there were happier times: on 18 February she wrote in her diary: 'Day after day has passed with no trouble between us. The cloud of madness has rolled over.' Two and a half months later Alyse once again:

> felt buried in a dim, disconsolate trouble. . . . When I saw them coming toward me, Gamel with her arm in his, leaning on him, then drawing away when she saw me, I got the full sense of how intimate they were together when I was not there, how happy she *would* be with him were I dead. Yet Llewelyn loves me dearly, this I know . . . he loves me, he trusts me he depends on me . . . all [my] love of life vanishes . . . I am thrown into a relationship that is unnatural to me.

Hating her present situation, Alyse was powerless to change it, for she could not bear the thought of life apart from Llewelyn, and feared that if she did commit suicide the effect on Llewelyn's health would be catastrophic. At the same time her feelings for Gamel were wildly ambivalent, veering between consuming jealousy, and the tender compassion of moments when she 'longed to reach her and to absolve myself for having ever thought any treachery toward her'.

Gamel too was now finding the situation difficult. She was still deeply attached to Llewelyn, but dared not tell him that after her experiences the previous year she no longer wished to risk having his child. The fact that Llewelyn was now set on this, gradually undermined his role as her protector; and she began to draw closer to Alyse who, whatever her private feelings, had always treated her so kindly and generously. In April Llewelyn first began to worry that Gamel was turning away from him, and his standing may have been further diminished in her eyes by his temporary lack of success as an author. He was now busily reading for what he described in a letter to John as 'my most important book': a summary of his philosophy, and a practical guide for living which he was to entitle *Impassioned Clay*. But when *The Pathetic Fallacy* was published in May it received a generally hostile press, and in one paper, the *Daily Express*, the review was headed 'James Douglas Battles with an Atheist.'

Gamel Woolsey was not strong enough to strike out on her own; it needed the arrival of Gerald Brenan to separate her from Llewelyn.

Brenan was no stranger to complex sexual relationships; he had come to Dorset armed with an introduction to Theodore Powys, but he was also escaping from his unrequited love for the painter Dora Carrington, who was bound up in a *ménage-à-trois* with her husband Ralph Partridge and her employer Lytton Strachey. When Brenan arrived in East Chaldon he was looking for a wife, and it was a little ironic that his choice should fall on a woman who was also entangled in what was effectively another *ménage-à-trois*. It was during his first exploration of the village that Gerald Brenan:[71]

> saw a young woman walking very slowly with her eyes on the ground and stooping every now and then to pick up a flint. I guessed that she must be searching for prehistoric implements. . . . Her face struck me by its freshness and beauty, but her slow, lethargic movements and sad, dreamy expression modified this youthful image.

The young woman was Gamel Woolsey. The very next day Brenan met her at Theodore's, and 'felt immediately drawn' to this beautiful poet from South Carolina. The day after their meeting they had tea together, and from then on met every day, often going out for drives in Gerald's car.

Gerald was soon introduced to Llewelyn and Alyse, but although it was clear to him that Llewelyn was in love with Gamel, he himself found Theodore's brother 'so worn and racked by age and sickness' that it never entered his head to suppose that Gamel had ever had any strong feelings for him. Gamel said nothing to him about her relationship with Llewelyn, and within three weeks of their meeting Gerald had proposed marriage to her. She still did not tell her suitor the whole truth: it would have been extremely embarrassing to have admitted that she had come to England with the declared aim of bearing Llewelyn Powys a child, but, with tears of relief streaming down her face, Gamel explained her present unhappy situation, and what she now thought of as the threat to her health posed by the desires of a man with whom she was no longer in love. She agreed to marry Brenan, and reassured him on the following day that she was not still in love with Llewelyn. Later he found that 'she had no respect for the truth and believed in telling people not what she herself thought or felt but what they wanted to believe.' However, before he drove off to London she promised to meet him there in a few days' time.[72]

For some while Alyse had seen that Llewelyn was 'anxious, because his happiness is so precariously balanced on Gamel's feeling for Mr Brenan. This has stirred his passion and rivalry.' On 30 July, Llewelyn was still telling Alyse that he loved her best, but the following day he talked of going away if he found that Gamel did care for Brenan, 'so that he will not have to endure the torment of seeing her love another.' This was hard enough for Alyse to bear, and she wrote in her diary: 'Let me be free. . . . Though I know his face has the beauty of apple orchards under the sun, let me flee with my living soul!' But then came still more painful revelations, and on 1 August she recorded in her diary – clinging to it, in her own words, 'as a dying man in some Arctic zone might note at each hour the closing down of his days' – that:

> I sit here numb and strange and calm, only a continual ache that never stops in my heart. The truth has been said. He loves Gamel, desires her continually, is in torture lest he lose her. . . . Last night I lay awake hour after hour going over each incident of my death, yet I live; and I must not desert him until he is sure of Gamel. He suffers there and I suffer here, and we cannot help each other.

On 5 or 6 August, with Mr Brenan safely in London, Gamel for the first time admitted to Llewelyn that she was very fond of her new admirer. Llewelyn at once told Alyse, who recalled him lamenting 'He has won her from me.' She unselfishly declared 'that he must choose between them, and if he wanted to go with Gamel, she would do everything to help them and would never reproach him.' In a state of extreme agitation, he left for a further talk with Gamel, while Alyse, scarcely knowing where to turn, walked to Chydyok to pour out her troubles to Gertrude. Gertrude did her best to be reassuring, promising her a permanent home at Chydyok if the worst came to the worst, but adding that she thought it most unlikely that Llewelyn would ever desert her.

When she walked back to their cottage at White Nose, Alyse was relieved to find Llewelyn apparently 'quite tranquil as he told her that Gamel had "practically" made up her mind to merry Gerald.' However, it seems more likely that he was in a state of shock, for: 'next morning in desperate passion Llewelyn declared that he must go away immediately. He hurried to the village to say goodbye to Gamel and the same day left for London; after packing their luggage, Alyse followed the next day.' They stayed for a short while with Bertie, while Llewelyn wrote anguished letters to Gamel, in one of which he begged her:

> Do say over and over that we will be happy again, that I will always be your own true love. Oh Gamel! I do love you so. Do take your temperature ever so carefully and make sure it is all

right . . . I love you so, I love you so. . . . Do make Mr Brenan promise that if he does win you he will never separate us, will allow us to be together. . . . I don't think that I have ever been so tormented. I can't bear to think of you, yet think of you all day long.

Your Lulu.

Then on 14 August Alyse and Llewelyn sailed for America, and when they arrived in New York she set out for her parents' house in Connecticut, while Llewelyn travelled to John's house at Phudd. The happiest part of Llewelyn's love affair with Gamel was over. Gamel later wrote a sonnet lamenting that things had ended badly between them, but adding:[73]

And yet we had all men have ever had!
'Happy for ever after' is no more
Than happy for a day when one is dead.
Life is fulfilled in love. Though it is gone,
The halcyon nested once on the blue hill,
The heart received all that the summer shone.

CHAPTER FOURTEEN

1930–1932

John in upstate New York with Phyllis, 1930–2 • *his unusual
behaviour* • *publishes* Dorothy M. Richardson, *1931*, A
Glastonbury Romance, *1932.*
*Theodore in England, hears of his son Dicky's death in Africa, October
1931* • *publishes* The White Paternoster, *1930*, Unclay, *1931*, The
Two Thieves, *1932.*
*Llewelyn unhappily in love with Gamel, lives with Alyse in upstate
New York, August 1930 to March 1931, and to West Indies
February–March 1931, then to England, March 1931* • *poor, moves
from the White Nose to Chydyok, October 1931* • *publishes* A
Pagan's Pilgrimage, *1931*, Impassioned Clay, *1931.*
Gamel 'marries' Gerald Brenan, 1931 • *Gamel in Dorset, 1931–2.*

Llewelyn had arrived at his brother's house in a thoroughly over-
wrought condition. Temporarily separated from Alyse as well as from
Gamel, he found it difficult to sleep, and wrote to his wife after one
particularly nervous night: 'my heart pounded like it did in the cell of
Mount Carmel and I seemed to be hot and cold and my thoughts
always going.' He talked of returning almost immediately to England,
and added: 'I feel so harassed, I am driven, and yet I love you so.' Soon
afterwards he wrote again to Alyse, telling her:

> It is a kind of madness. I think of [Gamel] and it seems madness
> to let anything separate us . . . when I so *yearn* for *her*. Then I go
> out into the night . . . and my knowledge of my way is suddenly
> destroyed and our love is with me again and I remember our
> years together and how you *are my nature* . . . then once in the
> lighted room will come back the old longing for Gamel and the

knowledge that if he . . . *marries* her . . . there will be no
possibility . . . of my having a child by her.

Llewelyn now wrote 'Pride',[1] a long poem about his love affair with
Gamel. In it he describes their first meeting, their first separation, and
their reunion in England, where he looked at her and 'Suddenly in the
sea mist was the face of a lost mother.' Then, describing the 'immortal
anguish' of their most recent parting, he tried to come to terms with his
misery by declaring: 'Then was I proud . . ./ I have taught her, I have
taught her *to trust the earth.*'

However, when Alyse joined Llewelyn at Phudd Bottom, she found
that he was not yet 'cured' of what she described in her diary as his
'summer madness', and she recorded sadly: 'I walk beside him less real
than the wind that stirs in the trees.' With characteristic generosity of
spirit she had written to Gamel Woolsey telling her of Llewelyn's
misery, and asking Gamel to send for him; and now her own unhappiness was made harder to bear when she contrasted it with the evident
love between John and Phyllis. At the beginning of September Alyse
and Llewelyn left Phudd, having accepted an invitation from Edna St
Vincent Millay and Eugen Boissevain to stay on their country estate.

From Phudd it is a drive of no more than a dozen miles to the hamlet
of Austerlitz, from where a road winds eastward through the Berkshire
mountains until it reaches a broad valley and the lands of Steepletop.
High up to the left of the road stands Steepletop itself, the imposing
mansion built by Boissevain when he created the new estate; and on
the right of the road, lower down but still with fine views across the
valley, is the older cottage which had been placed at the Powys's
disposal. Here Llewelyn's spirits began to revive. He had always
greatly admired the beautiful and vivacious Edna St Vincent Millay,
and in her husband Eugen Boissevain he found a kindred spirit,
described by Alyse as 'adventurous, quixotic . . . [facing] life as an
eagle faces its flight'. There were delightful walks to be enjoyed in the
surrounding forests; there was the good news that the American
edition of *Apples Be Ripe* had sold 4,000 copies since its publication in
the summer; and, above all, there was a letter from Gamel Woolsey
telling Llewelyn how much she still loved him: for 'No sooner had
Llewelyn left her than she yearned to have him back.' Gerald Brenan,
returning to Dorset to look for Gamel, who had failed to keep her
promise to join him in London, found her staying with Gertrude, and
'distressingly ill'. Gertrude, who was not generally given to metaphysical fancies, carefully explained to him:

that the love between Llewelyn and Gamel transcended all other loves, having something supernatural that could never be quenched. Its burden was more than Gamel's frail health could sustain, but Gerald's devotion had arrived opportunely to save her. Thus Gerald found himself rescuer rather than lover.

Llewelyn received Gamel's love-letter on Thursday, 11 September, and Alyse noted in her diary: 'now that he knows she loves him best he turns back to me.' At first he was too overjoyed to write, but on Saturday he sent two letters in reply. 'My darling Gamel,' he began the first, 'I carry your letter in my pocket. Whenever I am alone I read it and re-read it . . . I think of you all the time'; and in the second he added: 'Edna is very sweet to me. . . . She does all she can, yet not what I want. I want to be at your side in the lanes and roads and fields again. I want to be walking in silence near you. I want to be pulling you back to kiss you where we aren't seen.' On Sunday he wrote again recalling their love-making in Patchin Place, and saying: 'I wish I could have those hours again . . . and tell you proud stories of forgotten days and kneel before you in the firelight as if you were my mother. For you have been my mother, my maiden.' Because he was so happy after receiving Gamel's letter, he was not unduly alarmed when on the following Wednesday a letter arrived from her in which she made it clear that she was going to stay with Mr Brenan. The letter was to Alyse, but it was Llewelyn who replied, writing to Gamel as her 'father' and 'Master', commending her choice of Mr Brenan, and approving the match, while adding that she should allow nothing 'to lessen our love for each other', as it was 'a rare thing on earth'.

For a while there were no further letters from England, and Llewelyn became uncertain again, while Alyse wrote 'I exist in a perpetual pain lest I am depriving Llewelyn of his happiness. I think of her as he must be thinking of her and I have no other reality.' Boissevain tried to provide his guests with some distraction by driving them over to spend an evening with John and Phyllis, but they took their preoccupations with them. John became aware of this when he went for a walk with Llewelyn before supper. Llewelyn bathed in a deep pool, and then, when he was drying himself, he mentioned the possibility of John supplicating the nymph of the pool on his behalf. The conversation turned at once to Gamel Woolsey, and soon afterwards, as they were walking home, John suddenly caught hold of his brother: 'he held my arm', Llewelyn wrote to Gamel, and shouted at the top of his voice, so that the words echoed across the dusky ragged meadows and broken-down hedges, *Save Gamel and Lulu*. I was afraid of those wild strange sounds in the darkness and yet thrilled also to hear *our names* TOGETHER sounding through the night. It was the new moon he had seen for a single moment between the clouds. This he took as the most fortunate omen for us. Yet I could not be reassured

On 2 October another letter arrived from Gamel. Once again Llewelyn was in good spirits, and Alyse reaped the benefits of his increased happiness, writing in her diary on 6 October: 'when he returns to me as he has today . . . how my heart lifts! . . . Did he love another too? What did that matter! At that moment his heart was mine.' Gamel had taken Llewelyn's advice and sent a collection of her poems to Grant Richards, who was to publish them the following year as *Middle Earth*. In the melancholy title poem she described herself, like Llewelyn at that time, as existing in a state of constant uncertainty, for:[2]

> . . . there was nothing that I knew,
> Nothing that told me false from true.
> It is not heaven, it is not hell,
> This world between them where I dwell.
> With secret pain, with open mirth,
> I go my way on middle earth.

Llewelyn and Alyse spent the last three weeks of October in New York. Llewelyn found Patchin Place haunted by memories of his first meetings with Gamel; and these memories could not be dispelled either by Alyse or by the companionship of his old flame, 'Meg'. He wrote to Gamel: 'You have rid me of the lust for other girls. I am no longer careless, I cannot make love. Sitting among red sumach bushes I caught one swift glimpse of Meg's intimate body and yet I remained unmoved. . . . See how my old philosophy of life falls about me.' In another letter about Meg he wrote: 'I used to love her, but how differently, how differently from this love that has so much pain in it.'

A combination of emotional anguish and occasional bouts of high temperature had prevented Llewelyn from doing much serious work since his arrival in America, but at the beginning of November, back at Steepletop, he was able to continue writing *Impassioned Clay*,[3] the 'trumpet-call to youth, something of a Devil's Handbook' that he had begun in Dorset. In this long essay Llewelyn shows how short and precious our lives are, by setting them within the context not only of the vast and enduring astrological universe, but also of the huge geological tracts of time which lie in earth's past, and may lie in her future. Unfortunately, as man's consciousness developed, he learned what it was to be afraid: hence the darkness of religious superstition; and, despite the clear light of Greek civilisation, the western world has been very largely overshadowed by the morbid, Pauline version of Christianity. This imposes restraints which make happiness difficult to achieve. But, Llewelyn argues, happiness should be the aim of every action. Liberty must be tempered by compassion, and some deference must be paid to tradition and the law; but 'Our personal conduct should principally be regulated by the natural response of our being to each situation as it arises.' In particular, there must be no room for jealousy; and 'we must be indulgent in our attitudes to sex. This is the heart of the matter. All opponents of freedom are aware of this.'

The story of Llewelyn's own private life shows how difficult it is to live according to his philosophy without causing suffering to others. At the beginning of December, when *Impassioned Clay* had been completed, he received a stinging personal attack from Louis Wilkinson, who accused him of such a degree of subjectivity that even his friends:[4] 'can't depend on you for even a moment's effort if that effort is not agreeable. It's not "morality" that one demands – but the kind of objectivity that makes the satisfaction of other people a matter of interest.' However, Alyse believed in her husband's philosophy, and did her utmost not to show any signs of jealousy. She told Llewelyn that he and Gamel 'would never be parted', and wrote once again to Gamel 'saying that I want her and Llewelyn to go away together.' It was impossible not to suffer when 'always her letters come, and his go to her, and he will draw his out of his pocket like a shy, nervous schoolboy, and yet', Alyse wrote, 'I feel for him a kind of tender pity.' Llewelyn was not quite so selfish as Louis maintained: the happier he was, the more kindly he treated Alyse; and he was always ready to give his advice to anyone who was ill or unhappy and came to him for help.

Llewelyn and Alyse continued to see a good deal of John and Phyllis, and spent two nights at Phudd Bottom on 7 and 8 November. Llewelyn found his brother 'in very good spirits and his nerves in good case but he does not look so well.' John had given a short course of lectures in New York that autumn, and the travelling and lecturing had been bad for his stomach. He was happier and healthier living quietly with

Phyllis and working on *A Glastonbury Romance*, of which he had now completed some 550 manuscript pages.[5]

At the heart of *A Glastonbury Romance*[6] are the mediaeval legends about the Holy Grail, the cup from which Jesus Christ drank at the Last Supper, and which was then used by Joseph of Arimathea to receive His blood at the Cross. According to some accounts, Joseph had brought the Grail to Glastonbury, and there founded the earliest Christian Abbey. Glastonbury was further connected with Grail legends because of strong associations between Glastonbury and Arthurian Romance. Arthur's knights were supposed to have searched for the Holy Grail, and according to Gerald of Wales, writing in the twelfth century, Glastonbury, surrounded by low-lying countryside, was the Isle of Avalon to which Arthur had been carried after his death; indeed, he declared that the tombs of King Arthur and Queen Guinevere had actually been discovered at Glastonbury during the reign of Henry II. But the Grail legends, as they appear in Arthurian Romance, are not wholly Christian in origin, as John Cowper Powys had found out during the summer of 1929, when he spent the voyage from Southampton to New York in reading and re-reading the classic *Studies in the Arthurian Legend* by John Rhys.[7] 'What really allured me about the Holy Grail', he later wrote, 'were the unholy elements in both its history and its mystery; in other words the unquestionable fact that it was much older than Christianity itself.' The quest by Arthur's knight, Perceval, for the Grail was, in its original form, of a pagan character, and there are clear links between the Grail and the magical cauldrons of Celtic mythology.

Finding the Grail to be associated both with Christian and with pre-Christian mythology led Powys to believe that Glastonbury is one of the great religious centres of the world, one of the 'reservoirs of world-magic' comparable with Jerusalem, Rome, Mecca or Lhassa, where some fragment of the hidden truth occasionally breaks through into the world as we perceive it, in the form of some new revelation. None of these revelations tell us the whole truth, for 'no one Receptacle of Life and no one Fountain of Life poured into that Receptacle can contain or explain what the world offers us'; a truth which he expresses in another way in the closing pages of *A Glastonbury Romance*, when he writes:

> the great goddess Cybele, whose forehead is crowned with the
> Turrets of the Impossible, moves through the generations from

one twilight to another; and of her long journeying from cult to cult, from shrine to shrine, from revelation to revelation, there is no end. . . . The powers of reason and science gather in the strong light of the Sun to beat her down. But evermore she rises again . . . those 'topless towers' of hers are the birth-cries of occult generation, raised up in defiance of Matter, in defiance of Fate, and in defiance of cruel knowledge and despairing wisdom.

This novel is about the influence in one particular place of the unseen upon the seen. It is a vast, sprawling work of genius, true to the artistic beliefs which Powys had outlined in *Suspended Judgments*,[8] when he wrote that novel-writing is a 'large and liberal art'; that a book must have 'a four-square sense of life-illusion, a rich field for my imagination to wander in at large, a certain quantity of blank space, so to speak, filled with a huge litter of things that are not tiresomely pointing to the projected issue'; and that characters in a romance 'must be penetrated through and through by the scenery which surrounds them and by the traditions, old and dark and superstitious and malign, of some particular spot upon the earth's surface.' It is also set firmly within the context of the philosophical beliefs which Powys had detailed in *The Complex Vision*. In the very first paragraph of the novel, we are informed of something passing 'between the soul of a particular human being', one John Crow, 'and the divine-diabolic soul of the First Cause of all life'; and later the Holy Grail is described as 'a morsel of the Absolute and a broken-off fragment of the First Cause', which, as a result of 'the creative energies pouring into it from the various cults' associated with Glastonbury, 'had grown to be more of an independent entity'.

There is little trace of a formal plot: how could there be, in a book whose heroine is the Grail? Instead there are many individual stories, bound together chiefly by the fact that they take place largely in and around Glastonbury, the mystical 'land of twilight and death'. The novel actually begins in the Norfolk landscape of Powys's childhood holidays, where John Crow and his cousins have gathered to hear their grandfather's will. But their grandfather has left his entire fortune to his secretary John Geard, an heretical preacher from Glastonbury, known because of his constant references to the blood of Christ as 'Bloody Johnny'.

Geard, whose strange beliefs and larger-than-life personality make him very like Powys himself in late middle age, is a prophetic figure who taps ancient reservoirs of power to revive a dead child, and to cure a dying woman of cancer. Returning to Glastonbury, he stages a Passion play which includes not only the traditional scenes of Christ's trial and death on the Cross, but also scenes from Cymric mythology and the Arthurian cycle of legends. This is part of his plan 'to make Glastonbury the centre of the Religion of all the West'. Other characters with clearly autobiographical elements include the Welsh antiquary Owen Evans, who is writing a life of Merlin, and suffers dreadfully from sadistic thoughts; John Crow himself, with his 'cerebral' love-making and ambivalent sexuality; and Sam Dekker the vicar's son, whose father is rather like Powys's father, and who experiences a period of saintly or masochistic resignation similar to that experienced by Powys in his early twenties.

Powys deals kindly with these four characters modelled so particularly upon elements in himself. Evans is cured of his sadism, and protected by the love of a good woman; John Crow is allowed a vision of King Arthur's sword Excalibur, and a happy marriage; Sam Dekker is allowed a vision of the Grail, which cures him of his selfish and narrow-minded ascetic scruples; and Johnny Geard also sees the Grail as he is drowning in flood-water, happy to die because he has experienced all that this world can offer him, and looks forward to '"the next dream"'.

While John Cowper Powys worked on the vast panorama of this masterpiece, his brother Theodore was busy writing short stories. His novel, *Kindness in a Corner* had appeared earlier in 1930, *Unclay* was due out the following year, and a collection of his stories, *The White Paternoster*, had recently been published. Sylvia Townsend Warner visited him at this time and was relieved to find a calmer and happier household than the one which she had visited briefly the previous August.[9] Although Francis was still at home, his health was a great deal better; Violet was pleased to have company; and Theodore was delighted to see someone who understood and admired his work. But he maintained his regular routine, and on the first evening of her visit, Sylvia at first pretended to be asleep so that he could prepare to set off for his usual 7 o'clock walk with a clear conscience. Then, when he was ready, she 'forgot to be . . . the tactful guest' and asked if she could go with him:[10]

It was a pitch-black night. He walked in it with absolute
certainty and I held on to his arm and let myself be guided by

him. We walked up the valley, very slowly, and in silence. At
last he said: 'This is my favourite time for a walk.' Presently he
said: 'Are you afraid of the dark?' I was about to answer that I
was not when a loud unearthly sigh came out of the darkness,
apparently proceeding from a spot about two yards away. We
both started violently. Theo tucked my arm more closely under
his and quickened his pace. . . .

I looked back over my shoulder. He felt the movement, and
said: 'It's too dark to see if it's following us, whatever it is.'

This statement, so full of common-sense, might have been
heartening; but he undid the good work by adding: 'Perhaps it's
as well we can't.'

Gamel Woolsey, who had stayed for a while at Chydyok with
Gertrude, had now left East Chaldon. She had a minor lung infection,
and Gerald Brenan had removed her to a sanatorium in Norfolk, where
she stayed for a number of weeks before being pronounced cured.
Brenan himself lived in lodgings nearby, so that he could see Gamel
every day;[11] meanwhile she corresponded regularly with Llewelyn,
who was frantically excited when he heard that she intended 'to stay at
East Chaldon in December and . . . *look for a house in Dorset!*' He
imagined taking her to Montacute and showing her 'every hidden
place of my childhood', and his letters soon became full of 'middle
earth' dreams and visions. In one of them, Gamel became the heroine
of an Arthurian romance; in another, he described how in a dream he
had met Gamel walking in the woods near Steepletop, wearing her
Russian dress. She had taken him to a cottage guarded by a Wyvern
with a golden collar, and they had made passionate love; after which,
as Llewelyn wrote to her:

> I forgot everything and must have become unconscious with the
> joy of my body, for when I was once more aware, I was lying in
> your arms, my breast upon your breasts, your large lovely
> breasts with the exquisite hazelnut nipples I know so well – *in a
> swooning dream of loving you.* I think my spirit had really for long
> moments entirely lost itself in yours. You see I had never known
> what it was to love till I met you. I never knew that I should
> meet the *girl of my dreams* actually alive

Alyse continued to be desperately unhappy, and Llewelyn himself
was depressed when on Christmas Day he received a merely formal

message of love and good wishes from Gamel. On New Year's Eve the situation became worse, as Alyse noted in her journal:

> We used to form a little world – now the wind shrieks through the gaps, and Llewelyn's eyes drive me far, far away. In the morning I gave Llewelyn Gamel's letter to me, which I had for several days and not dared to give him in which she said she would not leave Mr Brenan, and it worked in him like a *raging fever*.

In January 1931, Gerald Brenan took Gamel to Italy. Llewelyn wrote her more dream letters from America, but her replies kept him at a safe emotional distance, without totally discouraging him:

> Lulu, I do so hope you are well and not unhappy. It is such a long time since I have heard from you, and I cannot tell how you are. And I do hope Alyse is better and is happier. I do grieve and worry about her, and the injury I have done your life together. For you know you always told me that you were perfectly happy with Alyse. And you always would have been if I had not come. . . . I seem to have been a fatal element all my life, Lulu. But I never willingly harmed anyone, you know.

Llewelyn was in so tortured a condition during much of January that he did no work and could think of little else but the possibility of persuading Gamel to leave Gerald and go away with him. Alyse, in whom he confided without apparently realising that he was hurting her, felt as though she were 'being dragged over stones to be thrust down a precipice and left dying alone'. But she loved Llewelyn very greatly; and towards the end of the month, thinking only of what Llewelyn was suffering, she wrote another letter to Gamel *'imploring her to change'*.

After Alyse had visited her parents in February, Llewelyn, needing distraction, suggested that they should go on a voyage to the West Indies. So for several weeks they left winter behind, voyaging among 'the Leeward and the Windward islands as far as Trinidad'. One of the most impressive sights of their tour was the ruined city of St Pierre, destroyed by a volcano, and more striking than Pompeii, 'its streets broader and its crumbling walls higher'. Alyse wrote of their holiday:

> Never has [Llewelyn] been a sweeter companion than when we walked together under the tropical sun elated by the novel

scenes, the startling primitive colours, the hot mid-summer air, the black faces, musical voices, and swaying figures of the natives, the yellow sands and palm trees, the dense forests with their strange fruits.

In the evenings, Llewelyn 'sank back into his reveries', and Alyse was uncomfortably aware that he would have preferred Gamel by his side; 'and yet', she wrote bravely,

we could be happy too, happy until the evenings came down upon us, and we sat at the stern of the boat under the stars gazing out into our anxious futures; Llewelyn caught into his dream, his tragic loss, his uncertain hopes – and I isolated and alone, yet longing to lift his trouble, feeling my bones melt with love and pity.

By mid-March Llewelyn and Alyse were back in New York state; and at the end of the month they sailed for England. When they reached their cottage at East Chaldon, Llewelyn was delighted to find a letter from Gamel waiting for him. She was now expecting Gerald's child, and towards the end of April she and Gerald 'went through a marriage ceremony of [their] own devising' in Rome.[12] However, they intended to return to Dorset before long, and Llewelyn, who had felt saddened to be back in a countryside where 'every slope and hedge and tree whispers . . . of our snatched hours', began once more to look forward to solitary picnics with Gamel on the Downs.

Gamel's return was delayed until mid-June after she had suffered yet another miscarriage; and while he was waiting for her Llewelyn found it impossible to settle down to any serious original work. However, he began reading for a proposed abridgement of Andrew Clark's five volume *Life and Times* of the seventeenth-century antiquary Anthony à Wood; and in the afternoons he resumed his walks with Theodore, and they spoke of love and death. Llewelyn had recently had a terrible vision, as he lay awake one night in his shelter, of 'a skeleton walking across the horizon on the rim of a nearby hillock', which had reminded him how soon death comes to us all; and Theodore talked about the death of Louis Wilkinson's mother who had been so kind to him during his schooldays. 'Perhaps', said Theodore, 'we will presently come to see death as safety'; and when Llewelyn commented that the idea of death was 'Not so pleasant when you read in Anthony à Wood of the filthy rotting corpses', he replied that he found it necessary to think of the unpleasant aspects of death, or he would long for it too much!'[13]

The short stories which Theodore wrote reflect his melancholy state of mind. In one of them, *In Good Earth*, the hero, his ambition and lust equally thwarted, realises that the grave is the best place for him; and now Theodore told his brother that he himself was 'naturally dead. . . . Romance keeps me alive – when it is taken from me I am driven back to my natural prison.' In another story, *The Two Thieves*, Theodore painted a terrible picture of sadistic lust; and he told Llewelyn: 'it is lust . . . that is my ruin.' Now fifty-five years old, and feeling his age, he added: 'Girls are all the same, I suppose – [they] would rather be off with a young boy, anyone at all rather than with me. Of course I am more gross than you, always was. I don't want anything intellectual – I want little animals' roguery. I don't like ladies.' He also wrote 'God', one of his finest short stories, philosophical, witty, and curiously moving, in which he enters the mind of a young child who comes to believe that his father's top hat is God; and when the child grows up he falls in love and marries a village girl very much like Theodore's own wife Violet. But he had almost come to the end of his writing. On 23 July he told Llewelyn: 'I do not now want to talk. I have nothing to say. I want to remain quiet and let time pass'; and, a few days later: 'I respect my melancholy. I respect my resignation. I respect the peace of God which comes from lying back on Nature. All hope is dangerous. It is best to live in a drugged indifference.'[14]

There was no such drugged indifference for Llewelyn: the previous month Gamel and Gerald had returned from Italy, and settled in a cottage at West Lulworth, only three miles from the White Nose; and on 12 June, after days of excitement during which he had found work of any kind impossible, Llewelyn met Gamel on the Downs. Gerald had been indignant earlier in the year when he discovered that Gamel was still writing love-letters to Llewelyn, especially since she told her former lover that she was 'utterly miserable' with her new partner. Gerald was certain, because of 'her almost continual good spirits', that this was quite untrue, but had to accept her explanation that 'she was afraid that if Llewelyn felt she was forgetting him he might have a haemorrhage.' Now, on their first walk together, Llewelyn begged not to be separated from Gamel, and Gerald, remembering his own unhappy experiences with Carrington, never prevented his wife from meeting her former lover.

Gerald appears to have suffered much less than Alyse who, returning one day from Weymouth to join Llewelyn, Gamel and Gerald for tea at the White Nose, felt for a moment that she:

> could not, I could not, *I could not* go into that gate – rather would
> I drown in the salt waves; yet down the steps I walked nearer
> and nearer . . . and she stood before me, so pale, so full of good
> intentions. . . . I looked at Llewelyn sitting a little flushed and
> as if his wits were straying, but he was happy . . .

Some of their meetings were very much more difficult than this. On
16 June, Alyse and Llewelyn visited the Brenans to find that 'Gamel
was in bed. She was pale with that Asiatic look she sometimes has that
suggests a knowledge of the secret arts of love. Llewelyn could hardly
bear to look at her.' And when Gamel and Gerald both made it clear
that they disliked a poem which Llewelyn had quoted, 'he looked so
crushed, so rebuffed. And going back up the valley such misery
descended on us, such bitter trouble, that death alone seemed to
promise release.' It was extremely hard for Llewelyn to have to depend
so much upon Gerald's generosity, while Gamel was often provok-
ingly elusive, and although there were the usual summer distractions,
with visits to and from family and friends, the strain on Llewelyn's
health was considerable, and he suffered from headaches, bouts of
dizziness, and palpitations of the heart.

On the other side of the Atlantic, in his retreat at Phudd Bottom,
John also had been in poor physical health. However, his mind was
calm, and even in February, when he had been compelled to spend
much of each day lying on his back,[15] he had been able to make good
progress on *A Glastonbury Romance*, writing to Littleton: 'I expect this
silence and hush & solitude is splendid for my book. I have, what
I've never had before, *real time* to write in, hours and hours of time.'[16]

John and Phyllis now acquired a spaniel which they named 'The
Black';[17] and when John's health was better he took this dog on the
daily walks which became part of his routine: one before breakfast, one
after his morning's work, and another longer one before his evening
meal. But although his days followed a pattern, they were rarely dull:
for John heightened his enjoyment of life by developing customs and
rituals associated with quite ordinary activities, and he used his
powerful imagination to dramatise and transform his surroundings.
Some of his behaviour must have seemed extremely eccentric to the
local farmers, but it was generally in accordance with the philosophical
beliefs and the code of conduct which he had set down in *The Complex
Vision* and elaborated in other works such as *The Meaning of Culture*. He
had written about 'the illusion of dead matter';[18] so it was not illogical to

give his walking sticks names and personalities, and arrange to take them out at particular times of day.[19] Writing that it was 'the privilege of the solitary stoical soul . . . to live surrounded by the essences of the exclusive universe of its choice',[20] there was no reason why he should not believe that thought *by itself* could be a powerful tool; and so when he had posted his letters, he would seek to ensure that they reached their destinations safely by pressing his head against the mailbox while he muttered secret incantations over them. Still open-minded about the possibility of life after death, he would turn from the mail-box, cross over the road, and press his forehead against the gatepost of the cemetery while he prayed for the souls of the dead.[21] His walks were made magical by his belief in 'the boundless polytheism of the universe. . . . From every plant and from every stone there emanates a presence.'[22] From one tree he believed that he drew strength;[23] a large rock became a symbol of powerful natural forces;[24] and when, far up on the hillside above Phudd, John discovered twenty enormous heaps of stones, he liked to think that they were ancient Indian mounds,[25] and developed an elaborate series of rituals connected with them. One day that summer, when Marian was staying with them, her son Peter, now nine years old, decided to follow his uncle, and stalked him up the hillside from tree to tree. He had no idea how important John's private world had become to him; but when John discovered that he was being followed, and that his prayers and observances were being watched, he burst into a furious mind-searing rage which haunted his nephew for nearly fifty years.[26]

Other visitors during the summer included Edna St Vincent Millay and her husband, who on one occasion drove John and Phyllis over to Steepletop for the day;[27] and Mr Schuster who, seeing the already enormous length of John's unfinished manuscript, talked of making substantial cuts to *A Glastonbury Romance*, and of publishing it in two parts.[28] John also kept up a vast correspondence, and was now exchanging letters with Dorothy M. Richardson. He found it easy to write to her with all the frankness of an intimate friend,[29] and in a long essay he described her admiringly as one of the 'very few great fiction writers . . . who . . . are also original philosophers'.[30]

Phyllis was not always very well, but she enjoyed gardening, and was helped with the cooking and the cleaning by an elderly German lady, one of Marian's discoveries, who stayed with them for five months before they felt that she had become too tyrannical, and replaced her with a local woman.[31] John worked hard despite his bouts of bad health,[32] and by mid-October Mr Rosenberg, one of Schuster's senior men, was able to travel up from New York to collect the completed manuscript of *A Glastonbury Romance*.[33]

Rosenberg took an interest in manuscripts in their own right, and suggested to John, who had managed to sell the manuscript of *Wolf Solent*, that they should ask whether Theodore had any manuscripts for sale.[34] Theodore was pleased to find another source of income, and on 21 October sent John a letter of thanks[35] which was remarkably calm in view of the tragic news which he had recently received: the body of his son Dicky had been found dismembered in the African bush, and first reports suggested that he had been partially devoured by lions.[36] The truth was still more horrible, as it was a case of murder: Dicky had been attacked by some disaffected native warriors, who had speared him and then torn him apart.[37] By an unpleasant coincidence Theodore's novel *Unclay*, with Death as its central character, had only just been published, and the shock of his son's death made further writing seem even less important than it had done before. The three stories which Theodore had written in the spring were published under the title *The Two Thieves* in 1932, but for twelve months or more his literary work appeared to be entirely at an end.

Llewelyn and Alyse were feeling particularly impoverished when Alyse's third novel *Hester Craddock* was published in the autumn of 1931, but unfortunately it was no more of a commercial success than her husband's publications that year. *A Pagan's Pilgrimage*, published in the spring, had in Llewelyn's words 'starved' them; and in October, with few hopes for *Impassioned Clay* – another disaster – they wisely decided to move into the half of Chydyok which Gertrude and Katie had left unoccupied. As Llewelyn explained: 'We would then have got down as low as possible and will be in a position to let these storms blow over. . . . It is a shame, but often it is more happy to go down than up.'

Llewelyn enjoyed the actual move, and by 22 October he and Alyse had settled in and were entertaining Theodore to tea.[38] Although they had less money, they managed not to appear poor: they regularly used silver cutlery, they had 'beautiful pottery and porcelain', and their upstairs living-room was furnished with 'eighteenth-century Chippendale, and was full of books and paintings'.[39] Llewelyn's shelter had also been moved from the White Nose. It was set up not far from Chydyok on the north side of a prehistoric earth circle, and Llewelyn was pleased to think that 'except possibly for an occasional shepherd, I am the first human being to lie here since neolithic days.'[40]

Llewelyn's relationship with Gamel remained awkward and unsatisfactory. On 14 November, for example, Gamel sent a telegram asking Llewelyn to lunch, but was then so unresponsive that when he returned to Alyse she found him 'more freed . . . than he had been almost since we had been here'. Perhaps Gamel realised that she had been too cold towards him, for later the same day 'another telegram arrived asking us to supper', wrote Alyse in exasperation, 'and his love for her forces his pride to submit and my love for him bows my pride as well.' When they arrived they found Gamel 'ambitious for her book', *Middle Earth*, which would soon be published, and 'smelling strongly of scent, in her apple blossom dress, with a long Sorrento scarf of silk'. After an evening of tedious conversation Llewelyn and Alyse walked home 'in sadness and silence'.

While his books sold badly, and his friendship with Gamel became increasingly difficult to sustain, Llewelyn drew closer to Alyse. On 22 November, she walked to meet him in the moonlight, after he had been out for another painful supper with the Brenans, and found him 'so surprised to see me, and [he] kissed me again and again . . . he talked so beautifully of the relief of coming out into the wide night.' Llewelyn was also grateful at this time for the friendly comments of those who still appreciated his writing. 'What a lovely letter you wrote me', he told Ann Wilkinson; '. . . I feel as if I had one disciple and in having such a one am content to wander on through the harvest fields, white with harvest.' Clifford Musgrave, 26-year-old chief librarian of the Yeovil Public Library, was another admirer, who called on him every three or four weeks with his wife Margaret. Their conversations were friendly but formal, Llewelyn insisting for two years that he and Alyse should be addressed as Mr Powys and Miss Gregory. Margaret found Miss Gregory 'wonderful. She had such a way with young girls. She talked about books and drew me out'; but there was more than twenty years' difference in their ages, and Alyse also seemed to her to be 'very old-fashioned. Her hair was long and done up, and she wore no make-up. She wore very good quality clothes, of the tweedy kind. She had a cape and always wore a hat, sometimes trimmed with a bit of swathed voile. She was a bit like Virginia Woolf in her clothes and manner.' Margaret also observed Llewelyn, and noticed in particular his: 'bright blue-grey eyes which lit up with a terrific radiance when he thought of some great idea, or when he saw something which he thought was wonderful. They were rather piercing eyes, and he would fix them on your face when you were speaking to him.'[41]

Having moved to Chydyok, Llewelyn and Alyse inevitably saw a great deal more of both Gertrude and Katie. Gertrude still painted, and occasionally travelled to Paris for a holiday;[42] but at Chaldon she appeared to outsiders to be 'very much the great lady . . . always visiting the sick, or taking fresh milk or honey to people who were ill.'[43] Alyse believed that Gertrude had 'in ultimate things the most disillusioned mind of any one of the family'; but she never forgot that Gertrude had once offered to protect her, and wrote warmly of her as a combination of 'earth mother' and 'Chinese sage' with 'her compassionate heart, and her cool wisdom'. Alyse noticed that Llewelyn turned to Gertrude for advice, but that he suspected her of preferring Theodore to himself, and that his favourite was Katie, whom he 'treasured . . . with a life-long homage'.[44] Katie in turn adored Llewelyn, and told Alyse that she envied women who were able to give themselves completely to him.[45] Her own private life during 1932 was as turbulent as ever: a special friendship with Valentine Ackland, known as 'Molly', seemed threatened by the arrival on the scene of Sylvia Townsend Warner;[46] and she embarked on a passionate love-affair with a local fisherman called Jack Miller.[47]

Katie and Gertrude had Christmas dinner with Llewelyn and Alyse, and joined them again to see in the New Year of 1932. Shortly afterwards Llewelyn received a letter from the young American artist Lynd Ward, who had illustrated *Impassioned Clay*, and who now wrote asking him to write another book which could be issued as the first publication of a new cooperative venture, set up in New York as the Equinox Press. Llewelyn agreed, and broke a rest of several months to begin work on *'Now that the Gods are Dead'*, another philosophical essay, in which he declared that 'The secret of life lies in our own individual poetic vision.'[48] He also wrote a number of shorter articles and essays, some of which he sent to the *American Spectator* at the invitation of Theodore Dreiser. The payment was small, and he asked Dreiser crossly: 'Am I to have my soul damned over these cursed essays at the price of $10 a fling?'; but he added that he would 'submit *under protest*, for you are publishing a fine brave paper.' Llewelyn called his essays 'sling shots'; and, aware of the gulf between his own philosophical views and those of his eldest brother, he wrote: 'Take it, old Man of Phudd, for they are meant for thee.'

John Cowper Powys spent January 1932 at Phudd Bottom, correcting the proofs of *A Glastonbury Romance*, which Schuster now intended to publish in the early spring in a single large volume of more than 1,100 pages.[49] John had high hopes for its success, and dreamed of winning a Nobel Prize.[50] In the meantime he was already planning his next novel, which was to be as grand in scope as *Glastonbury*, and was to be set in Weymouth and Portland. Llewelyn sent him some up-to-date information about that area of Dorset, and in February John also wrote to Littleton asking for 'any old tumbled to bits guide-books', saying that he was '*insatiable* over materials of this sort'.[51]

When advance copies of *A Glastonbury Romance* arrived in mid-March, John sent one to his youngest sister Lucy, to whom the novel is dedicated; and one to Llewelyn,[52] who was extremely impressed and told Louis Wilkinson:

> Truly I think it is wonderful – more bawdy and blasphemous than anything any of us have yet written and yet a deeply religious book, so thickly religious that it swallows the Anglican faith as if it were a gnat – swallows up Christianity itself as though it were a single egg of caviare.

Before long a copy of *A Glastonbury Romance* was on its way to his brother Littleton, but he was displeased by what he found. Not only was there an inaccurate reference to their former Sherborne teacher Mr King,[53] but a clear association between Sherborne School and John's fictional 'Greylands School',[54] said to have been the school which scarred one of the characters in the novel for life, as 'Bullied at Greylands – always bullied'.[55] Littleton was very upset by this attack on their old school, but John defended himself by writing: 'I cannot agree with the policy of crying "hush" in the presence of abuses because they touch a well-loved institution.' He added:[56]

> I fear in matters of this kind between Littleton and Johnny its like those old Chess Games and drawing ships *versus* 'Volentia Army' – its the heart speaking & carrying the head away on its tide. You are an emotional Conservative. I am an emotional Radical. And . . . so in a sense I fear it will be to the end of the story.

Although he felt confident about the success of *A Glastonbury Romance*, John Cowper Powys appreciated that his publishers were taking a considerable risk in publishing one of the longest and most disturbingly original novels ever written, and he knew that they were also spending a great deal of money on advertising; so at the beginning of April he himself travelled in to New York City to give interviews and sign copies of his book. He also gave a lecture on *A Glastonbury Romance*, as the first of three lectures which he had allowed Keedick to arrange for him, and which he thought of as his farewell to the lecture-platform.[57] The second lecture, on Faust, was attended by his friends Masters and Dreiser; and the third not only by his publishers Richard Simon and Max Schuster, but, fittingly enough, by the man who had arranged so many of his American lecture tours, Arnold Shaw.

Despite the efforts made both by his publishers and by Powys himself, *A Glastonbury Romance* was a financial disaster. Provincial reviews were moderately encouraging, but only one New York reviewer could find anything good to say about this new novel;[58] and, sadly, there was no praise at all for what can now be recognised as one óf the most remarkable of Powys's achievements: a description of sexual relationships which far surpasses D. H. Lawrence in its maturity and understanding. By 10 June Powys was 'In despair over the bad sale of my Glastonbury', and his publishers had commissioned him to write a short philosophical work, in the hope of recouping some of their losses.

John Cowper Powys began writing this new book, *A Philosophy of Solitude*, while also working on his Weymouth novel, but despite a diet so smooth that he had to rely on daily enemas to open his bowels,[59] his ulcer became very troublesome,[60] and by mid-July he had decided that he was overworking, and setting himself an impossible task. The novel was laid aside until the autumn, when he had completed the philosophical work. By this time he had had a chance to rethink his novel in the light of the failure of *A Glastonbury Romance*; and, in a move which compelled him to adopt higher standards of artistic control, he decided to rewrite 'from the very start my Weymouth Romance: for I'd made it too big, too long & since Glastonbury won't sell I *must* write shorter . . . this foundation . . . was huge . . . and I must get all the stones nearer the Centre now.'[61]

CHAPTER FIFTEEN

1932–1934

John in America, 1932–4 • *completes* Weymouth Sands, *July 1933* • *begins* Autobiography, *August 1933* • *news of libel suit against him, April 1934* • *moves with Phyllis to England, June 1934* • *publishes* A Philosophy of Solitude, *1933*.
Theodore in England • *little writing* • *adopts 'Susan', January 1933.*
Llewelyn in England • *very ill, June 1932, July 1933, and March 1934* • *publishes* Now that the Gods are Dead, *1932*, Life and Times of Anthony à Wood, *1932*, Glory of Life, *1934*, Earth's Memories, *1934*.
Louis Wilkinson publishes Swan's Milk, *1934*.

Theodore Powys praised John's *A Glastonbury Romance*, but declared that he himself was much happier for having given up writing altogether.[1] He had managed to come to terms with his elder son's death; and some idea of how he had got through the difficult months immediately afterwards can be found in a letter which he wrote to Louis Wilkinson in January 1932 to commiserate with him over the sudden death of his wife Ann Reid. 'The only thing to do' he advised his old friend, 'is to go on eating and drinking like an Animal. Merely and only that. There is nothing else to be done.'

Then towards the end of the summer the household at Beth-Car was unexpectedly increased when Violet, who was still upset by the loss of Dicky, and had always wanted a girl,[2] agreed to look after a pleasant young baby.[3] The child, born on 4 August 1932, was formally adopted by Theodore and Violet on 20 January 1933, as Theodora Gay Powys. Contained in Theodora's own unpublished typescript 'Portrait of T. F. Powys', there is a remarkably dramatic but at present unpublishable account of her parentage and very early life.[4] Count Potocki makes further similar allegations in his book *Dogs' Eggs*.[5] Whether these were retailed to Theodore at the time of the adoption remains very obscure, but in any case Violet had quickly become extremely fond of the little girl, whom she and the rest of the family began calling Susan, a less forbidding name than Theodora;[6] and Theodore, who had always loved small children, was soon to be seen pushing Susan's pram along the lanes near Beth-Car.

For the first five months of 1932 Llewelyn had been hard at work on his books and essays. By 1 March he had completed *Now that the Gods are Dead*,[7] and he also finished his abridgement of the *Life and Times of Anthony à Wood*. But towards the end of June there was an alarming incident: Llewelyn suddenly felt giddy, and then vomited blood. Alyse was terrified, but they were both so accustomed to the idea of Llewelyn spitting blood that no doctor was sent for, and Llewelyn simply lay as still as possible on his bed. Gamel, who came at once, wept to see him looking so unwell. Earlier in the year she had been drawing closer to Alyse and further from Llewelyn,[8] but now she came to visit him almost every day.

During July Llewelyn's health improved, and Gamel's visits became less frequent, but he was grateful to Alyse for her devoted nursing, and she explained in her journal on 6 August that she had made few entries lately because: 'the days pass and Llewelyn and I are happy together, as happy perhaps as we have ever been. He is no longer sad if he does not see Gamel, and when he does see her he returns to me with his whole being delighted to be at home again.' 'Whatever has passed', she added a month later, 'we are still dear to each other'; and together they gardened, went for walks, bathed, lay naked in the sun, and 'were very happy'. Early in August they had visited Max Gate, where Hardy's widow introduced them to Dr Marie Stopes, the then notorious advocate of birth-control; and they enjoyed the company of their old friends Louis Wilkinson and Bernie O'Neill.[9] After these visits they spent a few days in London, where Llewelyn mixed business with pleasure, calling on Frank Whitaker, the editor of *John o'London's Weekly*.

They returned to Dorset to find that Gamel, who had undergone a breast operation, was fully recovered, and that she and Gerald were planning to spend the winter in Spain. To Alyse the Brenans 'both seemed faraway, indifferent, anxious only to be gone as quickly as possible from England.' She noted on the morning of 21 September that Llewelyn now seemed to be 'untouched by the fact that they are going', but she felt profoundly sorry for him. Not only had Gamel grown cold towards him – Gerald had told Alyse privately that Gamel now 'felt a certain resentment toward Llewelyn' – but she herself had begun to feel that Llewelyn 'never reaches the core of my being'. Now, as Gamel turned to go, Alyse:

> felt such a sudden love for her, this beautiful, remote girl, that I bent down saying 'dear Gamel' and gave her one last kiss, and so sweet a smile came into her face as she gave my cold hand a clasp with her hot one that I was touched to the heart, and for long kept my eyes upon her until with a blind wave of her hand she disappeared.

At first Llewelyn brooded over Gamel's departure, and would come to kneel by Alyse to be comforted, but before long his sorrow was outweighed by fears for his health: he was suffering from dizzy spells, and in mid-October he went with Alyse to consult a doctor. When the doctor heard that Llewelyn had vomited blood in the summer, he told them that he was clearly suffering from a stomach ulcer, and must eat only soft food in future; moreover, he must be aware 'that such a condition might lead to mortal bleeding, or even to cancer.'

Llewelyn and Alyse were both badly shaken by this news: Alyse was thrown into a fit of depression, while Llewelyn, who had for some time endured a punishing combination of physical ill-health and the emotional strain of an unhappy love-affair, drifted dangerously close to a complete breakdown. Not long after his visit to the doctor, he wrote to Rivers Pollock about an odd experience which for a while made him think that he was going mad:

> Yesterday I saw with clear eyesight the head of a fairy float up to the sky – the size of a small apple. I saw it very clearly as I lay awake in my shelter and said to myself this vision invalidates my senses. It seemed to be lifted off a faded rusty dock.

More encouraging news, which must have helped Llewelyn through this crisis, was that he soon had two new books in print: *Now that the Gods are Dead* was published in a limited edition in New York, and Llewelyn was delighted with Lynd Ward's illustrations, telling him that he had 'caught the spirit of what I have tried to say'; while the *Life and Times of Anthony à Wood* was published in London, and led to an invitation to Llewelyn to travel to Oxford in December to attend a luncheon at Merton in honour of Wood's tercentenary. Llewelyn accepted the invitation, though he told Pollock afterwards that when he met some of the Fellows of the college he 'detected the same shallow suspicious attitude to Wood as they showed him in the old days'.

At the time of his Oxford visit, Llewelyn Powys had called on Robert Gibbings, who was then associated with the Golden Cockerel Press, and who hoped to illustrate one of Llewelyn's long essays, *Glory of Life*. On New Year's Day 1933, when Gibbings was visiting Llewelyn at Chydyok, Llewelyn was well enough to walk with him over the downs to lunch with Louis Wilkinson at West Lulworth, and several days later he attended the christening of Theodore's adopted daughter. However, his health continued to be very variable, and he did not feel well enough to make the journey to Wool Station to say goodbye to his sister Katie: she was setting out for Africa, where she spent ten months with their brother Will, before deciding that she could never be an intimate friend of Will's wife Elizabeth, and returning home to Gertrude and to Chydyok.[10]

Llewelyn continued to find it very difficult to earn a living, and much of his best work was being sold very cheaply to the local *Dorset Echo*. Some of his essays were taken by the *Spectator*, the *Cornhill Magazine*, and the *Manchester Guardian*, and he went on sending work to the *American Spectator*, though, as he wrote to Dreiser:

> I confess I do feel a certain chagrin when I contemplate your colleagues and how they have played the b. . . with me. They want essays; they don't want essays. They will accept two turned into one . . . and then they will postpone its publication, or indeed not publish it at all. . . . I must sing only at the approved moment, and then get a turd for my pay

John Cowper Powys found it impossible to write essays to supplement his meagre income from royalties,[11] but in January 1933 he heard that *A Glastonbury Romance* had at last been accepted by an English publisher, John Lane;[12] but he was not told when it would be published, and in the meantime everything depended on the success of *A Philosophy of Solitude*, published in America on 9 February.[13] Fortunately, it sold well, and on 23 March John wrote to Littleton telling him that it had been 'a "non-fiction" best-seller for one week anyway, in Chicago and in Washington!' But his royalty was only 20 cents per copy,[14] and when in that month a number of banks closed their doors he and Phyllis lost the small amount of money they had left in an account in Philmont,[15] and had to rely for a while on loans from their neighbour Mr Krick,[16] whose young nephew Albert had been employed by them during the previous twelve months.[17]

Albert Krick saw more than anyone else of John and Phyllis during these years; his pride in himself was deliberately increased by John, who deferentially addressed him as 'Master', and he was powerfully impressed by the strength of John's feeling for the down-trodden. Even when he was short of money, John would give freely to anyone who approached him with a hard-luck story; and once, when Dreiser was visiting him, he became so concerned about an ash tree which was being leaned on by a willow, that he paid Albert $5 to cut down the willow. Albert also observed John's daily routine and eccentric habits: in the mornings, he liked to walk up to a clearing on the hillside facing east, from where he could watch the sunrise; he wore rubber boots summer and winter, keeping his shoes for a very occasional trip to New York City; and when a white kitten which belonged to them died, he asked Albert to bury it, and conducted an elaborate funeral service including an oration in which he quoted Shakespeare, declaring: 'The evil that men do lives after them, The good is oft enterred with their bones, and so it is with Whitey'![18]

John was now working desperately hard on his new novel, eventually to appear as *Weymouth Sands*, hoping that if he could complete it by 15 July 1933[19] it would be published that autumn. His letter-writing was a great hindrance to his work, but at the beginning of May he told at least one of his numerous correspondents, Eric Barker, that he should expect no more letters until *Weymouth Sands* had been delivered to the publishers.[20]

In *Weymouth Sands*,[21] the most haunting and poetical of John Cowper Powys's major novels, there is no central plot but, as in *A Glastonbury Romance*, there are many stories linked together chiefly by the fact that they are set in the same town. There is also a considerable element of nostalgia: John had known and loved Weymouth ever since his father took him there for seaside holidays,[22] and his own nostalgic feelings are made most explicit through the character of Magnus Muir, a middle-aged Latin tutor who recalls the days when his father, clearly modelled on Powys's father, lived at Penn House – the very house where Powys had spent those early holidays. But Weymouth is also seen as a place of mystery: a meeting point not only between the land and the sea, but between the temporal and the eternal, the visible and the invisible. Muir himself feels that he is in 'a strange phantasmal Weymouth, a mystical town made of a solemn sadness . . . a town built out of the smell of dead seaweed, a town whose very walls and roofs were composed of flying spindrift and tossing rain.'

Other characters have similar experiences: the love-affair between the attractive young Perdita Wane, and the coastal trader 'Jobber' Skald, is one of the principal stories in the book; and, soon after they meet for the first time, a gesture of Skald's, as he throws a pebble into the water, becomes for Perdita a moment when the 'spiritual screen . . . between our existing world of forms and impressions and *some other world* . . . suddenly gr[ew] extremely thin.' Later, Perdita's room seems 'transitory' and 'insecure'; and, as she listens to the sea, 'It chill[s] her consciousness with the ebb and flow of vast non-human forces that cared nothing for human plots and counter-plots.' Her new awareness of the transitory nature of human life is of great importance: if we are 'awake all the time' we may savour every experience of life to the full, even if its pleasures are short lived, as Powys reminds us in a memorable description of the sands at night-fall:

> Itself invisible, the after-glow of the sunset gave the sands an incredible look of enchantment. Some of the pools and canals in the wet sand that the children had made gleamed as though, ere they were deserted, buckets of liquid gold had been poured into them. . . . But by degrees the golden reflections died away and a curious chilliness . . . established itself there . . . the chilliness of a cemetery across which a gay procession of intruders has come and gone.

Two of the characters in *Weymouth Sands* are of special interest, since Powys admitted that they had been given 'certain characteristics and peculiarities' of his own. One is Magnus Muir, who combines nostalgia for the past with fear that he will end his days in a mental hospital, but he does have the ability, when depressed, to 'seiz[e] upon some dominant or poetical aspect of the physical present . . . and [draw] . . . from it a fresh, a simple, a childish enchantment'; and the other is the eccentric prophet Sylvanus Cobbold, worshipper of the sun, the sea and the sky, with his 'oracular mutterings', his 'ritualistic nod[s]' and his chanting of 'ponderous metaphysical runes'. Powys defends all these by explaining that: 'To Sylvanus' own mind his peculiarities were a simple, direct, categorical way of living upon the earth, that had no connection with affectation or nonsense or silliness. In fact he regarded them as an evidence of shrewd common-sense.' He has established 'a certain rapport between himself and the cosmos'; and increasingly has come to feel 'as if his real home were . . . in some Cimmerian twilight'. Sylvanus is scolded by his brother Jerry, just as John was by Llewelyn, for deceiving his listeners: 'Dead we shall all be,' says Jerry, 'dead as those Dinosaur bones . . . found at Ringstead Bay. . . . I . . . have peeped behind that Curtain . . . and *there's nothing there*!' But Sylvanus persists in offending not only his brother, but the whole of respectable society by publicly declaiming his beliefs, and by seducing young girls: though he does no more than hold them in his arms, believing that he can 'fumble and grope towards the world's mystery through the more receptive souls of women'.

While John was writing the last chapters of *Weymouth Sands*, his brother Llewelyn was living with Alyse what she described as a life 'full of a delicate, dream-like quality'. Although he still loved Gamel, he was no longer tortured by his passion for her: he told Alyse towards the end of April that there was in Gamel 'something worldly, almost calculating', and that 'it gave him a sense of power, the fact that she was no longer able to hurt him.' When one evening Alyse felt a lover's sadness, and 'asked him how he reconciled himself to the knowledge of illness and death', he replied that:

> we had to think that all was anyway lost, and that what we had now – these dear days – were given to us like a miracle, and he kissed me with such grave and deep and true love . . . and our hearts were united with a mysterious and inarticulate tenderness and understanding.

In June they went on holiday to Dartmoor for ten days, but Llewelyn, who had for some months been aware that he was coughing much more than usual, foolishly walked too far. On their return to Dorset, he was compelled to go to bed, and wrote to Dreiser that 'my old consumption has revived to torment me after a quarter of a century.' Alyse placed him on a new regimen: plenty of sun-bathing, together with a diet mainly of fruit, nuts and vegetables. For six weeks his health improved, and he wrote to John: 'My temperature is nearly steady now. I walk naked over the hills delighting in the summer sunshine.' He also told John about a recent nightmare in which 'I was waiting in some great station and you came in and were flushed and excited and they said you were ill . . . I hope you are all right.' In reality it was Llewelyn who was about to be extremely ill.

On 19 July 1933 Llewelyn had his worst attack of blood-spitting since the one which had followed his walk round the walls of Jerusalem in

1928; and although he appeared to make a rapid recovery, his tuberculosis was once again very active and highly dangerous. In the early hours of 4 August he woke Alyse, who roused herself and watched in horror as:

> suddenly he began to have a hemorrhage – the blood coming up and up from his chest, filling his mouth, his body shaking, as if singled out and alone, he was fighting nature. . . . The attacks continued and continued until way into the morning. I sat by him hour after hour with the light gradually coming and the sun at last shining down upon the golden corn.

For several days Llewelyn lay very close to death, unable to get his breath 'because I had no dry lungs to breathe and it seemed I coughed against my naked spine'; but there was no weakening of his hatred for the church. At his request permission was obtained for him to be buried on the downs, and one night he whispered to Alyse that he wished 'to be buried with flexed knees like the Romans, not with crossed arms'. The Brenans had returned from Spain in May, and each day Gerald collected ice from the fishmonger's and brought it up to Chydyok to be applied to Llewelyn's chest. Alyse slept by Llewelyn's side: he told her 'I am happy when you are near me, my darling. You have a strong spirit'; and Gertrude shared with Alyse the work of nursing. At last the immediate crisis was over, and towards the end of August, though still too weak to sit up, Llewelyn was able to write to John with the news that his fever had 'abated a little'.

John had first heard that Llewelyn was seriously ill on 12 or 13 August, when he had the news in a telegram from Alyse. At once he laid aside his work, offered up special prayers to various heathen divinities, and began re-reading everything that Llewelyn had ever written.[23] Two weeks later there was a touching exhibition of friendship from Eugen Boissevain and Edna St Vincent Millay: they had only just heard of Llewelyn's illness from Arthur Ficke, and Eugen descended on John with plans for making an immediate journey with him to England. John accompanied Eugen to Steepletop where Eugen and Edna, both in a high state of emotional excitement, wrote telegrams in which *he* put himself and his wealth entirely at Llewelyn's disposal, and *she* promised to visit him at a moment's notice.[24] Earlier in the year they had also been thinking of travelling to Dorset,[25] but now John knew that Llewelyn had improved a little, and in view of this a journey to England seemed unmerited. However, Edna dedicated her latest volume of poetry, *Huntsman, what Quarry* to Llewelyn Powys and Alyse Gregory, and included a poem, 'The Ballad of Chaldon Down',[26] in which she imagined what it would be like for Llewelyn to be visited by 'A Lady come from over the sea',

> [Who] found a track without a name
> That led to Chaldon, and so came
> Over the downs to Chydyok,
> All for to say good-day to me.
>
> All for to ask me only this –
> As she shook out her skirts to dry
> And laughed, and looked me in the eye,
> And gave me two cold hands to kiss:
> That I be steadfast, that I lie
> And strengthen and forbear to die.

Llewelyn did strengthen, but it was a slow process, and in September he sent a note to Gamel saying that he still was not well enough to see her, and that 'I try to write, but every muscle in my hand trembles.' However, he began marking passages in the writings of Thomas Hearne for a volume which, if published, would have been a companion to his *Anthony à Wood*; and Bodley Head had accepted *Earth Memories*, a collection of his essays with wood-cuts by Gertrude, for publication in 1934. More good news came from the Golden Cockerel Press, where Robert Gibbings had completed the illustrations for Llewelyn's 9,000 word philosophical essay *Glory of Life*, also to be published in 1934, but in an expensive limited edition of 277 copies.

In *Glory of Life*,[27] Llewelyn Powys argues once again in favour of a religion founded upon a poetic appreciation of existence. There is no room, he states, for belief in God, for hopes of a life after death, or for trust in any ordained moral order. Deliberate cruelty is the only unpardonable sin, and personal fulfilment the principal virtue. The 'most vital aspect' of this fulfilment, he asserts, 'has to do with sex. How continually one hears people say, "You make too much of sex . . ." [but] It is the backbone of all life. . . . Whenever mutual attraction exists between two people it is a life-disavowal to reluct from joy.'

John had recently advised Llewelyn that having said all he needed to say about religion and morals, he should return to the work of transforming his personal recollections into literature,[28] for which Llewelyn had shown that he had an outstanding gift. In the light of this advice, Llewelyn began planning an autobiographical novel about his love-affair with Gamel Woolsey. John was asked to suggest names for the heroine, and sent his brother a long list[29] from which Llewelyn selected Dittany Stone; and on 27 October, after 'walk[ing] in his dressing gown just far enough to get a distant glimpse of the sea because he thought it would bring him fortune', Llewelyn began work on *Life and Death*.

Although he wrote very rapidly, and had soon completed a first draft of several chapters, he became ill again and was once more confined to bed. This time Llewelyn felt a 'nervousness which', as he confessed to Gamel, 'is very humiliating to me . . . no thoughts philosophical can avail to reduce my anxiety.' He had clearly been working too hard, and he was obliged to put aside his novel and concentrate on writing the kind of 'very short and utterly "perfect" articles' which he knew that he could sell to the *Dorset Echo*. Despite trouble with his eyesight, he told Rivers Pollock that: 'These do not seem to tire me. I have a mania for doing this. I like the idea of giving to the Dorset labourers and shepherds and furze cutters the *very best writing* and it thrills me when I hear of some essay being discussed in a Dorset tavern.'

Theodore had done little writing until the autumn, when he composed several short stories,[30] but he had had a very exhausting year. Violet, having encouraged him to adopt Theodora, or 'Susan', found that the work of looking after a baby again at the age of forty-six was almost too much for her. In March she was very ill, and Theodore, whom Llewelyn found 'over worked and anxious and pale', had to employ a nurse to look after her for several weeks.[31] When Violet recovered from this illness, she found it difficult to find assistance in the village, and began sleeping extremely badly.[32] In December Theodore was still doing much of the work of looking after Susan, and told Louis Wilkinson:

> My mornings are all occupied with Baby, and my evenings are too, after 6.45, and I go to bed as soon after eight o'clock as I can. For Baby is often awake again at 6 and then I go to Violet's room to give her the bottle. She has not enough teeth to eat proper food yet.

Theodore was working hard, but had very little income, and he had to ask John and Marian not to send gifts of clothes for Susan, because he could not afford to pay the import duty.[33] Much earlier in the year he had considered applying for help to the Royal Literary Fund, but delayed his application for twelve months when he learned that they would wish to have details of his income for 1932, a year in which his total income had been unusually large at about £300. During 1933 he would have had to manage on not much more than a third of that sum,[34] but for the intervention in the autumn of David Garnett who, together with other admirers, promised him £90: a third of it almost at once, and the remainder within six months.[35]

John Cowper Powys, not so ill as Llewelyn or so exhausted as Theodore, but just as short of money as both of them, had succeeded in completing *Weymouth Sands* and in despatching it to his publishers by 23 July 1933,[36] only eight days later than the deadline to which he had been working. It was a blazing hot summer, and while Phyllis's mother was visiting them[37] – her father had died in Kansas earlier in the year[38] – John planned to relax for a week or two. He intended to walk, read, and catch up with correspondence, but he was soon worrying that Simon and Schuster would be too sluggish to get *Weymouth Sands* into print by 1 November.[39] This was essential, for they would pay him nothing for the book until six months after publication, and he could only survive on his current earnings until the end of April 1934.[40]

In the meantime, John began work on his next book, which he was determined should be one of the most highly original autobiographies of all time.[41] In July he had told Llewelyn that he was considering how to achieve this. He had already thought of the unusual and perhaps rather masochistic idea of including nothing but praise for everyone who appeared in the book apart from himself! Another idea was to include no women; and although he at first thought that this would be insincere, as women had been so important to him,[42] he later changed his mind, explaining to Littleton that 'the leaving out of *all women* completely leaves me free to devote much more time to sensations and ideas and also to the men I have known.' In any case, he would have had to leave out many of the women in his life if he was to fulfil his declared aim of writing his autobiography in such a way 'that no one's feelings whether living or dead could possibly be hurt.'[43]

In particular, John wished to avoid giving any offence to his wife Margaret: indeed, having spent so many years working himself almost to death in a possibly misguided but certainly heroic endeavour to preserve Margaret in her cocoon of middle-class respectability, it would have made no sense suddenly to expose her to all kinds of unpleasant gossip; and this would have been inevitable if he had gone into any detail about many of his relationships with women. John had not even told his brother Littleton about his life with Phyllis Playter because he felt certain that Littleton's wife Mabel, who had always disliked Margaret, would enjoy gloating over her misfortunes.[44] Revelations about his relationships with other women would not only distress Margaret, but could be very embarrassing for the women involved, and might endanger current friendships such as that with Frances Wilkinson. There were of course some women who could safely have been mentioned; but since his autobiography was bound to be considerably unbalanced in this respect, it made a good deal of sense to turn a handicap into an advantage, and deliberately to seek originality by mentioning '*not one single woman* not even our mother – not even our sisters'.[45]

Towards the end of August, when John Cowper Powys had completed the first chapter of his *Autobiography*, he received extremely discouraging news from Simon and Schuster about *Weymouth Sands*: one of the editors thoroughly disliked it, and there was no chance of it being published by 1 November as John had requested. They eventually decided to publish *Weymouth Sands* the following year, but there was a very worrying period during which John thought that he and Phyllis would have to leave Phudd Bottom[46] and settle in rooms nearby[47]; and Phyllis was in particularly low spirits, eating very little,[48] and hating the extremes of climate to which they were exposed each summer and winter.[49] For a while, John even revived his dream of settling in Wales where, steeped in Welsh culture and tradition, he would write the long historical novel[50] – 'I see it as an extraordinary book', he told Littleton – which might be his greatest work. There he would live 'for the rest of my days'; and there, at last, he would be 'buried in the land of my fathers!'[51]

The more John thought about moving to Wales, the more difficulties he imagined, and he was especially worried that by living openly with Phyllis Playter, he would create a terrible scandal which would embarrass his wife and overshadow his son's career.[52] When better news about *Weymouth Sands* arrived, he 'let this Welsh idea recede in my mind';[53] and, encouraged by Edgar Lee Masters, took a train to New York to demand more favourable terms and an advance on his royalties.[54] The personal approach produced better results than letter-writing had done; John and Phyllis were able to remain at Phudd, and they both became more cheerful about the future.

John spent the last part of 1933 writing his *Autobiography*, correcting proofs of *Weymouth Sands*, and trying to deal with an ever-increasing weight of correspondence.[55] He also wrote one long article attacking vivisection, and another in praise of Columbia County, in which he revealed that he had now named 'every stump and stone, every rock, swamp and rivulet in this virginal Arcadia'; and that, despite Phyllis's dislike of the winter months at Phudd, he himself considered them to be 'the real culmination of our life here . . . the heavenly Nirvana that is to free us from the teasing bustle of Being. . . . We are *what we are* in the Winter in unapproachable felicity.'[56]

While John and Phyllis spent the Christmas of 1933 isolated from their families and most of their friends in a land which John described as 'hushed, silent, dead, sepulchred in white snow',[57] there was a considerable gathering of the Powys family in Dorset. Theodore and Violet were at Beth-Car, with their adopted daughter Susan; Llewelyn and Alyse were in one half of Chydyok, while in the other were not only Gertrude and Katie, but also Bertie and his second wife Faith; and staying at Down Barn, another rather isolated building in the area, were Will and Elizabeth, recently arrived from Africa. Another visitor to Dorset that Christmas was one of the family's oldest friends, Louis Wilkinson, who was staying at a nearby hotel with his third wife Diana.

Louis was in a cheerful mood, and when he visited Llewelyn he amused him so much that, fearing a haemorrhage, Llewelyn 'had to dismiss him very soon because of speechless laughter'. Louis also took Diana to tea at Beth-Car, where he was asked for his opinion on some Marsala wine which Will had given Theodore for Christmas. Louis told Theodore that he had written an autobiographical novel *Swan's Milk*, which was due to appear in the spring. He had written it under his customary pen-name Louis Marlow, and his own identity had been further disguised by the name 'Dexter Foothood'; but John, Theodore, Llewelyn and other members of the Powys family appeared in the book under their own names. Llewelyn, the only member of the family to be invited to read *Swan's Milk* in typescript, described it to Theodore Dreiser as 'packed with rascality about the Powys family and deriding Jack . . . but I admire it and have sponsored it on its cover.' The title recalled an incident in which Llewelyn had made it clear that he believed swans *could* be milked, but generally Llewelyn had been well treated. What really attracted him, however, were the thoroughly unconventional views which made it 'a scandalous book'. In his appreciation, Llewelyn wrote: 'Although I personally resented several of Mr Marlow's references to my own family and was 'deeply hurt' by his malicious representation of my brother John, I scarcely remember ever having read a book with more relish and entertainment.' He was furious when he received an advance copy and found that the qualifying clause in this statement had been removed, and he wrote angrily to Louis:

> I have always recognised the fact since the publication of *The Buffoon* that you intended to revenge yourself upon Jack subtly and insidiously in season and out of season – with 'I mean no harm Master' always upon your lips . . . now by a piece of clever knavery which I was too trustful to guard against I am presented to the world as giving my unqualified assent to the crowning stroke of this monstrous campaign of disparagement against my own brother and the man I love and admire and am astonished by more than anyone else I have known in my life upon earth.

This might very well have ended their long friendship, but for the fact that Louis protested that he was not responsible for the deletion, and insisted on the missing words being restored before the book went on sale.

After spending Christmas at Down Barn, Will and Elizabeth had remained in Dorset for about six weeks before travelling to America, where they spent a fortnight with John and Phyllis at Phudd Bottom. John was now two-thirds of the way through his *Autobiography*, and had recently been writing about the onset of Llewelyn's tuberculosis in 1909, and their winter journey to Clavadel. This was part of a chapter entitled 'Europe': as John explained to Littleton, 'I am taking matters in sections. . . . Dates, my dearest friend, were ever my weak point and I am simply letting them go to the devil!'[58] The lack of accurate dating, though it makes hard work for a biographer, in no way detracts from the superlative quality of both this and the preceding eight chapters. Powys had told the important stories of his youth, and frankly outlined the development of his most secret manias and obsessions; he had also written vivid character sketches of some of his friends and family; and although he had concentrated almost exclusively upon the males, he had been prepared to bend his own rules a little: in the chapter he was now writing, for example, he could not resist including a portrait of Frances Gregg at the time when she was the sylph of his dreams. Unfortunately, the concluding chapters of the *Autobiography* are marred by his reticence about his private life, and what had been begun so brilliantly becomes increasingly rhetorical, verbose, and unrevealing.

It was more than twenty years since John had last seen Will, and he felt as though he were meeting a new member of his family for the first time.[59] The two brothers got on well together, and since John was once again feeling extremely poor,[60] he was most interested by Will's stories, based on up-to-date experience, about how much more cheaply it was possible to live in England than in America.[61] Will promised John that if he decided to take Phyllis to England, they could begin their stay in Down Barn, since he was intending to make it his permanent base in Dorset, and had rented it for twelve months despite the fact that he would shortly be returning with Elizabeth to Africa.

By the beginning of March 1934 John and Phyllis had put their cottage up for sale, and were scanning a Dorset newspaper so that they could look out for a suitable apartment in one of the major towns. John had agreed that Phyllis's mother and aunt should be encouraged to live near them when he and Phyllis were settled in England,[62] and he now wrote to his wife saying that he would soon be returning to England, and might eventually have three women with him: but they would be his nurses rather than his mistresses, and if Margaret was still afraid of scandal he would move with them to a remote part of Britain or the Continent.[63]

The *Dorset Echo*, which John and Phyllis were now having sent to them, contained two essays a month written by Llewelyn, whose book of essays, *Earth Memories*, was published in England the day before Louis Wilkinson's *Swan's Milk*. But Llewelyn's health remained extremely uncertain. At the beginning of March he was once again spitting blood; and Alyse, quietly desperate, noted in her journal that: 'he is too delicate to survive another hemorrhage. He says he would be carried off in a second.' When John heard the news of Llewelyn's set-back, he wrote a letter to him calling on God to allow them to meet again;[64] and then, knowing Llewelyn's views about the uselessness of such prayers, John chafed him for his lack of belief.[65] He himself had begun to feel that a new religious age was dawning, and had recently written to Dorothy Richardson telling her that various strange items reported in the newspapers seemed to him to be a sign that the day of the ancient mythological beliefs had come round again.[66]

Then, in the first week of April, John Cowper Powys heard the alarming news that both he and John Lane of the Bodley Head, who had published the English edition of *A Glastonbury Romance*, were being threatened with legal action by the owner of the underground caverns known as Wookey Hole which had featured in the novel. The owner was convinced that he had been portrayed as the grasping Philip Crow; while his legal representatives asserted that John's description of the caverns would deter respectable people from paying to see them.[67] This made John and Phyllis complete their arrangements for leaving America as rapidly as possible. John finished his *Autobiography*, Phudd Bottom was sold, and, having said goodbye to their friends they sailed from New York on 1 June 1934, arriving in Southampton nine days later. After settling in with Phyllis at Down Barn, also known as Rat's Barn, John travelled up to London, where he met Littleton Alfred, and went on to seek the best legal advice on how to face the charges against him.

CHAPTER SIXTEEN

1934–1936

John with Phyllis in Dorset • settles libel suit out of court, March 1935 • moves to Corwen, North Wales, July 1935 • writes Maiden Castle, *1935–6 • begins* Morwyn, *1936 • becomes a Welsh Bard, May 1936 • publishes* Weymouth Sands, *1934 (published in England as* Jobber Skald, *1935),* Autobiography, *1934,* The Art of Happiness, *1935,* Maiden Castle, *1936.*
Theodore publishes Captain Patch *and* Make Thyself Many, *1935.*
Llewelyn in Dorset • seriously ill, July – August 1934 • loses libel case, January 1935 • very ill, September 1935 • corresponds with Rosamund Rose, 1935–6 • leaves with Alyse for Switzerland, September 1936 • publishes Dorset Essays, *1935,* Damnable Opinions, *1935,* The Twelve Months, *1936.*
Louis Wilkinson publishes Welsh Ambassadors, *1936 • A. R. Powys (Bertie) dies, March 1936.*

The solicitors whom John Cowper Powys consulted were both expensive and discouraging. If John's remarks were adjudged to be libellous, he would have to pay a great deal of money even if it could be proved that the remarks had been made accidentally and without forethought. He therefore had to face the prospect of bankruptcy. The trial would not take place for some months, but for the time being the Bodley Head cautiously postponed publication of *Weymouth Sands* for fear of similar problems. This turned out to be a wise move: the local man whom John hired to compare his fictional account of Weymouth with the real life of the town discovered that one of John's invented characters, 'Sippy' Ballard, the town clerk, almost exactly matched a real-life official.[1] At last, after numerous alterations, John's novel was published in 1935 as *Jobber Skald*: a thoroughly misleading title, drawing attention to just one of the several important strands in the book.

Llewelyn had recovered enough during April to be able to go out for short walks, and to enjoy a visit from Edna St Vincent Millay and Eugen Boissevain, but he had to wear dark glasses because his eyes were bad; and when Alyse tried to build up his strength by giving him 'food with some real nourishment in it', he suffered from the most appalling headaches. When John and Phyllis first arrived in Dorset, they were shocked by his appearance,[2] and during June and July 1934 John regularly walked over to Chydyok, and read aloud to his brother from the works of Milton, Bunyan, and Thomas Deloney. These visits were very important to Llewelyn, who wrote that:

> If he stays it will be the crown of my life. He seems well and his
> spiritual vitality is enormous and his flame undimmed. . . . He
> agreed that true religion had nothing to do with morals . . .
> putting back his noble head he looked at me with a proud smile
> full of a wise irony. 'I like,' he said 'to associate religion with
> immorality.' I do love him and honour him so much and I
> cannot believe that with such a witch doctor abroad on the
> downs any great misfortune can come to me.

Llewelyn told John about his recent correspondence with the White House. He took a keen interest in international affairs, and had recognised at an early stage the dangers to world peace posed by Hitler and Mussolini. Knowing that Mrs Roosevelt admired his writing, Llewelyn had sent a letter 'asking her in her bed chamber to beg the President to make some utterance on behalf of Democracy to which everybody of liberal opinions could rally all over the world.' Much to Llewelyn's pleasure, the president himself had replied, though he declared rather cautiously that he had 'a horror of being accused of preaching'.

Llewelyn also told his brother the story of his involvement in a curious case of purely local interest, concerning the management of a local home for mentally backward girls. While Llewelyn and Alyse were away in America, Sylvia Townsend Warner and her close friend Valentine Ackland, usually known as Molly, had been prompted to investigate the home when a girl ran away from it, and they had not been pleased by what they found. Llewelyn took a considerable interest in Sylvia and Molly and their activities, partly because he found something about their relationship which excited him: 'Sylvia', he wrote to Molly, 'must see you often when you look very lovely: I hope she will make you tired tell her from me.'[3] Now in 1934 another girl had fled from the home, and Llewelyn decided that the time had come for some positive action. He drew up a petition suggesting that the present controllers of the home were not 'suitable persons', and asking for 'the whole case . . . [to be] thoroughly investigated by the Dorset County Council'. However, when the petition reached the Dorset County Council, no attempt was made by the councillors to launch an impartial inquiry; instead Llewelyn received a solicitor's letter accusing him of 'falsely and maliciously publishing' defamatory statements about the controllers, and demanding an apology if he wished to avoid legal action.

He refused to apologise, since he was determined that there should be a proper investigation, and soon writs for libel had been taken out not only against him, but also against James Cobb, a farmer who had helped to collect signatures, and Sylvia and Molly, who had written separate letters endorsing the petition. The case would not be called at the Dorchester Assizes for some months; in the meantime John, whose own dealings with the legal profession were making him cynical, warned Llewelyn that he 'must have an expensive elderly weighty lawyer or the Judge *would not so much as listen*, so besotted are they by all the inside politics of the profession.'

Llewelyn became increasingly worried by his libel case, and on 22 July he wrote about it to Gamel. She had recently arrived to spend the summer in Dorset with her husband and the child they had adopted, who was in fact Gerald's four-year-old daughter by a Spanish girl. Gamel and Gerald came at once to Chydyok, accompanied by the poet Arthur Waley and his friend Beryl de Zoete. Their visit was too stimulating and exhausting for Llewelyn, though for once Alyse was blind to what was happening, having eyes chiefly for Gamel. 'Gamel stole in first,' she wrote in her journal that evening,

> so fearful, so as I had known her in the old days – and my heart both rushed forward and shrunk back. . . . Gamel went into the house and I waited for her, and suddenly when I saw her so nervous, so anxious I could not refrain from kissing her, and the tears came to her eyes and she said 'Alyse, you are a lovely person'. But Llewelyn does not understand.

Only a few hours later, Llewelyn had another major haemorrhage. He lay seriously ill until the end of August, and Alyse, who nursed him, was overworked and herself became ill with neuralgia. John was a great support to them both; he visited them every day and once dashed all the way to the village to fetch Alyse the bottle of Burgundy which he hoped would relieve her pain.

After visiting Chydyok, John would walk back across the downs to Rat's Barn. It was a peaceful and mysterious old building, with its massive walls, its high rafters, and its resident owls which flew out hunting each night; but the facilities were primitive, and he disliked being so close to the dangerous cliffs from which he morbidly imagined himself or Phyllis falling to their death. So they began searching for an apartment for the winter,[4] and on John's 62nd birthday, he and Phyllis moved into lodgings above a grocer's shop at 38 High East Street, Dorchester. This was a convenient location, as John had made a 'rough tentative beginning' to a new novel, to be set in Dorchester; but only four days after the move a letter arrived from Simon and Schuster, John's New York publishers, proposing that he should write a popular book on 'the art of happiness'. 'This is the first time in my days', wrote Powys in his diary, 'that I have received an offer of this sort. I have written to say I would certainly do it, putting aside my Dorchester Romance – just begun – until I have finished it.'[5]

In *The Art of Happiness* John Cowper Powys argues that the key to happiness lies in the power of controlling one's own thoughts, and explains various psychological devices by which unhappiness may be kept at bay. Conventional religion is dismissed in favour of a worship of the elements, but no one is condemned for finding comfort where he may: for this is a book of practical wisdom rather than of philosophy, and Powys says that 'from my own point of view the more conjuring tricks we have in our pilgrim's wallet the better.'[6]

Sometimes John found it difficult to work, as he was often visited by friends and family,[7] and he also enjoyed wandering about the country-side near Dorchester, recalling childhood memories.[8] But he made reasonable progress, and towards the end of November he took a short holiday, spending a day in Weymouth with Phyllis, Littleton and Mabel; and then travelling on alone to Norfolk to see Frances Wilkinson, before rejoining Phyllis at a London hotel.[9] On their return to Dorchester, John resumed work on *The Art of Happiness*, which he completed on 2 January 1935.

Since September, Llewelyn's health had been gradually improving, and his fever left him when, on John's advice, he spent seven days 'absolutely at rest like a trappist monk, I didn't speak or write or read, but lay freezing like a rabbit.' However, he was incensed to learn that John had been praying to a Christian saint on his behalf. After some angry letters, in one of which he told John that his judgement was unbalanced, Llewelyn calmed down enough to write to his brother:

> I am always a believer in your supernatural native powers, and half a believer in your sticks and stones and fields of grace, and even to your prayers to Jesus in the damp straw, but you have no idea how deep my distaste for Christianity and its ecclesiastical rogueries – my whole moral nature revolts from its teaching and practise, and it was when I found you praying to 'Church Saints' instead of to the stone of Fal that I felt in some way betrayed and *weakened*.

Financially, Llewlyn was being considerably weakened by legal fees already amounting to £125, and he wrote to Gamel, now back in Spain again, that 'All my prudence and thrift and foresight and backsight seem utterly demoralised by this Law suit.' Ironically enough, his original object in drawing up a petition, which was to ensure that there was an official investigation into the girls' home, had already been achieved: the Ministry of Health had inspected the home, and promised to continue to keep an eye on it. However, the legal proceedings against Llewelyn, James Cobb, and Sylvia and Molly had to take their course.

In December 1934 Theodore wrote to Louis Wilkinson: 'Llewelyn is certainly better – I touch wood. He is more merry. He has had good luck with his writing, I think. He has a good chance to win the libel case too.' Llewelyn himself told James Cobb 'I believe now all will be well'; but when the trial was finally fixed for 17 January 1935 the strain began to show on both Llewelyn and Alyse. She looked horribly unwell,[10] and he suffered from 'slight discolouration', but, as he wrote to Arthur Ficke about the trial at Dorchester:

> I have set my heart on getting in if I can and am to be carried over the downs in an armchair placed in a dog cart like some buggerly Buddha for the populace to bawl after and the seagulls to molest. . . . On the village green I am to be met by Mrs Thomas Hardy's car and conveyed to the Antelope where John has bespoken a room – no. 18 – and will be waiting for me. The next day, all being well, I shall appear in court

He did so, and the national press took up the story: that Sunday, the *News of the World* was advertised on posters bearing the legend: DYING MAN IN DORSET ASSIZE DRAMA', and another Sunday newspaper asked for an article on the 'Meditations of a Dying Man' – though they rejected what he wrote, a beautiful summary of his poetic philosophy, as 'over the heads of the average reader'. Unfortunately, the jury's verdict was also unfavourable, and Llewelyn and his co-defendants were each fined £100 with costs. Llewelyn's total losses, when lawyers fees had been added, came to £573 8s 3d, an appalling sum which would have effectively ruined him but for the recent death in Norwich of his Aunt Etta, who had left each of her nephews and nieces around £1,000. Five days after the trial, Llewelyn was once again lying in bed in his shelter at Chydyok, 'pestered', as he put it, 'with this whoreson blood-spitting and a low fever'; but he soon revived; and on 10 February he wrote to Gamel in Spain:

> Gamel, I am getting well very fast. I can actually feel my life sap pouring back into all my bones. It is a very strange experience and very rare and exultant. Think of being allowed *more* life. Think of seeing you next summer and coming away with you next year to Spain. What fun to travel all together!

Llewelyn recovered from the trial more rapidly than John or Phyllis, who had both been ill with worry, especially as their own legal battle remained unresolved. John determined that in his Dorchester novel he would 'bring in local places but be very careful about any *libel danger* after all these terrible libel suits';[11] and at last he was able to settle out of court, by paying an agreed sum of damages. His total loss was only a little less than Llewelyn's,[12] and but for Aunt Etta's legacy he would have been bankrupt.

After these costly legal disputes, Phyllis had reacted strongly against England as a whole,[13] and John wanted to live in a place where he was less likely to be disturbed by visitors. They began to think once more about John's dream of returning to the land of his ancestors; and at this moment they were visited in Dorchester by the young novelist James Hanley and his wife, who lived in the little village of Cynwyd a mile or two from Corwen in North Wales. The Hanleys strongly encouraged them to move, and promised to find them a temporary home from which they could look for something more permanent. In mid-May, therefore, John and Phyllis travelled up to Cynwyd, where they stayed in a gipsy's bungalow for several weeks, and by the beginning of June they had found what they were looking for.[14]

The town of Corwen lies in the Vale of Edeyrnion, on the southern side of the River Dee, and in 1935 a local land-owner was building Cae

Coed, a small group of cottages on a hillside to the west of the town. They had been designed to the highest modern standards,[15] with their own bathrooms, and with electricity laid on, and John and Phyllis were lucky enough to secure the tenancy of Number Seven, which was still being built near the top of the slope.

In June, they returned to Dorset to await the completion of their new home, and they discovered that while they were away Llewelyn's health had taken another turn for the worse. In March he had felt well enough to spend several weeks with Alyse at Brunswick Terrace in Weymouth, and, besides making many expeditions around the town in an old-fashioned bath chair, he had been able to walk up and down the esplanade: 'I shake hands with everybody I see,' he wrote trium- phantly to Arthur Ficke, 'whether worker or shopkeeper, as a man might do *who has risen from the grave*. Ho! Ho! my life returns. The spring is coming and I am happy to be alive.' But in the early summer, back at Chydyok, Llewelyn caught a bad cold and began spitting blood again. John now found his brother lying in bed all day, though despite this he was in good spirits; his eyes were not so bad as they had been the previous year, he was busy writing essays, and he absolutely refused to see a doctor, telling John that he relied upon some strange concoc- tion prescribed for him years ago by one of the native physicians at Gilgil in Africa.[16] Llewelyn had also been considerably encouraged by some good reviews of his latest collection of philosophical essays, *Damnable Opinions*.

John and Phyllis had returned to Corwen by 3 July, and they stayed for a few days at the Owen Glendwr Hotel while furniture was moved in and the final touches were put to 7, Cae Coed.[17] When they moved in, they found that from the back of the cottage they could walk directly up into the Berwyn mountains. From the front windows, they looked across the valley of the Dee towards an ancient walled enclosure dating back to pre-history. For John, it was like finding himself in a waking dream. Their cottage stood in the centre of the lands once ruled by the Princes of Powys from whom he believed that he was descended; and his mind reverted to his plans for writing a long historical novel, which he now intended should be set in North Wales and have Owen Glendower as its hero.[18] However, he still had to finish his Dorchester romance, and he spent much of the rest of the year working on it.

In *Maiden Castle*,[19] as in his two previous novels, John Cowper Powys deals with the occult, or the hidden reality of things, but the sinister tone of *Maiden Castle* comes as an unpleasant shock after the magical healing of the Grail in *A Glastonbury Romance*, and the nostalgic enchantment of *Weymouth Sands*. Maiden Castle itself is the prehistoric site fortified by massive earthworks which lies just outside Dorchester, and the main character in the novel, Dud No-man, an historical novelist, is one of Powys's most obvious self-portraits. Dud's curious name not only protected Powys himself from another libel suit, but was a way of characterising a man 'whose mind was so morbid, and whose virility was so weak, that he could neither "love" as other men or feel angry as other men.' *Maiden Castle* is concerned with human relationships as well as the occult: Dud No-man falls in love with a circus-girl, Wizzie Ravelston, whom he rescues from her brutal employer; and the story of Dud and Wizzie is a thoughtful reworking of Powys's own experiences as a younger man – experiences omitted from his recent *Autobiography* – when he had found that most of the women with whom he became sexually involved were first irritated and then repelled by his failure to consummate their relationship.

But more important than Dud's meeting with Wizzie is his meeting with the other central character in the novel, Enoch or Uryen Quirm, who turns out to be his father, and who may be seen as a projection of the darker and more powerful side of Powys's own personality. Seeming to Dud No-man like some Celtic corpse-god, Uryen not only calls Shaftesbury by its old name of Palladour, but has a sinister mania for visiting Maiden Castle; and when prehistoric votive offerings are found there by archaeologists, he declares: 'these things are like dark-finned fish embedded in ice. *They have life in them that can be revived.*'

Uryen Quirm believes that not only the votive images, but the ancient sites themselves are centres of occult power, and he confides in his son: 'Just think of it, lad, . . . Mai-Dun, Poundbury, Maumbury Rings, all coming slowly back to life!' It was not long since Powys had been writing to Dorothy Richardson about signs that the world was entering a new age, in which ancient beliefs would once more come into their own; and now he shows us Dud No-man gradually becoming less sceptical about Uryen's beliefs, and beginning to make strange speculations of his own connecting Dorchester with the next astrological era: 'Dorchester . . . its secret goes back far beyond the Romans! The Camp on the Waters. That's why it's lucky to live here when we're moving into Aquarius.'

Dud No-man is told by his father that: '"Uryen" is no Celtic word but far older – a word belonging to that mysterious civilisation . . . possessed of secrets of life that Aryan science has destroyed.' It is this civilisation which is presumed to have built Avebury and Stonehenge, and to have made 'Mai-Dun . . . a civilised *polis*, long before the Romans came'. Dud No-man himself looking up at the great earthworks of Maiden Castle, wonders:

> whether it really *is* possible that if I'd come along this road ten thousand years ago I should now be gazing up at the Cyclopean walls and towers and parapets of a great, peaceful city of a far nobler civilisation than ours, where war and torture and vivisection were unknown, where neither the pleasures of life were denied nor the paths to immortality discredited?

If this Golden Age is to be restored, Uryen Quirm and others like him must break through to 'the Power of the Underworld', but this is a difficult and dangerous task, and Dud No-man decides that it is not for him: however, like John Cowper Powys, he will never 'close . . . his mind to the "intimations of immortality" that . . . were so thick about him.'

It was now almost forty years since *Odes and Other Poems* had appeared in print, and, between them, John and his brothers Theodore and Llewelyn had had more than sixty books published. However, apart from a slim and not very helpful volume by William Hunter on *The Novels and Stories of T. F. Powys* (1930), there had been no attempt at a general appreciation of any of their work. This gap was now filled by R. H. Ward's critical study *The Powys Brothers*; while for those who were interested in more biographical details than had appeared in John's *Autobiography* or in his own *The Buffoon* or *Swan's Milk*, Louis Wilkinson was commissioned to write a book about the three brothers based on his long friendship and correspondence with them all. Despite having been unkindly treated by Louis in the past, John did not hesitate to give his approval to Louis's plans;[20] and Theodore and Llewelyn also gave Louis a free hand to quote from their letters to him. Louis came to stay at the Dairy Farm at Chaldon during the summer of 1935 while he was writing his new book, and he frequently visited Llewelyn and read sections of it to him. Other members of the Powys family were less enthusiastic: Bertie, a man of great distinction in his own field, was irritated by the title *Welsh Ambassadors*, pointing out that the Powys family had had nothing to do with Wales for at least four hundred years; and Littleton, who had found some of Louis's comments in *Swan's Milk* highly offensive, became more and more unhappy as the publication date for *Welsh Ambassadors* approached.[21]

In the meantime, Llewelyn was working as hard as his health allowed. In the autumn of 1935 a volume of his *Dorset Essays* was published and generally well received by the critics, though it had sold fewer than a thousand copies by Christmas; and the poetic essays which he had been contributing to the *Daily Herald* were collected and published in 1936 by the Bodley Head. They appeared under the title of *The Twelve Months* and were illustrated by Robert Gibbings. Llewelyn also found time to send thoughtful letters of advice and encouragement to those who asked for his help. To one young man of twenty, who had read *Damnable Opinions* and who wanted some practical advice on how to live according to Llewelyn's philosophy when he was compelled to spend most of each day in an office, Llewelyn wrote:[22]

> 'Hide your real life.' Concentrate with passionate intensity upon developing your mind. . . . Read. . . . Unless you are absolutely certain you have found a girl with tastes like your own *do not marry*. Take all sexual pleasures you can but be very careful about the Pox and never under any circumstances take any unfair advantage of a girl or leave her in the lurch. . . . Bring analysis and philosophic thought to bear upon all the incidents of the day however petty and tiresome. Never explain, *never complain*. Have confidence in yourself. You have a margin of freedom *convert it into a golden margin*.

Another admirer with whom Llewelyn began a more prolonged correspondence was Mrs Rosamund Rose, who wrote in November 1935 praising his *Dorset Essays*.[23] The following month she told him about a serious illness from which she was suffering, and Llewelyn, who had been attracted by her personality, replied sympathetically:[24]

> This is most distressing news – I shall be truly enormously happy to hear all is well. You seem to me a very sensitive and rare woman and very brave and just such a one who should live for many seasons bringing a grace and heightening to life – to human life so often gross and clumsy.

Earlier in 1935, Llewelyn was visited by the young poet Kenneth Hopkins. Llewelyn was too ill to see him for more than a few minutes, but he told him to 'Burn always with an intense flame, think always of beauty, never of the plaudits of men. Be proud of your calling as a member of the pilgrim band of poets.'[25] Hopkins found Powys looking older than his fifty years,[26]

> for his face was lined by illness and his eyes were deep set. He had a mass of curly, almost white hair, and a thick beard. The hand he held out to me was thin, with the blue veins clearly visible. His voice was not strong, but I thought its slow, rich tones the most remarkable I had ever heard.

Other meetings followed, and a considerable volume of correspondence in which Llewelyn Powys was at great pains to comment upon Kenneth Hopkins's poems, and to give him detailed advice about his life as a writer.

During the summer, when Llewelyn had often enjoyed Louis Wilkinson's company, he was also visited by Gamel, and pledged himself in a subsequent letter to remain 'Your attached and loving friend until the years of [my] life are complete.' For some time he had seen nothing of Theodore, who had been one of the signatories of Llewelyn's unlucky petition, and had somehow got it into his head that Llewelyn was very angry with him about the libel case. But he did see Francis Powys and his wife Minny, and 'was as nice as I could be to both' of them; and he was also visited by his sister Marian, who came over from New York with her son Peter to spend the summer in England.

In late August, Marian and Peter travelled up to Corwen to visit John and Phyllis. No doubt they heard about Francis and Minny's recent visit;[27] about John's explorations along the River Dee;[28] about excursions to the ruins of Valle Crucis Abbey, and to the Eisteddfod at Caernarvon;[29] and how Phyllis disliked the local shop-keepers, but was fascinated by the Welsh character and customs.[30] John found Peter 'extraordinary nice, tactful & diplomatic', and admired the way he coped with Marian, whom he himself described as: 'undoubtedly the most Nietzschian woman it's even been my lot to meet.'

After her departure, John settled back into the routine he had established for himself: dealing with his vast correspondence; reading, with the help of translations, a passage from the Welsh Bible, and a passage from Homer; taking two long walks every day,[31] and working on *Maiden Castle*. In September he was visited by Littleton and Mabel;[32] and towards the end of November Louis Wilkinson arrived and made them laugh by reading extracts from *Welsh Ambassadors*.[33] Phyllis was saved from over-work by the device of sending their guests out to eat their main meal of the day at an hotel in the town,[34] but John was worried about her health, and pleased when it was decided that her mother should come over from America to live next door to them.[35]

In September, Llewelyn had spent another totally silent week at John's request, but the following month he and Alyse were thoroughly alarmed when his temperature rose to 102 degrees, and he began suffering from night sweats for the first time for twenty-five years. He stopped work and refused to see visitors, and when he was a little better he wrote to John saying that he was now thinking of going out to Switzerland as soon as he was strong enough to travel.[36]

John also heard from Theodore, who had not been without his troubles:[37] in the early autumn Violet had been ill in bed for three or four weeks, leaving him to look after both her and Susan, and making it impossible for him to read quietly in his study, which was now his favourite occupation. However, a collection of his short stories had been published as *Captain Patch*; another story, *Make Thyself Many*, was published separately in a limited edition; and, more important, the government had granted him an income of £60 a year as a pension on the Civil List.

Despite the weakness in his heart which had prevented him from being enlisted during the Great War, Theodore appeared to be in better health than most of his brothers: in mid-January 1936 John, Littleton, Bertie and Llewelyn were all laid up with one illness or another. Bertie, who had always been so fit, was now the third of the brothers to suffer from a stomach ulcer, and the experience seems to have upset his mental balance. He absolutely refused to give up work, and when his wife 'pleaded with him and said "You will kill yourself,"' he replied very oddly: 'You will be grievously bruised but Time will heal the scar.'

It was now, early in 1936, that *Welsh Ambassadors* was published. John and Phyllis were full of praise for Louis's achievement; but although Llewelyn wrote Louis a generally admiring letter, he was almost as upset as Littleton by the portrait of their father. Louis had suggested an underlying sadism in the Rev. C. F. Powys's character, and Llewelyn at once wrote to *The Times* to announce that: 'All my recollections testify to the essential underlying gentleness of my father's character.'[38] When Littleton's autobiography, *The Joy Of It* was published less than two years later, it could be seen that he had devoted a good deal of space to 'correcting' Louis on this and other interpretations of character; but *Welsh Ambassadors* remains the more penetrating account of the Powys family, and when Katie compared

Louis's book with Littleton's, she felt that the first illuminated her memories, while the second made them depressingly dull.[39]

During February, John, Littleton and Llewelyn were all in better health: Llewelyn was hard at work on some essays, and John made some corrections to the typescript of *Maiden Castle* before sending copies to London and New York.[40] Bertie, however, was very ill, but his nerves had been affected by the war, and he was so terrified by the prospect of receiving treatment in hospital[41] that he continued journeying round the country as if there was nothing wrong with him.[42] The result was a stomach haemorrhage, after which he had to enter a nursing home. Unfortunately, it was too late to save him, and the manner of his death was particularly gruesome. He could not bear to use an enema to relieve the constipation caused by his stomach trouble,[43] his body became 'slowly poisoned by absorption', and on Sunday 8 March he lost consciousness and soon afterwards died.

Llewelyn was so shocked by the news that he was unable to sleep for several nights. John travelled down to Hindhead, where he hardly recognised his dead brother's features, so sadly were they altered. Then the coffin was nailed up, and John was driven behind the hearse all the way to Dorset,[44] where the funeral service took place in the church of Winterbourne Tomson, whose restoration Bertie had himself supervised. Llewelyn was not well enough to attend, but Alyse went in his place. She travelled with Theodore whom, as she told Llewelyn, she found full of a kind of morbid good humour in the presence of death:

> The clergyman was late in coming, the church was very draughty, and Alyse said, 'Why are we waiting?' 'Waiting,' said Theodore as he turned up his collar, 'for *somebody else* to die.' Observing Littleton's face contorted with emotion, he remarked, 'Cows soon forget to blare for their calves,' . . . He was a trifle put out by Rivers Pollock's saying, 'Why, how odd you look in a bowler,' but even here Theodore was not nonplussed and said to Alyse, 'It is what the King wears, isn't it?' John arrived late in the little church in a red shirt and it seemed, so Alyse said, that his spiritual flame-like power was so great that he might have raised the dead. He kissed Alyse *eight times*.

Llewelyn still wrote to Gamel, but he was now conducting a more passionate correspondence with Rosamund Rose. Mrs Rose's illness had led to a spell in hospital, but by the end of January she was back at her home, Leweston Manor near Sherborne, when Llewelyn wrote that he was 'going to put on a different jacket', and become her 'philosophical tutor'. He added: 'you are born sensitive and poetical – these are rare gifts and because you possess this *everbody loves you* . . . but [you] must be discerning and discriminating.'[45] Soon afterwards she visited Chydyok, from where Llewelyn wrote on 2 February saying that Alyse regarded her as '"a real discovery" – and you *are*; you *are*, you are – I shall teach you a thousand things – will send you books and papers *and never let you go.*'[46] Six days later he wrote again, saying that if he became well he would go walking with her, and she could 'suddenly become a little girl again, with white breasts cold as mushrooms under your holland frock and strange marginal thoughts in your beautiful head.'[47] After this, she began to write to him as 'darling Lulu', and on St Valentine's Day he told her: 'There is nothing about you that does not delight me and that I do not love – I would like to be near you *every* moment of the day.'[48]

In May, Rosamund visited Chydyok a second time. Alyse warmed still more to her 'very rare kind of beauty' telling Llewelyn that Rosamund had 'some impregnable spiritual chamber' of her own;[49] while Llewelyn wrote her letters on three consecutive days, telling her in one of them: 'I am so happy, to have seen you and to find it is *all* true – and my dreams were true dreams. I shall never see enough of you – your Lulu. I won't ever be a trouble to you – or ever make Alyse unhappy: but oh! my heart so dances over the hills to you.'[50] When Rosamund began to worry about their correspondence, feeling that she was being deceitful to Alyse, Llewelyn first suggested that she burn their letters,[51] and then wrote: 'I must never try to join my dreams to a world of reality – that is very clear – until I have made myself quite well . . . in future you will listen to me talking on matters that have to do with the poetry of nature.'[52] Their love-affair remained entirely in the mind, though in his letters to her it was not long before Llewelyn had decided that 'the poetry of nature' might very well include pages of detailed erotic fantasy.[53] Rosamund presumably enjoyed these pages, for she made no further move to prevent Llewelyn from writing to her, and she looked after all his letters most carefully; though ten years later she protested to Alyse that her feelings for Llewelyn had been entirely spiritual, and that at the time of their correspondence her sexual longings were being satisfied by another man.[54]

In early May Katie spent ten days with John and Phyllis at Corwen, and while she was there the local Eisteddfod took place. Apart from the usual celebrations, there were to be Druidical ceremonies within a circle of standing stones, ceremonies at which John was among those who were to be honoured. The proceedings opened to the sound of thunder rolling among the mountains, and Katie and Phyllis watched in pouring rain[55] while John was installed as a bard under the title Ioan Powys.[56]

When the ceremonies were over, John returned to work on *Maiden Castle*. It had been rejected by two English publishers already, and this disposed him to accept most of the cuts which Schuster was now demanding.[57] By 18 June he had revised the edited version, which was to be published in New York in the Fall, and a few days later he began work on a new novel.[58]

John Cowper Powys had been strongly opposed to vivisection for many years: he had written passages condemning the practice in many books, including *Wolf Solent* and *Maiden Castle*, and there had been a particularly sustained attack in *Weymouth Sands*. Now, partly in the hope that a 'committed' work would meet with Frances Wilkinson's approval,[59] he started writing 'my anti-vivisection story', *Morwyn*.[60]

Powys himself, very thinly disguised, is the hero of this new book, a weird fantasy which is at times so strange and sinister that Frances Wilkinson, far from approving of it, described it as 'drenched in evil'.[61] As the story opens, the hero is walking up towards the Berwyns, feeling annoyed, just like John,[62] by the thought of 'the miles of barbed wire that confine this part of our mountain range to certain plump totem-birds and their dedicated keepers.'[63] The dog at his side, Black Peter, is clearly modelled on John's dog 'The Black', now known as 'The Old' or 'The Very Old'; and in his imagined role as a half-pay captain, Powys is visiting a house on the slope above Cae Coed where Morwyn, a sylph-like nineteen-year-old girl, is on holiday with her father, the vivisector. The elderly captain had hoped to go for a walk with Morwyn: he loves her, and realises that she loves him; and it is difficult not to see in their relationship similarities to the one between John Cowper Powys and Phyllis Playter. She is described as not pretty, but highly attractive; at times she becomes nervous, and needs soothing, but she is devoted to him, despite the considerable difference in their ages, and when he himself is upset, and clings to her, he feels: 'a strange sensation of infinite safety and security . . . together with a feeling as if I were back once more, for all my grey hairs, and conscious too of its fathomless beatitude, safe from life's horrors, in the blessed womb of the woman who bore me.'

Much to the captain's annoyance he, Morwyn and Black Peter are joined on their walk by the vivisector. When they have all climbed up the mountain-side, and are looking back at the River Dee, a meteorite strikes the slope above them, and they are carried down through the earth to the vast caverns of Hell. The vivisector is killed by the fall, but his spirit survives, and is soon at home: for Hell is reserved for those who have been cruel, and who can now enjoy themselves watching on giant television screens the vivisection experiments currently being carried on in the upper world.

Pursued by the vivisectors, who are prepared to leave their screens for the chance of torturing live people and a live dog, Morwyn and the captain escape with the Welsh Bard Taliesin, who is hunting for Merlin, to the deepest regions of Hell. Here Merlin briefly awakes to save them from their pursuers, and they enter an area where Rhadamanthus, the Judge of the Golden Age, watches over the cauldron of rebirth, and the mounds where Saturn and the Earth Mother lie sleeping until the dawn of a new Golden Age, when science and the pursuit of truth will no longer be worshipped at the expense of the individual conscience. Socrates then explains that mankind took a wrong turning when, in the time of Friar Bacon's experiments, 'The soul of a wise man, the conscience of a good man, became no longer the test.' At length Morwyn's father has a change of heart, and sets off with Morwyn to preach against vivisection in America, while the captain is escorted back to Wales to await their return.

After working for two weeks on *Morwyn*, John travelled south to spend a month at Down Barn with not only Phyllis and 'The Very Old', but also Phyllis's mother and aunt, both of whom now lived next door to them in Cae Coed. He found Llewelyn looking healthier, working hard,[64] and able to enjoy short walks.

On 13 August, a few days after John had returned to North Wales, Llewelyn celebrated his fifty-second birthday; his birthdays had become memorable events in the locality: he liked to give presents to everyone, and he would send 10s. to the landlord of the Sailor's Return so that anyone coming in after seven in the evening could drink his health.[65] Everything seemed to be going well: they were relieved to hear that Gamel and Gerald had escaped from the dangers of the Spanish Civil War, and were on their way home to England;[66] and

Llewelyn was looking forward to spending November and December at Clavadel in Switzerland.

Towards the end of September, however, as Alyse wrote to Kenneth Hopkins, 'Mr Powys had a rather serious haemorrhage of the lungs . . . owing to having seen too many people and is unable to write any letters and is, indeed, very ill.'[67] Alyse now thought that there was very little chance of their going to Switzerland, but Llewelyn, determined that he should be well enough to travel, abandoned all his work and lay still for many days. At last, on 1 December, he and Alyse and Gertrude were driven to Bournemouth in a car lent by Rosamund Rose, and went on by train first to London, and then to Dover. At Dover they said good-bye to Gertrude, and although they planned to be back within six months,[68] it would be three years before Alyse returned, and Llewelyn had now left England for the last time.

CHAPTER SEVENTEEN

1936–1939

John in North Wales, writing Owen Glendower, *1937–9* • *visited by Dreiser, summer 1938* • *lectures at Bridgend, December 1938* • *publishes* Morwyn, *1937*, The Pleasures of Literature, *1938.*
Theodore in Dorset • *publishes* Goat Green, *1937* • *suffers a mild stroke, spring 1938.*
Llewelyn with Alyse to Switzerland • *reaches Clavadel, December 1936 and stays with Lisaly Gujer* • *visited by Gamel, August 1937* • *Llewelyn writing* Love and Death, *1937–8* • *very ill, December 1937* • *publishes* Somerset Essays, *1937*, Rats in the Sacristy, *1937*, The Book of Days, *1937*, Love and Death, *1939* • *very ill from 19 November 1939* • *dies, 2 December 1939.*

After disembarking at Calais, Llewelyn Powys and Alyse Gregory travelled through a moonlit night across France and into Switzerland. In the early hours of 2 December 1936 their train arrived at Lausanne, where they broke their journey for several days in order to move into rooms found for them by Dr Frey, the man who had treated Llewelyn so many years ago at Clavadel. Frey's up-to-date report was encouraging, but he told Llewelyn to travel on to Clavadel in a wheel-chair, and then to remain in bed until he came to make another examination on 16 December.

Before leaving England, Llewelyn and Alyse had arranged to stay with Lisaly Gujer, who still remembered Llewelyn from his previous visits to Clavadel. She had had an exhausting job looking after an old German professor for the past fifteen years, and was now stout, lame and asthmatic. However Llewelyn had been 'the great romance of her life' and she was eagerly looking forward to caring for him.[1] When Llewelyn and Alyse arrived at Clavadel, in a heavy snow storm, Lisaly met their train. Alyse's first impression was 'that I should never, never find anything in common with her', but gradually she came to appreciate Lisaly's 'desire to please Llewelyn', and her 'will of iron'. On New Year's Day, 1937, Alyse wrote in her journal: 'She has a childish disposition, offended at one moment and interfering at the next, but she has a good heart and an inexhaustible energy devoted entirely to our service.' Llewelyn's health began to improve at once in the mountain air, and when Dr Frey examined him on 10 January, he 'declared that he would "make old bones".'

Optimism about his health made him worry less about what he described to his sister Lucy as 'days so disastrous' in his writing career. John Lane's bankruptcy had swallowed up Llewelyn's royalties on *Dorset Essays*, and *The Twelve Months*, which had already received some reviews, was suddenly withdrawn from publication for the same reason.[2] He was also having no luck in America, where none of his books had been published since 1932, partly because one literary agent whom he dealt with had absconded, while the next one failed to answer his letters for eight months.

John Cowper Powys had been having better luck: after being rejected by seven publishers, *Maiden Castle* had at last been accepted for publication in England by Cassells, and they were to publish it in its entirety.[3] By the third week in January 1937 John had completed *Morwyn*,[4] which Cassells also agreed to publish later in the year, and he at once busied himself with a volume of essays to be published by Schuster the following year as *The Pleasures of Literature*.

In February John took a short holiday from his work, travelling to London and staying for a few days in lodgings in Dorset Square[5] with his sister Gertrude. She was in London for an exhibition of her paintings; at the private view John and their brother Littleton helped her to look after their guests,[6] including many old family friends such as Louis Wilkinson and Bernie and Belle O'Neill; and a few days later, much to John's surprise and delight, one of the visitors to the exhibition was their former governess Miss Beales.[7]

In May 1937 first Louis Wilkinson and then Gertrude went out to Switzerland to visit Llewelyn, and found him very much better than they dared to hope. His digestion was delicate, and he still had to observe a strict diet, but tuberculosis no longer compelled him to lie in bed all day. At the beginning of March he had been well enough to join Alyse: 'for a drive in a sleigh to see an avalanche. It was my first outing in three years and I was in a joy to be free';[8] and soon he was going on walks, and enjoying meeting ordinary people. 'I like the Swiss so much', he wrote enthusiastically. 'I like their beards, their cows, their wine, their cheese – an honest hearty people and great lovers of freedom.' By mid-March his health was so good that he had decided to stay at Clavadel for another twelve months, if necessary, in the hope of a complete recovery. By July, Alyse was writing cheerfully in her journal about walking with Llewelyn 'up the mountain':

> We walked through the meadows and on the mountain uplands as if in a dream. Llewelyn was carried away by all that he saw, aware of the miracle of being able to move freely once more; holding my hand and stopping to kiss me; and I could say to myself, 'At this moment I know what happiness is!'

With Llewelyn in better health, Alyse was able not only to take German lessons, but also to begin writing her collection of philosophical essays, *Wheels on Gravel*; while Llewelyn's literary career was also prospering. The Bodley Head, thoroughly reorganised, had published *Twelve Months*, and later in the year were to publish a volume of *Somerset Essays*; Watts were bringing out a collection of essays appropriately entitled *Rats in the Sacristy*, about men whose thought was profoundly anti-Christian; while from The Golden Cockerel Press came *The Book of Days*, a handsome limited edition in which each day of the year was illustrated by a quotation from Llewelyn's writings; and the news from New York was also good; Van Wyck Brooks had taken charge of Llewelyn's affairs in America, and was writing the introduction for an American edition of *Earth Memories*.

All these books had been written before Llewelyn came to Clavadel. He was still writing an occasional essay, but his main task now, taken up at Alyse's suggestion, was to work on *Life and Death*, the autobiographical novel which he had laid aside some three and a half years previously. Now renamed *Love and Death*, it begins with Llewelyn becoming ill at Chydyok in the spring of 1933, and remembering his love for Gamel Woolsey, who appears as 'Dittany Stone', and how he finally lost her to Gerald Brenan, who appears as 'Randal Pixley'. Alongside extracts from Gamel's poetry, there are some fine descriptions of Dittany, whose 'presence seemed in an odd way to suggest not only the world of mediaeval mortals but also the mediaeval fairy world';[9] but Llewelyn was no longer passionately in love with Gamel, and the novel lacks conviction. The triangle of conflicting loves and loyalties between Llewelyn, Gamel and Alyse which had made their relationship most dramatic in real life was also missing, because Llewelyn had set his story in pre-war Montacute, long before he had met and married Alyse Gregory, and there was no comparable figure in the novel to take her place. The vignettes of life at Montacute are the most deeply felt paragraphs in the book: Llewelyn was still dreaming sadly about his dead brother Bertie, and now in his imagination he was able to recall him to life, to wander with him once again through a wood full of cowslips, and to describe many other details of their shared childhood. *Love and Death* ends in fantasy: Llewelyn 'remembers' how Dittany died in 1914 after an accident, and how Randal soon afterwards shot himself. Then, returning to 'the present' of 1933, Llewelyn lies sick at Chydyok, and despite Alyse's tender nursing, dies after a severe haemorrhage.

In reality Gamel was still very much alive, and in August 1937 she arrived at Clavadel to spend ten days with Llewelyn and Alyse. Llewelyn was pleased to see her, and Alyse was overjoyed, writing in her journal: 'I thought I had never looked on a more beautiful face, and I felt, after the constant restraint I am under with Lisaly, immeasurable relief to be able to talk with her . . . we are bound together in some incommunicable way.' Lisaly, however, was thoroughly upset by Gamel's arrival, and was furious with Alyse when one evening she allowed Gamel and Llewelyn to walk home together after they had all been out on the mountainside for the afternoon.

Llewelyn was still writing to Rosamund Rose, though his letters had become less intimate now that there was so little chance of their meeting, and Alyse had begun to play an important part in their relationship, just as she had done in Llewelyn's relationship with Gamel. She now wrote to Rosamund, who had been unwell:[10]

> I think of you constantly – and with such anxiety. Never a day passes that Llewelyn and I do not say to each other 'I hope Rosamund is all right'. I can't bear to think that your eager, sensitive, proud, generous, capricious, . . . reckless and unique spirit should be held down by illness.

Llewelyn also wrote regularly to John, who was delighted to hear about the improvement in his health.[11] Shortly after returning to Corwen from Gertrude's exhibition in London, John had heard sad news about his former lecture-manager, Arnold Shaw, who had died in New York;[12] and in the spring there had been a disappointing report by Littleton of a visit to John's wife and son at their new home in

Wiston, Sussex. Margaret was looking drab, elderly, and very unwell. She appeared to find conversation an effort, and apart from a brief period of gardening she spent most of each day hidden away in well-warmed quarters in a separate part of the house. But she appeared to be utterly dependent on her son, and Littleton thought that there would be no chance of his marrying while she was alive.[13]

Littleton came up to Corwen in June, and learned that John and Phyllis had been having Welsh lessons,[14] and that John had been asked to undertake an official duty at the Corwen Eisteddfod. This involved reciting a short Welsh poem,[15] and was a welcome distraction from some unexpected financial worries. John had been working hard on the first chapter of his great Welsh romance, *Owen Glendower*, but had to put it to one side when he heard the professionally devastating news[16] that Schusters had totally rejected *Morwyn*, and expected him to rewrite approximately half of *The Pleasures of Literature*. Without the advance royalties which he had been expecting, he was once more very short of money.

In July he forgot these worries for a while and took Phyllis down to stay in East Chaldon for a few weeks. While they were in Dorset, they travelled over to Montacute with Gertrude; and, on another occasion, John was driven to a left-wing literary meeting by Katie and some of her friends. He had recently had all his teeth taken out, and had refused to have false ones in their place, but this did not prevent him from giving a spirited talk![17]

When he returned to Corwen, John worked hard on *The Pleasures of Literature*, but the financial strain was considerable. Katie came up for a short holiday towards the end of the summer, but found it impossible to relax in the tense atmosphere.[18] A little later, when the English edition of *Morwyn* was published, and Louis Wilkinson wrote an admiring letter, John was particularly pleased 'as I'm so poverty-stricken just now that I can't send anybody a free copy.'

Other Powys publications in the autumn of 1937 included *From the Ground Up*, a posthumous collection of Bertie's architectural papers, and Littleton's autobiography, *The Joy Of It*. Theodore's only publication for the year was *Goat Green*, a story of sixty pages written some years previously and now published for the first time by the Golden Cockerel Press. Violet had been ill again,[19] and Theodore spent a good deal of time looking after her and Susan. He had learned that it was best to take domestic difficulties as lightly as he could, whatever his real feelings; and when one of his Chaldon friends, the sculptress Betty

Muntz, accused him of camouflaging his true nature with the mantle of Mr Woodhouse in Jane Austen's Emma, he looked at her:[20]

> as if I had suddenly revealed intimate knowledge of some long buried secret, and he said rather tersely, 'Ah, you've found me out.' Then, instantly, his delightful roguish twinkle followed and he said in his mildest and most Woodhouse-like voice, 'Well, my dear, the function of a mantle is to protect, is it not? And to camouflage is to disguise, I believe? I think I could hardly have chosen better, do you agree?'

At Clavadel during the summer and early autumn Llewelyn had been showing a notable lack of caution. Alyse recorded that he was moving 'with a kind of rushing eagerness, throwing himself into every little incident as a girl throws herself into the arms of a lover'; but his long walks on the mountainside overstrained him, and by October his health was deteriorating and he was suffering from headaches and palpitations of the heart. Alyse once more became anxious and unhappy, and her state of mind was not improved by reading aloud to Llewelyn the early chapters of the manuscript of his *Love and Death*: 'it gave me a strange sensation – pitiful, sad – as if all human relations were made of air and illusions. I was so overcome when I read the first part of the love affair, knowing that he had Gamel in his mind, that I could not go on for a long time . . .' Llewelyn reproved her, saying that he was '*amazed*' that she should take 'so "narrow" a view over this book – a *domestic* view', and that he would burn what he had written if she was distressed by it. Realising that she must conceal her emotions, Alyse made suggestions for some alterations to the novel, 'and I praised it *very* much and he is happy now about it.' But that evening she wrote bitterly in her journal: 'There is no truth except in the uncaring heart of nature. . . . Deep in his heart he is proud to have hurt me, and deep in my heart I know that I have never truly yielded my spirit to him.'

Although Llewelyn was confined to his bed for a few days in October, by mid-November he was writing to Katie: 'I am pretty well again now. . . . I walk very firm and strong and feel vigorous. . . . I think I shall be all right if I do not over tire myself again with these huge walks.' Unfortunately this was not to be the case. Llewelyn was now enjoying the company of the artist Ernst Ludwig Kirchner, a refugee from Nazi Germany; and on 2 December 1937, immediately after a picnic expedition with Kirchner, he suffered a severe haemorrhage. Three days later, Alyse wrote:

> Llewelyn is still very very ill with the bleeding still going on. The doctor comes and gives him injections of calcium which shock his system from head to foot. When I see the little toys he brought for the [local] children's Christmas – the chocolate Santa Claus – *I am drowned in pain*.

Gradually the immediate danger passed. Louis Wilkinson went out to Switzerland, and telephoned Bernie O'Neill on 16 December to say that Llewelyn was now spending much of each day asleep.[21] On Christmas Day Alyse bravely went ahead with the Christmas party which had been planned for the peasant children, but for several months Llewelyn was extremely ill. His flesh wasted away because he could eat so little and for a while his eyesight was too poor for him to read or write; it was not until the beginning of April 1938 that he really began to recover.[22]

Theodore who had been dreadfully worried about Llewelyn's health was now very unwell himself. Susan, then aged only four-and-a-half, recalled years later how she and Violet were eating breakfast in the kitchen, when Theodore entered and complained of feeling ill. Soon afterwards, he collapsed and fell to the floor. For a few moments he was unconscious, and Violet ran out of the house with Susan to find help. Will Powys was on holiday in England, staying at Rat's Barn, and he was driving into the village with some of his family when he passed Violet and Susan running along the road, and stopped his car to find out what the matter was. Soon Theodore had been carried up to bed, and when a doctor had been summoned they learned that he had had a stroke.[23] Luckily it had been a slight one, and, as Llewelyn wrote to a friend, 'his mind and body [are] unaffected'. But he had to remain in bed for some time, and when he was allowed up again he suffered from occasional giddiness, and from a continually aching head.[24]

When John heard the news of Theodore's illness, he tried to encourage him by sending him letters detailing as many instances as he could discover in which people had made full recoveries from a first stroke, and never suffered from a second one.[25] Although John was still feeling poor, he and Phyllis had only kept one room properly warmed throughout the winter,[26] he was in good enough health to go for regular walks, and he was working as hard as ever. Towards the end of 1937 he had resumed work on *Owen Glendower*, but in January 1938 he had to lay it aside yet again, for both Schusters and Cassells had decided that John's *The Pleasures of Literature*, which now had eleven essays in it, would have more appeal if it were a substantially larger book.[27] So, having already rewritten much of it, John now had to spend still more time writing another nine long essays.

In April, John Cowper Powys's routine was enlivened by a visit from Kenneth Hopkins, who was out of work, and had decided that 'Rather than hang about out of work in Bournemouth I would be a tramp! I would shuffle along the lanes and support myself by selling my poems from door to door!' Before setting out, he wrote to Llewelyn about his plans, and received an encouraging reply wishing him luck and adding: 'May the strong influence of the sun and sweet influence of the moon and magical influence of the stars be ever with you . . .' He spent a night at Corwen before setting out again on the road to London; and John was highly impressed by the romance of his journeying.[28]

Will Powys went over to Switzerland in May to visit Llewelyn, who was still confined to bed. Will himself had been in hospital earlier in the year, to be examined after having begun to suffer from the family stomach trouble, and he delighted Llewelyn by describing in detail a visit to his bedside by Gamel Brenan who was living with her husband near Marlborough. Alyse's bitterness about Gamel's appearance as Dittany in *Love and Death* had been swept away by the severity of Llewelyn's recent illness, and in March she had written in her journal: 'We are always happy when we are alone together. I have been going over his new book with him, and I do not see how I could ever have been distressed by it.' Will found that Llewelyn was once again busily writing essays for the English papers, and although he was disappointed that *Somerset Essays* had sold fewer than 700 copies, and *Rats in the Sacristy* fewer than 200, he had been pleased by the excellent reviews which greeted the American publication of *Earth Memories*. While Will was at Clavadel, Llewelyn was also visited by Reginald Marsh, and received a third visit from Louis Wilkinson, who went through *Love and Death* 'word for word' to suggest improvements.

Will returned to Dorset, to rejoin his wife and children at Rat's Barn; and in early July he drove to Corwen and back to collect John, Phyllis, and 'The Very Old',[29] who had been invited by Gertrude and Katie to spend a week at Chydyok. Bernie O'Neill and Louis Wilkinson also came down from London, and on one memorable day the six of them were joined for tea by Littleton, who had driven over from Sherborne. Theodore could not be present, because he was still too ill to cope with groups of people,[30] but Littleton was in such good health that when he went for a ramble with John and Bernie, he lifted John over an awkward fence, and even carried Dr O'Neill on his back for a few yards.[31] The news about his wife Mabel was less favourable: she was shortly to have an operation for breast cancer, but she was already very ill, and the outlook was poor.[32]

Marian, like her brother Will, had decided to visit Llewelyn at Clavadel; and in July she crossed the Atlantic with her son Peter, and went straight to Switzerland. Llewelyn had been getting dressed each day since 4 June, sitting in the garden to enjoy the company of the village children, and even going on very short walks. But he was extremely weak: on 11 June he had described himself in a letter to Gamel as 'like a new-born calf with my knees trembling if I stand to look at a flower'; a few days later there was the depressing incident of his friend Kirchner's suicide, and Alyse found him 'suddenly so old and frail', and noted that because she loved him so much she was 'doomed', so long as he remained ill, 'to unremitting punishment'. Marian was also distressed to see her brother 'so frail'. Llewelyn himself was chiefly pleased not by Marian herself, but by Peter, who was now sixteen years old and six feet tall. 'He is extraordinarily attractive', wrote Llewelyn to Rivers Pollock, who had recently visited Clavadel, '– a really exciting human being, very good looking, very intense and open to life. I don't know when I have been more drawn to anyone. I longed to protect him.'

On 13 August 1938 it was Llewelyn's fifty-fourth birthday, and four days later he received a letter from John explaining that he had not forgotten his brother's anniversary, but that he had been fully occupied not only with Marian and Peter, who had come on to him from Clavadel, but also Theodore Dreiser. Marian had persuaded Dreiser to call on John when she had coincided with him earlier in the year in her voyage across the Atlantic.[33] Now, as Llewelyn learned, 'He had come fresh from Barcelona. He flew there from Paris carrying a portmanteau of Petit Magdalenes for the fighters [in the Spanish Civil War], and like Goethe went to the firing line "to see what it was like".' After the noise of battle, Dreiser was enchanted by the peacefulness of the Welsh countryside through which they walked while John showed him where his ancestors 'had lived and died, or passed into the spirit world. . . . For he sensed that some of them were still here on the moors at night.' Some months later, Dreiser wrote from California: 'Dear Jack, Dear Phyllis . . . I see Corwen and the heather-carpeted mountain above, and the valley and the river – and know you have as good a world as anywhere. The felicity of a true, mental companionship! To how many in any century, does that come?'[34]

Having arrived at Corwen, Marian immediately began making plans for John and Phyllis to travel out to Switzerland to see Llewelyn, and although John was very nervous about the idea,[35] they would have gone but for another serious illness in the family. Will Powys was staying in Corwen with his wife and two of their children when he was taken ill, and rushed into hospital at Ruthin. While he was there, a gastric ulcer perforated his stomach, and he would have died but for an emergency operation.[36] Elizabeth Powys stayed with John and Phyllis until Will was well enough to travel,[37] and by that time, although John had received some £20 from Llewelyn and Alyse towards the expenses of the journey,[38] he had realised that he and Phyllis could not really afford to travel to Switzerland. *Morwyn* had sold very badly; he had spent the American advance on *The Pleasures of Literature*, and doubted whether he would receive a great deal more from that book, and he was less than half way through *Owen Glendower*.[39] An idea for collaborating with his old friend Edgar Lee Masters on some articles came to nothing,[40] and the only good news was that through the intervention of Gerard Casey, a young correspondent of his, Powys was to receive a substantial fee for a lecture on 5 December at Bridgend in South Wales. 'Ten Guineas! Think of that', he wrote to Louis Wilkinson, '– & the old gentleman without teeth too! . . . when I tell you that I'm to lecture on *Welsh Mythology* you can believe, teeth or no teeth, these great musical Rugger-lads will get their money's worth!' When Llewelyn heard how poor John had become, he sent him by return of post a substantial sum of money which John put to one side, for use in an emergency.[41]

Another reason for John's failure to reach Clavadel that autumn was the threat of a European war.[42] John was particularly alarmed by the prospect because he had taken Elizabeth Powys and Phyllis to the local cinema where they had seen *Things to Come*,[43] H. G. Wells's frightening prediction of a future war in which whole cities would be obliterated by aerial bombardment. John was even prepared to believe in the wisdom of the Munich agreement between Chamberlain and Hitler,[44] until Llewelyn wrote that he himself: 'would have gone to war rather than be bullied and I would never agree to making an alliance with these tyrants unless they changed their manners.'

Llewelyn had also been hoping for a visit from Gamel, but the war scare deterred her from leaving England. After some blood spitting in

September, Llewelyn had spent most of October in bed, correcting proofs of *Love and Death* which, after being corrected by John as well as by Louis, had been accepted for publication by the Bodley Head. Working on this novel had made Llewelyn write rather more warmly to Gamel than he had done for some time, but after she received a letter from him in which he quoted two passages about 'Dittany', she wrote very slightingly to Alyse about Llewelyn's book, saying:[45]

> I have seen two pages of Lulu's novel he sent me – something about Dittany – the flower & a girl. You know what Lulu is – tomorrow it will be a white owl and the month of May. Lulu is in love with life and the visible world – those are his real paramours – . . . Let's walk to Davos by ourselves again, and talk the hours by.

In another letter, Gamel told Alyse not to worry about Llewelyn's book: it had been 'a trouble' to her too, and what she was really looking forward to was Alyse's *Wheels on Gravel*,[46] which was published that autumn with a dedication to her and – at Llewelyn's request[47] – an introduction by John Cowper Powys.

In November Llewelyn's health improved for a while, and he described to Van Wyck Brooks what must have been one of the very last long walks of his life:

> Today I walked further than I have for a year and if I can once *walk again* I shall live. Autumn in these high mountains is wonderful, the larch trees golden amongst the firs and when they stand by themselves they rise out of a carpet yellow and round as a guinea, caused by the fallen needles. I saw a badger that some rogue of a hunter had killed . . . even in death it looked a nobler beast and its eye teeth much finer and sharper than I had remembered.

But in mid-November came two days of blood spitting, followed by a period of lying quietly in bed, not even daring to work, for fear of another haemorrhage. When he felt well enough to receive visitors, Alyse allowed him to see the novelist Ethel Mannin, who had been corresponding with Llewelyn, and had now come all the way to Switzerland to visit him. Despite his illness, he still made a striking impression, Miss Mannin recalled. She felt nervous as she climbed the staircase of 'the châlet-like little house', and was shown into a bedroom 'with a tall stove, and a bed in the corner'. But then came:[48]

the swift awareness of a bearded, pointed face, a fine head,
sensitive hands, kindly, amused eyes. Suddenly I was no longer
nervous, but strangely stirred. There was a light in the room
that did not come from the windows, that was neither sunlight
nor the light off the snow. . . . I have never known such charm
. . . charm that kindles the senses like sunlight.

By Christmas Llewelyn was still in bed, though he had once more
taken up his essay writing, and on Christmas Day he was able to enjoy
watching some of his favourite village children come to tea.

John and Phyllis spent Christmas at Corwen, and John was extremely pleased to have a Christmas letter from Theodore, advising
him not to get too involved with articles or lectures, but to concentrate on completing his historical novel. 'Yes you are right', John
replied, adding that:[49]

For the last month **letters** have been one of my bothers and
handicaps; for *answering* them has taken me all morning and the
best part of the afternoon so I haven't been able to *get to my work*
till *after tea*. . . . They are due to my having for 30 years been a
sort of *secular clergyman* . . . and feeling proud of giving spiritual
advice to so many young persons. . . . But I must get drastic . . .
so I *will*, even at this *second*, only *post this to you* and then turn at
once to my *Owen Glendower* letting the un-answered letters . . .
talk to each other on the shelf and tell their troubles to *each other*.

In *Owen Glendower*,[50] John Cowper Powys tells how the Welsh prince
of that name rebelled against Henry IV of England in the early years of
the fifteenth century, and although Owen himself occupies the centre
of the stage far less often than his adherent and distant cousin, the
young scholar Rhisiart, it is the romance of heroic and hopeless
rebellion which lies at the novel's heart. Such a rebellion is full of an
occult significance, and when Owen formally throws off his allegiance
to Henry IV he shows his awareness of the fact that he is also
challenging fate and destiny by taking a 'magic globe', covering it with
a wolf-skin, and then raising a great axe and bringing it 'crashing down
upon the hidden crystal'.

Owen has been inspired by stories he has heard about the remote
past of the Welsh people, and when, with Rhisiart, he visits the site of
Mathrafal, an ancient Welsh stronghold, he declares:

there's no name . . . that can compare with Mathrafal . . . our fathers were bards as well as warriors . . . they gathered up their ignorance into the most magical names ever invented by man. . . . Our fathers flung into this name all their beating against the gates of the mystery that bowed them down, as it bows us down! . . . I feel as though in the dust of Mathrafal there lives forever . . . all the voyaging desires . . . of the people of this land.

Once, he believes, there was 'a great city with granite walls and marble towers' at Mathrafal, inhabited by a people who 'worshipped the Great Serpent'; and sometimes he has 'felt the rush of the souls of the dead' in that place.

But in launching an armed rebellion, heroic though this is, Owen may have acted against the best interests of the people whom he is trying to defend from their oppressors, and he becomes increasingly aware of this, saying to himself on one occasion:

the way of life of the first people was far wiser, far freer . . . there were no princes, no rulers then, but only the men of the land, living at peace together and worshipping peaceful gods. . . . What is Prince? A word! And what does that word mean? Blood and ashes!

The rebellion means 'blackened towns and ruined villages', and a compulsion 'to go on, on, on – till every head you've trusted lies low, and every heart you've loved is broken!'

The chief cause of Owen's eventual defeat is that he fails to be as utterly ruthless as his cause demands, but, Powys tells us, it is in defeat that Owen learns the true 'secret of the land' of Wales, which lies in 'the *mythology of escape*'. Successful resistance to oppression depends upon being 'able to escape into . . . the world *outside the world*', which is, in part, the world of legend. Rhisiart and others who are present at Owen's death feel that they have come 'close to a crack in the visible; a crack through which the invisible was blowing an ice-cold blast on its phantom horn.' From being a mere Prince of Powys, Owen Glendower has become a Prince of Welsh legend, and, in his own way, a part of the lost world of Mathrafal.

John Cowper Powys's writing of *Owen Glendower* was briefly interrupted by a lecture on Owen which he delivered to a local society on 10 February,[51] but he still answered a great many letters,[52] and he also had a number of visitors. C. Benson Roberts, for example, arrived at Corwen in mid-April, with the poet Huw Menai; and Nicholas Ross, an American who had once heard Powys lecture at Boston, arrived in June despite Powys's warning that:

> your aged heathen Guru is [now] a toothless demi-semi-invalid, living on liquids, not having had a normal ordinary action of the bowels for ten years and with a fixed and rigorous routine of walking and drinking tea to which I add a crumb of stale white bread.

But Powys enjoyed these visits: Ben Roberts and Huw Menai's arrival, and their journey with him to the ruins of Valle Crucis, were a welcome distraction not only from his work, but also from the grief which he felt over the recent death of 'The Very Old'; while the two men eased his financial worries by promising to arrange more lectures.[53] Nicholas Ross, thirty-three years old, was handsome and charming, and although in religious matters he was irritatingly narrow-minded, the similarity between his devotion to Catholicism,[54] and Rhisiart's romantic devotion to the cause of Glendower was so striking that John addressed him as Rhisiart for the rest of their long friendship.

John continued to write regularly to Llewelyn, and at the beginning of May he and Phyllis received a copy of Llewelyn's newly published *Love and Death*. Phyllis was particularly excited, because the novel had been dedicated to her, and she believed that Llewelyn had thereby made her immortal.[55] She was not alone in thinking highly of *Love and Death*, but the majority of the London critics disliked it, sales were poor, and Llewelyn was unable to find an American publisher.

Reading so many unfavourable reviews was an unhappy experience for Llewelyn, who wrote a long essay attacking 'Modern Town Critics'; however, he was consoled by many admiring letters, especially cherishing one from Gamel Brenan, who had written warmly despite her earlier lack of enthusiasm. Llewelyn wrote to her 'I want no one but one person to feel excited by this book. I was thrilled by what you said of it, for it was my garland of sunny dandelions, that at the end of all, I laid at your feet, my darling of darlings.'

Gamel had spent a week at Clavadel in February, but Alyse had been saddened to find her looking 'older, very thin and pale', and she told Alyse privately that 'she had often long periods of extreme melancholy and thought frequently of suicide.' Although she managed to write kindly to Llewelyn about *Love and Death* when he sent her a copy, she then could not bring herself to answer his letters for several months; and when eventually she did, it was to reveal not only that she was desperately unhappy, but also that, in reality, *Love and Death* had given her pain rather than pleasure. Llewelyn at once wrote her a wise and loving letter, not disguising his sadness 'that I should read your words about my book after what you have said before,' but making it clear that he bore her no grudge, and only desired her to be more cheerful:

> Do, do remember that the future remains open and unknown, and that no day should be held to be cheap. It is a dismal thing to hold beauty and love lightly. To me it is incredible. You have health and bread and wine and can still see the moon and the sun and the stars . . . you are so lovely, and your mind can be so subtle, and your hand holds to poetry as few hold to that clue in life's labyrinth. . . . Let the worst happen – there are still chances of happiness.

Llewelyn himself had few such chances left. His digestion would never again be strong enough for him to get well between bouts of high temperature and blood spitting. Any unusual exertion was dangerous, and at the beginning of May he made himself very ill by overworking:

> at my old pastime of cross-stitch. Was ever anyone such a Fool? I began doing a little bag for my favourite peasant child aged 10 . . . and then got interested and gave up writing, worked 8 hours a day, and suddenly found I had a temperature of a hundred and have had to stay quiet ever since.

But he was always determined to get what pleasure he could out of life. Later in the month, he resumed his writing, and enjoyed a fourth visit from Louis Wilkinson, whom he described in a letter to his sister Lucy as 'very well and as good company as ever and very tender of me.'

At the end of June, John Cowper Powys briefly left his Welsh retreat to attend an anti-vivisection meeting in London;[56] and then in mid-July, after Littleton had sent him some money for a proper holiday,[57] he and Phyllis set out for Dorset. They travelled separately, for Littleton Alfred was on his way back from an Irish holiday, and John spent forty-eight hours with him in South Wales. Then he went on to join Phyllis at Chaldon, where they saw the usual gathering, and John was pleased to find Theodore better than he had been the previous summer.[58] From Chaldon they travelled up to London, where they visited the ballet, and Phyllis helped John to cope with the intricacies of the London Library; and on to Cambridge, where John showed Phyllis round his old college.[59]

Returning to Corwen, John resumed work on the final chapters of *Owen Glendower*, and he wrote to Llewelyn on 2 October telling him that the sum of money he had sent him was still untouched: he had been commissioned by a London journal to write a series of articles on religious orators, and this would provide him with living expenses until *Owen* was completed.[60]

When England declared war on Germany in September 1939, travelling was restricted, and Gertrude and Katie were no longer able to travel to Switzerland to see Llewelyn as they had planned. John's son Littleton Alfred volunteered to be an army chaplain, and another vicar and his family moved in with Margaret for the duration.[61] John, who had very mixed views about the war, regarding it as both necessary and evil, read no newspapers, but listened to the king's speeches on the wireless.[62] For Alyse, as a convinced pacifist, the outbreak of war was particularly terrible; while for Llewelyn, with his hatred of the dictators, it came as a relief: his chief fear had been that 'England might not stand firm for I would rather see England fall honourably than live by sagacity alone.'

Llewelyn had survived the summer: by the end of June he had been able to get dressed and sit in the garden, where he had 'lovely hours . . . watching the cat and the butterflies and watching the children play with my Noah's Ark on a wide wooden table'; but he had never been able to take more than very short walks, and in September he was back in bed again. Now, on 2 October, he wrote:[63]

> Miss Gregory goes over once a day for the news and I remain waiting for her in my bed – impatient for my tea and idly hoping that the news will not be too bad. If I think Switzerland is to be invaded then I wake up with a start. For the rest I continue writing occasional pieces easily, indolently – the real pinch of poverty – the crab's claw pinch not having been felt as yet.

During October he improved a little, as he had done in the summer, and enjoyed signing the sheets of a limited edition of a collection of his autobiographical essays,[64] published the following year by the Silver Horse Press as *A Baker's Dozen*. On the last day of the month Alyse wrote in her journal: 'Llewelyn and I have been so happy together – as we might have been in our earliest days. He has been able to take little walks and we have had so many hours of united companionship, with no spectres to separate us.' But in November, as he tried to build himself up by 'eating *every day* a little very good cured ham with a little cream each morning in my porridge,' his stomach began to hurt, and he suffered from palpitation of the heart. However, he began making lists of Christmas presents for members of his family, and for nine of the village children at Chaldon;[65] and on the same day wrote his last letter to Gamel, who had welcomed his recent letters of consolation, and talked of coming out to Switzerland as soon as such a journey was possible. He told her about the Swiss children, saying that he could not give them too much attention, for 'They seem to lead me very near to our secret garden and often as I play with them I seem to be playing with you'; and he added: 'The part of your life that I know is but a parcel of ground, but I do so hope that you go to it sometimes.'

Three days later on 19 November, he was dressing for a walk when, as had happened at Chydyok in June 1932, he suddenly felt giddy and then vomited blood. As before, a stomach ulcer was responsible, but this time his condition was too serious for him to survive. He endured for twelve more days, fed by injection, and sustained by blood transfusions, but he was too ill for an operation to be successful, and gradually he grew weaker. When Llewelyn realised that death was inevitable, he asked Alyse for pen and paper, and wrote:

> This then is my last word to the men and women, to the boys and girls, and even to the little children that I always so loved. Love Life! Love every moment of life that you experience *without pain*. Now that my hours so sharply shorten (and I never was dull to passing moments) I look back to the most inconsequential and accidental of them with the liveliest regret and yearning *to have them again*.

He began to feel that the efforts made to prolong his life were unnatural: 'They are dragging me the wrong way', he said to Alyse; and again: 'I long for the sweet web of dust.' Towards the end, as Alyse later recorded,

> His mind went continually back to his childhood, and particularly to his days with his brother Bertie when they were boys together. . . . The only words he ever uttered that betrayed an emotion other than a complete surrender to his destiny were 'I am a little disconsolate,' and these were spoken

as a boy might speak who has learned that a decision has gone against him.

On the night of 1 December, the doctor gave him an injection to help him sleep. He never woke again, but died in the early hours of the following day.

Later in the morning of 2 December, a grief-stricken Alyse managed to summon up enough presence of mind to send a telegram to John Cowper Powys. Llewelyn had recovered so many times from being seriously ill that news of his death seemed quite unreal to John.[66] Without a word, he handed the telegram on to Phyllis and to Gamel Brenan, who by coincidence was staying with them at Corwen.[67] For a while, they were all in a state of shock; and the circumstances of Llewelyn's death, far away in another country during war-time, meant that there were none of the usual family rituals to absorb some of that shock. After a while, John sat down to write a letter to Gertrude, and told her that he was thinking of building[68] a cairn to their brother's memory on the slope of the mountain above Cae Coed; and a few days later he wrote to Nicholas Ross explaining that Llewelyn's death had 'made one of those HOLES in the ground that these bombers make,' for:

> Llewelyn was by far the most alive of all of us, and had a
> special-affect-relat-cont-link with each separate one of us, men
> and feminines alike. He was and is, the special darling of the
> family. . . . Llewelyn has had his epoch of being my brother
> Littleton's companion in special, my brother Berty's companion
> in special, and John's (your humble old servant's) as well.

The shock was one from which Alyse never wholly recovered. On 4 December, two days after Llewelyn's death, she recorded in her journal that she had:

> looked for the last time at Llewelyn's dead body. I kissed his
> clay cold brow and knelt beside the body that was my whole
> universe, that *is* my whole universe.
>
> *The cold! How shall I bear my heart without its heat?*
> *My clay without its soul? . . . I am alone –*
> *More cold than you are in your grave's long night,*
> *That has my heart for covering, warmth and light.*

Gamel, returning to her Wiltshire cottage, wrote to Alyse saying that she and Gerald would be very happy for Alyse to live with them, and adding: 'Don't let us ever lose each other – let us always be together whenever we can. I love you always with my deepest love – and your personality always moves & delights me. . . . Dear dear Alyse I always loved you so much and always shall –'.[69] When the news of Llewelyn's death reached Chaldon, Katie also thought at once of Alyse, and wrote three warm letters in rapid succession, imploring Alyse to return to live next door to Gertrude and herself at Chydyok.[70] Alyse welcomed the thought of being close to the maternal Gertrude, who had offered her protection in the past, and in any case, she had little real choice: a further letter from Gamel, though stating that 'we would truly love to have you', pointed out twice that the grandly named Bell Court was in fact a *'little* cottage', and added that they had visitors, so there would be no room for Alyse until March![71]

Towards the end of December 1939, Alyse arrived at Chydyok, where she was warmly welcomed by her two sisters-in-law. She had hoped to bring Llewelyn's ashes back with her, but war regulations compelled her to leave them behind in Switzerland, where they remained for the duration. When the war was over, the ashes were brought home, and buried on the Downs between Chydyok and the sea. The place is marked by a large block of Portland stone, carved by Betty Muntz, and inscribed with the words:[72]

LLEWELYN POWYS

13 AUGUST 1884

2 DECEMBER 1939

THE LIVING THE LIVING HE SHALL PRAISE THEE

The obituaries were mixed: there was a friendly one in *The Times*, but a very hostile one in *The Daily Telegraph*. Alyse attempted to sum up Llewelyn's place in modern literature for her own satisfaction. His defects, she believed, were his tendency to reflect his reading of Charles Lamb and Walter Pater, his inclination to overdramatise, and the ferocity of his attacks upon Christianity:[73]

> But these defects ride as lightly on the main body of his work as
> sea frit on an incoming ocean roller. The bent of his mind is
> sturdy, poetical, and philosophic, and he combines those two

characteristics without which no work of art can for long
endure – passion and detachment.

Her belief that *Love and Death* was his masterpiece now seems misguided. Llewelyn is likely to survive not as a novelist but as a writer of
essays, the best of which, as Malcolm Elwin has written, 'reveal a
philosophical poet relating the pleasures of his senses in the purest
prose of his time'[74]; and as a writer of autobiography. His finest
achievements include *Skin for Skin*, the African essays in *Ebony and
Ivory*, and his collections of *Dorset Essays* and *Somerset Essays*; while
many readers will continue to find comfort and inspiration in the poetic
philosophy of *Impassioned Clay*, *Now That the Gods Are Dead*, and *Glory of
Life*.

On Christmas Eve 1939, while he was still deeply upset by
Llewelyn's death, John Cowper Powys completed his long historical
novel *Owen Glendower*. He went up to 'the top of Mynydd y Gaer and in
a sort of Phoenix Nest of prehistoric heavy-as-meteor stones', he wrote
the final nostalgic paragraphs, in which Owen's son Meredith comes to
terms with his father's death, and imagines the ravens of Edeyrnion
'flying towards the mounded turf and the scattered stones that were all
that was left of Mathrafal.'[75]

CHAPTER EIGHTEEN

1940–1963

John and Phyllis in North Wales • writes Porius, *1942–50 alongside other works, some 'pot-boilers' • helped by Royal Literary Fund, 1944 • very ill, September 1945–March 1946 • from autumn 1950 published by Macdonalds • the fantasies of his later years • autumn 1954 moves from Corwen to Blaenau Ffestiniog • contented old age • from 1961 his health fails • publications include:* Owen Glendower, *1940,* Mortal Strife, *1941,* The Art of Growing Old, *1944,* Dostoievsky, *1946,* Obstinate Cymric, *1947,* Rabelais, *1948,* Porius, *1951,* The Inmates, *1952,* In Spite Of, *1952,* Atlantis, *1954,* The Brazen Head, *1956,* Lucifer, *1956,* Up and Out, *1957,* Homer and the Aether, *1959,* All or Nothing, *1960 • dies 17 June 1963.*
Theodore and Violet move from East Chaldon to Mappowder, Dorset, summer 1940 • his friendships with Dr Jackson and Charles Smith MD • publishes Bottle's Path, *1946,* God's Eyes A-Twinkle, *1947 • dies 27 November 1953.*
Other deaths include Frances Wilkinson, 1941 • Margaret Powys, 1947 • Gertrude Powys, 1952, Littleton Alfred Powys, 1954 • Littleton Powys, 1955 • Katie Powys, 1962.

Each morning, John Cowper Powys followed the rough pathway which led up the mountains behind his cottage. It was 'a beautiful walk between patches of whortle-berries and heather with groves of larches and little fir trees . . . and, far in the distance in a blue mist, fold upon fold of mountain ranges',[1] and now, each morning, he carried up stones, so that by the third week in January 1940 he had already 'constructed . . . quite a Cairn or Cromlech or Carnedd to Lulu's Memory'. At home, he worked hard correcting the typescript of *Owen*

Glendower, and, when that task had been completed, and the typescript posted to London, John began writing what he described to Nicholas Ross as 'one of my little tracts': this was *Mortal Strife*, a philosophical justification for the war against Germany.

In April, Alyse arrived in Corwen for a fortnight. She found Phyllis 'so open to sympathy, so full of generous goodness, so sweet to me'; and John 'full of a goodness that seems to have no reserves. P. says he never utters a cross, impatient, or unkind word.'[2] North Wales was far more peaceful than Dorset, where there were soldiers and guns and searchlights all along the coast; but soon, even in Corwen, the war began to seem dangerously close, and John stopped walking on the mountain, having become afraid that a German parachutist might suddenly descend on him while he was alone in the wilds.

At the beginning of June, Alyse found the streets of Weymouth filled with French soldiers from the beaches of Dunkirk. Theodore's black joke, made the previous autumn, that any German airman who dropped a bomb on Chaldon would be drummed out of the service for incompetence, began to seem less amusing;[3] and, in spite of having lived there for twenty-seven years, Theodore decided to sell Beth-Car and move inland to somewhere quieter and less exposed.

Mappowder, the small village which he chose, lies in the heart of Dorset well away from every main road and every centre of population. Immediately beyond the church, separated from the graveyard by a stone wall, is a little bungalow with only 'two small bedrooms, a kitchen and bathroom, and the one living-room';[4] and here, by the middle of July 1940, Theodore and Violet were established in somewhat cramped quarters with their adopted daughter Susan, most of their furniture from Beth-Car, and their thousands of books. Their new home was called 'The Rectory Lodge';[5] and beside it a drive ran up to the large house which was occupied by Dr Samuel Jackson, a well-read gentleman of sixty-two who had lectured at Manchester University before retiring to the country to become Rector of Mappowder.[6] He and his wife invited the Powyses to a meal soon after their arrival.[7] Dr Jackson was only two years younger than Theodore; he was delighted to discover in his new parishioner a man of such intelligence and originality, and the two men soon became friends, lending each other books[8] and going for walks together. Theodore had not altered his unorthodox religious beliefs, but he had always been happy to find spiritual comfort in the rituals of the church, and before long he was attending church each week-day to read through a service with his new friend. He did not attend on Sundays however, because he was still suffering from the after-effects of his stroke, and any gathering of people tended to make him feel ill.[9] He settled down into a peaceful routine of reading, walking and contemplation which, apart from periods of extreme ill-health,[10] or periods when he decided to educate Susan at home,[11] remained relatively unaltered until his death thirteen years later.

As well as hearing about Theodore's move to Mappowder, John Cowper Powys heard news about a dramatic change in his son Littleton Alfred's career. Suddenly converted to the Roman Catholic faith, he had 'thrown up his commission as an army Chaplain and his living as a Rector', and was 'studying to become a secular Priest' in Wigan.

No English publisher had yet been found for *Owen Glendower*, but Schusters published it in New York on 25 January 1941. By this time John had completed *Mortal Strife* and sent it to London, but Jonathan Cape offered him only £50 for what had been a year's work, and the worry connected with negotiations for a higher fee brought on John's dyspeptic trouble:[12] for the next twelve months he suffered almost daily from what he described in his letters as 'acid drops'.

The war raged on: from his bedroom window, John had seen '"fireworks" over Chester', and among his numerous visitors was George Lewin, a Jewish bookseller who had been bombed out of his London home;[13] while at Chaldon, Gertrude, Katie and Alyse grew used to seeing the skies filled with searchlights, and a bomb blew in the ceilings of Rat's Barn; Francis Powys was reasonably safe in the Royal Army Pay Corps; but Oliver Wilkinson was in the navy, and his father Louis, feeling that he himself should witness the historical drama at first hand, risked the bombs and rented a top floor apartment in the heart of London. In the event, he survived; it was his first wife Frances, together with their daughter, who was killed by a bomb in Plymouth in April 1941. Louis was shocked by the news, but admitted that he also felt relieved.[14] His marriage to Frances had been one of the least happy and creditable episodes in his life, and even after they had parted he had been troubled by her constant struggles against poverty and ill-health, so that her death removed a substantial burden from his mind. Frances was more truly mourned by Theodore,[15] who recalled her efforts to help him with his writing when he was still virtually unknown, and who wrote sadly to John about her death. John himself must have been still more deeply moved: he was happy and secure with Phyllis, and, as he had once told Llewelyn, was in love with her mind, but Frances had been the great romantic passion of his life, and now she was gone beyond recall.

John heard in June that Jonathan Cape had accepted a revised version of *Mortal Strife*, and that John Lane at The Bodley Head had accepted *Owen Glendower*. This was welcome news, as he had less than £15 left in the bank,[16] and was currently working, as hard as ill-health and deteriorating eyesight would allow, on a modern novel set in Corwen. This experiment was a failure, and after 'two separate false starts' he abandoned the idea in favour of 'reading and studying . . . for a long historical Romance à la my 'Owen' . . . ON THE DARK AGES, – epoch from 475 to 525 A.D., centering around the figure of Boethius.' He began writing this new novel on 18 January 1942, and he wanted it 'to be very good and very long and very true. . . . I must read for it and go slow, go slow with it. (A page or two a day, no more.) Only half an hour every day, something like that, while I earn my living as I can.'[17]

To do this, it was necessary for Powys to write what he called pot-boilers. Since August 1941 he had been working for Cape on 'a modern *De Senectute*', eventually to be published as *The Art of Growing Old*; and, while finishing it in the summer of 1942, he asked Laurence Pollinger, his London literary agent, to arrange more commissions for him. Soon he was engaged in writing an essay on *Finnegan's Wake*, completed in early November, and a two hundred page book on *Dostoievsky*, written at enormous speed and completed in March the following year. By then he had already accepted another commission, this time to write for the Bodley Head 'a book called "Introducing Rabelais", with my own translations from the original! What do you think of that?' he asked Louis Wilkinson, adding: 'Lucky I've got Phyllis, eh? – who *is* good at French.' Unfortunately these projects often took up more time than he had anticipated, and as he explained in October 1942: 'I am celebrating the octave of becoming a Septuagenarian by racing against time in the completion of pot boilers so that my money won't be gone before a trifle more comes in! . . . I have had to give up Welsh and Homer.'[18]

By July 1943 Powys was managing to write his *Rabelais* and his dark-ages novel on alternate days, but he was suffering from eczema,[19] and was eventually forced to hold his pen between the wrong fingers to be able to write at all.[20] He began to be seriously worried that his advance money would run out long before *Rabelais* was finished, but

Littleton sent him a generous sum[21] which tided him over for the rest of the year.

Early in 1944 Powys was once again compelled to put everything but *Rabelais* to one side, but Pollinger received £100 from Cape, who at long last had published *The Art of Growing Old*; and, although at first he was most reluctant to do so, fearing that if his publishers heard of it they would pay him lower advances, John eventually applied for a grant from the Royal Literary Fund. On 22 April he received a cheque from the fund for £100, and wrote to Louis, who had first suggested that he apply, that it was 'an incredible relief and comfort. . . . I can now finish "Rabelais" in peace & pleasure & then get on to my Romance.'

In the meantime, he had enjoyed a few days at Valle Crucis Abbey with Littleton Alfred, who had recently been ordained a priest: 'an actor', John described him, 'in the secula seculorum, oldest of all Mystery-Plays!' He was now working in Bath, and his mother, also a convert to the Roman Catholic faith, lived close by, and was apparently enjoying life more than she had done for years.[22]

For the rest of 1944, John worked steadily on his books, though there were a few diversions when family and friends came to visit him: he was particularly pleased when Gertrude arrived in October and 'painted a Wonderful Portrait of me . . . old Mr John lying on his couch in profile writing the last pages of his Rabelais'; and he also enjoyed the company of the poet Redwood Anderson, who was now living in Corwen. In November came news that the Bodley Head would take *Dostoievsky*, and in December *Rabelais* was completed and sent to Pollinger.

In the new year of 1945, John and Phyllis became 'immersed' in an autobiographical play by Oliver Wilkinson in which, according to his father, Frances Wilkinson appeared:[23]

> both as a monster and as a victim: she excites keen pity and
> strong reprobation [while her] . . . love of power, her
> megalomania, her passionate and even ferocious wish to be set
> above all others, and they doing homage to her genius of
> character and brain, are shown as pathological maladies.

As he read on, John found this portrayal very hard to accept: in mid-February he wrote to Louis about Frances and Phyllis, saying that he had 'really & truly only loved 2 women in all my mortal days', and soon afterwards he told Louis that while he was 'still as deeply impressed as ever' by the '*power*' of Oliver's play, 'some psychic

outward force, or more likely some inward inhibition suddenly interrupted my reading of it!'

At the end of May there was a visit from Louis Wilkinson, and in
August John spent another extremely enjoyable holiday with his son
Littleton Alfred at Valle Crucis Abbey. Littleton celebrated Mass each
day, and in the river which runs beside the ruins he caught trout for
them to eat, while John kept the kettle filled with water from the spring
which the monks had used hundreds of years before.[24]

There was still no news of publication dates for his *Rabelais* or his
Dostoievsky, but a second grant from the Royal Literary Fund meant
that he was able to concentrate on what he called his 'Dark Ages
romance' without being distracted by financial worries.

Writing at the height of his powers, but with great self-indulgence –
'What I like far best myself in my writings', he told Louis, 'are my
longest novels & romances because I tell myself stories then and just
ramble on, losing myself & my – – – – – – personality in those I'm writing
about' – John Cowper Powys was creating in *Porius* an adult version of
the endless fairy tale with which his father had entertained him in his
childhood. However, even in its enormously long unedited state,
Porius covers only the first eight days of the story which Powys had
originally intended to write, and he never reached the figure of
Boethius around whom the novel was originally going to revolve!

Porius appears at first to be firmly set in the year AD 499 in the valley
of Edeyrnion, where Porius himself is the son of a British chieftain loyal
to Arthur, but soon it develops into an elaborate and compelling
fantasy, as Powys conjures up a world of dark forests and occult
secrets, in which it is possible for an owl to be transformed into a
bird-maiden; in which there is an aboriginal race of giants, the Cewri,
from one of whom Porius is descended; and in which Merlin, or
Myrddin Wyllt, Arthur's adviser, is really Saturn or Cronos, God of the
Golden Age.

Porius[25] was conceived while Britain was at war with Nazi Germany,
and throughout the novel there is a sustained attack upon 'the power
of fanaticism, whether spiritual or temporal, to pervert human nature
and suppress the natural freedom of the soul.' In the Golden Age,
Powys tells us, there was an 'anarchical' matriarchy – something of a
contradiction in terms! – and he shows us in Porius and his father
two men who are wise enough, in his view, to leave important
decisions to their womenfolk whenever possible, and to drift happily
upon the tide of events. John also attacks Christianity as fiercely

as his brother Llewelyn could have wished: Myrddin Wyllt, was 'God before the Three-in-One conquered heaven; and [he] made people happy before cruelty and love and lies ruled the earth'; while Myrddin declares that:

> The Golden Age can never come again till governments and rulers and kings and emperors and priests and druids and gods and devils learn to un-make themselves as I did, and leave men and women to themselves! And don't *you* be deceived . . . by this new religion's talk of 'love'. I tell you wherever there is what they call 'love' there is hatred too and a lust for obedience!

Porius comes to understand that his 'real life' lies in his 'cavoseniargizing', an invented word for a mental trick by which he 'embrace[s] . . . the . . . elements', immersing himself in the inanimate objects round about him, so as 'to feel this first and last sensation of the human soul and body in harmony'. Taliesin, with his 'babyish abandonment to pure unadulterated sensation' is the poet of this natural harmony, and he recites verses in which he advocates Powys's recipe for happiness, with:

> The ending forever of the Guilt-sense and God-sense,
> The ending forever of the Sin-sense and Shame-sense,
> The ending forever of the Love-sense and Loss-sense,
> The beginning forever of the Peace paradisic,
> The 'I feel' without question, the 'I am' without purpose,
> The 'It is' that leads nowhere, the life with no climax,
> The 'Enough' that leads forward to no consummation,
> The answer to all things, that yet answers nothing . . .

There is another element in *Porius* which seems to have been of particular, though in this case, largely unexplained importance to Powys: it concerns the relationship between Porius and the aboriginal giants, the Cewri. At a crucial moment in the story Myrddin has magically halted an unequal battle between a small group of Arthur's supporters and the massed forces of the forest people, when a mist comes down from the mountain, and 'two gigantic figures' pass by. A man and his beautiful daughter, they are the last of the Cewri, and their smell is described as 'mysteriously attractive . . . and such as, once inhaled, might leave behind . . . a desperate, unspeakable craving . . . such as a particular kind of person . . . might follow to destruction.' Porius has always had a 'nostalgic longing for some vague feminine creature inhabiting the mountains'; and when he first smells the giants in the mist, it reminds him 'of the smell of the tadpoles – especially when they were dying or dead – which he had carried as a child to certain wayside puddles at the foot of the Gaer.' Although Porius sees that the giants carry away corpses from the battlefield to eat them, this does not prevent him from being strongly attracted to the female giant. There is a 'rush of magnetic intimation' between them, after which Porius experiences a personal crisis, as he suddenly feels that his mind has become powerful enough to take decisive independent action. Before long he has mated with the giant he desires, but then she dies, after receiving a blow from the other giant which was meant for Porius; and her father carries her dead body away, leaping with it into a lake where he too meets his death. This bizarre episode, with its giants associated with nostalgic longing, with sexual desire, and with savagery, and with its explicit reference to an important episode in his own childhood concerned with tadpoles and his father's anger, must rank as one of the most highly personal passages in all Powys's writing.

In mid-September 1945, with *Porius* far from completed, John Cowper Powys had a serious attack of his old illness: an ulcer led to haemorrhaging,[26] and he was rushed into hospital at Wrexham,[27] where he had to stay for a month. Theodore, hearing news of his brother's illness at a time when John's life still hung in the balance, was pleased to learn that he was not at all agitated and therefore, Theodore reckoned, must be mentally prepared for death.[28]

Theodore, as preoccupied as ever with death, often went to meditate in the church, and had spent some time getting to know the names on the tombstones in the churchyard. He also continued to read, and 'His reading in the last years was almost entirely restricted to the Bible and Christian devotional and mystical works.' In these works, by men such as Jeremy Taylor, George Fox, Eckhart and Tauler, Theodore made marks against passages in which 'the mystical "way" of negation, of silence, of inwardly stripping to the barest essentials . . . receives emphasis.'[29] Alyse visited him once or twice a year, and on one occasion he teased her by saying that he went to the services 'because he looks on at this religion as a survival of savagery – and because he finds the kneeling position beneficial to his health'! Alyse also noted 'his extreme dependence on and supreme contempt for Violet and Susie'; and his 'fantastic conceptions of people': he told Alyse, no doubt seeking reassurance, 'that John hates him, that Violet wishes him dead, that Littleton is eaten up with snobbish ambition; and yet he is open to persuasion and shifts his ground easily.' Theodore had made another new friend since moving to Mappowder: this was his doctor, Charles Smith MD, who came from nearby Sturminster Newton.[30] Soon he was visiting Theodore simply to enjoy his company; they went for walks together, and sometimes Dr Smith would take him for a run in his car. On one occasion he drove him to the very outskirts of Montacute, though he went no further, because his passenger felt that it would be too painful an experience to revisit his childhood home.[31]

Theodore wrote to John in December 1945, telling him with characteristic melancholy that he supposed they both *might* survive a little longer, and that dying would be a strange experience![32] He had learned that there was now a rock dedicated to him on the slopes above Corwen, and although he did not believe in the gods and goddesses whose aid John invoked, he had found it comforting to think of his brother kneeling by the rock and including him in his prayers each day, and he could not help being disturbed by the fact that John's illness had temporarily put an end to the observance of this ritual.[33]

For several months after leaving hospital, John Cowper Powys was bed-ridden, and when he wrote to Louis Wilkinson on 4 March 1946 he was still very unwell:

> Raw eggs seem the only thing I can always safely digest & *they alone* never give me nausea or vomiting or indigestion, but I tell you if you saw me NAKED you'd be a bit startled if not shocked, so thin & skeleton-like . . . have I grown! . . . I'm as weak as a newly-dropt lamb. . . . I can still *just* shave standing up but I find it exhausting. I force myself to dress, lest I get weaker; & to totter – literally! – some 50 yards or less up our lane before 'breakfast'.

A week later he was so ill that there was talk of his re-entering hospital, but he disliked the idea of returning to Wrexham,[34] and when a specialist was called in for a second opinion, he was allowed to remain at home, but 'ordered . . . to drink NEAT, all I can get of PURE OLIVE OIL.' This new treatment was so efficacious that by the beginning of August John was walking up the mountain each day before breakfast, and working hard again on *Porius*; though he had to be careful with his eyesight, as he was now 'practically Blind in my right eye from Cataract'.

But John did not work on *Porius* alone. Towards the end of 1946, with

Dostoievsky at last in print, Powys was writing *Obstinate Cymric*,[35] a collection of essays mainly on Welsh subjects, in which he talks of 'We Aboriginal Welsh People', links Welsh legends with 'the mystical Saturnian Age', and points to similarities between the Taoist doctrines of China and the calm philosophy of the ordinary Welsh people. The final essay in the volume, 'My Philosophy Up To Date As Influenced By Living In Wales', is a valuable companion-piece to *Porius*. Stating that, as a philosopher, he is 'proud to be the sort of *empiric* who is called a quack, a charlatan, and even a mountebank because he insists on accepting the immediate . . . *contacts with life*, as his starting-points', Powys tells us 'to live for sensation rather than for fame or success or art or religion or science or humanity'. He also confesses that each morning he prays '"to" or "at" a lichen-covered rock which has come to represent for me the great spirit of the mysterious poet Taliesin', and advocates 'a *mysticism of Nature*'. *Obstinate Cymric* was completed early in 1947, and published that autumn by the Druid Press of Carmarthen. John was also commissioned by Macdonalds to write a preface to Sterne's *Sentimental Journey*. Eric Harvey, one of the directors, liked John's work so much that he doubled his payment from £50 to £100, and also invited him to write a preface to *Tristram Shandy* for a similar sum.

During 1947 John enjoyed visits from numerous relatives, including Littleton, Littleton Alfred, Marian and Will, but not all the family news was good. One snowy day in January Theodore, now an old man of seventy-two, tumbled over on a slippery road, hurting his ankle so badly that he could not move, and was forced to lie there for some time before being rescued by a passing motorist.[36] Then on 28 February John's wife Margaret died, and was buried a few days later at Bath. Although they had been separated for so long, John had devoted much of his life to looking after her interests, and the news came as a considerable shock.[37] In the spring there was another death in the family: Littleton's first wife, Mabel, had died of cancer in the autumn of 1942; and now his second wife, the novelist Elizabeth Myers, whom he had married a year afterwards, died also, at the early age of thirty-four. In a letter of sympathy, Theodore sent Littleton a quotation from the Arabic:

> In the Garden of Life a bird sang on the
> highest branch, and then soared away.

They had been married only three and a half years, but it had been a real love-match, and they had been wonderfully happy together, despite a difference of almost forty years in their ages, and despite their ill-health: he was lame with arthritis when they first met, and she was already ill with tuberculosis. A few weeks before Elizabeth's death, John heard from Louis that Bernie O'Neill, one of the last of their 'Circle', and one of John's oldest friends, had died in hospital. John wrote sadly to Louis: 'As you well say, 'tis the greatest loss we will all, I guess, be destined to know, save, of course, of our (in each case) particular day-to-day mate & companion.' Phyllis, however, remained in good enough health, though sometimes exhausted by the strain of looking after not only John but the two old ladies next door; while John, deep in the mysterious world of *Porius*, boasted to a correspondent that he had been restored by drawing upon the magical influences which lingered above his Welsh valley.[38]

John Cowper Powys spent most of 1948 working on *Porius*, though he wrote one or two articles, kept up his usual correspondence, and was visited not only by both Littletons – much to John's alarm, Littleton Alfred had taken to arriving by motor bike – but also by his nephew Peter Powys Grey. The other event of the year was the publication in May of John's *Rabelais* by the Bodley Head. The end of *Porius* continually receded, though by 28 December 1948 John announced that he was 'just thinking of the *last sentences*' in what he now called 'my long long 499 AD *semi-hist-novel* about Corwen'. By mid-February 1949 he was at last working on the final paragraphs of the thirty-third and final chapter,[39] after working on Porius over a period of seven years, and completing more than 2,800 pages of manuscript.

The spring and summer of 1949 were spent in revising the typescript of *Porius*; while John also planned his next works: the writing of 'a pure popular thriller about an escape from Bedlam' was to alternate day by day with the writing of a book on Aristophanes. By September 1949 the revised typescript of *Porius* had been sent to London, where it was placed by the Bodley Head in the hands of one of their readers, Norman Denny.[40] A copy of the typescript was also sent to Schusters in New York. There followed an anxious period of waiting; and when the news did come, it was bad. Schusters totally rejected *Porius*; and on the morning of 5 December Powys received a most unflattering letter from Denny, who admitted that 'embedded in this mountain of verbiage there really is a book', but suggested that the novel needed cutting by approximately one thousand pages. In particular, he found the story of

Porius and the giants 'distasteful . . . [and] . . . utterly unconvincing', and demanded that the Cewri should be altogether cut out.[41]

His self-confidence considerably shaken, Powys's first reaction was to write a submissive letter to Denny, telling him that he intended to obey his instructions precisely;[42] but very soon he was having second thoughts, and on 7 December wrote again to Denny, telling him that he would only reduce the length of *Porius* on the condition that it should be published within twelve months, and adding that he absolutely refused to remove the giants: if all the magical elements in *Porius* were cut out, the novel would be ruined, for it had deliberately been written in the light of a non-scientific view of the universe. More fantastically, Powys claimed to be an organ of communication from the departed spirits of the men of the fifth century, and asserted that he had been present at the events which he described![43]

John was clearly in an exhausted state of mind or he would not have allowed the fancies of his private world to be stated so categorically in a business letter. Phyllis too had seemed very tired that autumn, when Lucy and Katie visited Corwen,[44] but the general strain on their household was considerably reduced when on 28 November Phyllis's aunt Harriet died at the age of eighty-six.[45] John, hard at work reducing *Porius* by about a third, described himself as 'in my own grave eating a third of my own bones', but he completed the task by the end of March 1950,[46] and by the beginning of May Denny had approved the shorter version.

During the period of silence which followed, Powys began a correspondence with the author Henry Miller, who remembered attending his lectures in New York way back in 1917,[47] had admired him ever since, and was soon to write of him:[48]

> To encounter a man whom we can call a living book is to arrive
> at the very fount of creation. He makes us witness of the
> consuming fire which rages throughout the universe entire and
> which gives not warmth alone nor enlightenment, but enduring
> vision, enduring strength, enduring courage.

By the end of August it had become clear to Powys that despite Denny's letter of approval, the Bodley Head 'found my long "historic" – no! no! *not* historic, "*mythologised*" rather! . . . unpalatable to their taste', and the shortened version was sent to Macdonalds. Malcolm Elwin, who had commissioned Powys's prefaces to works by Sterne, wrote a lengthy but favourable report of some seven to eight thousand words on *Porius*; and, taking the trouble to travel up to Corwen to meet Powys, reported to his director, Eric Harvey, that Powys was 'not merely the greatest man I had ever met, but his goodness equalled his greatness.' Harvey was similarly impressed when he too made the pilgrimage to North Wales,[49] and by the end of the year Powys was writing gleefully: 'I've signed up with him and have had advance royalties and the book is to appear *next summer*.'

In the meantime, laying aside his idea for a book on Aristophanes,[50] Powys worked on his new novel *The Inmates*: 'a "Pot-Boiler"', as he described it, 'about a thrilling and happy escape from a *Lunatic Asylum*'. He was still engaged on this task when in the summer of 1951 he heard that his correspondent Nicholas Ross, or 'Rhisiart' was to be married, and he promised to celebrate his wedding day by performing 'at the Ogof-y-Rhisiart, somewhere between the stone of Aristophanes and the heap of stones of Rabelais . . . the oldest of all Druidic rites according to the strict rule of Phythagoras!' He promised more such white magic when he heard that Francis Powys and his wife, now known as Sally rather than Minnie, planned to open what became 'The Powys Bookshop' at Hastings on the Sussex coast.[51]

Porius was published in August 1951, and, perhaps because readers of *Owen Glendower* were expecting a similar historical novel, sales were good. Within six weeks several thousand copies of the ordinary edition had been sold, together with nearly forty-five of an expensive limited edition of two hundred copies. Macdonalds immediately agreed to take *The Inmates* for publication in 1952, and exchanged letters about Powys's two new projects:[52] a volume of practical philosophy entitled *In Spite Of*, which he had written by the summer of 1952, and which was published in 1953; and another novel, a 'long Romance about ODYSSEUS in his extreme old age, hoisting sail once more from Ithaca.'

Unfortunately by the late summer of 1952, when John Cowper Powys began writing this new romance, which at first he called 'Odysseus' but which was later published as *Atlantis*, he was himself in his eightieth year. He had been unpleasantly reminded of the passing of time in April when his younger sister Gertrude had died after a short illness at the age of seventy-five. His brother Littleton, aged seventy-seven, was now crippled with arthritis, and was about to have an operation for a cataract; while John himself had only one passable eye, and for more than four years had felt it prudent, before setting out on any long walk, to write into a special diary kept for that purpose an 'elaborate description of where to go to find my DEAD BODY in case I fell (as they love to call it) "in my tracks".' Powys's imagination was still as powerful as ever, and in *Atlantis* there are many remarkable scenes involving gods and monsters and legendary creatures, but his powers of artistic control were on the wane. As usual in one of his novels, there is a large cast of human characters, but in *Atlantis* the reader must also contend not only with the personalities of such things as a stone pillar, a wooden club, an olive-shoot, a moth and a fly, but with an overwhelming proliferation of names from Greek mythology. Powys's themes, such as the benefits of matriarchy, and the wickedness of priests and of a modern science which condones vivisection, have all been more than adequately explored in the earlier novels; and even readers who are excited by the idea of Atlantis may be too discouraged to get through the necessary three-quarters of the novel before Odysseus actually sets sail from Ithaca, and may never read the striking descriptions of his descent to the drowned world of Atlantis – which Powys recognised as 'the best part of the book' – and the story of his ultimate arrival at the island of Manhattan.

While John was writing *Atlantis* during 1952 and 1953 he enjoyed a visit from Henry Miller, but much of the news which reached him from the outside world was distressing. His sister Lucy, only sixty-two, had moved to Mappowder, where she had been enjoying long walks across the fields with Theodore,[53] but in the autumn of 1952 she had to enter hospital suffering from tuberculosis. Then came the news that John's son Littleton Alfred had been involved in an accident on his motor bike. He had not been killed, and was mentally alert, but the accident appeared to have triggered off a wasting disease in his muscles. Closer to home, Phyllis's mother was extremely ill, and she died in April 1953. Meanwhile Littleton Alfred had to stay in hospital, and by September that year had deteriorated so much that he could not even move his hands, and it was difficult to make out what he was saying.[54] There was also bad news about Theodore's health. During the early part of 1953 Theodore became so feeble, and his eyesight grew so poor, that he no longer felt that it was safe to go out walking without either Violet or Susan; and by the summer he was so ill that he had to go into hospital in Sherborne, and was only released in August when it became clear that he was a dying man, and that it would be kinder to allow him to spend the remainder of his life at home. For the next three months he remained in bed, nursed by Violet and Susan, who were greatly assisted by Francis's wife Sally.[55] Louis Wilkinson came to visit his old friend, and later wrote:[56]

> When I last saw him very soon before his death and when he knew he was near to death, of which he had talked and written so much, he was serene, he was at peace and content. He talked like himself with the freedom and ease of his later years; he comforted me with the reassurance of his own mind and Spirit.

Any suspicions or resentments he may once have harboured against his eldest brother had vanished completely, as the particularly warm letters he had written to him during 1950 and 1951 reveal,[57] and he now told Louis: 'I love Jack more than anyone.' Nine or ten days before his death, he grew less serene and peaceful, and his friendship with Dr Jackson ended on an unhappy note when Theodore refused to accept Communion from him.[58] Some days after this, Theodore's mind began to play tricks on him, and in one particularly vivid hallucination he imagined that Bernie O'Neill's wife, who had been dead for many years, had come to visit him. Not long after this alarming experience, he lost consciousness for the last time.[59] On 26 November Katie came over from Mappowder, but Theodore did not appear to recognise her;[60] and on the following day he died, less than a month before his seventy-eighth birthday, drinking at last the 'good wine' for which he had so much longed.

Three months later, Littleton Alfred Powys died at the comparatively early age of fifty-one.[61] Not long before his death he was driven out to North Wales to see his father for the last time, and although conversation was impossible, he enjoyed listening to John reading some poems.[62]

John Cowper Powys was deeply affected by the deaths of Theodore and Littleton Alfred: he threw himself into a frantic correspondence with his brother Littleton,[63] and worked extremely hard on his novels. By March 1954, with *Atlantis* completed and due for publication in the autumn, he was writing a new novel, to be published in 1956 as *The Brazen Head*. The central element in this story, set in thirteenth-century Wessex, is the blasphemous attempt by Friar Roger Bacon to create life by inventing a brazen head that will utter oracles. The novel is full of strange scenes, some of them nightmarish, and far more unpleasant than anything to which Frances Wilkinson had taken exception in *Morwyn*. There is also a strikingly autobiographical description of the philosopher Albertus Magnus, of whom Powys writes that he knew:[64]

by instinct that there were sleeping devils in the intricate
corridors of his mind that it would be dangerous to disturb . . .
it was imperative for him to avoid this region of his mind at all
costs . . .

It is perfectly possible for an energetic and powerfully
galvanic will to win renown for its owner, while the deepest part
of the personality which that towering will-power has to carry
along with it . . . may be secretly twitching and quivering with
all manner of maniacal distastes and repugnances.

'All my life,' thought Albertus Magnus, 'I've been escaping
from myself . . .' . . . there can be little doubt that this supreme
teacher's frightful necessity to keep his own malady in the
background had something to do with the desperate fervour of
his way of teaching.

No doubt the continuing spate of minor works which poured from
John's pen during the last fifteen years of his life owed something to his
continuing wish to lose himself in his characters, a wish which he had
once explained in a revealing letter to Louis Wilkinson:

being an actor & self-conscious thro' and thro' and being really
scared of thinking of myself or facing myself, I always run away
– in fact my whole life is a running away from myself . . . I *hate*
the idea of my 'personality' . . . I tell myself stories . . . and just
ramble on . . . losing myself and my —— personality in those
I'm writing about.

Certainly he was under less financial pressure. In April 1954 he assured
Louis Wilkinson that he was 'quite all right financially', not only
because Macdonalds had given him an advance on a reprint of
Visions and Revisions, but because he was making money from the sale
of old manuscripts, and he stood to benefit from his son's will.

By the summer of 1954 it had become clear that he was no longer a
welcome tenant at Cae Coed, where the landlord wanted to sell his
property with vacant possession,[65] and he had also begun to feel that
Corwen was becoming too noisy and popular. So that autumn he spent
£165 on a 'blessed little two-storied house – all staircase and window-
sills' at Blaenau Ffestiniog, a somewhat sinister slate- and granite-
quarrying little town high up in the mountains some distance to the
west. This tiny semi-detached dwelling, on the very edge of the town,
with a stream running down beside it, had been found for John and

Phyllis by Gerard Casey, the man who had once arranged for John to lecture in South Wales, and who had for many years been a member of the family, having married Lucy's daughter Mary. Known simply as 1, Waterloo – though as John pointed out: 'There is only 2 Waterloo – no more!' – their new home needed a good deal of money spent on it, but even when the price had effectively been more than doubled,[66] it was still very good value. It was certainly much smaller than their house at Corwen, being 'essentially two rooms, one up and one down'[67] but before moving in during April 1955, they had managed to distribute many of their possessions among the family, and they sent some of their library to the Powys Bookshop at Hastings.[68]

For much of each day John Cowper Powys wrote busily in the upper room at 1, Waterloo, where he lay on a couch beside the window. From here he could look out across the town to the broad sweep of the Moelwyn mountains; and at first, in the early mornings, he would set out for long walks, writing to Louis on one occasion:

> there *are* aspects of this town that are 'grim' but there are also
> small grassy valleys with streams of water running thro' them
> from which to look up at the grim mountain precipices all round
> towering above you as you lie on some sun-warmed rock
> listening to the water, & watching white sea-gulls and hay-fields
> and reedy marshes.

Visitors found their way to him even in this remote place; and during the summer and early autumn he saw Eric Harvey, Malcolm Elwin, Oliver Wilkinson, and several members of his family including his brother Will and his sister Lucy. In the evenings Phyllis read to him, as she had done for many years 'all the most exciting *modern* fiction', from the novels of Graham Greene to the detective stories of Simenon.

Then on 27 September 1955 came news of his brother Littleton's death. 'Without any psychic feeling', John wrote,

> my mind was concentrated on him the whole time that morn, &
> it was exactly as I set out on my walk that he died – and all the
> time I lay under a lightning-struck oak tree by the stream where
> I go I recalled one event after another of our fishing excursions
> as boys at Northwold, Norfolk.

Often written off as the dull one of the Powys brothers, Littleton had not only lived a good and worthwhile life as a schoolmaster, but had frequently come to the emotional or financial rescue of his more

unstable brothers and sisters; and something of his quality has been
permanently captured in lines by one of his pupils at the Sherborne
Prep., Louis MacNeice, who wrote of him as:[69]

> . . . a gentle Knight.

Owen, who once was a walking belfry, the Sun
Strode through his lips and boomed in his steps when first
At the age of ten I watched the wild flowers run

Into his fingers, and all Dorset burst
In bird song round his head, trill, twitter, chirp and chaff.
Whom now I find in a cottage, half immersed

In lameness, deafness, blindness. But the half
That can still greet me greets me full, the voice
Comes strong as a gong as ever, and the laugh

As deeply ingrained and warm. Rejoice, rejoice,
Was always Owen's motto, on two sticks
He still repeats it, still confirms his choice

To love the world he lives in.

Within two weeks of hearing about Littleton's death, John himself was
feeling old and ill, and he wrote to Louis, who now became his
principal correspondent, 'my vital strength has completely collapsed! It
must be my heart . . . I keep having to sit down and gasp for breath for a
minute or two.' He avoided seeing a doctor, and the crisis passed, but
he reduced his long walks from two or two and a half hours to twenty
or thirty minutes, and began for various reasons to feel that he was
now leaving maturity behind, and entering a kind of second childhood.

For one thing, he found that 'my Age first removing the desire, and
secondly my conscience . . . have ended entirely erotic cerebralism.'
For another, he believed that he gained an important insight into his
own nature when, at the request of Gamel Brenan, who lived near him
in Spain, Augustus John came to Blaenau Ffestiniog in December 1955
to make some drawings of him. Powys found the visit exciting, and:

> was seized with pure Hero-worship, a sort of ecstasy, and leapt
> up from my seat & kissed his forehead & it didn't bother or
> worry or perturb him any more than if I'd been Heracles
> saluting Zeus his Dad! . . . His final drawing was simply of my
> very soul. . . . From A. J. I've learnt to boldly follow that

321

element in my nature which might be called babyish 'innocence'.

Powys's memory was also becoming unreliable: he lived more than ever for the sensation of the moment, and even while sustaining himself chiefly on raw eggs and two bottles of milk a day, managed to find the very 'greatest pleasure' in drinking 'strong tea with heaps & heaps & heaps of sugar & dry bread, but only about 3 or 4 large mouthfuls.' He also discovered that he had developed 'a mania for Babies and Toddlers of 3 and 4 and 5 and 6 – in fact second Childhood being happy playing with First Childhood!' Among these 'Toddlers' was the young son of one of Powys's new friends: Raymond Garlick, poet, school-teacher, and editor of the *Anglo-Welsh Review*, who had settled in Blaenau only about a year before John and Phyllis.[70] For more than five years Garlick was a regular visitor to 1, Waterloo, where he climbed the steps to the upper room to find Powys at his work, lying on his couch between the window-ledge, now 'full of small framed photographs of members of his family, and postcards of Hardy and Pius XII among others', and 'a tray on a small table, bearing various talismanic objects – a Greek coin, a small china owl, the bird sacred to Minerva: he once said to me, "I must be the only person living who prays to both Jehovah and Pallas Athene."'[71] He remained a confirmed polytheist, but had now come to believe, like his brother Llewelyn, that there was no life after death. Another growing conviction, and one which he had long recognised as the wishful thinking of an old man, was that he had not only Jewish blood – in itself highly unlikely – but also Negro blood, which he claimed to have inherited 'Because of that affinity of the Welsh to the Berbers whose capital was Marrakesh in North Africa'.

John and Phyllis's other new friends in Blaenau Ffestiniog were Vera and John Vaughan, an unmarried sister and brother who lived in an ancient house which had been inhabited by their family for more than four hundred years; and visitors during 1956 included Jacquetta Hawkes, J. B. Priestley's wife; and Professor G. Wilson Knight, who was soon to become a leading authority on John Cowper Powys's work as a novelist, poet and philosopher. Wilson Knight had recently reviewed Powys's *Lucifer*, the long poem originally entitled *The Death of God* which Powys had written in 1905, and which had just been published for the first time by Macdonalds.

1956 also saw the publication of *The Brazen Head*, and the republication of *Visions and Revisions*; while Powys completed *Up and Out* and *The Mountains of the Moon*, two 'very short book[s] of the *space adventure* type'. These were published in one volume in 1957 under the title of the story, *Up and Out*, in which Powys:

> describes in some large details the collapse of the Human Race under the Hydrogen Bombs, and then an encounter in empty space with both God and the Devil who are persuaded to join a pair of earthlings and all the stars in committing One Grand Final Universal Suicide by leaping into another Dimension where they disappear & perish.

While writing these weird stories, Powys was in fact in a particularly happy frame of mind. A bequest from Littleton had finally liberated him from all his financial worries;[72] he had been entirely clear of his dyspeptic troubles since moving to Blaenau Ffestiniog; and for some time he had been free from his virtually life-long compulsion to make love to himself while he dreamed up sadistic images.[73] His mind often went back to the days of his childhood, and to atone for having long ago cut up some worms, he now picked up any that he found on the road, carrying them to safety;[74] and he wrote many revealing letters to Louis Wilkinson, in one of which he spoke of the strong sexual feelings he had once had for Nelly, Katie, and Marian.[75]

In September 1956 John Cowper Powys began working on *Homer and the Aether*, which he described to Nicholas Ross as 'a FREUDIAN PARAPHRASE OF THE ILIAD', and in which Powys retells the story of the Iliad, with additional passages in which an 'imaginary thought-reader, the immortal Aether', is brought in to discuss Homer's motives and intentions. In the autumn of 1957 Raymond Garlick found Powys 'living in the Iliad, which is quite as real to him as the *Observer* and the *Sunday Times* which lie beside his copy.'[76] After being visited by Juanita Berlin, a friend of Robert Graves, Powys was also taking an interest in Graves's most remarkable book, *The White Goddess*, which Graves had sub-titled 'A historical grammar of poetic myth'. He found the mythology fascinating, but he and Graves had crossed swords many years in the past – as he had with Graves's friend Siegfried Sassoon[77] – and he found it a disagreeable experience seeing things which were so important to him being strained through another's mind.[78]

Homer and the Aether was completed by January 1958, and published the following year. In the meantime Powys had written *All or Nothing*, 'a *Space-Fiction* tale . . . about life in the *Milky Way!*' which Macdonalds indulgently published in 1960. In the summer of 1958 he was also presented with the Bronze Plaque of the Hamburg Free Academy of Arts: the only public honour received during his life-time thus came to Powys from abroad! On the day that Rolf Italiaander made the presentation, Powys was also visited by Glen Cavaliero, already a great admirer of Powys's work,[79] and the man who was later to write the first systematic critical study of his fiction. Other visitors during 1958 included Louis Wilkinson,[80] who had just published a volume of John's letters to him; Gamel Woolsey and Marian Powys.

Gamel and Gerald Brenan were living in Spain, but Gamel liked to return to England each year to see her friends. Among these friends were Bertrand Russell, with whom she visited John and Phyllis,[81] and of course Alyse Gregory. Alyse and Katie had at last moved from Chydyok, far too remote and isolated for women now in their seventies. Alyse had accepted an offer from Rosamund Rose, the woman to whom Llewelyn had once written so passionately, to live in a cottage near her farmhouse in the Devonshire village of Morebath,[82] and there she stayed for the last ten years of her life. Katie had found a cottage in Buckland Newton,[83] not far from Mappowder, and her youngest sister Lucy was able to look after her as she succumbed first to arthritis and then to heart-trouble.[84] Alyse travelled over to see Katie sometimes,[85] and in 1958 Marian visited her,[86] after first flying to Kenya to see Will, and then travelling to Blaenau Ffestiniog to see John: a remarkable series of journeys for a woman of seventy-six who was herself suffering badly from arthritis,[87] and had long retired, after rising to be one of the world's foremost authorities on lace.

By the beginning of 1959 Powys had completed *All or Nothing*, and he spent the rest of the year on several short fantasies, none of which were published until some years after his death. He told Nicholas Ross that in writing the first of them, *You and Me*, he had 'at the back of my mind in this rather confusing book . . . to indicate the strange link which I have discovered there is between babies who have just come into this world and old men who are just . . . going out . . .' By July he was working on *Real Wraiths*, 'a book about the adventures of Four Ghosts. . . . I find it very thrilling', Powys wrote, 'to imagine myself a ghost along with other ghosts.' Then in mid-August he began *Two and Two*[88] a bizarre fantasy full of Greek mythology, metaphysical speculation, and space-travel. Towards the end of 1959 he was writing another story, as yet unpublished; and on 26 December he told Benson Roberts: 'I am absurdly well for my age: 87 last Oct 8th.'[89]

Early in 1960 he caught 'Asian' Flu, and although he could still dream up stories, the disease weakened him 'in every way . . . all I can do' he wrote in April, 'is go to sleep or lie on my back breathing heavily with my mind all puzzled confused bewildered.' In mid-July he was 'still too weak to leave this little house & go even for a small stroll'; but by September he was well enough to receive Eric Harvey, his wife Elizabeth, and their seven-year-old twins; and on 16 November he wrote to 'Rhisiart' that:

> For a whole fortnight every morn between 9.30 and 10.30 I have climbed up to the bottom of our wild waterfall . . . and sat down to rest up there on a cloth cap I carry for that purpose as well as my dead brother's walking stick which I call 'Sherborne'.

Harvey had told Powys that Macdonalds were to publish a new edition of *Wolf Solent*, and that Christmas John gathered his failing powers together to write a preface, which he found 'like writing a commentary on my whole life as it was, as it is, and as it probably will be, before I die.'[90] He had reconciled himself to there being no life after death, but he began to wish that he had grandchildren to survive him.

During 1961 he grew weaker, and abandoned his walks. However, he was well enough to write occasional letters and in the autumn he enjoyed a visit from his sister Lucy accompanied by her daughter and son-in-law, Mary and Gerard Casey.[91] In 1962 Katie died; and in March that year John began a letter to 'Rhisiart': 'Well my old Friend we certainly, you and I are living just now on the same. . .' but was unable to complete it; and Phyllis added: 'John . . . does not seem to have a cold or anything else tangible the matter with him. But he is not himself, and very far away, and won't take anything but milk and Complan.' He recovered a little in the summer; Louis Wilkinson visited him, and found him in quite good spirits, and with his mind clear, though he lay on his couch the whole time, and dozed off occasionally as old men do.[92]

A year later, in March 1963, when Powys was in his ninety-first year, Clifford Tolchard wrote asking for an article, but Phyllis had to reply that 'J.C.P. . . . does not write anything now.' In April the sculptor Oloff de Wet came to Blaenau Ffestiniog to prepare a head of John Cowper Powys, which was later cast in bronze. He found John in a cheerful frame of mind, singing the Sherborne School song, and reading out one of the long poems he had created for Taliesin in *Porius*; but he was 'happier to listen . . . than to be engaged in conversation', and when he did speak to de Wet at length, it was of some whimsical fantasy that was running through a failing mind.[93] In June he entered the local hospital in Blaenau Ffestiniog. On the seventeenth of the month, the day of John Cowper Powys's death, Gerard Casey was at his bed-side, and listened to him 'singing John Peel in his last day of life. . . . That last day his old head looked inexpressibly noble against the pillows in his bed. . .'[94]

In his preface to *Wolf Solent*, Powys had written:

> Whatever death may mean, and none of us really know, I have come to the conclusion for myself that when I die it is the complete and absolute end of me. I am now satisfied that when I lie dying I shall be feeling a perfect contentment in the sure and certain knowledge that no consciousness of mine will continue after my last breath.

At his death, however, John Cowper Powys left behind him a body of work in which there still flames the spirit of his idiosyncratic genius. It is in the nature of that genius to inspire passionate feelings, and many critics have responded to Powys's work with excessive admiration or excessive dislike. Powys himself came to recognise that his primary gifts were as a novelist rather than as a poet, although a handful of his poems are memorable. But even if one largely discounts the poetry, the apprentice-work of the early novels, the minor critical and philosophical works, and those books written when his powers were on the wane, one is still left with an impressive achievement. This includes that philosophical *tour de force*, *The Complex Vision*; an outstanding *Autobiography*; and a number of fine novels including six major works: *Wolf Solent*, *A Glastonbury Romance*, *Weymouth Sands*, *Maiden Castle*, *Owen Glendower*, and *Porius*.

John Cowper Powys had spent much of his life in the United States of America, and in North Wales, but he and his literary brothers will always be particularly associated with Dorset. Llewelyn's ashes already lay under a block of stone at the top of the cliffs near Chaldon, and Theodore had been buried in the heart of Dorset in the churchyard at Mappowder. Now John was cremated, and his ashes were taken to Chesil beach, where he had set a shipwreck scene in *Weymouth Sands*, and there they were scattered upon the waters of the deep.

Afterword

Louis Wilkinson died in September 1966. The body of work which he left behind has many fine qualities, but it is unlikely to be read except by those who are primarily interested in the Powys brothers. Violet Powys moved from the Lodge to another house in Mappowder, and when she died in 1966 she was buried in the same grave as Theodore. Alyse Gregory committed suicide in 1967. She was then in her eighty-fourth year, and did not wish to live to become a burden to others. Before she took an overdose, she lay down on Llewelyn's cloak, having first placed a picture of Gertrude where it would be the last thing she saw before she died. Gamel Woolsey died of cancer in January 1968. She was an original though minor poet, and much of her work has now appeared under the imprint of Kenneth Hopkins's Warren House Press. Marian Powys died of cancer in New York State in 1972. Will Powys outlived his wife and one of his sons, and died on his farm in Kenya in 1978. Lucy Penny, née Powys, still lives in Mappowder, where I have had the pleasure of visiting her. She is the last survivor of Charles and Mary Powys's sons and daughters. Her own daughter Mary died in 1980, but Lucy is cared for by her son-in-law Mr Gerard Casey, and her niece Isobel Powys Marks lives nearby. Miss Phyllis Playter lived until her death in March 1982 at 1, Waterloo, Blaenau Ffestiniog, where I once had the pleasure of calling upon her in the home which she had shared with John Cowper Powys.

Abbreviations

1 Unpublished sources

COLGATE
: The Powys collection in the Everett Needham Case Library, Colgate University, Hamilton, New York 13346. The Collections Librarian, to whom I owe much, is Bruce M. Brown.

ELWIN
: Documents in the possession of Evelyn Elwin, widow of the biographer Malcolm Elwin, who wrote *The Life of Llewelyn Powys*. These documents include: ELWIN: *John to Llewelyn*, by which I refer to copies of letters from John Cowper Powys to Llewelyn Powys 1925–39; and a typescript of the version of those letters, edited by Malcolm Elwin, with some explanatory linking passages, but as yet unpublished.

SYRACUSE
: George Arents Research Library, Syracuse University, New York State: from Powys, John Cowper, 1872–1963, Papers 1890–1972, 6 boxes, 1 pkg.; and from their Eric Barker collection.

TEXAS
: The Powys collection in the Humanities Research Center in the University of Texas at Austin. I was given considerable help by the Research Librarian Ellen S. Dunlap and her assistant Cathy Henderson.

YALE
: University of Yale Library MS Vault RICHARDSON, Series 1, Box 11, Folder 2, Powys, John Cowper, 76 ALS to Dorothy Richardson 1930 Jan. 19–1952 Oct. 21. The present author did not visit this collection personally, but was lent photocopies of some letters.

2 Published sources

Advice to a Young Poet
: R. L. Blackmore (ed.) *Advice to a Young Poet*, the correspondence between Llewelyn Powys and Kenneth Hopkins (Fairleigh Dickinson University Press, 1969).

329

A Pagan's Pilgrimage	Llewelyn Powys, *A Pagan's Pilgrimage* (Longman, Green, London, 1931).
Autobiography	John Cowper Powys, *Autobiography* a new edition with an introduction by J. B. Priestley and a note on writing the autobiography by R. L. Blackmore (Colgate University Press, Hamilton, NY, 1968).
Black Laughter	Llewelyn Powys, *Black Laughter* (Macdonald, London, 1953).
Brenan	Gerald Brenan, *Personal Record 1920–1972* (Cambridge University Press, 1979).
Confessions	John Cowper Powys and Llewelyn Powys, *Confessions of Two Brothers* (The Manas Press, Rochester, NY, 1916).
Essays	Belinda Humfrey (ed.) *Essays on John Cowper Powys* (University of Wales Press, Cardiff, 1972).
Hopkins	Kenneth Hopkins, *The Powys Brothers, A Biographical Appreciation* (Warren House Press, North Walsham, 1972).
John to Llewelyn	Malcolm Elwin (ed.) *Letters of John Cowper Powys to his Brother Llewelyn*, vol. 1 (Village Press, London, 1975).
John to Louis	Louis Wilkinson (ed.) *Letters of John Cowper Powys to Louis Wilkinson 1935–1956* (Village Press, London, 1974).
John to Roberts	C. Benson Roberts (ed.) *Letters from John Cowper Powys to C. Benson Roberts* (Village Press, London, 1975).
John to Ross	Arthur Uphill (ed.) *John Cowper Powys: Letters to Nicholas Ross*; Selected by Nicholas and Adelaide Ross (Bertram Rota, London, 1971).
John to Tolchard	Clifford Tolchard (ed.) *Letters to Clifford Tolchard from John Cowper Powys*; with a Memoir by Clifford Tolchard (Village Press, London, 1975).
Letters of Llewelyn	Louis Wilkinson (ed.) *The Letters of Llewelyn Powys* with an introduction by Alyse Gregory (The Bodley Head, London, 1943).
Life of Llewelyn	Malcolm Elwin, *The Life of Llewelyn Powys* (The Bodley Head, London, reprinted 1949).
Recollections	Ed. and with an introduction by Belinda Humfrey: *Recollections of the Powys Brothers: Llewelyn, Theodore and John Cowper* (Peter Owen, London, 1980).
Skin for Skin	Llewelyn Powys, *Skin for Skin* (Village Press, London, 1975).
Soliloquy	Theodore Francis Powys, *Soliloquies of a Hermit* (Village Press, London, 1975).
So Wild a Thing	Llewelyn Powys, *So Wild a Thing, Letters to Gamel Woolsey*, ed. as a narrative by Malcolm Elwin (The Ark Press, Somerset, 1973).
Still the Joy of It	Littleton C. Powys, *Still the Joy of It* (Macdonald, London, 1956).

Swan's Milk	Louis Wilkinson, writing as Louis Marlow, *Swan's Milk* (Faber & Faber, London, 1934).
The Cry of a Gull	Michael Adam (ed.) Alyse Gregory, *The Cry of a Gull, Journals 1923–1948*, with a tribute to Alyse Gregory by Evelyn Hardy (The Ark Press, Somerset, 1973).
The Joy of It	Littleton Powys, *The Joy of It* (Chapman & Hall, London, 1937).
The Verdict of Bridlegoose	Llewelyn Powys, *The Verdict of Bridlegoose* (Village Press, London 1975).
Welsh Ambassadors	Louis Wilkinson, writing as Louis Marlow, *Welsh Ambassadors: Powys Lives and Letters*, with an introduction by Kenneth Hopkins (Village Press, London, 1975).

Notes

Introduction

In the course of preparing for this biography, I have read and noted an enormous number of books, and thousands of manuscript documents. However, it would take ten years to read everything which has ever been written about the Powys brothers, and inevitably there will be occasions – I hope not many – when I have unwittingly given an unpublished source precedence over a published one; and there may also be occasions when I have arrived independently at a conclusion which has at some stage been put forward by someone else. I should like to assure any scholar whom I may have offended that small errors of this kind have not been made deliberately, and, if pointed out to me, will certainly be put right in any future edition of this work in which alterations are possible.

In order to avoid weighing down the book with detailed footnotes, I will throughout this section list initially those works from which I have drawn the bulk of my references for the chapter in question. The remaining notes will normally be to lesser-known and less accessible sources. However, in view of the difficulties of tracing information from collections of articles, I feel that it will be right to give full references for extracts from *Essays, Recollections*, and numbers of *The Powys Review*. Hopkins's *The Powys Brothers* has been of value throughout, but I will refer to that work only when drawing from it material which has not appeared elsewhere. When discussing books written by the Powys brothers, I have included in a single note all those pages from which quotations have been taken, as a matter of courtesy to any literary critics who may wish to challenge my conclusions. All unpublished sources will be given.

Chapter One 1797–1885

Unless otherwise indicated, the information in this chapter is drawn largely from: *Autobiography; The Joy Of It; Still The Joy Of It; Life of Llewelyn*.

1 TEXAS: John Cowper Powys to Trevor Moilliet 29 January 1957. The masochistic strain appeared more obviously in Pippa than in her mother.
2 *The Powys Review*, no. 8, 1980–1, Mary Barham Johnson, 'The Powys Mother', p. 62.
3 Ibid., p. 59.
4 Ibid., p. 58–9.
5 Ibid., p. 59.
6 Ibid., p. 62.
7 Ibid.

8 *John to Louis*, p. 369.
9 TEXAS: Littleton Powys to Charles Powys, 31 March 1879.
10 SYRACUSE: For John's comment on this see John Cowper Powys to Norman Denny, 6 September 1949.
11 *Essays*, p. 314.
12 Ibid.
13 Unpublished 'Portrait of T. F. Powys' by his adopted daughter Theodora Gay Powys, p. 100.
14 A. B. Gourlay, *A History of Sherborne School* (Sawtells, Sherborne, 1971) pp. 126–7.

Chapter Two 1885–1894

Unless otherwise indicated, information in this chapter is drawn largely from: *Autobiography; The Joy Of It; Still The Joy Of It; Life of Llewelyn.*

1 Llewelyn Powys, *A Baker's Dozen* (Village Press, London, 1974) p. 29.
2 Littleton Powys, *The Powys Family* (Western Gazette, Yeovil, 1952) p. 11.
3 A. B. Gourlay, *A History of Sherborne School* (Sawtells, Sherborne, 1971) p. 127.
4 Ibid., p. 187.
5 Unpublished 'Portrait of T. F. Powys' by his adopted daughter Theodora Gay Powys mentions a book given to Theodore as a leaving present in April 1889, p. 5.
6 *John to Tolchard*, p. 43.
7 COLGATE: John Cowper Powys to Louis Wilkinson, 7 April 1959.
8 *John to Ross*, p. 164; *John to Louis*, pp. 344, 345.
9 ELWIN: *John to Llewelyn*, 12 October 1932, gives the date at which John wrote this story as 1886.
10 Littleton Powys, *The Powys Family*, p. 12.
11 A. B. Gourlay, *A History of Sherborne School*, pp. 183–5.
12 COLGATE: John Cowper Powys to Louis Wilkinson, 16 February 1959.
13 Derek Langridge, *John Cowper Powys: A Record of Achievement* (The Library Association, London, 1966) pp. 4–12.
14 Unpublished 'Portrait of T. F. Powys', p. 5.
15 Oliver Wilkinson, in a telephone conversation with the present author, 23 October 1981.
16 Louis Wilkinson, writing as Louis Marlow, *Swan's Milk* (Faber & Faber, London, 1934) p. 44.
17 ELWIN: Littleton Powys to Malcolm Elwin, 26 August 1944: it was during the winter of 1890–1 that Littleton nicknamed Theodore 'Bob'; Theodore later nicknamed Littleton 'Tom'.
18 COLGATE: John Cowper Powys to Louis Wilkinson, 12 January 1959.
19 TEXAS: John Cowper Powys to Trevor Moilliet, 29 January 1957.
20 Four of them appeared in *The Shirburnian* between 1891 and 1892, and are reproduced in D. Langridge, *John Cowper Powys*, pp. 12–16.
21 TEXAS: John Cowper Powys to Austin and Gwyneth Johnson, 21 July 1961, shows that John also idolised his contemporary Bertrand Russell, then an undergraduate of Trinity College Cambridge, but they did not actually meet until many years later.
22 Llewelyn Powys, *Ebony and Ivory* (The Richards Press, London, 1960) p. 108.

23 ELWIN: Alyse Gregory to Malcolm Elwin, 8 September 1964.
24 Littleton Powys, *The Powys Family*, p. 15.
25 Llewelyn Powys, *Ebony and Ivory*, p. 109.
26 Ibid., pp. 108–10.
27 Ibid., p. 110.
28 *The Powys Newsletter, THREE*, 1972–3 The Reverend Charles Francis Powys, 'Harvest Thanksgiving', (Colgate University Press, Hamilton, NY,).
29 ELWIN: Alyse Gregory to Malcolm Elwin, 8 September 1964.
30 *Essays*, p. 105.
31 ELWIN: Alyse Gregory to Malcolm Elwin, 8 September 1964.
32 TEXAS: Gertrude Powys to Mary Powys, 12 October 1897, confirms that the present name of the farm is unchanged from the days when Theodore owned it.
33 TEXAS: Gertrude Powys to Mary Powys, 15 and 19 July 1893; and John Cowper Powys to Mary Powys, nd 1893.
34 TEXAS: Frances Beales to Gertrude Powys, 21 July 1893.

Chapter Three 1894–1899

Unless otherwise indicated, most of the information in this chapter is drawn largely from: *Autobiography; Life of Llewelyn; Letters of Llewelyn; John to Llewelyn.*

1 West Brighton was just beginning to be called Hove.
2 TEXAS: Llewelyn Powys to Mary Powys, nd; spelling just as it appears!
3 SYRACUSE: John Cowper Powys collection, box 5, contains five notebooks of a play dating from 1894.
4 John Cowper Powys, *Odes and Other Poems* (Village Press, London, 1975) p. 12; previous quoted Coleridge-like line, p. 42.
5 Ibid., p. 44.
6 John Cowper Powys, *Poems* (Village Press, London, 1975) p. 47.
7 Ibid., p. 121.
8 This suggestion was first made by Malcolm Elwin in his introduction to *John to Llewelyn*, p. 14.
9 John Cowper Powys, *Wolf Solent* (Penguin Books, Harmondsworth, 1964) p. 113.
10 Ibid.
11 Ibid., p. 73.
12 TEXAS: John Cowper Powys to Gertrude Powys, 7 May 1951; no precise date is given for this holiday, but other members of the Powys family were staying nearby.
13 John Cowper Powys, *Wolf Solent*, p. 196.
14 Malcolm Elwin makes clear in his introduction to *John to Llewelyn*, p. 14 that the details of Louis Wilkinson's story are highly speculative and unreliable, but Louis confirmed the underlying truth of the story to Glen Cavaliero, see n. 15 below.
15 Glen Cavaliero in a letter to the present author, 23 October 1981, relates this story as it was recounted to him by Louis Wilkinson.
16 Derek Langridge, *John Cowper Powys; A Record of Achievement* (The Library Association, London, 1966) p. 67.
17 COLGATE: John Cowper Powys to Louis Wilkinson, 18 August 1958.
18 John Cowper Powys, *Poems*, p. 16.
19 Ibid., p. 82.

20 TEXAS: John Cowper Powys to Littleton C. Powys, 16 August 1943.
21 TEXAS: John Cowper Powys to Austin and Gwyneth Johnson, 21 July 1961.
22 John Cowper Powys, *Poems* p. 10.
23 Ibid., p. 107.

Chapter Four 1899–1907

Unless otherwise indicated, the information in this chapter is drawn largely from: *Autobiography; Life of Llewelyn; Letters of Llewelyn; John to Llewelyn; Swan's Milk; Welsh Ambassadors.*

1 Littleton C. Powys, *The Powys Family* (Western Gazette, Yeovil, 1952) p. 14.
2 Llewelyn Powys, *A Baker's Dozen* (Village Press, London, 1974) p. 40.
3 Ibid., p. 41.
4 Oliver Wilkinson in a telephone conversation with the present author, 23 October 1981.
5 TEXAS: John Cowper Powys to Glyn Hughes, 26 July 1957.
6 COLGATE: John Cowper Powys to Louis Wilkinson, 18 August 1958.
7 COLGATE: John Cowper Powys to Louis Wilkinson, 9 October 1957.
8 *Essays*, p. 317.
9 TEXAS: John Cowper Powys to Gertrude Powys, nd.
10 ELWIN: Sylvia Townsend Warner to Alyse Gregory, 22 June 1967.
11 *Essays*, pp. 315–17.
12 *John to Louis*, p. 210.
13 COLGATE: see for example John Cowper Powys to Theodore Powys, 25 May 1903.
14 COLGATE: E. E. Bissell to Tom Davies, 8 February 1967.
15 Llewelyn Powys in *Confessions*, p. 186.
16 Ibid., p. 187.
17 Ibid., p. 188.
18 TEXAS: see for example Llewelyn Powys to Littleton C. Powys, 5 March 1902, 26 May 1902, 10 July 1902.
19 COLGATE: John Cowper Powys to Louis Wilkinson, 29 August 1958.
20 *John to Ross*, pp. 129–30.
21 COLGATE: John Cowper Powys to Louis Wilkinson, 14 [?] 1959.
22 Llewelyn Powys in *Confessions*, p. 190.
23 *The Powys Newsletter ONE*, 1970 (Colgate University Press, Hamilton, NY).
24 Peter Powys Grey, in conversation with the present author, October 1980; see also TEXAS: John Cowper Powys to Gertrude Powys, 19 September 1940, which throws another light on this.
25 COLGATE: John Cowper Powys to Louis Wilkinson, 9 October 1957; toned down a certain amount by COLGATE: John Cowper Powys to Louis Wilkinson, 25 January 1958.
26 *John to Ross*, p. 159.
27 Littleton C. Powys, *The Powys Family*, p. 14.
28 SYRACUSE: Powys collection, box 2.
29 *The Powys Newsletter ONE*, 1970, Isobel Powys Marks, 'The Powys Family Magazine' (Colgate University Press, Hamilton, NY); the story itself is reprinted in *The Powys Newsletter TWO*, 1971.
30 John Cowper Powys, *Lucifer* (Village Press, London, 1974) pp. 63, 119, 107, 75, 49, 53.

31 This photograph, in the possession of Isobel Powys Marks, was seen by the author on 28 August 1981.

32 *The Powys Review*, no. 4, 1978–9, Llewelyn Powys, 'Conversations with Theodore Powys, Summer 1931', p. 12.

33 Theodore Francis Powys, 'God' in *The Two Thieves* (Chatto & Windus, London, 1932) p. 179.

34 Theodore Francis Powys, *An Interpretation of Genesis* (Chatto & Windus, London, 1929) pp. 90, 99, 13, 78–9.

Chapter Five 1907–1910

Unless otherwise indicated, the information in this chapter is drawn largely from: *Autobiography, Life of Llewelyn, Letters of Llewelyn, John to Llewelyn, Confessions, Welsh Ambassadors, Skin for Skin.*

1 H. M. Icely, *Bromsgrove School through Four Centuries* (Basil Blackwell, Oxford, 1953) pp. 107–16.

2 Llewelyn Powys, *Swiss Essays* (John Lane, London, 1947) p. 140.

3 Derek Langridge, *John Cowper Powys: A Record of Achievement* (The Library Association, London, 1966) see p. 53. During the summers of 1908 and 1909 Powys lectured for the Oxford delegacy in Dresden and Leipzig. He gave twelve lectures each year: in the first year, on the poets and prose writers of the nineteenth century; and in the second, on Shakespeare.

4 COLGATE: Theodore Francis Powys to Louis Wilkinson, 3 January 1909 and 27 December 1910.

5 ELWIN: Alyse Gregory to Malcolm Elwin, 14 June 1967.

6 Littleton C. Powys, *The Joy Of It* (Chapman & Hall, London, 1937) p. 150.

7 John Cowper Powys, *Romer Mowl and Other Stories* (Toucan Press, Guernsey, 1974) p. 13.

8 TEXAS: Bernard Price O'Neill to Gertrude Powys, 10 October 1909.

9 TEXAS: Llewelyn Powys to Mary Powys: a large collection of picture postcards.

Chapter Six 1910–1914

Unless otherwise indicated, the information in this chapter is drawn largely from: *Autobiography; Life of Llewelyn; Letters of Llewelyn: John to Llewelyn; Welsh Ambassadors; Skin for Skin.*

1 *Recollections*, Appendix, pp. 266–70.

2 *Essays*, Appendix 1 (a), pp. 317–19.

3 *Recollections*, Appendix, p. 268.

4 Oliver Wilkinson in conversation with the present author, 26 September 1980, said: 'they were not a solidly united family – this is a myth.'

5 Ibid.

6 Llewelyn Powys, in *Confessions*, pp. 239–40.

7 Photograph in the possession of Isobel Powys Marks seen by the present author, 28 August 1981.

8 Oliver Wilkinson in conversation with the present author, 26 September 1980.

9 Ibid.

10 *The Powys Review*, no. 2, winter 1977, Oliver Marlow Wilkinson, 'John Cowper Powys in Love', pp. 61–2.
11 Llewelyn Powys, in *Confessions*, p. 240.
12 TEXAS: Alyse Gregory, 'Notes on Catherine Edith Philippa Powys'.
13 TEXAS: Stephen Reynolds to Katie Powys, 29 December 1912.
14 TEXAS: Alyse Gregory, 'Notes on Catherine Edith Philippa Powys'.
15 TEXAS: Mary Powys to Katie Powys, 27 January 1914.
16 Llewelyn Powys, 'The Stunner' in *Ebony and Ivory* (Richards Press, London, 1960) pp. 104–5.
17 Llewelyn Powys, *Damnable Opinions* (Watts & Co., London, 1935) p. 20.
18 *The Powys Review*, no. 2, op.cit., pp. 62–3.
19 TEXAS: Bernie O'Neill to Gertrude Powys, 10 May 1913; and Gertrude Powys to Mary Powys, 21 May 1913.
20 ELWIN: Alyse Gregory to Malcolm Elwin, 22 February 1956.
21 For a full account see *The Powys Review*, no. 5, Anthony Dyer, 'William Powys: an appreciation'.
22 ELWIN: Alyse Gregory to Malcolm Elwin, 1 July 1944, in which she describes photos of Marion Linton.

Chapter Seven 1914–1915

Unless otherwise indicated, the information in this chapter is largely drawn from: *Autobiography; Life of Llewelyn; Letters of Llewelyn; John to Llewelyn; Confessions; Black Laughter; Soliloquy.*

1 TEXAS: Charles Francis Powys to Katie Powys, 21 May 1914.
2 ELWIN: from the original version of an introduction by John Cowper Powys to Llewelyn Powys's *A Baker's Dozen*, (Village Press, London, 1974).
3 *Recollections*, Francis Powys, 'Mr. Weston's Good World', p. 123.
4 Hopkins, p. 35.
5 ELWIN: op. cit.
6 TEXAS: op. cit.
7 John Cowper Powys, *The War and Culture* (Village Press, London, 1975) p. 69.
8 Besides the reference in *John to Llewelyn*, p. 174, see TEXAS: John Cowper Powys to Gertrude Powys, 28 October 1914, for Marian's outrageously provocative behaviour.
9 *Recollections*, Maurice Browne, 'John Cowper Powys in America and Sussex', p. 178. For another account of John as a lecturer see Frances and Louis Wilkinson, writing as Louis Wilkinson, *The Buffoon* (Village Press, London, 1975) p. 143.
10 John Cowper Powys, *Visions and Revisions* (Village Press, London, 1974) pp. 167–8, 31, 143, 183.
11 *Welsh Ambassadors*, p. 250.
12 John Cowper Powys, *Wood and Stone* (Village Press, London, 1974) pp. vii–viii, 313, 81, 402, 568.

Chapter Eight 1916–1918

Unless otherwise indicated, the information in this chapter is drawn from: *Autobiography; Life of Llewelyn; Letters of Llewelyn; Black Laughter.*

1 TEXAS: Theodore Francis Powys to John Cowper Powys, 16 December 1915.
2 Hopkins, p. 53.
3 Theodore Francis Powys, *Mr. Tasker's Gods* (Trigon Press, Beckenham, 1977), pp. 17, 74, 103, 17.
4 TEXAS: Theodore Francis Powys to John Cowper Powys, 25 April 1916.
5 TEXAS: ibid., 27 May 1916.
6 COLGATE: Theodore Francis Powys to Louis Wilkinson, 22 June 1916.
7 Ibid., February 1917.
8 COLGATE: Theodore Francis Powys to Louis Wilkinson, 10 September 1916; and TEXAS: Theodore Francis Powys to John Cowper Powys, 23 August 1916.
9 John Cowper Powys, *Wolf's Bane* (Village Press, London, 1975), pp. 30, 47, 13.
10 Louis and Frances Wilkinson, writing as Louis U. Wilkinson, *The Buffoon* (Village Press, London, 1975) pp. 31, 33, 86, 51, 50. It is interesting to note that John had thought of himself as 'a bitter subject for a book' in a letter to his brother Llewelyn in 1911 (see Chapter Six, p. 86).
11 TEXAS: Theodore Francis Powys to John Cowper Powys, 1 May 1916.
12 Oliver Wilkinson in conversation with the present author, 26 September 1980.
13 John Cowper Powys, *One Hundred Best Books* (Village Press, London, 1975) p. 65.
14 John Cowper Powys, *Rodmoor* (Macdonald, London, 1973), pp. 423, 438, 248, 252, 438, 1, 42, 388, 111, 113, 456, 460.
15 TEXAS: e.g., Theodore Francis Powys to John Cowper Powys, 23 August 1916.
16 Ibid., 29 September 1916, 23 November 1916.
17 John Cowper Powys, *Suspended Judgments* (Village Press, London, 1975) pp. 14, 9, 425, 286–7, 198; see also pp. 284–6, 294, 411, 234.
18 Ibid., p. 178; and following quotation pp. 40–1.
19 Marian Powys, *Lace and Lace Making* (New York 1953); see dust jacket.
20 The letter on p. 207 of *John to Llewelyn* appears from internal evidence to be misdated, and should read 6 July 1917, not 6 July [1916].
21 John Cowper Powys, *Suspended Judgments*, p. 330.
22 John Cowper Powys, *Mandragora* (Village Press, London, 1975) p. 64.
23 Oliver Wilkinson in conversation with the present author, 26 September 1980.
24 Ibid.
25 Oliver Marlow Wilkinson in *Men of Mystery* ed. Colin Wilson (W. H. Allen, London, 1977) p. 94.
26 TEXAS: Theodore Francis Powys to John Cowper Powys, 7 May 1917.
27 John Cowper Powys, *Mandragora*, p. 140.
28 *John to Ross*, p. 60.
29 *The Powys Review*, no. 5, Anthony Dyer, 'William Powys: an appreciation', p. 81.
30 TEXAS: Theodore Francis Powys to John Cowper Powys, 27 May [1917].
31 TEXAS: Littleton Powys to Theodore Francis Powys, 6 April 1917.

32 TEXAS: Theodore Francis Powys to John Cowper Powys, 4 January 1918.
33 TEXAS: Theodore Francis Powys to John Cowper Powys, [?] 1918.
34 ELWIN: Alyse Gregory to Malcolm Elwin, 14 June 1967.
35 TEXAS: e.g., Theodore Francis Powys to John Cowper Powys, 7 May 1917.
36 TEXAS: Theodore Francis Powys to John Cowper Powys, 2 July 1917.

Chapter Nine 1919–1921

Unless otherwise indicated, the information in this chapter is drawn largely from: *Autobiography; Life of Llewelyn; John to Llewelyn; Letters of Llewelyn; Welsh Ambassadors; The Verdict of Bridlegoose.*

1 Llewelyn Powys, *Ebony and Ivory* (The Richards Press, London, 1960) pp. 37–51.
2 Ibid., p. 37.
3 TEXAS: Theodore Francis Powys to John Cowper Powys, 24 November 1918.
4 TEXAS: Theodore Francis Powys to John Cowper Powys, 16 February 1919.
5 TEXAS: Theodore Francis Powys to John Cowper Powys, 2 March 1919.
6 This and the following two paragraphs are largely drawn from Oliver Marlow Wilkinson, 'A Rival to Jack' in *Recollections*, pp. 184–5.
7 Oliver Marlow Wilkinson in a telephone conversation with the present author, 28 November 1980.
8 John Cowper Powys in *Confessions*, p. 43.
9 Oliver Marlow Wilkinson in conversation with the present author, 26 September 1980.
10 John Cowper Powys, *The Complex Vision* (The Village Press, London, 1975) pp. xxiv, 13, 18, 57, 83, 150–1, 194, 254, 35, 335, 337.
11 *Recollections*, p. 181.
12 As n. 9 above.
13 *Recollections*, p. 183.
14 As n. 9 above.
15 *Recollections*, p. 184.
16 Ibid.
17 TEXAS: Theodore Francis Powys to John Cowper Powys, October 5 1919; there were some delays due to a railway strike.
18 Llewelyn Powys, *Ebony and Ivory*, p. 33; this volume also includes 'How it Happens'.
19 TEXAS: Theodore Francis Powys to John Cowper Powys, 5 December 1919.
20 For further information about this meeting see *Two Essays by Llewelyn Powys* (The Toucan Press, Guernsey, 1971) p. 483; published as no. 70 of 'Monographs of the Life, Times and Works of Thomas Hardy'.
21 TEXAS: Theodore Francis Powys to John Cowper Powys, 1 March 1920.
22 Llewelyn gives a July date in *The Verdict of Bridlegoose*, but we know that John was at Burpham in June [*John to Llewelyn*, p. 281]; and an end of April date is suggested by John's letter in *John to Llewelyn*, p. 280.
23 John Cowper Powys, *After My Fashion* (Pan/Picador, London, 1980) p. 214; the date of writing is not known to me, but internal references to Prohibition (p. 264 and p. 169) suggest that at least part of the novel was written after January 1920. The summers of 1920 and 1921 therefore seem most likely; and I have inclined to the former because it appears to have been written before John came under the happy influence of Miss Phyllis Playter.

24 TEXAS: Theodore Francis Powys to John Cowper Powys, 1 March 1920.
25 Oliver Wilkinson in a telephone conversation with the present author, 28 November 1980.
26 Peter Powys Grey in conversation with the present author, 16 October 1980.
27 TEXAS: Theodore Francis Powys to John Cowper Powys, 24 November 1920.
28 Ibid., 21 December 1920 and 27 January 1921.
29 Ibid., 24 November 1920.
30 Ibid., 8 November 1920.
31 Ibid., 22 December 1920.
32 Ibid., 16 November 1920.
33 Ibid., 11 November 1920.
34 *The Powys Review*, no. 5, Michael Pouillard, 'T. F. Powys and the theatre', pp. 45–6.
35 TEXAS: Theodore Francis Powys to John Cowper Powys, 21 December 1920.
36 *The Powys Review*, no. 5, op. cit., p. 36.
37 TEXAS: Theodore Francis Powys to John Cowper Powys, 16 November 1920.
38 Ibid., 27 January 1921.
39 ELWIN: Alyse Gregory to Malcolm Elwin, 2 October 1946; in *The Verdict of Bridlegoose*, Lydia Gibson was called 'Nan' by Llewelyn Powys.
40 TEXAS: Gertrude Powys to Katie Powys, 21 August 1920.
41 Llewelyn Powys, *Dorset Essays* (The Bodley Head, London, 1935) p. 102.
42 *The Powys Review*, no. 5, Sylvia Townsend Warner, 'Theodore Powys and some friends at East Chaldon, 1922–1927: A narrative and some letters', pp. 13–14.
43 Ibid., pp. 14–15.

Chapter Ten 1921–1923

Unless otherwise indicated, the information in this chapter is drawn largely from: *Autobiography; Life of Llewelyn; Letters of Llewelyn; John to Llewelyn; Welsh Ambassadors; The Verdict of Bridlegoose.*

1 For John Cowper Powys's previous friendship with Mr Playter, Kenneth Hopkins in a telephone conversation with the present author, 31 December 1980. On the strength of ELWIN: *Letters to Llewelyn*, pp. 288–9, it appeared that John first met Phyllis Playter in November 1921. However, the author has been advised by Mr Jeffrey Kwintner, who has seen John's diaries, that their first meeting was in fact during March that year.
2 Donald Kerr in conversation with the present author at the Powys Society Conference, Norwich, September 1980, recalling a conversation with Miss Phyllis Playter earlier that year.
3 *Recollections*, Belinda Humfrey, Introduction, p. 31.
4 As n. 2 above.
5 *Recollections*, p. 31.
6 John Cowper Powys, *Samphire* (Village Press, London, 1975) p. 51.
7 Nicholas Joost, *Schofield Thayer and The Dial* (Carbondale 1964) shows that Alyse Gregory was managing editor of *The Dial*, February 1924 to June 1925 [information from Kenneth Hopkins].
8 John Cowper Powys, *The Owl. The Duck. and – Miss Rowe! Miss Rowe!* (Village Press, London, 1975) p. 5.

9 See Evelyn Hardy's tribute to Alyse Gregory in *The Cry of a Gull*, p. 9; and see p. 7 for 'a rebel and an agnostic' in next paragraph.

10 The quotation in this paragraph is from *The Powys Review*, no. 3, 1978, Rosemary Manning, 'Alyse Gregory: A biographical sketch', p. 85. The other information comes from both this source and that in n. 9 above.

11 'her lover for a while' from Llewelyn Powys, *So Wild a Thing*, p. 15; the other information in this paragraph from *The Cry of a Gull* and *The Powys Review*, no. 3, op. cit.

12 *Recollections*, Alyse Gregory, 'The character of Llewelyn Powys', p. 74.

13 ELWIN: Alyse Gregory to Malcolm Elwin, 20 October 1946.

14 Llewelyn Powys, *So Wild a Thing*, p. 15.

15 TEXAS: John Cowper Powys to Gertrude Powys, 29 April (no year) refers to this visit to Chaplin and to the performances of *The Idiot* which we know were in April and May 1922. Otherwise it might have seemed more likely that this visit took place in the spring of 1923.

16 Derek Langridge, *John Cowper Powys, A Record of Achievement* (The Library Association, London, 1966) pp. 92–5; Reginald Pole was credited as co-adaptor after helping to prepare John's adaptation for the stage.

17 Peter Powys Grey in conversation with the present author, October 1980.

18 Ibid.

19 COLGATE: John Cowper Powys to Louis Wilkinson, 9 October 1957.

20 *The Powys Review*, no. 5, 1979, Sylvia Townsend Warner, 'Theodore Powys and some friends at East Chaldon, 1922–1927: A narrative and some letters', p. 15. The information in the rest of this paragraph and the next is taken from the same article, pp. 15–20.

21 Ibid., p. 15.

22 Theodore Francis Powys, *The Left Leg* (Chatto & Windus, London, 1923) p. 79.

23 The information in this paragraph comes from Sylvia Townsend Warner's article in *The Powys Review*, no. 5, op. cit.; from Hopkins, pp. 77–8; and from TEXAS: John Cowper Powys to Theodore Francis Powys, 14 October 1922.

24 Theodore Francis Powys, 'Abraham Men' in *The Left Leg* (Chatto & Windus, London, 1923) p. 294.

25 *Recollections*, David Garnett, 'Mrs Ashburnham's Scotties', p. 137.

26 TEXAS: Theodore Francis Powys to John Cowper Powys, 24 December 1922.

27 Ibid., 14 October 1922.

28 *The Powys Review*, no. 2, 1977, 'John Cowper Powys in America to T. F. Powys: Letters 1923–1929', p. 67.

29 John Cowper Powys, *Psychoanalysis and Morality* (The Village Press, London, 1975) pp. 12, 22.

30 John Cowper Powys, *James Joyce's Ulysses – An Appreciation* (Village Press, London, 1975) p. 21.

31 There is only indirect evidence for this visit: in *John to Llewelyn*, p. 343, where Powys says that 'The Old Man' (i.e. Colonel Wood) 'could make nothing of her'; this suggests that Phyllis visited California; and might be tied in with John referring to Phyllis as though present on p. 332 (though that is ambiguous).

32 TEXAS: Llewelyn Powys to Littleton C. Powys, from 4, Patchin Place, nd.

33 *The Powys Review*, no. 2, op. cit. p. 69.

34 TEXAS: John Cowper Powys to Gertrude Powys, 24 June 1923.

35 *The Powys Review*, no. 5, op. cit., p. 24.

36 *The Powys Review*, no. 2, op. cit., p. 68.

37 TEXAS: Llewelyn Powys to Littleton C. Powys, 23 July 1923.
38 Littleton C. Powys, *The Powys Family* (Western Gazette, Yeovil, 1952) p. 13.
39 Ibid., p. 17.
40 TEXAS: Gertrude Powys to Katie Powys, postcard, 3 August 1923.
41 *The Cry of a Gull*, p. 19.
42 TEXAS: Llewelyn Powys to Littleton Powys, 23 July 1923.
43 TEXAS: Gertrude Powys to Katie Powys, 23 March 1924.
44 Ibid., 4 November 1923.
45 TEXAS: Theodore Francis Powys to John Cowper Powys, 24 December 1922.
46 COLGATE: Theodore Francis Powys to Louis Wilkinson, 3 November 1923, details the expenses to which Theodore was put, which Louis Wilkinson edited out of *Welsh Ambassadors*, pp. 181–2.
47 *The Joy Of It*, p. 204.
48 Ibid., p. 205.

Chapter Eleven 1923–1925

Unless otherwise indicated, the information in this chapter is drawn largely from: *Life of Llewelyn*; *Letters of Llewelyn*; *John to Llewelyn*; *Welsh Ambassadors*; *The Verdict of Bridlegoose*; *The Cry of a Gull*.

1 *Recollections*, Sylvia Townsend Warner, 'Theodore Powys at East Chaldon' pp. 132–3.
2 Ibid., p. 135.
3 *Recollections*, David Garnett, 'Mrs. Ashburnham's Scotties', p. 138.
4 *Recollections*, Sylvia Townsend Warner, pp. 133–4.
5 Theodore Francis Powys, *Mockery Gap* (Chatto & Windus, London, 1925) pp. 10 and 11.
6 *Recollections*, Sylvia Townsend Warner, p. 128.
7 Ibid., p. 129.
8 Ibid., p.130.
9 TEXAS: John Cowper Powys to Gertrude Powys, 18 November 1923.
10 TEXAS: Alyse Gregory, 'Notes on Catherine Edith Philippa Powys'.
11 TEXAS: Gertrude Powys to Katie Powys, Christmas Day 1923; and see TEXAS: John Cowper Powys to Gertrude Powys, 18 November 1923, for his warning that she should not worry about 'success'.
12 TEXAS: Gertrude Powys to Katie Powys, 23 March 1924.
13 TEXAS: Llewelyn Powys to Littleton C. Powys, 20 May 1924.
14 See Chapter Ten, n. 7.
15 *The Powys Review*, no. 3, 1978, Rosemary Manning, 'Alyse Gregory: A biographical sketch', p. 86.
16 TEXAS: Theodore Francis Powys to John Cowper Powys, 21 October 1920.
17 *As You Like It*, Act II, scene vi.
18 COLGATE: John Cowper Powys to Louis Wilkinson, Tuesday 14 [Ap? May?] 1959.
19 John Cowper Powys, *Ducdame* (Village Press, London, 1974) pp. 3, 264–5.
20 TEXAS: Theodore Francis Powys to John Cowper Powys, 30 January 1925.
21 ELWIN: Alyse Gregory to Malcolm Elwin, Saturday 1944 [no month].
22 Ibid., 8 December 1944. Betty's father was the curator of the Metropolitan Museum of Art.
23 *The Powys Review*, no. 3, op. cit., p. 87.

24 TEXAS: John Cowper Powys to Gertrude Powys, 6 October 1924.
25 Ibid. But Alyse continued throughout her married life to be known as 'Miss Gregory'.
26 TEXAS: Theodore Francis Powys to John Cowper Powys, 12 December 1924, talks of such a tea being planned. These 'Volentia teas' were a recurring feature of family life.
27 Ibid.
28 *The Powys Review*, no. 5, 1979, Sylvia Townsend Warner, 'Theodore Powys and some friends at East Chaldon, 1922–1927: A narrative and some letters', p. 25.
29 Ibid., pp. 25–6.
30 TEXAS: Theodore Francis Powys to John Cowper Powys, 30 January 1925.
31 *The Powys Review*, no. 5, op. cit., p. 31.
32 TEXAS: Theodore Francis Powys to John Cowper Powys, 12 April 1925.
33 For a brief survey of T. E. Lawrence's life see the present author's *Lawrence of Arabia and His World* (Thames & Hudson, London, 1976; Charles Scribner's Sons, New York, 1976). While the present author was researching that life, he read a letter in the British Museum from T. E. Lawrence to George Bernard Shaw or his wife Charlotte, in which he praised Theodore Powys's work. Lawrence may have heard of the Powys family and their writings (he was also interested in Llewelyn's work) from their mutual friend Thomas Hardy; or from the Garnett family: David Garnett's father, Edward Garnett, was working on an abridgement of *Seven Pillars of Wisdom*.
34 In *Recollections*, pp. 125–6, Theodore's son Francis Powys tells an amusing story about Theodore mistaking T. E. Lawrence for a tax inspector, at a time when he was 'having trouble with the tax authorities over the tax on Armorial Bearings and the crests had been removed from all the family silver just before this visit.' In the view of the present author, very considerable doubt is thrown on the reliability of this story – no doubt an old family joke, perhaps running together two separate incidents, and the truth long forgotten – by the documentary evidence. This shows that T. E. Lawrence first visited Theodore in or before April 1925; while Theodore was busy removing crests from the family silver as late as October 1932 (TEXAS: letters from Theodore to John, 12 April 1925, and 14 October 1932).
35 ELWIN: *John to Llewelyn*, 18 February 1925.
36 Ibid.
37 Ibid., 22 February 1925.
38 *The Powys Review*, no. 3, op. cit., p. 86.
39 Ibid., p. 88.
40 ELWIN: Alyse Gregory to Malcolm Elwin, 8 December 1944.
41 *So Wild a Thing*, p. 13.
42 ELWIN: *John to Llewelyn*, 13 March 1925.
43 Ibid., All Fools' Day 1925.

Chapter Twelve 1925–1928

Unless otherwise indicated, the information in this chapter is drawn largely from: *Life of Llewelyn; Letters of Llewelyn; Welsh Ambassadors; The Cry of a Gull; So Wild a Thing*.

1 ELWIN: *John to Llewelyn*, 2 June 1925.
2 Ibid., 4 January 1926.

3 TEXAS: Gertrude Powys to Katie Powys, 2 September 1925.
4 TEXAS: Theodore Francis Powys to John Cowper Powys, 2 July 1925.
5 *Recollections*, Alyse Gregory, 'A Famous Family', p. 60.
6 ELWIN: *John to Llewelyn*, 23 November 1925.
7 Ibid., 13 December 1925.
8 Ibid., 2 June 1925.
9 Ibid., 24 July 1925.
10 Ibid., 23 November 1925.
11 Ibid., 2 June 1925.
12 Ibid., 14 August 1925.
13 Ibid., 25 September 1925.
14 Ibid., 10 September 1925.
15 Ibid., see for example 24 July and 23 November 1925.
16 Ibid., 10 September 1925.
17 John Cowper Powys, *Wolf Solent* (Penguin, Harmondsworth, 1964), the quotations come from the preface, p. 11 and from pp. 264, 83, 245–52, 426, 623, 630, 617, 633. The novel was at first called 'Mystery', then 'An Ounce of Civet', and then 'The Quick and the Dead'. Seven or eight chapters were written before he began a lecture tour.
18 ELWIN: *John to Llewelyn*, 2 June 1925.
19 *The Powys Review* no. 7, 1980, John Cowper Powys, 'Wolf Solent; a letter from John Cowper Powys to his brother Llewelyn', p. 57–8.
20 ELWIN: *John to Llewelyn*, 3 December 1925.
21 Ibid., 27 August 1925.
22 Ibid., 3 December 1925.
23 Ibid., 31 December 1925.
24 TEXAS: Theodore Francis Powys to John Cowper Powys, 29 September 1925.
25 Theodore Francis Powys, *Mr. Weston's Good Wine* (Heinemann Educational, London, 1974). This edition was first published in 1967, with a penetrating introduction by David Holbrook to which I am very much indebted. The quotations come from pp. 35, and 146.
26 TEXAS: Theodore Francis Powys to John Cowper Powys; see letters of 29 September 1925, 16 January 1926, 18 August 1926.
27 Ibid., 3 December 1925.
28 ELWIN: *John to Llewelyn*, 3 October 1925.
29 Kenneth Hopkins identifies Thayer as the man referred to, in a marginal note in his copy of *Letters of Llewelyn*, p. 129.
30 ELWIN: *John to Llewelyn*, 19 March 1926. This information comes from a portion of the letter which has been edited out of the version which may eventually be published. For more on Patrick, see of course *Autobiography*, pp. 564–5.
31 ELWIN: *John to Llewelyn*, 19 March 1926.
32 Ibid., 10 April 1926. This information comes from a portion of the letter which has been edited out of the version which may eventually be published.
33 Ibid., 3 May 1926.
34 Ibid., 10 May 1926.
35 COLGATE: Theodore Francis Powys to Louis Wilkinson, 14 May 1926.
36 *John to Louis*, p. 315.
37 ELWIN: *John to Llewelyn*, 11 June 1926.
38 Ibid., (probably misdated) 9 April 1926. John had been planning to see Frances the previous month, when the General Strike ruined his itinerary;

there is no *proof* that he visited her, but it seems likely that he did: she must have been more important to him than a visit to Cambridge! Proof will probably appear when the correspondence between John and Frances is eventually published.

39 *Recollections*, H. P. Collins, 'Louis and Lulu', p. 82; Frances at this time was unsuccessfully trying to have two books published: an autobiographical novel which was less than flattering to Louis; and a collection of short stories, most of which had previously appeared in American magazines.

40 TEXAS: John Cowper Powys to Littleton Powys, 6 June 1926.

41 ELWIN: *John to Llewelyn*, 15 June 1926.

42 See for example *John to Llewelyn*, p. 367.

43 ELWIN: *John to Llewelyn*, 11 June 1926.

44 Ibid., 17 June 1926, 12 July 1926.

45 ELWIN: Alyse Gregory to Malcolm Elwin, 8 December 1944.

46 ELWIN: *John to Llewelyn*, 2 October 1926.

47 Ibid., see 19 August 1926.

48 Ibid., 7 October 1926.

49 Ibid., 20 January 1927.

50 Ibid., 11 February 1927.

51 Ibid., 2 April 1927.

52 Ibid., 15 November 1927.

53 Ibid., (for how John Cowper Powys passed the summer) 17 June, 17 July and 13 August 1927.

54 Ibid., 9 September and 30 September 1927.

55 Ibid., 15 November 1927.

56 *Brenan*, p. 221.

57 ELWIN: *John to Llewelyn*, 20 January 1927.

58 Gamel Woolsey, *Middle Earth* (Warren House Press, North Walsham, 1979) 'The House of the Moon' p. 27.

59 Gamel Woolsey, *The Last Leaf Falls* (Warren House Press, North Walsham, 1978), 'In All But Face I Am The Same', p. 11.

60 Gamel Woolsey, *Middle Earth*, 'Immutable' p. 45.

61 Ibid., 'For The Flesh' p. 33.

Chapter Thirteen 1928–1930

Unless otherwise indicated, the information in this chapter is drawn largely from: *Autobiography; Life of Llewelyn; Letters of Llewelyn; Welsh Ambassadors; The Cry of a Gull; So Wild a Thing; A Pagan's Pilgrimage.*

1 *The Powys Review* no. 3, 1978, Rosemary Manning, 'Alyse Gregory: A biographical sketch', p. 89.

2 Ibid., pp. 89–90.

3 ELWIN: see *John to Llewelyn*, 16 June 1928.

4 COLGATE: Katie Powys to 'Nan' Wilkinson, 22 January 1928 and 20 July 1928.

5 COLGATE: Theodore Francis Powys to Louis Wilkinson, 7 January 1928.

6 ELWIN: Alyse Gregory to Malcolm Elwin, 8 December 1944.

7 ELWIN: *John to Llewelyn*, 9 September 1928.

8 Ibid., 16 June 1928.

9 Llewelyn Powys, *Apples Be Ripe* (Longmans Green, London, 1932) pp. 17, 82, 71, 89, 216–7.
10 In addition we learn from *Recollections*, H. P. Collins, 'Louis and Lulu', p. 82, that Frances had now recovered from her cancer operation, and was editor of a staff magazine for John Lewis in Oxford Street, London.
11 ELWIN: *John to Llewelyn* a note by Malcolm Elwin.
12 Ibid., 9 September 1928.
13 TEXAS: John Cowper Powys to Gertrude Powys, 18 October 1928.
14 ELWIN: *John to Llewelyn*, 16 December 1928.
15 Ibid., 16 June 1928.
16 TEXAS: John Cowper Powys to Gertrude Powys, 18 October 1928.
17 *Recollections*, H. P. Collins, 'Louis and Lulu'.
18 ELWIN: *John to Llewelyn*, 16 December 1928.
19 Llewelyn Powys, *The Cradle of God* (Jonathan Cape, London, 1929) pp. 315, 229–30, 306.
20 ELWIN: *John to Llewelyn*, 4 March 1929.
21 Ibid.
22 Ibid., 16 December 1928.
23 Ibid., 18 January 1929.
24 Ibid., 10 May 1929.
25 Ibid., 16 December 1928 and 18 January 1929.
26 Ibid., 15 February 1929.
27 Ibid.
28 Ibid., 11 June 1929: from a portion of the letter which has been edited out of the version which may eventually be published.
29 Ibid., 11 June 1929.
30 *Recollections*, H. P. Collins, 'Louis and Lulu'.
31 Theodore Francis Powys, *Fables* (The Viking Press, New York, 1929) quotations from pp. 14, and 176–8.
32 Theodore Francis Powys, *Kindness in a Corner* (Chatto & Windus, London, 1930) pp. 232, 55, 33, 248.
33 COLGATE: Katie Powys to Nan Wilkinson, May 1929, 29 July 1929, 12 January 1930; and TEXAS: Littleton Powys to Katie Powys, 21 November 1929. Littleton opposed the move and asked how Gertrude would manage at Chydyok without her.
34 TEXAS: Littleton C. Powys to Katie Powys, nd.
35 COLGATE: Katie Powys to Nan Wilkinson, 21 October 1929, 30 March 1930.
36 ELWIN: *John to Llewelyn*, 11 June 1929.
37 Llewelyn Powys, *The Pathetic Fallacy* (Watts & Co., London, 1931) p. 106.
38 ELWIN: *John to Llewelyn*, 25 August 1929; partly from a portion of the letter which has been edited out of the version which may be published.
39 Ibid., a letter is quoted from Alyse Gregory to Malcolm Elwin.
40 TEXAS: John Cowper Powys to Gertrude Powys, 5 April 1929; see also ELWIN: *John to Llewelyn*, 12 July 1929.
41 ELWIN: *John to Llewelyn*, 12 July 1929.
42 Ibid., 8 August 1929.
43 *Recollections*, Oliver Marlow Wilkinson, 'A Rival to Jack', pp. 186–7.
44 See ELWIN: *John to Llewelyn*, 8 August 1919.
45 Ibid., 25 August 1929.
46 COLGATE: Llewelyn Powys to Miss Boyne Grainger, December 1929.
47 TEXAS: Theodore Francis Powys to John Cowper Powys, 28 May 1930.

48 Theodore Francis Powys, *Unclay* (Chatto & Windus, London, 1931) pp. 314, 282, 116, 66, 233–4.

49 TEXAS: Theodore Francis Powys to John Cowper Powys, 28 May 1930, from this one learns that Theodore resisted Llewelyn's efforts to persuade him to begin writing another novel.

50 ELWIN: *John to Llewelyn*, a portion of the letter of 25 August 1929 which has been edited out of the version which may eventually be published shows that on the voyage across the Atlantic John was busy reading and re-reading one of the books recommended by Gamel Woolsey.

51 John Cowper Powys, *The Meaning of Culture* (Village Press, London, 1974) pp. 90, 180.

52 Hopkins, p. 150.

53 ELWIN: *John to Llewelyn*, Autumn 1929.

54 Ibid., 14 November 1929.

55 Ibid., 19 January 1930.

56 Ibid., 21 February 1930.

57 Ibid., 4 March 1930.

58 Ibid., 21 February 1930.

59 John Cowper Powys, *In Defence of Sensuality* (Village Press, London, 1974) quotations from pp. 117, 9–10, 259, 141.

60 Derek Langridge, *John Cowper Powys, A Record of Achievement* (The Library Association, London, 1966), pp. 59–72. This quotation, p. 65.

61 John Cowper Powys, *An Englishman Upstate* (Village Press, London, 1974).

62 TEXAS: John Cowper Powys to Dr Guthrie, 19 May 1930.

63 ELWIN: *John to Llewelyn*, 10 July 1930.

64 Ibid., from the portion of the letter which has been edited out of the version which may eventually be published.

65 TEXAS: John Cowper Powys to Edgar Lee Masters, nd.

66 ELWIN: *John to Llewelyn*, 6 May 1930.

67 Ibid., 4 August 1930.

68 Ibid., 10 July 1930.

69 Ibid., 4 August 1930.

70 *The Powys Review*, no. 3, 1978, Rosemary Manning, 'Alyse Gregory: A biographical Sketch', pp. 90–1.

71 *Brenan*, p. 219.

72 Ibid., p. 231.

73 Gamel Woolsey, *Twenty-Eight Sonnets* (Warren House Press, North Walsham, 1977) from 'Of happy lovers there's no tale to tell', p. 26.

Chapter Fourteen 1930–1932

Unless otherwise indicated, the information in this chapter is drawn largely from: *Autobiography; Letters of Llewelyn; Life of Llewelyn; Welsh Ambassadors; So Wild a Thing; The Cry of a Gull; Brenan.*

1 TEXAS: Llewelyn Powys, 'Pride'.

2 Gamel Woolsey, *Middle Earth* (Warren House Press, North Walsham, 1979) p. 20.

3 Llewelyn Powys, *Impassioned Clay*, (Longmans, London, 1931) pp. 104, 108.

4 COLGATE: Louis Wilkinson to Llewelyn Powys, 4 December 1930.

5 TEXAS: John Cowper Powys to Gertrude Powys, 19 November 1930.

6 John Cowper Powys, *A Glastonbury Romance* (Pan/Picador, London, 1975) quotations in the next six paragraphs from pp. xii–xiii, 285, xiii, 118–20, 21, 748, 125, 739, 71, 1,104.

7 ELWIN: *John to Llewelyn*, 21 August 1929.

8 John Cowper Powys, *Suspended Judgments* (Village Press, London, 1975) pp. 114, 122–3, 322–3.

9 TEXAS: Theodore Francis Powys to John Cowper Powys, 7 August 1929.

10 *Recollections*, Sylvia Townsend Warner, 'Theodore Powys at East Chaldon', pp. 131–2.

11 TEXAS: John Cowper Powys to Gertrude Powys, 19 November 1930, suggests that Gertrude may have visited Gamel in mid-November.

12 They made private marriage vows to each other in a church on the Capitoline hill, and later Gamel changed her surname by deed poll from Woolsey to Brenan [see *Brenan*, p. 232].

13 The Powys Review, no. 4, 1978–9, Llewelyn Powys, 'Conversations with Theodore Powys', for the dating of these 'Conversations' see *The Powys Review*, no. 6, 1979–80, a letter from E. E. Bissell Esq., pp. 81–2; for the progress of Llewelyn's work see ELWIN: *John to Llewelyn*, 26 June 1931.

14 *The Powys Review*, no. 4, 1978–9, 'Conversations'.

15 TEXAS: John Cowper Powys to Edgar Lee Masters, Ash Friday 1931.

16 *Essays*, John Cowper Powys, 'Letters to Littleton C. Powys 1927–1934', p. 327.

17 COLGATE: Tape-recording of Albert Krick's reminiscences, dated 17 January 1980.

18 John Cowper Powys, *The Complex Vision* (Village Press, London 1975) pp. 248–69.

19 See for example, ELWIN: *John to Llewelyn*, 5 June 1931, 16 August 1931.

20 John Cowper Powys, *The Meaning of Culture* (Village Press, London, 1974) p. 109.

21 COLGATE: as n. 17 above.

22 John Cowper Powys, *The Meaning of Culture*, p. 180.

23 ELWIN: *John to Llewelyn*, 26 June 1931; information from a portion of the letter which has been edited out of the version which may eventually be published.

24 Ibid., 18 January 1932.

25 COLGATE: as n. 17 above.

26 Peter Powys Grey in conversation with the present author, 16 October 1980.

27 ELWIN: *John to Llewelyn*, 6 July 1931.

28 Ibid., 5 June 1931 and 26 June 1931.

29 YALE: John Cowper Powys to Dorthy Richardson, 19 January 1930 and 19 May 1931.

30 John Cowper Powys, *Dorothy Richardson* (Village Press, London, 1974) pp. 13–14.

31 ELWIN: *John to Llewelyn*: for Miss Playter's health and gardening, see 15 April 1931 and 5 May 1931; for the elderly German lady's arrival, see TEXAS: John Cowper Powys to Gertrude Powys, 28 March 1931, and for her departure ELWIN: *John to Llewelyn*, 6 August 1931, from a portion of the letter which has been edited out of the version which may eventually be published.

32 ELWIN: *John to Llewelyn*, 26 June 1931, 6 July 1931; and see also TEXAS: John Cowper Powys to Edgar Lee Masters, 4 September 1931 and John Cowper Powys to Dr W. N. Guthrie, 25 November 1931. One learns that John was

dyspeptic in June; that it was Miss Playter who went to New York in July finally to sever their links with Patchin Place, but that apart from a bad week at the end of August, John's health remained reasonably good until late November, when he was once more reduced to spending most of each day lying on his back.

33 ELWIN: *John to Llewelyn*, 12 October 1931.
34 Ibid.
35 TEXAS: Theodore Francis Powys to John Cowper Powys, 21 October 1931.
36 Unpublished 'Portrait of T. F. Powys' by his adopted daughter Theodora Gay Powys, p. 13.
37 COLGATE: cutting from *The Times* headed 'Nairobi', 8 November.
38 TEXAS: Theodore Francis Powys to John Cowper Powys, 21 October 1931.
39 *Recollections*, Mr and Mrs Roger Musgrave recording, 'Clifford and Margaret Musgrave: An Interview', pp. 90–1.
40 Llewelyn Powys, *Now that the Gods are Dead* (Bodley Head, London, 1949) p. 39.
41 *Recollections*, op. cit., pp. 88, 91, 88.
42 TEXAS: Gertrude Powys to Katie Powys, 24 April 1932.
43 *Recollections*, op. cit., p. 90.
44 *Recollections*, Alyse Gregory, 'A Famous Family', pp. 55–7.
45 TEXAS: Katie Powys to Alyse Gregory, Wednesday, nd 1932.
46 COLGATE: Katie Powys to Alyse Gregory, nd 1932
47 TEXAS: Katie Powys to Alyse Gregory, 8 March 1932. Katie also had an overdraft, largely as the result of trying to maintain her separate establishment at Sidmouth, and had to rely on Littleton to sort out her financial affairs, see TEXAS: Littleton C. Powys to Katie Powys, 8 September 1932.
48 Llewelyn Powys, *Now that the Gods are Dead*, p. 41.
49 ELWIN: *John to Llewelyn*, 18/19/20 January 1932.
50 *Essays*, John Cowper Powys, 'Letters to Littleton C. Powys, 1927–1934', p. 335.
51 Ibid., p. 329.
52 Ibid., p. 330.
53 Ibid., p. 331.
54 John Cowper Powys, *A Glastonbury Romance*, p. 917.
55 Ibid., p. 239.
56 *Essays*, op. cit., pp. 332–3.
57 TEXAS: John Cowper Powys to Edgar Lee Masters, 22 March and 7 April 1932; see also ELWIN: *John to Llewelyn*, 23 March and 15 April 1932.
58 ELWIN: *John to Llewelyn*, 15 April 1932.
59 TEXAS: John Cowper Powys to Gertrude Powys, 30 January 1932.
60 Ibid., 27 June 1932.
61 *Essays*, op. cit., p. 335.

Chapter Fifteen 1932–1934

Unless otherwise indicated, the information in this chapter is drawn largely from: *Letters of Llewelyn; Life of Llewelyn; Welsh Ambassadors; So Wild a Thing; The Cry of a Gull.*

1 TEXAS: Theodore Francis Powys to John Cowper Powys, 30 May 1932.
2 Isobel Powys Marks in conversation with the present author, 28 August 1981.

3 TEXAS: Theodore Francis Powys to John Cowper Powys, 23 November 1932 (dated 1931 in error).

4 Unpublished 'Portrait of T. F. Powys' by his daughter Theodora Gay Powys, pp. 13–14.

5 Count Potocki of Montalk, *Dogs' Eggs*, Part One, (The Shack Press, Les Faisses, 83-Draguignan, France, 1972) pp. 14–17.

6 TEXAS: Theodore Francis Powys to John Cowper Powys, 23 November 1932 (dated 1931 in error).

7 The date of completion is given in the book.

8 *Recollections*, Mr and Mrs Roger Musgrave recording, 'Clifford and Margaret Musgrave: An Interview', p. 88.

9 TEXAS: has a letter from Bernie O'Neill to Gertrude Powys, 3 September 1932, about his visit.

10 TEXAS: considerable correspondence from Katie Powys to Alyse Gregory, 1933; see in particular letters of 24 March, 10 April, 20 June, 10 October, 6 September and one nd. Katie hated the ostentation and constant socialising of the English settlers, and there seemed no prospect of earning her own living.

11 ELWIN: *John to Llewelyn*, 9 February 1933.

12 Ibid., 21 January 1933.

13 *Essays*, John Cowper Powys, 'Letters to Littleton C. Powys 1927–1934' p. 335–6.

14 Ibid., p. 336.

15 ELWIN: *John to Llewelyn*, 23 March 1933.

16 Ibid., from a portion of the letter which has been edited out of the version which may eventually be published.

17 ELWIN: *John to Llewelyn*, see, for example, 18 January 1932, 15 April 1932.

18 COLGATE: Tape-recording of Albert Krick's reminiscences, dated 17 January 1980.

19 *Essays*, op.cit., p. 336.

20 SYRACUSE: John Cowper Powys to Eric Barker, 2 May 1933.

21 John Cowper Powys, *Weymouth Sands* (Pan/Picador, London, 1980) quotations from pp. 39, 48–9, 53, 58, 260, 490, [prefatory] Note By Author, 39, 324 [the present author has amended the text from affection to affectation, believing that affection is either a misprint or a slip of JCP's pen], 271, 329–30, 272.

22 SYRACUSE: John Cowper Powys to Eric Barker, 2 February 1935, shows that John actually began writing his new novel with a pen which had belonged to his father.

23 ELWIN: *John to Llewelyn*, 13 August 1933.

24 Ibid., 29 August 1933.

25 Ibid., 9 February 1933.

26 Edna St Vincent Millay, *Huntsman, What Quarry* (Harper & Row, New York, 1933).

27 Llewelyn Powys, *Glory of Life* (Bodley Head, London, 1949) pp. 27–8.

28 ELWIN: *John to Llewelyn*, 7 May 1933.

29 Ibid., 25 September 1933.

30 TEXAS: Theodore Francis Powys to John Cowper Powys, 28 November 1933.

31 COLGATE: Theodore Francis Powys to Louis Wilkinson, 13 March 1933.

32 TEXAS: Theodore Francis Powys to John Cowper Powys, 28 November 1933.

33 Ibid.

34 COLGATE: Theodore Francis Powys to Louis Wilkinson, 9 February 1933.

35 TEXAS: Theodore Francis Powys to John Cowper Powys, 28 November 1933.
36 ELWIN: *John to Llewelyn*, 24 July 1933.
37 Ibid., 1 August 1933.
38 Ibid., 21 January 1933.
39 *Essays*, op. cit., p. 337.
40 ELWIN: *John to Llewelyn*, 11 August 1933.
41 Ibid., 7 May 1933, from a portion of the letter which has been edited out of the version which may eventually be published.
42 Ibid., 24 July 1933.
43 *Essays*, op. cit., pp. 339, 337.
44 ELWIN: *John to Llewelyn*, 29 September 1933.
45 *Essays*, op. cit., p. 337.
46 ELWIN: *John to Llewelyn*, 29 August 1933.
47 Ibid., 20 September 1933.
48 Ibid., 25 September 1933; there was not much incentive to cook, as John lived largely on bread and milk.
49 Ibid., 1 August 1933.
50 Ibid., 20 September 1933 and 29 August 1933.
51 *Essays*, op. cit., p. 338. ELWIN: *John to Llewelyn*, 24 July 1933, shows that the idea for a long historical novel was born when John noticed that although *A Glastonbury Romance* had been a commercial failure, *Anthony Adverse*, an enormously long historical novel, had been both a critical success and a best-seller.
52 TEXAS: John Cowper Powys to Gertrude Powys, 10 October 1933.
53 *Essays*, op. cit., p. 341.
54 Ibid., but see also TEXAS: John Cowper Powys to Edgar Lee Masters, 21 September 1933.
55 ELWIN: *John to Llewelyn*, 30 November 1933.
56 John Cowper Powys, *An Englishman Upstate* (Village Press, London, 1974) pp. 14, 16.
57 Ibid., p. 15.
58 *Essays*, op. cit., p. 342.
59 ELWIN: *John to Llewelyn*, 26 February 1934.
60 *Essays*, op. cit., p. 341.
61 TEXAS: John Cowper Powys to Edgar Lee Masters, 10 March 1934.
62 I have assumed this from the letter in n. 63 below, in which John makes it clear that when he settles in England he will have more than one woman with him.
63 TEXAS: John Cowper Powys to Gertrude Powys, 10 March 1934.
64 ELWIN: *John to Llewelyn*, 28 March 1934.
65 Ibid., from a portion of the letter likely to be excluded from the published work.
66 YALE: John Cowper Powys to Dorothy Richardson, 25 March 1934.
67 TEXAS: John Cowper Powys to Gertrude Powys, 6 April 1934.

Chapter Sixteen 1934–1936

Unless otherwise indicated, the information in this chapter is drawn largely from: *Letters of Llewelyn; Life of Llewelyn; Welsh Ambassadors; So Wild a Thing; The Cry of a Gull; Brenan; John to Louis*.

1 YALE: John Cowper Powys to Dorothy Richardson, 22 June 1934.
2 Ibid.

3 TEXAS: Llewelyn Powys to Valentine Ackland, nd 1934.
4 TEXAS: John Cowper Powys to Edgar Lee Masters, 4 August 1934.
5 Quoted in Malcolm Elwin's 'prefatory note' to John Cowper Powys, *Maiden Castle* (Macdonald, London, 1966) p. 7.
6 John Cowper Powys, *The Art of Happiness* (Village Press, London, 1975 p. 38.
7 TEXAS: John Cowper Powys to Edgar Lee Masters, 16 November 1934.
8 SYRACUSE: John Cowper Powys to Eric Barker, 10 November 1934.
9 TEXAS: Littleton C. Powys to Gertrude Powys, 23 November 1934.
10 ELWIN: *John to Llewelyn*, 8 January 1935.
11 John Cowper Powys, *Maiden Castle*, pp. 7–8.
12 TEXAS: John Cowper Powys to Edgar Lee Masters, 21 March 1935.
13 Ibid.
14 *Recollections*, James Hanley, 'John Cowper Powys: A Recollection' pp. 197–8.
15 Ibid., p. 198.
16 SYRACUSE: John Cowper Powys to Eric Barker, 8 July 1935.
17 ELWIN: *John to Llewelyn*, 3 July 1935.
18 TEXAS: John Cowper Powys to Edgar Lee Masters, 22 June 1935.
19 John Cowper Powys, *Maiden Castle* (Macdonald, London, 1935) pp. 121, 167, 174, 197–9, 254, 239, 230–1, 467, 496.
20 ELWIN: *John to Llewelyn*, 28 January 1935.
21 COLGATE: Albert R. Powys ['Bertie'] to Louis Wilkinson, 24 October 1935.
22 TEXAS: Llewelyn Powys to Arthur C. Abrahams, 30 March 1935.
23 TEXAS: Llewelyn Powys to Rosamund Rose, 6 November 1935.
24 Ibid., 29 December 1935.
25 *Advice to a Young Poet*, p. 81.
26 Kenneth Hopkins (ed.), *Llewelyn Powys: A Selection* (Macdonald, London, 1952) p. vi.
27 ELWIN: *John to Llewelyn*, 13 August 1935.
28 Ibid., 14 July 1935.
29 Ibid., 10 August 1935.
30 Ibid., 6 September 1935.
31 Ibid., All Souls' Day [2 November] 1935.
32 Ibid., 16 and 27 September 1935.
33 Ibid., 25 November 1935.
34 Ibid., 16 September 1935.
35 Ibid., 1 December 1935.
36 Ibid., All Souls' Day [2 November] 1935.
37 COLGATE: see Louis Wilkinson to Albert R. Powys, 21 September 1935.
38 *The Times*, 8 February 1936.
39 TEXAS: Katie Powys to Alyse Gregory, 10 November 1937.
40 TEXAS: John Cowper Powys to Edgar Lee Masters, 9 and 29 February 1936.
41 Ibid., 24 March 1936.
42 ELWIN: *John to Llewelyn*, 2 February 1936.
43 TEXAS: John Cowper Powys to Edgar Lee Masters, 24 March 1936.
44 ELWIN: *John to Llewelyn*, 15 March 1936.
45 TEXAS: Llewelyn Powys to Rosamund Rose, [?] February 1936.
46 Ibid., 2 February 1936.
47 Ibid., 8 February 1936.
48 Ibid., St Valentine's Day [14 February] 1936.
49 Ibid., 10 May 1936.

50 Ibid., 11 May 1936.
51 Ibid., 3 June 1936.
52 Ibid., 6 June 1936.
53 Ibid., see for example 1 September 1936.
54 TEXAS: Rosamund Rose to Alyse Gregory, 22 January 1946.
55 TEXAS: Katie Powys to Gertrude Powys, 17 May 1936.
56 Derek Langridge, *John Cowper Powys: A Record of Achievement*, (The Library Association, London 1966) p. 141.
57 TEXAS: John Cowper Powys to Gertrude Powys, 8 June 1936.
58 Malcolm Elwin, in his 'Prefatory Note' to John Cowper Powys, *Maiden Castle* (Macdonald, London, 1966) p. 8.
59 Oliver Wilkinson in conversation with the present author, 26 September 1980.
60 John Cowper Powys, *Maiden Castle*, p. 8.
61 As n. 59 above.
62 ELWIN: *John to Llewelyn*, see, for example, 8 July 1935.
63 John Cowper Powys, *Morwyn* (Sphere, London, 1977) p. 12; other quotations from pp. 148, 211.
64 SYRACUSE: John Cowper Powys to Eric Barker, August 1936.
65 ELWIN: Alyse Gregory to Malcolm Elwin, Saturday, n.d., 1944.
66 TEXAS: Gamel Woolsey to Gertrude Powys, 17 August 1936.
67 *Advice to a Young Poet*, p. 134.
68 ELWIN: *John to Llewelyn*, 17 February 1937.

Chapter Seventeen 1936–1939

Unless otherwise indicated, the information in this chapter is drawn largely from: *Letters of Llewelyn; Life of Llewelyn; So Wild a Thing; The Cry of a Gull; John to Louis; John to Rose; John to Roberts; Advice to a Young Poet.*

1 ELWIN: Alyse Gregory to Malcolm Elwin, nd 1944.
2 TEXAS: Llewelyn Powys to Van Wyck Brooks, 3 January 1937.
3 ELWIN: *John to Llewelyn*, Christmas Eve 1936.
4 TEXAS: John Cowper Powys to Gertrude Powys, 21 January 1937.
5 TEXAS: Gertrude Powys to Katie Powys, 2 February 1937.
6 Ibid., 7 February 1937.
7 ELWIN: *John to Llewelyn*, 17 February 1937.
8 TEXAS: Llewelyn Powys to Van Wyck Brooks, 1 March 1937.
9 Llewelyn Powys, *Love and Death* (The Bodley Head, London, 1950) p. 36.
10 TEXAS: Alyse Gregory to Rosamund Rose, 20 March/May [?] 1937.
11 See for example ELWIN: *John to Llewelyn*, 17 March 1937.
12 ELWIN: *John to Llewelyn*, 17 March 1937.
13 TEXAS: Littleton C. Powys to Gertrude Powys, 24 February 1937.
14 TEXAS: John Cowper Powys to Edgar Lee Masters, 19 June 1937.
15 TEXAS: John Cowper Powys to Gertrude Powys, 21 January 1937.
16 ELWIN: *John to Llewelyn*, letter marked by Mr Elwin, 13 August 1937, but in reality 13 July 1937.
17 Ibid., 26 July 1937.
18 TEXAS: Katie Powys to Alyse Gregory, 1 September 1937.
19 COLGATE: Katie Powys to Louis Wilkinson, 29 September 1937.
20 *Recollections*, Elizabeth Muntz, 'T. F. Powys: A Few Recorded Memories', p. 141.

21 TEXAS: Dr Bernard Price O'Neill to Gertrude Powys, 16 December 1937.
22 Some of this story is told in *Life of Llewelyn*, pp. 253–5, and in *The Cry of a Gull* p. 87; but see also ELWIN: *John to Llewelyn*, 12 April 1938.
23 Unpublished 'Portrait of T. F. Powys' by his adopted daughter, Theodora Gay Powys, p. 15.
24 TEXAS: John Cowper Powys to Edgar Lee Masters, 10 July 1938.
25 ELWIN: *John to Llewelyn*, 12 April 1938.
26 TEXAS: John Cowper Powys to Gertrude Powys, 2 June 1938.
27 ELWIN: *John to Llewelyn*, 31 January 1938.
28 Ibid., 12 April 1938.
29 TEXAS: John Cowper Powys to Littleton C. Powys, 13 June 1938.
30 TEXAS: John Cowper Powys to Edgar Lee Masters, 10 July 1938.
31 TEXAS: John Cowper Powys to Littleton C. Powys, 17 July 1938.
32 Ibid., 13 June 1938, 21 July 1938.
33 ELWIN: *John to Llewelyn*, 15 August 1938.
34 *The Powys Review* no. 6, 1979/1980, Marguerite Tjader, 'John Cowper Powys and Theodore Dreiser: A friendship', p. 20.
35 ELWIN: *John to Llewelyn*, 26 August 1938.
36 Ibid., 8 September 1938.
37 Ibid., 12 September 1938.
38 Ibid., 21 October 1938.
39 Ibid., 17 November 1938.
40 TEXAS: John Cowper Powys to Edgar Lee Masters, 9 December 1938.
41 ELWIN: *John to Llewelyn*, 22 November 1938.
42 Ibid., see 1 September 1938.
43 TEXAS: John Cowper Powys to Gertrude Powys, 16 September 1938.
44 ELWIN: *John to Llewelyn*, 20 September 1938.
45 *The Powys Review* no. 8, 1980/1981, Kenneth Hopkins (ed.), 'Gamel Woolsey to Alyse Gregory, some letters 1930–1957', p. 69. (Apostrophe on 'Let's' added by the present author.)
46 Ibid., p. 70.
47 ELWIN: *John to Llewelyn*, 26 November 1937.
48 *Recollections*, Ethel Mannin, 'A Visit to Davos in the Late 1930s', pp. 105–7.
49 *The Powys Review* no. 3, Summer 1978, assembled by Alasdair Tilson, 'J. C. Powys to T. F. Powys: some letters from Wales, 1935–1949', pp. 72–3.
50 John Cowper Powys, *Owen Glendower* (Pan/Picador, London, 1978) pp. 393, 413–4, 415, 417, 419, 644, 763, 889, 916–17, 925.
51 COLGATE: John Cowper Powys to Tom Hart, 10 February 1939.
52 See for example TEXAS: John Cowper Powys to Edgar Lee Masters, 28 April 1939.
53 ELWIN: *John to Llewelyn*, 15 April 1939.
54 Ibid., 10 June 1939, from a portion of the letter which has been edited out of the version which may eventually be published.
55 Ibid., 5 May 1939, from a portion of the letter which has been edited out of the version which may eventually be published.
56 From a combination of *John to Louis*, p. 48, and TEXAS: John Cowper Powys to Gertrude Powys, 2 July 1939, we learn that John stayed overnight with Francis and Minnie Powys, who were expecting Theodore's first grandchild; that he also saw Oliver Wilkinson and his charming wife, and Kenneth Hopkins, and he took Lucy Powys back to Wales with him for a short holiday.
57 TEXAS: John Cowper Powys to Edgar Lee Masters, 8 July 1939.

58 Ibid., 27 July 1939.
59 ELWIN: *John to Llewelyn*, 26 July 1939.
60 Ibid., 2 October 1939.
61 TEXAS: John Cowper Powys to Gertrude Powys, 5 October 1939.
62 TEXAS: Llewelyn Powys to Miss Valentine Ackland, nd.
63 TEXAS: Llewelyn Powys to [?], 20 October 1939.
64 Kenneth Hopkins, *Hal Trovillion and the Powys Brothers* (Warren House Press, North Walsham, 1978) (first appeared in ICarbS, vol. III, no. 2, Spring-Summer 1977).
65 TEXAS: Llewelyn Powys, an order to the Army and Navy Stores, 16 November 1939.
66 TEXAS: John Cowper Powys to Gertrude Powys, 2 December 1939.
67 Ibid., 1 December 1939.
68 Ibid., 2 December 1939.
69 *The Powys Review*, no. 8, 1980/1981, Kenneth Hopkins (ed.) 'Gamel Woolsey to Alyse Gregory', p. 71.
70 TEXAS: Katie Powys to Alyse Gregory, Friday, Sunday, and December 1939 (no full dates).
71 *The Powys Review*, no. 8, op. cit.
72 Hopkins, p. 254.
73 COLGATE: Alyse Gregory, *The Place of Llewelyn Powys in Modern Letters*.
74 *The Powys Review*, no. 7, quoted in Denys Val Baker, 'The Powys Family: Some memories of the mid-Forties, p. 87.
75 John Cowper Powys, *Owen Glendower* (Pan/Picador, London, 1978) p. 938.

Chapter Eighteen 1940–1963

Unless otherwise indicated, the information in this chapter is drawn largely from: *The Cry of a Gull; Brenan; Still The Joy Of It; John to Louis; John to Ross; John to Roberts; John to Tolchard*.

1 *Recollections*, Alyse Gregory, 'Recollections from Her Journals: 1940 and 1953', p. 208.
2 Ibid., p. 207.
3 YALE: John Cowper Powys to Dorothy Richardson, 4 September 1939.
4 *Recollections*, Mark Holloway, 'With T. F. Powys at Mappowder', p. 151.
5 TEXAS: Theodore Francis Powys to John Cowper Powys, 17 July 1940.
6 Information booklet in Mappowder Church.
7 TEXAS: Theodore Francis Powys to John Cowper Powys, 17 July 1940.
8 Ibid., 24 July 1940.
9 Ibid., 8 March 1940, shows that his head was still bad; the rest is an informed guess, though it is well-known that at this stage in his life he was particularly averse to large gatherings.
10 See for example TEXAS: Theodore Francis Powys to John Cowper Powys, 14 May 1942. From his adopted daughter's 'Portrait of T. F. Powys', p. 116, we learn that when he needed to calm himself, Theodore knitted woollen squares which Violet made up into shawls.
11 See for example TEXAS: Theodore Francis Powys to John Cowper Powys, 12 July 1942.
12 Ibid., 22 March 1941.
13 TEXAS: John Cowper Powys to Gertrude Powys, 23 September 1940.
14 TEXAS: Theodore Francis Powys to John Cowper Powys, 9 May 1941.

15 Louis Wilkinson, writing as Louis Marlow, *Forth, Beast!* (Faber & Faber, London, 1946), p. 40.
16 TEXAS: Theodore Francis Powys to John Cowper Powys, 9 May 1941.
17 In March 1941 he lectured for Professor Gwyn Jones on *King Lear* to the English Club of the Welsh College at Aberystwyth; and in the autumn of 1940 he had received a small inheritance from Warwick Powys, his distant cousin from New Mexico, and used this to travel south to visit family and friends.
18 *Recollections*, Gilbert Turner, 'John Cowper Powys', p. 214.
19 TEXAS: Theodore Francis Powys to John Cowper Powys, 8 June 1943.
20 YALE: John Cowper Powys to Dorothy Richardson, 8 December 1946.
21 TEXAS: John Cowper Powys to Littleton C. Powys, 16 August 1943.
22 YALE: John Cowper Powys to Dorothy Richardson, 23 August 1944.
23 Louis Wilkinson, writing as Louis Marlow, *Forth, Beast!* pp. 40–1.
24 TEXAS: John Cowper Powys to Gertrude Powys, 22 August 1945.
25 John Cowper Powys, *Porius* (Village Press, London, 1974) pp. 158, 308, 275, 276, 396, 402, 84, 414, 417–18, 486, 390, 507, 512.
26 TEXAS: Littleton C. Powys to Gertrude Powys, 21 September 1945.
27 COLGATE: Redwood Anderson to Louis Wilkinson, 12 March 1946.
28 COLGATE: Theodore Francis Powys to Littleton C. Powys, 24 September 1945.
29 *The Powys Review* no. 4, 1978/1979, Gerard Casey, 'A letter to the Editor' dated 5 December 1978, pp. 85–6.
30 *Recollections*, see both Alyse Gregory, 'The Character of Theodore', pp. 147–8, and Mark Holloway, 'With T. F. Powys at Mappowder', p. 155.
31 TEXAS: Theodore Francis Powys to John Cowper Powys, 26 August (no year).
32 TEXAS: Theodore Francis Powys to John Cowper Powys, 3 December 1945. He also told John that Chatto would be publishing the selection of his stories which appeared the following year as *Bottle's Path*; only three of the stories had not been printed before.
33 TEXAS: Theodore Francis Powys to John Cowper Powys, 28 March 1946 and 22 December 1946.
34 COLGATE: Redwood Anderson to Louis Wilkinson, 12 March 1946.
35 John Cowper Powys, *Obstinate Cymric* (Village Press, London, 1973) pp. 7, 73, 147, 143, 155, 164.
36 TEXAS: Theodore Francis Powys to John Cowper Powys, 12 March 1947.
37 TEXAS: John Cowper Powys to Gertrude Powys, 3 March 1947, informs us that Littleton Alfred advised John not to come down to the funeral; but John had the consolation of knowing that it was only recently that he and Margaret had corresponded with each other in the most amicable way.
38 TEXAS: John Cowper Powys to Elias Gillman, Boxing Day 1947.
39 COLGATE: John Cowper Powys to Miss Muller, 16 February 1949.
40 SYRACUSE: see John Cowper Powys to Norman Denny, 6 September 1949.
41 SYRACUSE: Norman Denny to John Cowper Powys, 4 December 1949.
42 SYRACUSE: John Cowper Powys to Norman Denny, 5 December 1949.
43 Ibid., 7 December 1949.
44 TEXAS: Katie Powys to Alyse Gregory, 10 September 1949.
45 SYRACUSE: John Cowper Powys to George L. Lewin, 30 November 1949.
46 SYRACUSE: John Cowper Powys to Norman Denny, 23 March 1949.
47 *Recollections*, Henry Miller, 'John Cowper Powys: A Living Book', p. 190.
48 Ibid., p. 194.

49 COLGATE: an article by Malcolm Elwin, perhaps in print; and see also *Essays*, Malcolm Elwin, 'John Cowper Powys and his Publishers', pp. 292–3.

50 On 20 October 1954 (*Letters to C. Benson Roberts*, Village Press, London, 1975, p. 100) and on 4 November 1954 (Langridge, *John Cowper Powys: A Record of Achievement*, p. 184) John talks of hoping to complete a translation of Aristophanes, which he has just begun, but whether or not he did complete it is unknown to the present author.

51 TEXAS: John Cowper Powys to Francis and Sally Powys, 22 August 1951.

52 TEXAS: John Cowper Powys to Trevor Moilliet, 24 September 1951.

53 Lucy Penny (née Powys) in conversation with the present author, 28 August 1981.

54 SYRACUSE: John Cowper Powys to Penn Kime (?), 17 September 1953.

55 Unpublished 'Portrait of T. F. Powys' by Theodora Gay Powys, pp. 44–6.

56 Louis Wilkinson, from information in Mappowder Church.

57 TEXAS: Theodore Francis Powys to John Cowper Powys, e.g. letters of 21 December 1950, 16 August 1951, 20 December 1951.

58 Unpublished 'Portrait of T. F. Powys' by Theodora Gay Powys, p. 43. Theodora's account on p. 85 suggests that Theodore had been out of sympathy with Dr Jackson for some time: prepared to meet him in church, but not to be involved in long private conversations if he could help it.

59 Ibid., p. 47.

60 COLGATE: Katie Powys to Louis Wilkinson, December 1953.

61 SYRACUSE: John Cowper Powys to George L. Lewin, 25 March 1954.

62 SYRACUSE: John Cowper Powys to Penn Kime, 21 June 1958; also COLGATE: John Cowper Powys to Louis Wilkinson, 14 June 1958.

63 SYRACUSE: John Cowper Powys to Penn Kime, 30 April 1954.

64 John Cowper Powys, *The Brazen Head* (Macdonald, London, 1959) pp. 268–9.

65 SYRACUSE: John Cowper Powys to Penn Kime, 25 June 1953.

66 TEXAS: John Cowper Powys to T. Evans, 30 September 1955.

67 *Recollections*, Raymond Garlick, 'Blaenau Remembered', p. 238.

68 Besides *John to Ross*, p. 124, see also SYRACUSE: John Cowper Powys to George L. Lewin, 28 September 1954.

69 Louis MacNeice, lines from 'Autumn Sequel' quoted in Littleton C. Powys, *Still the Joy Of It*.

70 *Essays*, Raymond Garlick, 'Powys in Gwynedd: The Last Years', p. 300.

71 *Recollections*, op. cit., p. 239.

72 COLGATE: John Cowper Powys to Christian Hewitt, 11 October 1960.

73 COLGATE: John Cowper Powys to Louis Wilkinson, 11 February 1935.

74 *Essays*, op. cit., p. 306.

75 COLGATE: John Cowper Powys to Louis Wilkinson, 11 February 1935.

76 *Essays*, op. cit., p. 309.

77 TEXAS: John Cowper Powys to Trevor Moilliet 7 July 1958.

78 Besides John Cowper Powys, *Letters to C. Benson Roberts*, p. 107, see COLGATE: John Cowper Powys to Louis Wilkinson, letters of 24 December 1957, 4 January 1958, 16 January 1958.

79 *Recollections*, Glen Cavaliero, 'Recollections of John Cowper Powys', pp. 251–5.

80 COLGATE: John Cowper Powys to Louis Wilkinson, 20 September 1958.

81 Ibid., 14 July 1958.

82 *The Powys Review* no. 3, Summer 1978, Rosemary Manning, 'Alyse Gregory: A biographical sketch, p. 96.

83 Francis Powys in conversation with the present author, 13 October 1981.
84 For Lucy's help see, for example, COLGATE: Katie Powys to Louis Wilkinson, 15 June 1961.
85 TEXAS: Katie Powys to Phyllis Playter, 8 October 1958.
86 COLGATE: Katie Powys to Louis Wilkinson, January 1958.
87 Ibid., 27 October 1957.
88 COLGATE: John Cowper Powys to Louis Wilkinson, 12 August 1959.
89 During the year, John had been visited by his brother Will, his nephew Peter Powys Grey, Louis Wilkinson, Gamel Woolsey and Gladys Ficke.
90 John Cowper Powys, *Wolf Solent* (Penguin, Harmondsworth, 1964) Introduction, p. 9.
91 TEXAS: John Cowper Powys to Austin and Gwyneth Johnson, 21 July 1961.
92 COLGATE: Tape-recording of Louis Wilkinson talking to Tom Davies, 17 May 1965.
93 Oloff de Wet, *A Visit to John Cowper Powys* (Village Press, London, 1974) p. 29.
94 *Recollections*, Gerard Casey, 'A Double Initiation', p. 172.

A note on
further reading

A list of the major published works by the Powys brothers, together with dates of first publication, has been provided in the elaborate chapter-headings. Under the heading of 'Abbreviations: 2, Published Sources', I have in effect provided a select bibliography for those readers who wish for advice before embarking on further reading. I would add that John's *Autobiography*, Llewelyn's *Skin for Skin* and Theodore's *Soliloquies of a Hermit* might be the best places to start.

Literary scholars who wish to consult specialist literature and who are not satisfied with the sources mentioned in my reference notes should consult the published bibliographies, beginning perhaps with Derek Langridge's excellent *John Cowper Powys: A Record of Achievement* (1964). For Theodore Powys there is Peter Riley's *A Bibliography of T. F. Powys* (1967); and for Llewelyn Powys there is a detailed bibliography in Malcolm Elwin's *The Life of Llewelyn Powys* (1946).

Although a biography of three writers inevitably includes some general critical judgments, it will be evident that the present work is a biographical study rather than a work of literary criticism. Those who wish for literary criticism should read Glen Cavaliero's first-class *John Cowper Powys: Novelist* (1973). G. Wilson Knight occasionally appears to make extravagant claims for John Cowper Powys, but his own articles and books are certainly the product of a brilliant mind: there are some thought-provoking essays by him in *Neglected Powers* (1971), while *The Saturnian Quest* (1964) was a pioneering work which remains essential reading.

I find it difficult to recommend any other full-length critical work. No doubt readers who are prepared to believe that in *Porius* John Cowper Powys was deliberately recreating the seven stages in the process of alchemy, and that *Porius* was written 'as a secret doctrine with a "secret" embedded in it that Powys made sure would remain hidden

359

to all but the few willing to follow him on his magic hunt', will be excited by Morine Krissdottir's *John Cowper Powys and the Magical Quest* (1980). There are many critical articles in the valuable *The Powys Review (1977–)*, but these are, as one would expect, of uneven quality: it was particularly ingenious of one recent contributor to suggest that 'despite its lack of military incident . . . *After My Fashion* is an attempt at a war novel on the grand scale.' (no. 8, p. 14).

Index

repays Littleton, 170; happy with Phyllis, 179, 190; summer at Burpham, 179; at Llewelyn's wedding, 181; relationship with son, 189; visits wife and son, 196; short of money, 198; looks after Gamel, 208, 210–11, 213; discusses legends with Gamel, 215–16, 218; meets Littleton, 219; visits Francis, 219; ill-health, 224–5; with Phyllis at Phudd Bottom, 226; eccentric rituals, 244–5; money troubles, 254–5, 261–2; advice to Llewelyn, 259; afraid of scandal, 262; caricatured in *Swan's Milk*, 264; re-union with Will, 265; sells Phudd Bottom, 265–6; returns to England, 266; Wookey Hole lawsuit, 266–7; visits Llewelyn, 268; moves to Dorchester, 270; prays for Llewelyn, 270–1; moves to Wales, 272–3; visited by Louis, 277; praises *Welsh Ambassadors*, 278; installed as bard, 281; money troubles, 288, 293; anti-vivisection, 281, 298; visits London, 298–9; builds cairn, 304; writes 'pot-boilers', 307; reaction to Oliver's play, 308–9; visits son, 309; illness, 311, 312; prays at rock, 312–13; correspondence with Henry Miller, 315; moves to Blaenau Ffestiniog, 319; Augustus John draws him, 321; plays with 'Toddlers', 322; sings, 325–6; death, 326

Works: *After My Fashion*, 131, 141–2, 177; *All or Nothing*, 323; *The Art of Growing Old*, 307, 308; *The Art of Happiness*, 164, 177, 192, 270; *Atlantis*, 316–17, 318; *Autobiography*, 261–2, 264, 266, 274; *The Brazen Head*, 318, 322; *The Complex Vision*, 133–6, 140, 144, 177–8; *The Confessions of Two Brothers*, 115; *Debate! Is Modern Marriage a Failure?*, 226; *Dostoievsky*, 307, 308, 309, 313; *Ducdame*, 177–9, 184; *Four Brothers: a family confession*, 192; *A Glastonbury Romance*, 224, 225, 227, 237–9, 249, 250, 254; *The Hamadryad and the Demon*, 59; *Homer and the Aether*, 323; *In Defence of Sensuality*, 225; *In Spite Of*, 316; *The Inmates*, 316; *James Joyce's Ulysses – An Appreciation*, 165; *Jobber Skald*, 267; *Life of Keats*, 79, 82; *Lucifer*, 60, 322; *Maiden Castle*, 273–5, 277, 281, 285; *Mandragora*, 124; *The Meaning of Culture*, 213, 215, 219, 224; *Mortal Strife*, 305, 306; *Morwyn*, 281–2, 285, 288, 293, 318; *The Mountains of the Moon*, 323; *Obstinate Cymric*, 313; *Odes and Other Poems*, 39; *One Hundred Best Books*, 118; *Owen Glendower*, 288, 290, 293, 295–6, 299, 303, 305, 306, 307; *The Owl The Duck and – Miss Rowe! Miss Rowe!*, 226; *A Philosophy of Solitude*, 250, 254; *The Pleasures of Literature*, 285, 288, 291, 293; *Poems*, 45; *Porius*, 307, 309–11, 312, 314, 315, 316; *Psychoanalysis and Morality*, 164; *Rabelais*, 307, 308, 309, 314; *Real Wraiths*, 324; *The Religion of a Sceptic*, 184; *Rodmoor*, 118–20, 177–8; *Samphire*, 151, 159; *The Secret of Self-Development*, 196; *Suspended Judgments*, 120–1; *Two and Two*, 324; *Up and Out*, 322–3; *Visions and Revisions*, 105, 106, 322; *The War and Culture*, 100, 104; *Weymouth Sands*, 255–7, 261–2; *Wolf Solent*, 26, 40–1, 184, 190–2, 212, 213; *Wolf's Bane*, 115; *Wood and Stone*, 111, 114, 177; *You and Me*, 324 assessment of achievements, 326; trace development of philosophy through – 27, 34, 53, 60, 73, 106, 133, 163–4, 206, 270, 312–13

Powys, Katie: birth, 20; 'highly-strung', 84; nervous breakdown, 91–2; farms near Montacute, 100; gives up farming, 168; visits America,